ANIMALS AND THE HUMAN IMAGINATION

Animals and the Human Imagination

A COMPANION TO ANIMAL STUDIES

EDITED BY AARON GROSS AND ANNE VALLELY

FOREWORD BY JONATHAN SAFRAN FOER

AND EPILOGUE BY WENDY DONIGER

COLUMBIA UNIVERSITY PRESS   NEW YORK

COLUMBIA UNIVERSITY PRESS

Publishers Since 1893

NEW YORK   CHICHESTER, WEST SUSSEX

cup.columbia.edu

Library of Congress Cataloging-in-Publication Data

Animals and the human imagination : a companion to animal studies / edited by
Aaron Gross and Anne Vallely.

p. cm.

ISBN 978-0-231-15296-9 (cloth : alk. paper)—ISBN 978-0-231-15297-6 (pbk. : alk. paper)—
ISBN 978-0-231-52776-7 (ebook)

1. Human-animal relationships.   2. Animals and civilization.   3. Animals—Study and teaching.
4. Other (Philosophy)   5. Animals—Public opinion.   6. Animals—Psychological aspects.
7. Animal welfare.   I. Gross, Aaron.   II. Vallely, Anne.

QL85.A537   2012

590—dc23   2011041790

c 10 9 8 7 6 5 4 3 2 1
p 10 9 8 7 6 5 4 3 2 1

To my father, Patrick Vallely, ever my guiding light.
—Anne Vallely

To Nicole Gross-Camp, who has inspired me more than she knows.
—Aaron Gross

Contents

FOREWORD
Jonathan Safran Foer IX
ACKNOWLEDGMENTS XIII

INTRODUCTION AND OVERVIEW:
ANIMAL OTHERS AND ANIMAL STUDIES
Aaron Gross 1

PART I
Other Animals: Animals Across Cultures 25

1. Hunting and Gathering as Ways of Perceiving the Environment
Tim Ingold 31

2. On Yeti and Being Just:
Carving the Borders of Humanity in Early Modern China
Carla Nappi 55

3. Pastoral Power in the Postcolony:
On the Biopolitics of the Criminal Animal in South India
Anand Pandian 79

PART II
Animal Matters: Human/Animal and the Contemporary West   113

4. Discipline and Distancing: Confined Pigs in the Factory Farm Gulag
Joel Novek   121

5. Boys Gone Wild: The Animal and the Abject
Cynthia Chris   152

6. Animal Heroes and Transforming Substances:
Canine Characters in Contemporary Children's Literature
Michelle Superle   174

7. The Making of a Wilderness Icon: Green Fire, Charismatic Species, and
the Changing Status of Wolves in the United States
Gavin Van Horn   203

8. Thinking with Surfaces: Animals and Contemporary Art
Ron Broglio   238

PART III
Animal Others: Theorizing Animal/Human   259

9. Being with Animals: Reconsidering Heidegger's Animal Ontology
Brett Buchanan   265

10. Heidegger and the Dog Whisperer:
Imagining Interspecies Kindness
Ashley E. Pryor   289

11. *The Lives of Animals*:
Wittgenstein, Coetzee, and the Extent of the Sympathetic Imagination
Undine Sellbach   307

12. Animal, All Too Animal: *Blood Music* and an Ethic of Vulnerability
Myra J. Hird   331

EPILOGUE:
MAKING ANIMALS VANISH
Wendy Doniger   349

CONTRIBUTORS   355
INDEX   361

Foreword

ANIMALS MATTER. ANIMALS MATTER BECAUSE THEY NOT ONLY live, but have *lives*—lives that we have every reason to believe are filled with joy and pain. But the way animal lives matter is always complicated by how we use animals to shape the landscape of our humanity, both materially and imaginatively. We often forget the degree to which our engagements with animals build the world in which our lives unfold from the very beginning. We feature animals in our stories of creation and our scientific accounts of evolution. We ask, with the philosophers of antiquity, what "separates man from the animal." We conduct hundreds of billions of dollars in trade associated with every conceivable kind of animal and animal product, build tourist industries around watching wildlife, and spend more than $40 billion internationally on food for our animal companions.[1] We have occupied a third of the land on the planet with animals we use for food or labor.[2]

As children we hear about animals in the stories our parents tell us before we go to sleep. We dream of animals. We watch animals in cartoons and documentaries, in zoos and aquariums, in national parks and backyards. In science class we learn about the DNA that unites all life. In English class we explore the meaning of human struggle by reading about Santiago's wrestling with a marlin in Hemingway's *The Old Man and the Sea* and learn lessons about equality from the villainous pig Napoleon in Orwell's *Animal Farm*.

Our views of animals are complex, varying tremendously depending on the species. In Western nations we learn that dogs are for companionship and fish are for dinner. We make a statement of our values by wearing fur trim or joining PETA, hunting or going vegetarian—or at least having opinions about such choices. We are fascinated by Jane Goodall's ethnography-like study of chimpanzees and take out patents on special breeds of genetically engineered mice to study cancer. We champion the virtue of compassion for animals while passing laws that exempt agribusiness from animal protection statutes. Our relations with animals are not rational, but they are significant. From the Lascaux cave paintings to the media's obsession with the dogs of political leaders, we think about who we are by thinking about what—or who—animals are.

That said, what we mean by "animals" isn't as clear as it may first seem. Even by the dictionary definition, humans both are and are not animals. I found myself confronted with the paradox of being and not being an animal in a new way when my son was born. Within moments of his birth he was breastfeeding. Without any explaining or experience, he knew what to do. At first I felt, with a primacy I'd never before experienced, a member of the human species. Watching him eat, all of my more particular identities—American, male, Jew, writer—fell away from me. But as I continued to watch him even my identification as human fell away. No watch on my wrist, no money in my wallet, no words. We were animals in that room, three of us: mother, father, child. I'm not exactly sure what I mean by that, but the moment is the best example of something that's happened to me only a few dozen times in my life. When thinking back to my most extreme experiences—extremes of terror, joy, pleasure, and pain—I think of them in the language of animality: "I howled like an animal"; "I hungered for it like an animal"; ". . . like a wounded animal"; ". . . like a blood-thirsty animal"; "I was an animal."

We are fortunate today that so many scholars are giving us new ways to think about animals, to think about ourselves. This important book guides us into this diverse literature and makes a compelling and intellectually rigorous case that our self-conception has always depended on how we imagine animal others. In these pages we realize how strange are our own understandings of animals—and our misunderstandings of ourselves. We learn how our thinking about humans through animals both unites and separates the different cultures of our planet. We are intrigued and revolted, surprised, and infuriated, and above all we are given an opportunity to think about what we, perhaps wrongly, call our humanity.

Jonathan Safran Foer

Notes

1. Worldwatch Institute 2010:14.
2. Steinfeld et al., 2006:xxi.

References

Steinfeld, H., P. Gerber, T. Wassenaar, V. Castel, M. Rosales, and C. de Haan. 2006. *Livestock's Long Shadow: Environmental Issues and Options.* Rome: United Nations Food and Agricultural Organization.

Worldwatch Institute. 2010. "State of the World 2010: Transforming Cultures." Washington, DC: Worldwatch Institute.

Acknowledgments

THE GERM OF AN IDEA FOR THIS VOLUME TOOK ROOT SOMETIME in 2006, over a lengthy phone conversation with my father. Animal issues is a topic over which we shared strong emotions and on which we would often talk at length. In my capacity as an academic I wanted to enter into the conversation on "the animal question" but was reticent because the topic was outside my field of scholarship. I likely would have let the idea lay idle had it not been for my father's forceful encouragement. Many things besides encouragement were essential to the success of this project, not least of which was connecting with Aaron Gross, whose depth of knowledge on the topic of animal issues is matched only by his profound and inspiring commitment to their well-being. Of course, a manuscript, however compelling the topic, is only as good as its content. I want to thank each of the authors for their extraordinary essays, as well as their patience and perseverance throughout the project's lengthy gestation period. A special thanks is also owed to Wendy Lochner, Senior Executive Editor for Religion, Philosophy and Animal Studies at Columbia University Press, for her initial enthusiasm and continued support, as well as to our editor, John Donohue, for his tremendous talent and most exacting eye. Closer to home, my gratitude to Stephen Quinlan for his steady support, his erudition, and his companionship is truly without limit. In a project that spans several years, the mind staggers over the multitude of persons and events that have been integral to the project's final fruition. But it was that encouraging phone conversation of 2006 with my father that ignited the project, and I had cherished the thought of celebrating the book's publication with him: *Beidh tú i gcónaí mar sholas treorach dom, m'athair ionúin.*

—Anne Vallely, September 2011

* * *

This work would not have been possible without the colleagueship and conversation partners I have benefited from through the American Academy of Religion's Animals and Religion Group: David Aftandilian, Barbara Ambros, Forrest Clingerman, David Clough, Celia Deane-Drummond, Heather Eaton, Christen Gutleben, Laura Hobgood-Oster, Kimberley Patton, and Paul Waldau, among others. I am similarly grateful to the supportive environment to explore these issues I found both at the University of California, Santa Barbara (particularly from my mentors Richard Hecht, Barbara Holdrege, and Elisabeth Weber), and at my present institution, the University of San Diego. I want to thank Jonathan Safran Foer and Wendy Doniger for their inspiring foreword and epilogue, and especially my coeditor, Anne Vallely, whose idea started this project and whose enthusiasm and insight have made the journey so enriching. Most of all, I want to thank the contributors, who without exception were a pleasure to work with and whose insights form the substance of this volume.

—Aaron Gross, September 2011

ANIMALS AND THE HUMAN IMAGINATION

Introduction and Overview

Animal Others and Animal Studies

Aaron Gross

Animals! The object of insatiable interest, examples of the riddle of life, created, as it were, to reveal the human being to man himself, displaying his richness and complexity in a thousand kaleidoscopic possibilities, each of them brought to some curious end.

—Bruno Schulz, *The Street of Crocodiles*

CONTEMPORARY THOUGHT HAS INCREASINGLY HIGHLIGHTED the tangled and circular ways that human communities everywhere imagine themselves—their subjectivity, their ethics, their ancestry—with and through animals. What is new today is not the general observation that humans do this, but a sense of the significant role animals play in the process of human self-conception.[1] Thinkers as diverse as the French philosopher Jacques Derrida, the South African novelist and Nobel laureate J. M. Coetzee, and the American theorist Donna Haraway have not only contributed to this "animal turn," but also helped initiate rigorous inquiries that are now bearing fruit in a diverse array of studies, some published here for the first time. "Animals," a term that proves surprisingly problematic, have moved from the shadows of our intellectual landscape and asserted their importance both as subjects in their own right and as part of the imagination of the human. Animals, this volume insists, are so deeply enmeshed in human self-conception that if they did not exist we would need to invent them.

Animal Studies as a Location of Resistance

Highlighting the "co-construction" of the categories human and animal is an attempt to question dominant Western articulations of the human/animal binary that overwhelmingly view this division of the world into human and animal as a fact. Far from being a datum given in the natural order, the human/animal binary has always been and remains unstable, disputed, and negotiated. As the first chapter in this volume by Tim Ingold demonstrates, many cultures do not even conceive of this bifurcation of the animate world into human persons and animal organisms. Still, to upset this usually reliable binary or even to take the full reality of animals as subjects seriously is no small task, thus the burden of a new inquiry: animal studies.

Many times, when we think we are challenging the human/animal binary we turn out to be reinforcing it. For example, in a number of contemporary discourses that tend to be labeled scientific, empirical, and experimental (e.g., the life sciences in general and the cluster of disciplines engaged under the heading of cognitive science) some scholars will unhesitatingly declare that we are "human animals" or that "humans are animals." More often than not, such scholars also feel that by making such assertions they have done their duty to disenthrone an outdated human exceptionalism that evolutionary theory and the like have rendered implausible. Such assertions are usually understood as a challenge to religious traditions such as Christianity that would want, at least in their dominant articulation, to say that humans are not animals but rather belong in a category all their own. Such religious persons would assert that merely being a unique kind of animal, as the science-minded are happy to grant, is not a sufficient marker of human difference (for every species is by definition unique, and the human is not like any other species). From the point of view of the present volume, to challenge the human/animal binary by calling members of the species *Homo sapiens* "human animals" is insufficient. I say this because very often such apparent challenges to the human/animal binary are working with the most classical and uncritical understanding of what constitutes a human or an animal. When certain voices assert that "humans are animals," they are not so much challenging the human/animal binary as challenging the idea that there is anything beyond animality (beyond the material world as known by modern science). That is, to assert "humans are animals" is a rejection of a *certain kind* of human exceptionalism. However, it is not a rejection of the division of the world into "the animal"—that is, the material world as known by science—and "the human"—that is, the material world imbued with something *more*: with soul as opposed to soulless beasts, with reason as opposed to irrational brutes, or with language and culture as opposed to animals that merely communicate and are driven by instinct. Often, to assert that "humans are animals" is precisely to accept the division of the world the human/animal binary implies. What is rejected instead is the reality of what religious practitioners call soul or the contention that *Homo sapiens* actually behave as rational subjects that freely create their own cultures. In many cases, to assert that "humans are animals" is to reinforce the dominant way of conceiving the category human and the category animal. Further, this assertion may also be an attempt to demote humans to the level of "the animal"—something that quite reasonably provokes unease. In such cases, the terms of thought are not changed at all, which is to say that real thinking has not begun.

The challenge of animal studies and of this volume is to think anew and in an interdisciplinary manner about the kind of being that members of the species *Homo sapiens* are and the kind of being represented by every other species. The challenge is to rethink our identity in the most radical sense by refusing to *assume* from the outset the usual categories of thought. And since the categories of human and animal are the most basic categories of Western ethics, the challenge extends to the rethinking of fundamental questions of morality, justice, and compassion. Animal studies is thus equally preoccupied with questions of ontology and ethics because it strikes at the roots of how both domains are conceived.

Just what would it mean to cease conceiving and experiencing our humanity as other than a special, higher kind of animality—as "an animal plus" (plus reason, plus speech, and so on)? Is it even possible to avoid thinking "man" by "beginning with his *animalitas*"?[2] As philosopher Matthew Calarco underscores in his important book *Zoographies*, "What thought will encounter once reliance upon these categories [human, animal] is surrendered cannot be known in advance."[3] Would "human" still be a useful word to describe ourselves if we could dwell outside the human/animal binary? Do we need to begin speaking of the "post-human" as a number of scholars have suggested?

More pointedly, is it even possible to upset the human/animal border from within the human or life sciences? The entire justification for separating the human sciences from the life sciences is the old idea that humans are a radically unique animal that cannot be studied with the same techniques used to explore the rest of the living world. Would poetry and fiction be more effective in helping us to rethink the human/animal border? Derrida goes so far as to argue that even the most innovative of the giants of continental philosophy— he singles out Martin Heidegger and Emmanuel Lévinas—have "dogmatically" repeated the human/animal binary despite aspects of their thinking that seem to want to go beyond it.[4] Much more will be said about Derrida's engagement with Heidegger on this point in part III of this volume in the chapter by Brett Buchanan. My point here is simply to emphasize the pervasiveness of the human/animal binary and the difficulty of analyzing and challenging it.

To take up the question of animal others and otherness is not so much to pick a theme as it is to adopt a location of resistance to dominant modes of human self-conception and dominant methods of scholarship. This volume, then, aims to contribute to the development of a *hermeneutics*—a critical lens like that offered by race or feminist theory.

Animal Studies

The present volume is an interdisciplinary and cross-cultural exploration of the phenomenon of human self-conception through animals, and through this critical engagement with animals, it provides an introduction to animal studies and simultaneously makes contributions from animal studies to a range of disciplines in the humanities and social sciences. Minimally, it provides both the necessary theoretical reflection and the diversity of exempla to convincingly show not only that "animals matter" as subjects in their own right (a point still in need of emphasis), but also that animal subjects and ideas about them are critical sites through which we imagine ourselves. The juxtaposition of the essays collected in this volume will help us better understand how humans imagine themselves through animal others in diverse contexts—and in ever-changing and telling ways. Those interested in examining the meaning of "human" or the question of subjectivity and, equally, those interested in what we problematically call human rights or animal rights should find value in considering the human/animal tangle explored here. More ambitiously, this volume is a contribution to the ongoing emergence of a discourse on animals, "animal studies," that cuts across fields in the human and life sciences—a discourse that has been paralleled by increasingly sophisticated discussions of and more robust concern for animals in popular culture. Scholars have been joined by journalists, novelists, politicos, and movie stars in creating a new "critical" awareness of animals that has had both important implications for their ethical status (for example, the question of the factory farm)[5] and implications for the broader significance of animals and our discourses about them. Especially because of the unusual diversity of disciplinary approaches assembled here, this volume can function as an introduction to animal studies.

While an introductory text for the nascent field of animal studies, the volume also is a contribution of animal studies to field-specific inquiries in a range of disciplines: anthropology, art history, children's literature, Chinese history, continental philosophy, gender studies, media studies, postcolonial studies, religious studies, South Asian studies, and sociology. In suggesting that critical attention to animals is both a theme and a hermeneutic lens, I am arguing that this volume can be viewed just as fairly as diverse disciplines gathering around the theme of animals (a work in animal studies) or a multifaceted, critical "animal hermeneutics" engaging concerns specific to multiple disciplines (a series of essays on animals contributing to different fields). For example, Joel Novek's "Discipline and Distancing: Confined Pigs in the Factory Farm Gulag" (chapter 4) finds in the hog factory farm a striking example of how certain processes—in this case disciplining and distancing—run roughshod over the human/animal divide. At this level Novek's piece can be read as a richly contextualized example of the intimate relationship between how we understand and treat human others and how we understand and treat animal others—often to the detriment of both. At the same time, however, Novek takes insights that emerge while attending to human/animal interactions and imports them into sociology, thereby enriching our understanding of important sociological concepts, namely, discipline and distancing. This twofold movement that both contributes to a new animal hermeneutics and engages problems in other fields with this hermeneutic is an important part of the ongoing formulation of animal studies as a distinct field of study.

Comparing and Theorizing Animal Others in Context

This volume both starts with and documents the basic observation that *across time and across cultures humans imagine themselves through animal others*. This general observation expands the significance of any particular instance of human self-conception through animals in two basic directions: (1) it provides a basis for comparative inquiries, and (2) it allows for the theorization and critique of the general phenomena of self-conception through animals.

Comparing different exempla of human self-conception through animals can be a powerful angle of analysis to consider a diverse range of issues with important social implications. For example, such comparative work might help us better understand why the human/animal binary is so often paired with the male/female binary and usually in ways that are good for neither women nor animals. Although it is not the focus of their inquiries, in the present volume

Cynthia Chris's consideration of how the human/animal border is deployed to imagine humanity on MTV's *Wildboyz* (chapter 5) and Carla Nappi's consideration of how that border is similarly deployed in the classificatory schemes of early modern China (chapter 2) both detail significant ways that gender is bound up with the process of self-conception through animals. Strikingly, these studies of two radically different contexts both uncover links between the human/animal binary and the male/female binary. What does considering such diverse examples together tell us about the potentially oppressive mechanisms of dividing the world into human/animal and male/female in the process of imagining humanity?[6] Such questions are raised by but cannot be answered within the present volume. The more limited aim of this volume is to sharpen our critical questions about the roles animals play in human self-conception, illustrate the significance of these roles in specific cultural contexts, and provide tools to respond to them.

Theoretically, the present volume draws on at least three different loci of scholarly discussions of animal others, all of which have become remarkably rich in the last decade. These loci include: (1) the vibrant discussions that have emanated from work in continental philosophy undertaken especially by Derrida, Heidegger, and, more recently, Giorgio Agamben (in this volume see discussions by Buchanan, Ron Broglio, Myra J. Hird, and Ashley E. Pryor); (2) the outpouring of interest in literary circles in the work of Coetzee on animals (Broglio, Pryor, and Undine Sellbach); and (3) the post-humanist discourse of scholars such as Donna Haraway (Chris, Hird, Novek, Anand Pandian, and Pryor). With some simplification we can consider these three circles of discussion, which often bleed into one another, as representative of three already partially developed pathways into a better understanding of animal others: continental philosophy, fiction, and cultural studies.

These trajectories are valuable taken in isolation, but the present volume brings these multiple angles of vision together in a triangulation that can better isolate the role of animal others in human self-conception. Interdisciplinarity of this kind is especially needed when considering animals because, as noted above, the human/animal binary governs the macrostructure of the academy by marking out the human as a unique phenomenon that requires methods of study—the human sciences—different from those methods required to examine inanimate matter or animal life, which are dealt with by the life sciences. If you are reading this volume as a student or professional scholar, the very context of your reading has already been determined by one particular Western conception of the human/animal binary. Our thoughts and experiences have already been shaped by our culture's human/animal binary well before we come to speculate about it. Thinking about that circularity can be enough to make one dizzy, but, as we will see, such vertigo can be productive.[7]

The most useful critical theorizations of animals both allow us to see the significant cultural and existential "work" of animals in specific contexts and provide resources to help with the vertigo induced by the fact that the question of the animal shapes the very discourses (like the scholarly disciplines represented in this book) that *later* come to discuss the animal. Consider, for example, Agamben's recent theorization of a persistent pattern of drawing a human/animal binary to imagine humanity throughout the long stretch of Christian intellectual history from Augustine forward. Agamben theorizes this human/animal binary as first "a mobile border *within* living man" without which "the very decision of what is human and what is not would probably not be possible."[8] He calls the troubling production of this binary an "anthropological machine" that executes the "practical political mystery of" separating the human from the animal, often in violent ways.[9] Agamben's anthropological machine can be a useful concept to understand a range of situations in which humans define themselves against animal others, but one of its most productive features is that it does not assume there is any way for those of us who wield this theory to actually stop the anthropological machine long enough to get outside its mechanisms. His work on the animal is marked by a vigilant returning to this basic problem, which makes him especially fecund for the purposes of the present volume. See the index for guidance to engagements with Agamben scattered throughout this collection.

Although this volume as a whole offers an open-ended exploration of human self-conception through other animals, each individual essay examines this phenomenon in a particular context or contexts. It considers this phenomenon, for example, in traditional northern hunting cultures (Ingold, chapter 1); in early modern Chinese taxonomies (Nappi, chapter 2); in colonial and postcolonial Indian methods of governance (Pandian, chapter 3); in Canadian agriculture (Novek, chapter 4); in American television (Chris, chapter 5); in English-language children's stories (Michelle Superle, chapter 6); in American environmental policy (Gavin Van Horn, chapter 7); in modern art (Broglio, chapter 8); in Western intellectual history (Buchanan, chapter 9); in contemporary relationships with pets (Pryor, chapter 10); in the process of drawing metaphors and analogies between humans and animals in contemporary Western thought (Sellbach, chapter 11); and in the way in which we conceive and relate to the microorganisms that coarse through our bodies and create the environments in which we dwell (Hird, chapter 12). By bringing this range of exempla together, it is our hope that we will not only make contributions to diverse fields, but also bring much-needed empirical data to discussions of the human/animal binary and the phenomena of human self-conception through animal others.

The "Always Already" Circle

This volume highlights the culturally specific, constructed nature of two categories—human and animal—while also taking seriously the reality of animals, what Coetzee calls the "lives of animals" (see Sellbach, chapter 11, for a discussion of Coetzee's phrase). How can these terms—"human" and "animal"—simultaneously form a basis for comparison *and* be critically scrutinized, even deconstructed? I'm not sure they always can be, but both intellectual moves are possible and are more powerful when juxtaposed. We can, at least, acknowledge that because of the unique way in which "animals"—the biological beings "out there"—are always already implicated in our self-conception, we have no way of completing the critical task of thinking in genuinely new ways about animals. Perhaps the best we can do is follow the lead of thinkers like Derrida by remaining vigilant on both fronts—problematizing the very categories we use to conduct our analyses and responding to the pragmatic reality of animal suffering. In the present volume, the utility of the categories animal and human is exploited as far as possible, but its limits are also given attention. As Ingold points out in chapter 1, the very idea of culture (and thus more than one scholarly field) is mired in a similar paradox: if categories are culturally constructed, how can we use culture (which is a category and therefore constructed) as if it is neutrally applicable to all human communities? To clarify, then, the basic observation that starts and guides this volume is that those beings *we know* as different animal species seem to invariably play a decisive role in human self-conception. Whether these others should be conceived of and imagined as "animals" remains an open question.

In the present context, this "always already" paradox can be somewhat mitigated by the fact that the basic process of distinguishing "natural kinds," *species*, does seem to be largely invariable. And although the taxonomies of species may differ wildly and the important groupings differ wildly (consider that in English "fish" refers to 27,000 different species, whereas "dogs" are one subspecies), there are few cross-cultural disagreements on what beings should count, for example, as *Canis domesticus*. In some contexts *Canis domesticus* is known as "dog" and is a companion, whereas in others *Canis domesticus* is more food than friend—but both communities will recognize the same beings as chickens and not chimpanzees or parrots if asked to differentiate (which may or may not be their habit). Thus we can fairly assume that "those beings we know as animals" are recognizable *at the level of species* across cultures in a way that "animals," "humans," "tree spirits," and "animal instincts" are not.

In any case, the point is that the logical circle cannot be evaded. Even if we accept that there are basic human mechanisms that lead to shared recognition of species boundaries, the significance of those boundaries is up for grabs. Is the line, for example, between *Homo sapiens sapiens* and all other species *special* or is it no different, for example, than the line between *Gallus gallus* (the domestic chicken) and all other species? These are serious problems. At the same time, though, working over this circularity is part of the great interest of this volume and animal studies more generally. Whether we wish to exploit them for human benefit, study their use as symbols, or establish legal protections for them, we need to tolerate some dizziness to fully attend to animal others.

The Organization of This Volume

Although an extraordinarily wide range of times and places are engaged in this volume, the thrust is to bring this range of thought to bear on questions about animal others as they are unfolding today in the contemporary Western context. In keeping with this orientation toward providing a broad entry into research on animal others cross-culturally while also speaking particularly to the contemporary Western context, we have divided the essays into three parts:

    I.   Other Animals: Animals Across Cultures
   II.   Animal Matters: Human/Animal and the Contemporary West
 III.   Animal Others: Theorizing Animal/Human

I. Other Animals: Animals Across Cultures

Part I aims to contribute to important discussions about animal others in the study of hunter-gatherer (Ingold), East Asian (Nappi), and South Asian (Pandian) traditions, as well as to provide case studies for broader comparative reflections that help situate what is culturally specific and what is cross-cultural in human/animal interactions. A shortened version of Ingold's now-classic essay "Hunting and Gathering as Ways of Perceiving the Environment" provides an invaluable opening to the volume by demonstrating that many human communities lack even a conception of "animal" in the sense familiar to the modern West. Using the exempla of how "northern hunters, in particular the Cree of northeastern Canada, understand their relations to the animals they hunt," Ingold makes a foundational contribution to contemporary thinking about nature/culture and the imagination of the human. A substantial quotation is in order.

> Now Western thought, as is well known, drives an absolute division between the contrary conditions of humanity and animality, a division that is aligned with a series of others such as between subjects and objects, persons and things, morality and physicality, reason and instinct, and, above all, society and nature. Underwriting the Western view of the uniqueness of the human species is the fundamental axiom that *personhood as a state of being is not open to nonhuman animal kinds.* It is for this reason that we are able to conflate both the moral condition and the biological taxon (*Homo sapiens*) under the single rubric of "humanity." And for this reason, too, we can countenance an inquiry into the animal nature of human beings whilst rejecting out of hand the possibility of an inquiry into the humanity of nonhuman animals. . . . Human existence is conceived to be conducted simultaneously on two levels, the social level of interpersonal, intersubjective relations and the natural ecological level of organism-environment interactions, whereas animal existence is wholly confined within the natural domain. Humans are both persons *and* organisms, animals are solely organisms.
>
> This is a view, however, that Cree and other northern hunters categorically reject. Personhood, for them, is open equally to human and nonhuman animal (and even nonanimal) kinds.[10]

Ingold's chapter and his larger oeuvre, which constitutes more than twenty years of reflection on the meanings of animals, is crucially important in helping contextualize the cultural similarities and differences that emerge in human self-conception.[11]

Additionally, Ingold's anthropologically oriented inquiry is a potentially powerful complement to work on animals in continental philosophy, including the chapters that constitute part III. Much philosophical effort has been spent pointing out the limitations of the human/animal binary and exhorting us to think outside it. Ingold's work, by contrast, attempts to introduce us to a way of "apprehending" the world without the human/animal binary. Ingold's chapter is among the few scholarly works that does not merely tell of the radically different conceptions of nonhuman animal species that appear among hunting and gathering cultures, but which *evokes* in readers a glimpse of how a world without the human/animal border appears. Just how challenging that task can be is suggested in an intriguing manner in the chapter by Nappi.

Nappi's chapter explores the shifting borders between animals and humans in early modern China found in the changing classification of humanoid beasts (Chinese "Yetis"), "wild women," monkeys, and other inhabitants of the human-animal borderlands. Her research functions in almost a converse direction to Ingold. Whereas Ingold's work on the Cree gives a picture of a culture that conceptualizes humanity and animality in so radically different a manner that the very terms of comparison, "animal" and "human," fail us, Nappi's work gives a picture of a non-Western culture that reveals not only a deployment of the human/animal boundary that would be familiar to students of Western intellectual history, but many of the same anxieties around that border. Among other details, Nappi's essay shows how these border anxieties are worked out in relation to eating (a theme also prominent in Novek, chapter 4, and Broglio, chapter 8), and gender and sex differences (also prominent in Chris, chapter 5).

Chapter 3, by Pandian, can be helpfully understood as situated between Ingold and Nappi. If Ingold brings to us a radically different understanding of nonhuman species and Nappi brings us an unexpectedly familiar one, Pandian's work reminds us that even within a given time and place, multiple understandings of the human/animal operate in relation to and competition with one another. Highlighting symbolic and pragmatic relationships between, on the one hand, the managing of livestock and the governance of human communities and, on the other hand, between the managing of livestock and self-governance, Pandian provides a new angle of vision on the process of "subjection." He shows how both political and ethical mastery relate to the problem of "animal" impulses and function as part of a broader process of imagining the human subject. In compelling prose, Pandian examines the processes of subjection in the British colonial subjugation of the Tamils' Piramalai Kallar caste, which was managed as an animal herd, and the Tamils' own deployment of pastoral vocabularies in a "devotional poetics of selfhood." In a manner resonant with Novek's linkages between oppressive treatment of humans and animals (a theme that calls for more scholarly attention), Pandian considers how pastoral tactics and vocabularies can be deployed in the service of political control or poetic self-conception.[12]

II. Animal Matters: Human/Animal and the Contemporary West

That the meanings of "human" and "animal" are always underdetermined, always shifting, always works in progress is no mere intellectual curiosity. The messy and freighted instantiations of the human/animal binary are politically and pragmatically important in our daily lives. The human/animal binary can regulate food, gender roles, and basic issues of justice. Still, for most of us, it often appears like dividing the world into humans and animals is unproblematic in practice even if philosophers quibble. As the essays in this volume demonstrate, this impression is not correct.

One rough-and-ready way to make this veiled messiness visible is simply to make the well-known, but undertheorized observation that it was not long ago that debates were heard about whether blacks or women are fully human. And more recently, powerful elements of the U.S. government—in alliance with some university scholars—have tried to place "enemy combatants" on the animal side of the human/animal divide, denying them basic "human" rights like freedom from torture.[13] In an equally striking development, the Spanish parliament recently passed a first-of-its-kind resolution granting great apes basic "human" rights.[14] Intriguingly, two of the most vocal groups opposing the parliament's resolution were religious leaders and animal researchers.[15]

We draw attention to such charged observations not in order to turn too quickly to questions of justice (though that too would be something I "might also want to do, and something which would lead us to the center of the subject"),[16] but rather to highlight the relevance of animal studies, including the present volume, for pragmatic and political concerns that pervade daily life. The kinds of scholarship this volume represents not only have a wide significance within the academy, but can be relevant for those interested in guiding public policy, which, of course, frequently involves the regulation of animal bodies. Novek's and Van Horn's chapters deal with public policy directly—agriculture and wildlife management, respectively. As we noted above, Novek considers what in many ways is the most important event in contemporary human-animal relations, the rise of the factory farm.[17] Van Horn's historically rich and detailed article traces the complex interplay between the popular American perception and treatment of wolves—which ranges from disdainful violence to a religiously charged admiration—and related understandings of fundamental human relationships to the lands of the United States and to the wider biotic community. As Van Horn shows, these shifting perceptions—and their manipulation by politicians, ranchers, and activists—have been deeply influential on both federal management of wilderness and the evolution of conservation as a social movement. Similarly, both Pryor's and Hird's chapters in part III point us toward alternative conceptualizations of ethics.

In one or another way, all the articles in part II of this volume point to parts of our everyday lives influenced by the question of the animal. Chris (chapter 5) considers how contemporary American television, specifically the genre of wildlife documentary, is an unexpected vehicle for the construction of the human subject and humanity. She argues that the slapstick style humor of MTV's *Wildboyz* "tests not only the species barrier, but also destabilizes presumptive heterosexual subject positions by means of homoerotic play."[18] Chris's chapter can be productively read alongside her important book *Watching Wildlife*,[19] which looks more broadly at the rise of now ubiquitous animal-oriented television (Animal Planet, Discovery Channel, National Geographic Channel, etc.), demonstrating the important and sometimes troubling work this programming does to shape questions of gender, race, and sexuality.

Michelle Superle (chapter 6) utilizes the treasure trove of reflection on humans and animals embedded in children's literature to consider how discovering humanity through animality is a powerful tool deployed in children's stories to address issues of family belonging, maturation, and self-transformation. Superle's consideration of dog stories in particular suggests some fascinating ways in which literary animals and real animals interact, a theme that could be highlighted in a number of this volume's other essays. Humans may imagine and produce animals as root others, but the real-life correlates of these imaginations exist independently and have agency that can impinge upon our lives.[20] The presence in our lives of real dogs as companions and our words about them work upon us in complex ways and, as Superle's chapter shows, from an early age.

In a related manner, Ron Broglio (chapter 8) shows how artistic representations of farmed animals have played a role in the actual breeding of them, which, in turn, determines what kinds of animal agriculture will be possible. Going further, Broglio contrasts this objectifying, potentially violent representation of animals in nineteenth-century art with the contemporary efforts of many artists, most notably the collaborative artists known as Olly and Suzi (Olly Williams and Suzi Winstanley). Olly and Suzi are noteworthy for their attempts to use technology to safely paint large predators *in the predators' environment* and while the predators are in close proximity—for example, quickly painting sharks while in underwater cages (the artists are in the cage, not the sharks). Olly and Suzi want to be forced to adapt to the animal's environment rather than, as has been the norm, bringing the animal into the artist's environment. In so doing, they hope to move beyond animal art that is produced only through an objectification of the animals depicted.

Much of this volume asks the reader to similarly work to break out of a traditional Western mode of looking at animals as objects. Just as Olly and Suzi seek to initiate new artistic traditions in which animals are no longer objects of the artist's gaze, this volume aims to promote a new scholarly orientation in which animals can never be objects because they are already subjects who help make us who we are.

III. Animal Others: Theorizing Animal/Human

Part III contains four essays that examine some of the most penetrating and subtle thinkers to engage the question of the animal in the last century, principally Coetzee, Derrida, Haraway, and Heidegger. The central ideas and problems explored in these essays resonate throughout the volume and serve to sharpen the broader relevance of the preceding essays, each of which takes up a particular historical and spatial context.

Buchanan (chapter 9) and Pryor (chapter 10) critically engage the robust legacy of philosophical thought on animals that has emanated from Heidegger's philosophical exploration of subjectivity. Since Heidegger's work on animals has been a point of departure for Derrida (and for Agamben), a clear understanding of his work on animals, despite its sometimes disturbing features, is of special value. Drawing especially on Heidegger's most extensive discussion of animals in *The Fundamentals of Metaphysics*, Buchanan carefully lays out the significance of Heidegger's work on animals in the longer arc of Western thought from Aristotle to Descartes and presents a case for the productivity of Heidegger's thought against its many critics. Finding Heideggerian thought productive but insufficient, Pryor utilizes the theoretical resources provided by Heidegger, particularly in his *Parmenides Lecture Course*, to develop a theorization of "kindness" as it arises in human relationships with companion animals. Working with the accessible example of interactions between dog, trainer, and owner on the popular National Geographic television show *Dog Whisperer*, Pryor provides a concrete demonstration of how she understands "kindness" and how this understanding can help us think about the fraught human/animal binary.

Sellbach (chapter 11), drawing especially on the rich resources provided by Coetzee, examines one of the most pervasive ways that Western thought has imagined the human in relation to animals: the drawing of analogies between the two. Sellbach both diagnoses the often problematic nature of these analogies and proposes alternative, more productive ways of metaphor making in dialogue with a range of thinkers, including Stanley Cavell, Lévinas and, most especially, Ludwig Wittgenstein.

Where Buchanan, Pryor, and Sellbach work to import thought from philosophy and literature into animal studies in order to sharpen our thinking about animals, Hird (chapter 12) works in a slightly different direction. Drawing on science fiction literature and a plethora of scientific studies, Hird challenges this volume's focus on humans and other animals by highlighting the even more intimate entanglement of human life—indeed all life—with bacteria. Hird reflects on the ways in which all life is profoundly dependent on microorganisms: in its evolution, in the creation of environments in which life thrives, and even in the basic metabolic processes that sustain life. In light of this radical dependence, Hird invites us to consider an "ethic of vulnerability," a vulnerability that unites the whole of the animal kingdom.

Absent Referents and the Post-Animal

One danger of scholarly work on animals, including the present one, is that it can function to render "actual animals" absent.[21] The appearance of discussing animals can be given and words about animals can be spoken, but those words can be a misrepresentation or obfuscation of animals as we know them from empirical observation and common sense. It is to be expected that scholars in the humanities will often utilize attention to animals as a route to illumine aspects of humanity (which can make the animals themselves seem beside the point). The problem arises when this is the *only* way animals are discussed—when there is no one looking in the horse's mouth or even in the direction of the horse. I raise these points here at the end of the introduction because this volume's focus on human self-conception through animals could be deployed both to render animals absent and to make them present. I hope it will be the latter and that this volume will help in developing a critical stance whereby we begin to see when, how, and maybe why the transformation of animals into absent referents (beings made absent as they are being referenced) takes place. Such a critical stance would both illumine how we understand our own subjectivity and bring the subjectivities of animals into view.

This collection's most immediate purpose is to advance scholarship in the narrow sense of that term. Our hope is that juxtaposing the essays contained here can be used as (1) an entry point into the many possibilities of animal studies both as an area of study and as a critical lens, and (2) a particular exploration of the shifting boundaries of human self-conception through animals.

At the same time, we have selected essays that simultaneously (3) make contributions to their respective scholarly fields, not necessarily public policy. Nonetheless, there is a powerful way in which the kind of inquiries undertaken here are (4) a basic precondition for the more politicized act of "making present" and making policy.

To most fully make animals present we first need to understand how they are rendered absent. This inquiry has important implications for how we imagine ourselves as human beings (which is the focus of the present volume), but it also has profound and troubling implications for how we engage with the very real animals with whom we share our lives (as companions, food, workers, entertainment, and so on). We might want to understand, for example, how it has been acceptable to the American public that the nation's only legislation regulating animal use in scientific experiments, the Animal Welfare Act (which had unusually high public support), does not, in fact, apply to the overwhelming majority of animals used in research. Similarly, we might want to understand how America's only legislation regulating humane slaughter, the Humane Methods of Slaughter Act, similarly does not protect the overwhelming majority of animals slaughtered for food.[22] However one evaluates these situations in terms of justice, they call out for scholarly analysis. Scholars in the human sciences are well placed to explain, describe, or interpret *part* of these curious situations, for example, by recounting the various political wranglings that produce legislation. The work of this volume points to a *different*, still-evolving set of tools that scholars might use to explain these odd legal situations or other troubled, curious, or simply strange aspects of human treatment of animals. This volume shows us that to articulate views about animals—for example, to announce protection of their welfare in research or insist on humaneness in their slaughter—is likely to be as much about how humans understand themselves as about the stated legislative aim of protecting animals. Humaneness blurs into humanness.

Animal others are always already involved in human self-conception. Policy makers, concerned citizens, and others with a stake in public debates about animals will simply fail to understand—and thus fail to most effectively impact—public policies regulating the treatment of animals if they do not take into account the kinds of deeper currents shaping discourse about animals documented here. In sum, to make animals present, we first need to gain some purchase on how animal others are imbedded in human self-conception—in the human imagination (the landscape of our mind) and the imagination of the human (how we imagine the meaning of humanity). Interdisciplinary work in animal studies has a crucial scholarly service to perform in this regard.

Today it is common enough, at least in the emerging scholarly literature on animals, to argue that we should not forget "actual" animals in our scholarly work. Insofar as this is a call to incorporate data from ethology (the study of animal behavior), neuroscience, or other empirical fields into the human sciences and insofar as this is a call to responsibility, I would not wish to challenge the call. That said, this volume casts doubt on just how easy it is to talk about "actual animals" or make them "present." To fully engage "the animals themselves" it is not enough to simply consult an empirical study of animals, bring an animal into the classroom, or visit a farm. We would further, at very least, need to get outside of the human/animal binary. That would "mean no longer to seek new—more effective or more authentic—articulations" of the human and confronting what Agamben calls "the central emptiness, the hiatus that—within man—separates man and animal, and to risk ourselves in this emptiness: the suspension of the suspension, Shabbat of both animal and man."[23] We would need to pause, put to rest, or surrender the categories animal and human. As Calarco emphasizes, "Any genuine encounter with what we call animals will occur only from within the space of this surrender. If there are any properly philosophical stakes in the field of animal studies, I would argue that they lie precisely here, in the clearing of the space for the *event* of what we call animals."[24]

A final aim for this volume, then, is that by taking the reader on a tour, as it were, of the always already circle—by circling around the human tendency to self-conceptualize through animals in particular contexts—we might create a clearing where it is possible to see, and perhaps be seen, by those others that we all too quickly name animals. That is, we hope to contribute to the always ongoing human imagination of the others we call animals.

This volume, to condense it in a phrase, hopes to lead us toward what we might call a "post-animal discussion" of those beings we call animals. That is, attention to how a certain understanding of animality is implicit in our self understanding (and thus our understandings of language, symbol, myth, subjectivity, religion, etc.) can perhaps expose the naturalness of the category animal as illusory. Significantly, such a post-animal discourse would not be an aim in itself.

Achieving a post-animal discourse would be a kind of goal, a kind of end, but it is more importantly a beginning. The real prize lies in asking, "What's beyond the 'post'?"[25] In one sense we never can get "beyond the 'post.'" Adding this prefix to key categories (post-colonial, post-human, post-modern, etc.) is nothing other than the basic gesture of critical thought. The "post" asks us to see "beyond" our present categories, whatever they may be. A century from now, critical thought might require us to think post-post-animal—and the "posts" must continually be piled on. Beyond the post lie more posts. In another sense, though, asking what lies beyond the "post"—beyond the act of moving "beyond" extant categories—is to gesture at the pragmatic and scholarly task of resetting our perceptions of and engagements with the world in potentially productive ways. The categories of animal and human have done important intellectual work. In practical life we cannot at present proceed very far without some talk of human rights and animal welfare (or protection or rights)—such language has become unavoidable. Thus I do not propose that the actual word "animal" be avoided—that would achieve very little. Rather, moving "beyond the 'post'" lies in actually making that once-familiar word appear strange or, as Derrida has quipped, "stupid"[26] even as one continues to use the word. Beyond the "post" is our ability to proactively imagine ourselves and others anew.

It is in this way that this volume, although focused on humans and the humanities, might lead us back toward our most intimate and forgotten others. It is in this way that the twin processes of making the familiar strange and the strange familiar that run throughout this volume might be put, in the resonant words of historian of religions J. Z. Smith, "in the service of an urgent civic and academic agendum: that difference be negotiated but never overcome."[27]

Notes

1. "Human self-conception" is an imperfect phrase to describe the phenomenon under consideration here. In a sense this entire volume is meant to provide a picture of what human self-conception might be and so it cannot be defined in advance. Preliminarily, we can note that "human self-conception" is meant to simultaneously describe or at least gesture at two meanings: (1) the range of ways in which we consciously seek to discourse about (write, speak, paint, sculpt, etc.) and imagine ourselves in order to gain a grasp of the kind of beings we are, for example, philosophical discourse on subjectivity or an anatomical sketch of the human body, and (2) unconscious or entirely different modes in which more obscure aspects of human imagination are implicated in the processes that create the kind of being we are, for example, through language or through a basic responsiveness to other living beings.

2. Agamben 2004:73. As Agamben has recently highlighted, Heidegger's "Letter on Humanism" famously reproaches the Western tradition for "thinking man 'beginning with his *animalitas* and not in the direction of his *humanitas*'" (Heidegger 1998:247). Agamben ultimately challenges Heidegger on this point: "in what sense does Heidegger's attempt to grasp the 'existing essence of man' escape the metaphysical primacy of *animalitas*?" (Agamben 2004:73).

3. Calarco 2008:4.

4. Derrida 1995:279.

5. A prominent example of engagement with what I have called the question of the factory farm can found in newspaper editorials. For instance in 2008 the *New York Times* became the first major national paper to editorialize against intensive confinement farming as such (*New York Times* 2008).

6. The links between the treatment of animals and women has attracted scholarly attention for roughly twenty years, and their consideration could fill more than one volume. Especially since Carol Adams's *The Sexual Politics of Meat*, first published in 1990, feminist thought has examined the links between the objectification of women and animals and argued that similar mechanisms of oppression operate against both groups (Adams 2010).

7. Derrida masterfully engages the idea that reflection on the animal other can be dizzying in his most comprehensive work on animals, *The Animal That Therefore I Am* (Derrida 2008).

8. Agamben 2004:15 (emphasis added).

9. Agamben 2004:16. More specifically, Agamben argues that this machine marks this difference by denying the human a place or rank in the animal or human order; that is, the machine generates the human based on a lack that becomes the basis for a separation.

10. Ingold, chapter 1, this volume.

11. Other important works by Ingold that deal with animals include Ingold 1987, 1996, 2001, 2002, 2005, 2008a, 2008b, and an edited volume of other scholars' work (Ingold 1988).

12. Charles Siebert's *New York Times* article "The Animal-Cruelty Syndrome" provides an overview of pragmatic uses of the connection between animal and human abuse by law enforcement and government agencies (Siebert 2010). "The link between animal abuse and interpersonal violence is becoming so well established that many U.S. communities now cross-train social-service and animal-control agencies in how to recognize signs of animal abuse as possible indicators of other abusive behaviors. In Illinois and several other states, new laws mandate that veterinarians notify the police if their suspicions are aroused by the condition of the animals they treat. The state of California recently added Humane Society and animal-control officers to the list of professionals bound by law to report suspected child abuse" (Siebert 2010). There is a wide body of literature that discusses these connections; for further discussion see: Anderson 2006; Arluke 2007; Ascione 2005; Ascione and Arkow 1999; Heide 2003; Lockwood and Ascione 1998; Luke 2007; Roberts 2008. Some feminist scholarship, particularly the work of Carol Adams, covers similar ground by theoretically exploring the connections between violence against women and violence against animals; see Adams and Donovan 1995; Adams 1993, 1994, 2003, 2010. For an opposing position, see Goodney Lea 2007.

13. Gross 2011.

14. Glendinning 2008.

15. It is worth pausing over what at first seems like an odd alliance between (Christian) religion and science. This alliance, which often is evident in these two cultural institutions' responses to animal issues, could be considered a powerful example of the deeper unity of religion and science as they have (co)evolved in the modern West. Typically, the alliance is disavowed and misrepresented as a clash. For discussion see Derrida's classic essay "Faith and Knowledge: The Two Sources of 'Religion' at the Limits of Reason Alone," in which he suggests, "Perhaps we might be able to try to 'understand' how the imperturbable and interminable development of critical and technoscientific reason, far from opposing religion, bears, supports, and supposes it. It would be necessary to demonstrate, which would not be simple, that religion and reason have the same source" (Derrida 2002:66).

16. The citation is of Derrida (1995:278), who is playing off the dual meaning of "subject": subject as in human subject and as in subject matter. More importantly, Derrida here suggests that scholarly inquiry and political action on animals will both produce comparable critical perspectives on animals and, ultimately, on the human subject. The issues raised by Derrida's remark are especially important to animal studies as it puts itself in relation to political work on animals.

17. By calling the factory farm an event I aim both to signify the new configuration in human/animal relations that it initiated and to follow Derrida in raising critical questions about its meaning. Derrida writes, "However one interprets it, whatever practical, technical, scientific, juridical, ethical, or political consequences one draws from it, no one can deny this event any more, no one can deny the unprecedented proportions of this subjection of the animal. . . . Neither can one seriously deny the disavowal that this involves. No one can deny seriously, or for very long, that men do all they can in order to dissimulate this cruelty or to hide it from themselves, in order to organize on a global scale the forgetting or misunderstanding of this violence that some would compare to the worst cases of genocide . . . there are also animal genocides" (Derrida 2008:25–26).

18. Chris, chapter 5, this volume.

19. Chris 2006.

20. The question of animal agency is attracting increasing scholarly attention and, as we would expect, is connected to debates about human agency (the "structure-agency debate") in sociology and psychology. At stake is the meaning of agency itself. For a robust discussion of animal agency and references to the broader literature on agency, see Irvine 2004:127–133, 200.

21. I am indebted to Carol Adams for her development of the helpful category of the "absent referent." For discussion see Adams 1990:4–44; Adams 1994:16–17.

22. The Animal Welfare Act excludes mice and rats from legal protection. The Humane Methods of Slaughter Act excludes chickens, turkeys, and other poultry (which has been a mater of legal contention) and sea animals (which, as far as the editors know, has not been challenged).

23. Agamben 2004:92. Agamben argues that the Western tradition has imagined the human as suspended between humanity and animality. The "suspension of the suspension" is the suspension of this tradition of imagining humanity as held between poles of animality and idealized humanity.

24. Calarco 2008:4.

25. The question "what's beyond the 'post'" was originally posed by historian of religions Charles Long (Holdrege 2000:77–91).

26. Derrida 2009:68. In French the word *bête* can mean both stupid and beast.

27. Smith 2004:389.

References

Adams, Carol J. 1990. "The Sexual Politics of Meat." In *The Sexual Politics of Meat: A Feminist-Vegetarian Critical Theory*, 47–63. New York: Continuum.

——. 1993. *Ecofeminism and the Sacred*. New York: Continuum.

——. 1994. *Neither Man nor Beast: Feminism and the Defense of Animals*. New York: Continuum.

——. 2003. *The Pornography of Meat*. New York: Continuum.

——. 2010. *The Sexual Politics of Meat: A Feminist-Vegetarian Critical Theory*. 20th anniversary ed. New York: Continuum. Original edition, 1990.

Adams, Carol J. and Josephine Donovan, eds. 1995. *Animals and Women: Feminist Theoretical Explorations*. Durham, NC: Duke University Press.

Agamben, Giorgio. 2004. *The Open: Man and Animal*. Trans. K. Attell. Stanford, CA: Stanford University Press. Original edition, 2002 (Italian).

Anderson, David C. 2006. *Assessing the Human-Animal Bond: A Compendium of Actual Measures*. West Lafayette, IN: Purdue University Press.

Arluke, Arnold. 2007. *Brute Force: Policing Animal Cruelty*. West Lafayette, IN: Purdue University Press.

Ascione, Frank R. 2005. *Children and Animals: Exploring the Roots of Kindness*. West Lafayette, IN: Purdue University Press.

Ascione, Frank R. and Phil Arkow. 1999. *Child Abuse, Domestic Violence, and Animal Abuse: Linking the Circles of Compassion for Prevention and Intervention*. West Lafayette, IN: Purdue University Press.

Calarco, Matthew. 2008. *Zoographies: The Question of the Animal from Heidegger to Derrida*. New York: Columbia University Press.

Chris, Cynthia. 2006. *Watching Wildlife*. Minneapolis: University of Minnesota Press.

Derrida, Jacques. 1995. "'Eating Well,' or the Calculation of the Subject." In *Points . . . Interviews, 1974–1994*, ed. E. Weber, 255–287. Stanford, CA: Stanford University Press.

——. 2002. "Faith and Knowledge: The Two Sources of 'Religion' at the Limits of Reason Alone." In *Acts of Religion*, ed. G. Anidjar, 42–101. New York: Routledge.

——. 2008. *The Animal That Therefore I Am*. Trans. David Wills. Ed. Marie-Louise Mallet. New York: Fordham University Press.

——. 2009. *The Beast and the Sovereign*, vol. 1. Trans. G. Bennington. Ed. M. Lisse, M.-L. Mallet, and G. Michaud. Chicago: University of Chicago Press. Original edition, 2008 (French).

Glendinning, Lee. 2008. "Spanish Parliament Approves 'Human Rights' for Apes." *Guardian*, June 26.

Goodney Lea, Suzanne R. 2007. *Delinquency and Animal Cruelty: Myths and Realities About Social Pathology*. El Paso, TX: LFB Scholarly Publishing.

Gross, Aaron. 2011. "Detainee." In *Encyclopedia of Global Religion*, ed. M. Juergensmeyer and W. C. Roof. Thousand Oaks, CA: Sage.

Heide, Kathleen M. 2003. *Animal Cruelty: Pathway to Violence Against People*. Lanham, MD: AltaMira Press.

Heidegger, Martin. 1998. "Letter on 'Humanism'" (1946). In *Pathmarks*, ed. W. Mc-Neill, 239–276. Cambridge: Cambridge University Press. Original edition, 1967 (German).

Holdrege, Barbara. 2000. "What's Beyond the 'Post.'" In *A Magic Still Dwells: Comparative Religion in the Postmodern Age*, ed. K. Patton and B. Ray, 77–91. Berkeley: University of California Press.

Ingold, Tim. 1987. *Hunters, Pastoralists and Ranchers: Reindeer Economies and Their Transformations*. Cambridge: Cambridge University Press.

——, ed. 1988. *What Is an Animal?* London: Unwin Hyman.

——. 1996. "The Optimal Forager and Economic Man." In *Nature and Society: Anthropological Perspectives*, ed. P. Descola and G. Pálsson, 25–44. London: Routledge.

——. 2001. "Animals and Modern Cultures: A Sociology of Human-Animal Relations in Modernity." *Society and Animals* 9, no. 2.

——. 2002. "Humanity and Animality." In *Companion Encyclopedia of Anthropology*, ed. T. Ingold, 14–32. New York: Routledge. Original edition, 1994.

——. 2005. *Key Debates in Anthropology*. London: Routledge.

——. 2008a. "From Trust to Domination: An Alternative History of Human-Animals Relations." In *The Perception of the Environment: Essays in Livelihood, Dwelling and Skill*, ed. T. Ingold, 61–76. London: Routledge. Original edition, 2000.

——. 2008b. "Making Things, Growing Plants, Raising Animals and Bringing Up Children." In *Perception of the Environment: Essays on Livelihood, Dwelling and Skill*, ed. T. Ingold, 77–78. London: Routledge. Original edition, 2000.

Irvine, Leslie. 2004. *If You Tame Me: Understanding Our Connection with Animals*. Philadelphia: Temple University Press.

Lockwood, Randall and Frank R. Ascione. 1998. *Cruelty to Animals and Interpersonal Violence: Readings in Research and Application*. West Lafayette, IN: Purdue University Press.

Luke, Brian. 2007. *Brutal: Manhood and the Exploitation of Animals*. Urbana: University of Illinois Press.

New York Times. 2008. "The Worst Way to Farm." May 31.

Roberts, Mark S. 2008. *The Mark of Beast: Animality and Human Oppression*. West Lafayette, IN: Purdue University Press.

Siebert, Charles. 2010. "The Animal-Cruelty Syndrome." *New York Times*, June 13.

Smith, J. Z. 2004. *Relating Religion: Essays in the Study of Religion*. Chicago: University of Chicago Press.

PART I

Other Animals

Animals Across Cultures

P ART I INVITES US TO CONSIDER RELATIONSHIPS BETWEEN AND understandings of humans and animals that arise outside of Western contexts. We are confronted with profoundly distinct ways in which humans understand and relate to nonhuman animals, underscoring the contingency of our own. But we are also confronted with the striking persistence and importance of these relationships for human self-conception, however differently configured.

Tim Ingold's classic essay "Hunting and Gathering as Ways of Perceiving the Environment" (chapter 1) has been influential across several disciplines, including anthropology, ecology, and philosophy. As a brisk and especially lucid appraisal of contemporary anthropological writings on "nature," it is indispensable to the burgeoning field of animal studies. It would easily be at home in any of the three sections of this volume. As a prescient analysis of contemporary anthropological views on animals, it would work well in part II ("Animal Matters: Human/Animal and the Contemporary West"); as a powerful critique of the foundations of Western thought as they relate to the question of "the animal," it would be well placed in part III ("Animal Others: Theorizing

Animal/Human"). Our decision to include it here in part I is based on the fact that its insights are derived from, and so indelibly connected with, rich ethnographic material from traditions other than our own—in particular, hunter-gatherer communities of diverse tropical forest regions, the Cree of northeastern Canada, and Australian Aboriginal peoples. Serious consideration of other traditions not only reveals the tremendous variability in the ways animals are understood, engaged with, and conceived cross-culturally, but also sometimes points to—as Ingold forcefully argues in this essay—ways of being that are more reflective of, and compatible with, the basic conditions of life.

Ingold begins his essay by taking aim at the idea of nature as a "cultural construction," a claim so fundamental within anthropology as to have near canonical status, but one, Ingold insists, that is fundamentally incoherent. He spends the remainder of his essay persuasively demonstrating its rootedness in a tenacious, but problematic division between nature and culture that lies at the foundation of Western thought.

Western ontological dualism presupposes human beings to be unique among all living things in that we alone are in possession of "mind"—that creative and constructive cognitive apparatus that shapes, mediates, and imparts meaning onto the things of the world around us. All other forms of existence, animate and inanimate, are presumed to be devoid of this characteristic and therefore, although open to receive meanings bestowed upon them, have none of their own to disclose. To talk about "nature" as "constructed" is to implicitly accept this premise.

In making this argument, Ingold wants to do more than merely highlight the intransigence of Western ontological dualism with its presumption of human isolation and disengagement from life; he wants to discard it outright. He insists that, as hunter-gatherers routinely do, we must come to acknowledge human beings as "immersed from the start, like other creatures, in an active, practical and perceptual engagement with constituents of the dwelt-in world." Ingold argues that hunter-gatherers do not, as a rule, "see themselves as mindful subjects having to contend with an alien world of physical objects." The world, for them, is not a thing to be grasped conceptually and communicated representationally; rather, hunter-gatherers are embedded within the world and engage with it reciprocally. Ingold characterizes this as an "ontology of dwelling."

Importantly, the "ontology of dualism" and the "ontology of dwelling" do not represent alternative views of the world (a relativism that is generally held to be true within anthropology, but that, for Ingold, is a reaffirmation of the

Western position itself). Of the two, only ontological dualism denotes a mental conception or construct. An ontology of dwelling, by contrast, is an embodied perception describing the engagement and apprehension that arises from being in the world. It presupposes an engagement with constituents not only of the human but also of the nonhuman environment, which is to say, it describes the phenomenon of life itself.

Drawing on ethnographic material from hunter-gatherer societies, Ingold describes how, when life is acknowledged as engagement, a unity is assumed to underwrite the superabundance of life forms. Human and animal are understood to share a common existential status as "persons." Each person exists in a network of reciprocating persons; meaningfulness, which resides in the relational context of one's involvement in the world, is derived from the engagement of one with the other. But, according to Ingold, Western ontology is blind to this. Because of its a priori separation of mind from nature, meaningfulness is always construed as "laid over the world by the [human] mind" on an otherwise meaningless nature, including animals.

That life is given in engagement rather than disengagement is the central thesis underpinning Ingold's essay. This thesis informs the basis of his critique of Western ontological dualism and his defense of hunter-gatherer ways of being that are grounded in the reciprocal nature of life. An "ontology of dwelling," Ingold argues, is simply "a better way of coming to grips with the nature of human existence."

In sixteenth-century China the boundaries between animality and humanity were beginning to be carefully drawn, signaling a shift from a past marked by the relative fluidity of such categories. Monkey-men, Bigfoot-creatures, voracious wild-women, and other oddly shaped anthropoids posed problems for understanding "what kind of thing man was." In "On Yeti and Being Just: Carving the Borders of Humanity in Early Modern China" (chapter 2), Carla Nappi draws us into lively debates over the limits of being human through an analysis of the marvelous world of the *Bencao gangmu*, a sixteenth-century compendium of *materia medica*, which is composed of pharmaceutical lists and a classification of the natural world.

The *Bencao* became the focus of fascination and consternation for a period ill at ease with classificatory ambiguity. Its author, Li Shizhen, the celebrated founding father of modern science and medicine in China, undertook to catalog stones, plants, animals, and other objects of the natural world. Importantly, he also sought to understand the processes of metamorphosis, which it was believed gave rise to those ambiguous entities that defied easy classification.

Such beings revealed the transformative processes at work in the universe and were a source of fascination for Li. Of the many beings that puzzled him, humans were among the most problematic of all.

Human oddities were placed at the outer limits of the people category, stretching the border of what constituted the human form, but not breaching it. Similarly, human-like animals constituted anomalies within their classifications, but not challenges to them. Instead, it was the boundary group (*yulei, guailei*)—which closed the section on beasts (*shou bu*) and immediately preceded the one on people (*ren bu*)—that received most attention. It was here, Nappi writes, that beings "strange and unusual" were placed.

Nappi devotes detailed and delightful attention to itemizing these beings, describing their form and common traits. We learn that the liminal category distinction of being neither-Beast-nor-Human was largely determined on the basis of the appearance and habits of the beings, as well as on their demonstration of ethical behavior, all of which could be analogized to humans. But it was the issue of eating that played the most crucial role, constituting evidence of their nonhuman status.

That Bigfoot creatures and wild women ate human flesh was evidence of their nonhumanity, but Nappi argues that the evidence that they were eaten by humans was equally important. The fact that they were food for humans established them as nonhuman. Who or what could be legitimately defined as "food" became a central focus in the erection of a boundary between human and animal. Nappi discusses the ensuing debates that erupted over the traditional practices of consuming human body parts (hair, urine, flesh). These practices were now thrown into question, igniting debates over the vexing issue of what it means to be human.

As Nappi's essay compellingly shows, the formidable and meticulous efforts devoted to detailing, studying, and classifying those beings at the boundaries of the human and animal were an exercise in studying humanity itself.

Anand Pandian's "Pastoral Power in the Postcolony: On the Biopolitics of the Criminal Animal in South India" (chapter 3) is a theoretical engagement with the idea of animality and an ethnographic encounter with living animals.

Pandian's work builds upon Foucault's analysis of biopolitics and its association with pastoral power. In particular, Pandian explores Foucault's argument that the idea of pastoral power has played a central role in the emergence of contemporary biopolitics.

Foucault seeks to understand the processes by which individual lives have come under meticulous scrutiny and control in modern states and traces their roots to the "remote processes" of a pastoral modality of power. Foucault claims that the image of "pastoral power" served as a crucial and commanding meta-phor for conceptualizing a type of authority modeled on the relationship be-tween a figurative shepherd and his flock and served to justify the emergence of a form of collective governance characterized by both coercion and care (e.g., the institution of policing). Biopolitics is modernity's expression of pastoral power: characterized by micro-attention to the individual within a system of absolute control, it exercises its power through the management, supervision, and regulation of individual bodies—bodies that constitute the animality of the human.

Pandian departs from Foucault in his understanding of the significance of pasturage and in the scope of its application. Whereas for Foucault the "pasto-ral" served primarily as a metaphor for the rationalization of a particular form of power in the West generally, Pandian seeks to look at examples of pastoral practices in specific cultural contexts and at real material engagements with nonhuman animals that gave rise to pastoral metaphors. He contends that re-lationships between humans and animals are generative of meaningful con-cepts and images, and he insists that exploring the way in which animals are governed by humans is essential for an understanding of the many ways in which humans themselves have been not only metaphorically but also actually governed as animals in modern times. Furthermore, because the distinctions between humans and animals have been politically charged and generative of meaning in a great many historical periods and cultural traditions, Pandian seeks to broaden the scope of Foucault's analysis of the biopolitical to contexts beyond the modern West. In this way, he moves from a theoretical discussion of biopolitics to an engagement with its contemporary expression among the Kallar agricultural caste in south India, where animals, animality, and pastur-age are at the center of the people's historical imagination and of the concerns they live daily.

Pandian discusses how the Piramalai Kallar caste of the Cumbum Valley, now a dominant agricultural and buffalo-herding community in Tamil Nadu, was criminalized under colonial Britain's Criminal Tribes Act in 1918 for their alleged "bestial tendencies" and subjected to a tightly regulated system of pun-ishment and reward. As beings of "instinctual and impulsive criminality," the Kallars were deemed incapable of governing themselves and were controlled "in the manner of captive beasts." The goal of the colonial policy (a form of pastoral biopolitics) was to humanize its subjects; its target was understood to be animal in nature.

Pastoral care and restraint remain prominent idioms of contemporary Kal-lar biopolitics, and Pandian's discussion reveals the striking degree to which the moral self-conduct of villagers remains bound together with the moral governance of animals. However, unlike the animalization of human subjects of colonial British biopolitics, the moral states of virtue and vice are understood by the Kallar to be shared by humans and animals alike. Animals and people are bound together in a common moral universe in which hard work and restraint are praised as virtuous and asocial behavior condemned as immoral. That which is in need of governance, control, and "grazing" is the unrestrained rebellious and wild dimension of life, present in both humans and animals.

Pandian argues that ideas of animality constitute an important domain within our conceptualizations of pastoral power. More importantly, his work forces us to take seriously the idea that practical relations between human and nonhuman animals may constitute the very ground upon which diverse modes for governing life, including the governance of human societies, have emerged.

Anne Vallely

one

Hunting and Gathering as Ways of Perceiving the Environment

Tim Ingold

THAT NATURE IS A CULTURAL CONSTRUCTION IS AN EASY CLAIM to make, and it is one that figures prominently in recent anthropological literature. It is not so easy, however, to ascertain what might be meant by it. One of my principal objectives in this chapter is to demonstrate that this claim is incoherent. To illustrate my argument I shall consider the anthropological treatment of those peoples classically regarded as operating within a natural economy, namely, societies of hunters and gatherers. Comparing this treatment with the understandings that people who actually live by hunting and gathering have of themselves and their environments, I shall show that the latter systematically reject the ontological dualism of that tradition of thought and

An earlier version of this essay appeared in *Redefining Nature: Ecology, Culture, and Domestication*, edited by Roy Ellen and Katsuyoshi Fukui (Oxford and Washington, DC: Berg, 1996). *Note*: The version of the essay appearing here has been abbreviated by the removal of a section originally entitled "Perceiving the Landscape," which appeared in the original version prior to the section entitled "What Do Hunters and Gatherers Actually Do?" (p. 47 in this chapter). British spellings have been Americanized.

science which—as a kind of shorthand—we call "Western" and of which the dichotomy between nature and culture is the prototypical instance. I propose that we take these hunter-gatherer understandings seriously, and this means that far from regarding them as diverse cultural constructions of reality, alternative to the Western one, we need to think again about our own ways of comprehending human action, perception, and cognition and indeed about our very understanding of the environment and of our relations and responsibilities toward it. Above all, we cannot rest content with the facile identification of the environment—or at least its nonhuman component—with "nature." The world can only be "nature" for a being that does not inhabit it, yet only through inhabiting can the world be constituted, in relation to a being, as its environment.

Nature, Culture, and the Logic of Construction

Let me begin by outlining what I take to be a commonly adopted position within social and cultural anthropology. I admit that this has something of the character of a "straw man," and I am indeed setting it up in order to knock it down. Nevertheless, it is one that has proved remarkably resilient, for reasons that will become clear as we proceed.

Of all species of animals, the argument goes, humans are unique in that they occupy what Richard Shweder calls "intentional worlds."[1] For the inhabitants of such a world, things do not exist "in themselves," as indifferent objects, but only as they are given form or meaning within systems of mental representations. Thus to individuals who belong to different intentional worlds, the same objects in the same physical surroundings may mean quite different things. And when people act toward these objects, or with them in mind, their actions respond to the ways they are already appropriated, categorized, or valorized in terms of a particular, preexistent design. That design, transmitted across the generations in the form of received conceptual schemata, and manifested physically in the artificial products of their implementation, is what is commonly known as "culture."

The environments of human beings, therefore, are culturally constituted. And when we refer to an environment—or more specifically to that part of it consisting of animate and inanimate things—as "nature," then this too has to be understood as an artifact of cultural construction. "Nature is to culture," writes Marshall Sahlins, "as the constituted is to the constituting."[2] Culture provides the building plan, nature is the building; but whence come the raw materials?

There must indeed be a physical world "out there," beyond the multiple, intentional worlds of cultural subjects, otherwise there would be nothing to build with nor anyone, for that matter, to do the building. Minds cannot subsist without bodies to house them, and bodies cannot subsist unless continually engaged in material and energetic exchanges with components of the environment. Biological and ecological scientists routinely describe these exchanges as going on within a world of nature. It is apparently necessary, therefore, to distinguish between two kinds or versions of nature: "really natural" nature (the object of study for natural scientists) and "culturally perceived" nature (the object of study for social and cultural anthropologists). Such distinctions are indeed commonplace in anthropological literature: examples are Rappaport's, between the "operational" models of ecological science, purportedly describing nature as it really is, and the "cognized" models of native people; and, perhaps most notoriously, the much used and abused distinction between "etic" and "emic" accounts.[3]

In the formula "nature is culturally constructed," nature thus appears on two sides: on one as the product of a constructional process, on the other as its precondition. Herein, however, lies a paradox. Many anthropologists are well aware that the basic contrast between physical substance and conceptual form, of which the dichotomy between nature and culture is one expression, is deeply embedded within the tradition of Western thought. It is recognized that the concept of nature, insofar as it denotes an external world of matter and substance "waiting to be given meaningful shape and content by the mind of man,"[4] is part of that very intentional world within which is situated the project of Western science as the "objective" study of natural phenomena.[5] And yet the notion that there are intentional worlds and that human realities are culturally constructed, rests on precisely the same ontological foundation. The paradox may be represented as follows:

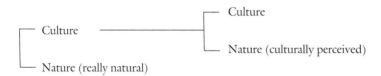

If the concept of nature is given within the intentional world of the Western scientist, then the concept of culture must—by the same token—be given within the intentional world of the Western humanist. Each, indeed, presupposes the other. Not only, then, must the concept of nature be regarded as a cultural construct, but so also must that of culture. As Carol MacCormack puts it: "Neither the concept of nature nor that of culture is 'given,' and they cannot be free from the biases of the [European] culture in which the concepts were constructed."[6] The fact that "culture" appears twice in this statement at once alerts us to a basic contradiction. For the references, in the second part of the statement, to culture and to the logic of construction take as "given" the very concepts that, in the first part of the statement, are said to be historically relative.

Nor can the problem be contrived to disappear by trying to have it both ways, as Kirsten Hastrup does when she suggests that instead of regarding nature as "either a relative cultural category or an objective physical framework around culture," it might better be seen as "both-and."[7] For then culture, too, must be both-and, both an objective categorical constructor and a relative category constructed. To attempt to apply this logic is at once to be caught in the vortex of an infinite regress: if the opposed categories of "nature" and "culture" are themselves cultural constructs, then so must be the culture that constructs them, and the culture that constructs that, and so on ad infinitum. And since, at every stage in this regress, the reality of nature reappears as its representation, "real" reality recedes as fast as it is approached.

In what follows I shall argue that hunter-gatherers do not, as a rule, approach their environment as an external world of nature that has to be "grasped" conceptually and appropriated symbolically within the terms of an imposed cultural design, as a precondition for effective action. They do not see themselves as mindful subjects having to contend with an alien world of physical objects; indeed the separation of mind and nature has no place in their thought and practice. I should add that they are not peculiar in this regard: my purpose is certainly not to argue for some distinctive hunter-gatherer worldview or to suggest that they are somehow "at one" with their environments in a way that other peoples are not. Nor am I concerned to set up a comparison between the "intentional worlds" of hunter-gatherers and Western scientists or humanists. It is of course an illusion to suppose that such a comparison could be made on level terms, since the primacy of Western ontology, the "givenness" of nature and culture, is implicit in the very premises on which the comparative project is itself established (see figure 1.1).

What I wish to suggest is that we reverse this order of primacy and follow the lead of hunter-gatherers in taking the human condition to be that of a being immersed from the start, like other creatures, in an active, practical, and perceptual engagement with constituents of the dwelt-in world. This ontology of dwelling, I contend, provides us with a better way of coming to grips with the nature of human existence than does the alternative, Western ontology whose point of departure is that of a mind detached from the world and that has literally to formulate it—to build an intentional world in consciousness—prior to any attempt at engagement. The contrast, I repeat, is not between alternative views of the world; it is rather between two ways of apprehending it, only one of which (the Western) may be characterized as the construction of a view, that is, as a process of mental representation. As for the other, apprehending the world is not a matter of construction

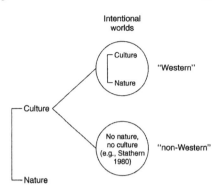

FIGURE 1.1. A comparison between "non-Western" and "Western" intentional worlds assumes the primacy of the Western ontology, with its dichotomy between nature and culture or between physical substance and conceptual form. *Source*: Author.

but of engagement, not of building but of dwelling, not of making a view *of* the world but of taking up a view *in* it.[8]

In the following sections I will move on to examine, in more detail, how this contrast has been played out in the context of Western anthropological studies of hunters and gatherers. First, I will consider how certain tropical hunter-gatherer peoples perceive their relations to their forest environment. Second, I will look at the way northern hunters, in particular the Cree of northeastern Canada, understand their relations to the animals they hunt. I conclude by showing how anthropological attempts to depict the mode of practical engagement of hunter-gatherers with the world as a mode of cultural construction of it have had the effect, quite contrary to stated intentions, of perpetuating a naturalistic vision of the hunter-gatherer economy.

Children of the Forest

In his classic study of the Mbuti Pygmies of the Ituri Forest, Colin Turnbull observes that the people recognize their dependence on the forest that surrounds them by referring to it as "Father" or "Mother." They do so "because, as they say, it gives them food, warmth, shelter and clothing, just like their parents," and moreover, "like their parents, [it] gives them affection."[9] This form of reference, and the analogy it establishes between the most intimate relations of human kinship and the equally intimate relations between human persons and the nonhuman environment, is by no means unique to the Mbuti.[10] Precisely similar observations have been made among other hunter-gatherers of the tropical forest, in widely separate regions of the world. For example, among the Batek Negritos of Malaysia, according to Kirk Endicott, the forest environment "is not just the physical setting in which they live, but a world made for them in which they have a well-defined part to play. They see themselves as involved in an intimate relationship of interdependence with the plants, animals and *hala'* (including the deities) that inhabit their world."[11] The *hala'* are the creator beings who brought the forest world into existence for the people, who protect and care for it, and who provide its human dwellers with nourishment. And again, among the Nayaka, forest-dwelling hunter-gatherers of Tamil Nadu, South India, Nurit Bird-David found a similar attitude: "Nayaka look on the forest as they do on a mother or father. For them, it is not something 'out there' that responds mechanically or passively but like a parent, it provides food unconditionally to its children."[12] Nayaka refer to both the spirits that inhabit the landscape and the spirits of their own predecessors by terms that translate as "big father" and "big mother" and to themselves in relation to these spirits as sons and daughters.

What are we to make of this? Drawing an explicit parallel between her own Nayaka material and the ethnography of the Batek and Mbuti, Bird-David argues that hunter-gatherer perceptions of the environment are typically oriented by the primary metaphor "forest is as parent," or more generally by the notion that the environment *gives* the wherewithal of life to people—not in return for appropriate conduct, but unconditionally. Among neighboring populations of cultivators, by contrast, the environment is likened to an ancestor rather than a parent, which yields its bounty only reciprocally, *in return* for favors rendered. It is this difference in orientation to the environment, she suggests, that most fundamentally distinguishes hunter-gatherers from cultivators, and it is upheld even when the former draw (as they often do) on cultivated resources and when the latter, conversely, draw on the "wild" resources of the forest.[13] In a subsequent extension of the argument, and drawing once again on Mbuti, Batek, and Nayaka ethnography, Bird-David proposes that hunter-gatherers liken the unconditional way in which the forest transacts with people to the similarly unconditional transactions that take place among the people of a community, which in anthropological accounts come under the rubric of sharing.[14] Thus the environment shares its bounty with humans just as humans share with one another, thereby integrating both human and nonhuman components of the world into one, all-embracing "cosmic economy of sharing."

But when the hunter-gatherer addresses the forest as his or her parent, or speaks of accepting what it has to offer as one would from other people, on what grounds can we claim that the usage is metaphorical? This is evidently not an interpretation that the people would make themselves; nevertheless—taking her cue from Lakoff and Johnson[15]—Bird-David argues that these key metaphors enable them to make sense of their environment and guide their actions within it, even though *"people may not be normally aware of them."*[16] There is a troublesome inconsistency here. On the one hand, Bird-David is anxious to offer a culture-sensitive account of the hunter-gatherer economy, as a counterpoint to the prevailing ecologism of most anthropological work in this field. On the other hand, she can do so only by imposing a division of her own, which forms no part of local conceptions, between actuality and metaphor. Underwriting this division is an assumed separation between two domains: the domain of human persons and social relations, wherein parenting and sharing are matters of everyday, commonsense reality; and the domain of the nonhuman environment, the forest with its plants and animals, relations with which are understood by drawing, for analogy, on those intrinsic to the first domain. In short, hunter-gatherers are supposed to call upon their experience of relations in the human world in order to model their relations with the nonhuman one.

The theoretical inspiration for this analytical tactic comes from Stephen Gudeman,[17] so let us turn to look at how he approaches the matter. Starting from the assumption that "humans are modelers," Gudeman proposes that "securing a livelihood, meaning the domain of material 'production,' 'distribution,' and 'consumption,' is culturally modeled in all societies."[18] Entailed in the notion of modeling is a distinction between a "schema," which provides a program, plan, or script, and an "object" to which it is applied: thus "the model is a projection from the domain of the schema to the domain of the object."[19] Comparing Western and non-Western (or "local") models of livelihood, Gudeman suggests that in the former, schemas taken from the "domain of material objects" are typically applied to "the domain of human life," whereas in the latter the direction of application is reversed, such that "material processes are modeled as being intentional."[20] But notice how the entire argument is predicated upon an initial ontological dualism between the intentional worlds of human subjects and the object world of material things, or in brief, between society and nature. It is only by virtue of holding these to be separate that the one can be said to furnish the model for the other. The implication, however, is that the claim of the people themselves to inhabit but one world, encompassing relations with both human and nonhuman components of the environment on a similar footing, is founded upon an illusion—one that stems from their inability to recognize where the reality ends and its schematic representation begins. It is left to the anthropological observer to draw the dividing line, on one side of which lies the social world of human modelers of nature, and on the other, the natural world modeled as human society.

In the specific case with which we are concerned, hunter-gatherers' material interactions with the forest environment are said to be modeled on the interpersonal relations of parenting and sharing: the former, assigned to the domain of nature, establish the object; the latter, assigned to the domain of society, provide the schema. But this means that actions and events that are constitutive of the social domain must be representative of the natural. When, for example, the child begs its mother for a morsel of food, that communicative gesture is itself a constitutive moment in the development of the mother-child relationship, and the same is true for the action of the mother in fulfilling the request. Parenting is not a construction that is projected *onto* acts of this kind, it rather subsists *in* them, in the nurture and affection bestowed by adults on their offspring. Likewise, the give and take of food beyond the narrow context of parent-child ties is constitutive of relations of sharing, relations that subsist in the mutuality and companionship of persons in intimate social groups.[21] Yet according to the logic of the argument outlined above, as soon as we turn to consider exchange with the nonhuman environment, the situation is quite otherwise. For far from subsisting in people's practical involvement with the forest and its fauna and flora in their activities of food-getting, parenting and sharing belong instead to a construction that is projected onto that involvement from a separate, social source. Hence, when the hunter-gatherer begs the forest to provide food, as one would a human parent, the gesture is not a moment in the unfolding of relations between humans and nonhuman agencies and entities in the environment; it is rather an act that says something about these relationships, a representative evaluation or commentary.[22]

In short, actions that in the sphere of human relations would be regarded as instances of practical involvement with the world come to be seen, in the sphere of relations with the nonhuman environment, as instances of its metaphorical construction. Yet those who would construct the world, who would be "modelers" in Gudeman's sense, must already live in it, and life presupposes an engagement with components not only of the human but also of the nonhuman environment. People need the support and affection of one another, but they also need to eat. How then, to stay with the same argument, do hunter-gatherers deal, actually rather than metaphorically, with nonhuman beings in the practical business of gaining a livelihood? They cannot do so in their capacity as persons, since nonhuman agencies and entities are supposed to have no business in the world of persons save as figures of the anthropomorphic imagination. Hence the domain of their actual interaction with the nonhuman environment in the procurement of subsistence must lie beyond that of their existence as persons, in a separate domain wherein they figure as biological objects rather than cultural subjects, that is as organisms rather than persons. This is the *natural* domain of organism-environment interactions, as distinct from the *social* domain of interpersonal relations. In figure 1.2 (upper diagram) this result is indicated schematically.

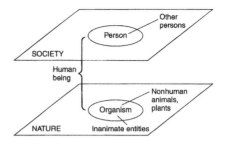

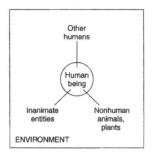

FIGURE 1.2. Western anthropological (top) and hunter-gatherer (bottom) economies of knowledge. *Source*: Author.

There is a profound irony here. Was not the principal objective to counteract that "naturalisation of the hunter-gatherer economy" that, as Sahlins comments, has formed the received anthropological wisdom, in favor of an account sensitive to the nuances of local culture?[23] Yet what we find is that such naturalization is entailed in the very stance that treats the perception of the environment as a matter of reconstructing the data of experience within intentional worlds. The sphere of human engagement with the environment, in the practical activities of hunting and gathering, is disembedded from the sphere within which humans are constituted as social beings or persons, as a precondition for letting the latter stand to the former as schema to object.

The consequences are all too apparent from the conclusion toward which Gudeman moves, in bringing his argument to a close: "In all living societies humans must maintain themselves by securing energy from the environment. Although this life-sustaining process amounts only to a rearranging of nature, a transforming of materials from one state or appearance to another, humans make something of this activity."[24] By his own account, then, the life-process of human beings, shorn of the diverse constructions that are placed upon it and that "make something" of it, is nothing more than a *rearranging of nature*.

In this connection, we may recall Sahlins's attempt to treat "economy" as a "component of culture," which led him to contrast "the material life process of society" to "a need satisfying process of individual behavior."[25] Hunting and gathering, by this account, are operations that take place in nature, consisting of interactions between human organisms with "needs," and environmental resources with the potential to satisfy them. Only after having been extracted is the food transferred to the domain of society, wherein its distribution is governed by a schema for sharing, a schema inscribed in the social relations that the economic practices of sharing serve to reproduce.[26] In the economy of knowledge, as conceived in general by Gudeman and specifically for hunter-gatherers by Bird-David, what applies to food applies also to sensory experi-ence. That experience, gained through human organism-environment interac-tions, provides the raw material of sensation that—along with food—hunters and gatherers "take home" with them. Carried over to the domain of interper-sonal relations, it too is assimilated to a social schema, to yield a cultural con-struction of nature such as "the forest is as parent."

In figure 1.2 this anthropological conception of the economy of knowledge is contrasted with that of the people themselves. In their account (lower dia-gram), there are not two worlds, of nature and society, but just one, saturated with personal powers and embracing humans and the animals and plants on which they depend as well as the features of the landscape in which they live and move. Within this one world, humans figure not as composites of body and mind but as undivided beings, "organism-persons," relating as such both to other humans and to nonhuman agencies and entities in their environment. Between these spheres of involvement there is no *absolute* separation—they are but contextually delimited segments of a single field. As Bird-David observes, hunter-gatherers "do not inscribe into the nature of things a division between the natural agencies and themselves, as we [Westerners] do with our 'nature: culture' dichotomy. They view their world as an integrated entity."[27] And so one gets to know the forest, and the plants and animals that dwell therein, in just the same way that one becomes familiar with other people—by spending time with them, investing in one's relations with them the same qualities of care, feeling, and attention. This explains why hunters and gatherers consider time devoted to forays in the forest to be well spent, even if it yields little or nothing by way of useful return: there is, as Bird-David puts it, "a concern with the activity itself," since it allows people to "keep in touch" with the non-human environment.[28] And because of this, people know the environment "in-timately, in the way one 'knows' close relatives with whom one shares intimate day-to-day life."[29]

That the perception of the social world is grounded in the direct, mutually attentive involvement of self and other in shared contexts of experience, prior to its representation in terms of received conceptual schemata, is now well established. But in Western anthropological and psychological discourse, such involvement continues to be apprehended within the terms of the orthodox dualisms of subject and object, persons and things. Rendered as "intersubjectivity," it is taken to be the constitutive quality of the social domain *as against* the object world of nature, a domain open to human beings but not to nonhuman kinds.[30] Thus, according to Trevarthen and Logotheti, "human cultural intelligence is seen to be founded on a level of engagement of minds, or intersubjectivity, such as no other species has or can acquire."[31] In the hunter-gatherer economy of knowledge, by contrast, it is as entire persons, not as disembodied minds, that human beings engage with one another and, moreover, with nonhuman beings as well. They do so as beings *in* a world, not as minds that, excluded from a given reality, find themselves in the common predicament of having to make sense of it. To coin a term, the constitutive quality of their world is not intersubjectivity but *interagentivity*. To speak of the forest as a parent is not, then, to model object relations in terms of primary intersubjectivity, but to recognize that at root, the constitutive quality of intimate relations with nonhuman and human components of the environment is one and the same.

Humans and Animals

The Waswanipi Cree of northeastern Canada, according to Harvey Feit, "say that they only catch an animal when the animal is given to them. They say that in winter the north wind, *chuetenshu,* and the animals themselves give them what they need to live."[32] This idea, that the nourishing substance of animals is received by humans as a gift, is widely reported among northern hunting peoples, but in what follows I shall confine my remarks to studies of two other Cree groups. Among the Wemindji Cree, "respectful activity towards the animals enhances the readiness with which they give themselves, or are given by God, to hunters."[33] And for the Mistassini Cree, Adrian Tanner reports that the events and activities of the hunt, though they have an obvious "common-sense" significance insofar as they entail the deployment of technical knowledge and skill in the service of providing for the material needs of the human population, are also "reinterpreted" on another, magico-religious level:

> The facts about particular animals are reinterpreted as if they had social relationships between themselves, and between them and anthropomorphized natural forces, and furthermore the animals are thought of as if

they had personal relations with the hunters. The idealized form of these latter relations is often that the hunter pays respect to an animal; that is, he acknowledges the animal's superior position, and following this the animal "gives itself" to the hunter, that is, allows itself to assume a position of equality, or even inferiority, with respect to the hunter.[34]

In short, the animals figure for these northern hunters very much as the forest figures for such tropical hunter-gatherers as the Mbuti, Batek, and Nayaka: they are partners with humans in an encompassing "cosmic economy of sharing."

Now Western thought, as is well known, drives an absolute division between the contrary conditions of humanity and animality, a division that is aligned with a series of others such as between subjects and objects, persons and things, morality and physicality, reason and instinct, and, above all, society and nature. Underwriting the Western view of the uniqueness of the human species is the fundamental axiom that *personhood as a state of being is not open to nonhuman animal kinds*. It is for this reason that we are able to conflate both the moral condition and the biological taxon (*Homo sapiens*) under the single rubric of "humanity." And for this reason, too, we can countenance an inquiry into the animal nature of human beings whilst rejecting out of hand the possibility of an inquiry into the humanity of nonhuman animals.[35] Human existence is conceived to be conducted simultaneously on two levels, the social level of interpersonal, intersubjective relations and the natural ecological level of organism-environment interactions, whereas animal existence is wholly confined within the natural domain. Humans are both persons *and* organisms, animals are solely organisms.

This is a view, however, that Cree and other northern hunters categorically reject. Personhood, for them, is open equally to human and nonhuman animal (and even nonanimal) kinds. Here, once again, is Feit on the Waswanipi:

> In the culturally constructed world of the Waswanipi the animals, the winds and many other phenomena are thought of as being "like persons" in that they act intelligently and have wills and idiosyncracies, and understand and are understood by men. Causality, therefore, is personal not mechanical or biological, and it is . . . always appropriate to ask "who did it?" and "why?" rather than "how does that work?"[36]

This rendering of the Cree perspective is echoed by Tanner, who points to the significant implication of the idea that game animals live in social groups or communities akin to those of human beings, namely, "that social interaction between humans and animals is made possible."[37] Hunting itself comes to be regarded not as a technical manipulation of the natural world but as a kind of interpersonal dialogue, integral to the total process of social life wherein both human and animal persons are constituted with their particular identities and purposes. Among the Wemindji Cree, qualities of personhood are likewise assigned to humans, animals, spirits, and certain geophysical agents. As Colin Scott writes: "Human persons are not set over and against a material context of inert nature, but rather are one species of person in a network of reciprocating persons."[38]

Though the ethnographic accounts offered by Tanner and Scott are in striking agreement, their interpretations are not, and it is revealing to explore the contrast between them. The problem hinges on the question of whether, when the Cree hunter refers to animals or to the wind as he would to human persons, he does so within the compass of what Feit, in the passage cited above, calls a "culturally constructed world." Tanner is in no doubt that they do. Thus he asserts that "game animals participate simultaneously in two levels of reality, one 'natural' and the other 'cultural.'"[39] On the natural level they are encountered simply as material entities, organic constituents of the object world to be killed and consumed. On the cultural level, by contrast, they are "reinterpreted" as anthropomorphic beings participating in a domain "modeled on conventional Cree patterns of social and cultural organization."[40] In terms of this analysis, then, animals are constructed as persons through their assimilation to a schema drawn from the domain of human relations. This is entirely in accord with Gudeman's theory of the cultural modeling of livelihood, which I discussed in the previous section. Indeed, Gudeman draws for ethnographic support, inter alia, on Tanner's study. "The Mistassini Cree," he writes, "construct their hunting and trapping activities as an exchange between themselves and animal spirits . . . and the exchange itself is patterned after ordinary human relationships, such as friendship, coercion and love."[41]

I have already shown, in the case of hunter-gatherer relations with the forest environment, how the constructionist argument is founded on an ontological dualism between society and nature, which in this instance reappears as one between humanity and animality. On one side, then, we have the world of human modelers of animals, on the other, the animal world modeled as human. If the people themselves profess to be aware of but one world, of persons and their relationships, it is because, seeing their own social ambience reflected in the mirror of nature, they cannot distinguish the reflection from reality. Now by all accounts, as we have seen, the dualism of humanity and animality, and the entailed restriction of personhood to human beings, is not endorsed by the Cree. This does not mean, of course, that they fail to differentiate between humans and animals. To the contrary, they are acutely concerned about such differences. For example, although humans may have sexual relations with certain other humans and may kill and consume certain nonhuman animals, the consequences of categorical confusion—of sex with nonhumans or killing fellow human beings—would be disastrous.[42]

The point is that the difference between, say, a goose and a man is not between an organism and a person, but between one kind of organism-person and another. From the Cree perspective, personhood is not the manifest form of humanity; rather the human is one of many outward forms of personhood. And so when Cree hunters claim that a goose is in some sense like a man, far from drawing a figurative parallel across two fundamentally separate domains, they are rather pointing to the real unity that underwrites their differentiation. Whereas Western thought sets out from an assumed dichotomy between the human and the animal and then searches about for possible analogies or homologies, the Cree trajectory—as Scott explains—"seems rather the opposite: to assume fundamental similarity while exploring the differences between humans and animals."[43] To posit a "metaphorical" equivalence between goose and man is not, then, to render "one kind of thing in terms of another,"[44] as Western—including Western anthropological—convention would have it. A more promising perspective is offered by Michael Jackson, who argues that metaphor should be apprehended as a way of drawing attention to real relational unities rather than of figuratively papering over dualities. Metaphor, Jackson writes, "reveals, not the 'thisness of a that' but rather that 'this is that.'"[45]

It follows that the equivalence can work both ways. It is not "anthropomorphic," as Tanner suggests,[46] to compare the animal to the human, any more than it is "naturalistic" to compare the human to the animal, since in both cases the comparison points to a level on which human and animal share a common existential status, namely, as living beings or persons. The move, if you will, is not from the literal to the figurative, but from the actual to the potential—for personhood, at root, is the potential to become a man, a goose, or any other of the innumerable forms of animate being. From this perspective, it makes no significant difference whether one renders animal actions in human terms or human actions in animal terms. As Scott puts it: "One might observe that a consequence of the sort of analogical thinking that I have been describing would be to anthropomorphize animals, but that would be to assume the primacy of the human term. The animal term reacts with perhaps equal force on the human term, so that animal behavior can become a model for human relations."[47]

This same argument can be applied, pari passu, to the metaphor "forest is as parent," considered in the last section. One could just as well say that "parent is as forest," for the force of the metaphor is to reveal the underlying ontological equivalence of human and nonhuman components of the environment as agencies of nurturance.

What humans and nonhumans have in common, for Cree as for other hunter-gatherers, is that they are *alive*. Ostensibly, and barring certain geophysical phenomena that Cree would regard as animate but that we might not, this is a conclusion with which Western thinkers would not disagree. Yet in Western biology, life tends to be understood as a passive process, as the reaction of organisms, bound by their separate natures, to the given conditions of their respective environments. This carries the implication that every organism is prespecified, with regard to its essential nature, *prior* to its entry into the life process—an implication that in modern biology appears in the guise of the doctrine of genetic preformation. With this view, personal powers—of awareness, agency, and intentionality—can form no part of the organism *as such*, but must necessarily be "added on" as capacities not of body but of mind, capacities that Western thought has traditionally reserved for humans. Even today, now that the possibility of nonhuman animal awareness has arisen as a legitimate topic of scientific speculation, the basic dualism of mind and body is retained—for the question is phrased as one about the existence of animal minds.[48] Consciousness, then, is the life of the mind.

For the Cree, life has a different meaning. Scott tells us that "the term *pimaatisiiwin*, 'life,' was translated by one Cree man as 'continuous birth.'"[49] To be alive is to be situated within a field of relations that, as it unfolds, actively and ceaselessly brings forms into being: humans as humans, geese as geese, and so on. Far from revealing forms that are already specified, life is the process of their ongoing generation. Every living being, then, emerges as a particular, positioned embodiment of this generative potential. Hence personhood, far from being "added on" to the living organism, is implicated in the very condition of being alive: the Cree word for "persons," according to Scott, "can itself be glossed as 'he lives.'"[50] Organisms are not just *like* persons, they *are* persons. Likewise, consciousness is not supplementary to organic life but is, so to speak, its advancing front—"on the verge of unfolding events, of continuous birth," as Scott renders the Cree conception.[51]

Now the ontological equivalence of humans and animals, as organism-persons and as fellow participants in a life process, carries a corollary of capital importance. It is that both can have points of view. In other words, for both the world exists as a meaningful place, constituted in relation to the purposes and capabilities of action of the being in question. Western ontology, as we have seen, denies this, asserting that meaning does not lie in the relational contexts of the perceiver's involvement in the world, but is rather laid over the world by the mind. Humans alone, it is said, are capable of representing an external reality in this way, organizing the data of experience according to their diverse cultural schemata. So when the Cree claim, as indeed they do, that the same events surrounding a hunt afford two possible interpretations, from the points of view, respectively, of the human hunter and of the animal hunted, the Western observer is inclined to regard the former as literal and the latter as figurative, "as if" the animal were human and so could participate with "real" humans in a common world of meanings. And this is precisely what Tanner does when he re-presents to us—his readers—as a "cultural" reality (as opposed to a "natural" one) what the Cree originally presented to him as a "bear reality" or "caribou reality" (as opposed to a "human" one).[52] Note that the distinction between natural and cultural levels of participation is not one that the Cree make themselves. According to Scott, Cree has "no word corresponding to our term 'nature,'" nor does it have any "equivalent of 'culture' that would make it a special province of humans."[53]

A creature can have a point of view because its action in the world is, at the same time, a process of *attending* to it. Different creatures have different points of view because, given their capabilities of action and perception, they attend to the world in different ways. Cree hunters, for example, notice things about the environment that geese do not, yet by the hunters' own admission, geese also notice things that humans do not.[54] What is certain, however, is that humans figure in the perceptual world of geese just as geese figure in that of humans. It is clearly of vital importance to geese that they should be as attentive to the human presence as to the presence of any other potential predator. On the basis of past experience, they learn to pick up the relevant warning signs and continually adjust their behavior accordingly. And human hunters, for their part, attend to the presence of geese *in the knowledge that geese are attending to them*. "The perceptions and interpretations of Cree hunters," Scott observes, "suggest that geese are quite apt at learning in what contexts to expect predation, at learning to distinguish predatory from non-predatory humans, and at communicating appropriate behavioral adaptations to other geese."[55]

In short, animals do not participate with humans qua persons only in a domain of virtual reality, as represented within culturally constructed, intentional worlds, superimposed upon the naturally given substratum of organism-environment interactions. They participate as real-world creatures, endowed with powers of feeling and autonomous action, whose characteristic behaviors, temperaments, and sensibilities one gets to know in the very course of one's everyday practical dealings with them. In this regard, dealing with non-human animals is not fundamentally different from dealing with fellow humans. Indeed the following definition of sociality, originally proposed by Alfred Schutz, could—with the insertions indicated in brackets—apply with equal force to the encounter between human hunters and their prey: "Sociality is constituted by communicative acts in which the I [the hunter] turns to the others [animals], apprehending them as persons who turn to him, and both know of this fact."[56] Humans may of course be unique in their capacity to *narrate* such encounters, but no one can construct a narrative, any more than they could build a model, who is not already situated in the world and thus already caught up in a nexus of relations with both human and nonhuman constituents of the environment. The relations that Cree have with the latter are what we outside observers call "hunting."

What Do Hunters and Gatherers Actually Do?

To this day, the anthropological status of hunters and gatherers has remained equivocal, to say the least. Though no one would any longer deny them full membership of the human species, it is still commonly held that in deriving their subsistence from hunting and trapping "wild" animals and gathering "wild" plants, honey, shellfish, and so on, they are somehow comparable in their mode of life to nonhuman animals in a way that farmers, herdsmen, and urban dwellers are not. Nothing is more revealing of this attitude than the commonplace habit of denoting the activities of hunting and gathering by the single word "foraging." I am not concerned here with the narrow sense of foraging in which it has sometimes been contrasted with collecting.[57] I mean rather to draw attention to the way in which "foraging" has been adopted in a very general sense as a shorthand for "hunting and gathering," ostensibly on the grounds of simple convenience. "Forager," it is argued, is less cumbersome than "hunter-gatherer," and the term carries no unwarranted implications as regards the relative priority of animal and vegetable foods, or of male and female labor.

But the concept of foraging also has an established usage in the field of ecology, to denote the feeding behavior of animals of all kinds, and it is by extension from this field that the anthropological use of the term is explicitly derived. Thus, introducing a volume of studies on "hunter-gatherer foraging strategies," Winterhalder and Smith note that "the subsistence patterns of human foragers are fairly analogous to those of other species and are thus more easily studied with ecological models."[58] And it is precisely the definition of human foragers as those who do *not* produce their food that legitimates the comparison: "Foraging refers inclusively to tactics used to obtain nonproduced foodstuffs or other resources, those not directly cultivated or husbanded by the human population."[59] In short, it appears that humans can be only either foragers or producers; if the former, their subsistence practices are analogous to those of nonhuman animals; if the latter, they are not. The producer is conceived to intervene in natural processes, from a position at least partially outside it; the forager, by contrast, is supposed never to have extricated him- or herself from nature in the first place.

I have argued in this chapter that the world as perceived by hunters and gatherers is constituted through their engagement with it, in the course of everyday, subsistence-related practices. These practices cannot be reduced to their narrowly behavioral aspect, as strategically programmed responses to external environmental stimuli, as implied in the notion of foraging. Nor, however, can they be regarded as planned interventions in nature, launched from the separate platform of society, as implied in the notion of production. *Neither foraging nor production is an adequate description of what hunters and gatherers do.* As an alternative, Bird-David suggests "procurement":

> Distinguished from "to produce" and "production," as also from "to forage" and "foraging," "to procure" (according to the Shorter Oxford Dictionary) is "to bring about, to obtain by care or effort, to prevail upon, to induce, to persuade a person to do something." "Procurement" is management, contrivance, acquisition, getting, gaining. Both terms are accurate enough for describing modern hunter-gatherers who apply care, sophistication and knowledge to their resource-getting activities.[60]

This is a suggestion I would endorse. The notion of procurement nicely brings out what I have been most concerned to stress: that the activities we conventionally call hunting and gathering are forms of skilled, attentive "coping" in the world, intentionally carried out by persons in an environment replete with other agentive powers of one kind and another. The point may be most readily summarized by referring back to figure 1.2. In the upper diagram, representing the Western ontology, foraging would be positioned as an interaction in the plane of nature, between the human organism and its environment, whereas production would appear as an intervention in nature from the separate plane of society. In the lower diagram, representing the hunter-gatherer ontology, there is but one plane, in which humans engage, as whole organism-persons, with components of the environment, in the activities of procurement.

My argument has been that the "naturalization" of the activities of hunting and gathering, as revealed in their apparently unproblematic redesignation as "foraging," is a product of the "culturalization" of the perceived environment. In the case of hunter-gatherers of the tropical forest, we have seen how their perception of the forest environment, as being in some respects like a human parent, has been interpreted anthropologically as due to the application of a schema for metaphorically constructing it, and how, as a result, the forest itself and hunter-gatherers' interactions with it come to be excluded from the domain in which they relate to one another as persons. In the case of the northern hunters, we have likewise seen how the assumption that in their capacity as persons humans can relate to animals only as the latter are represented within human intentional worlds leads to the placement of real encounters of hunting beyond the bounds of these intentional worlds, in a separate domain designated as "natural."

In short, a cultural constructionist approach to environmental perception, far from challenging the prevailing ecological models of hunting and gathering as foraging, actually reinforces them, creating by exclusion a separate logical space for organism-environment interactions wherein these models are appropriately applied. Those who oppose the designation of hunter-gatherers as foragers often do so on the grounds that it makes them seem just like nonhuman animals, without, however, questioning the applicability of the foraging model to the animals themselves.[61] I believe that by paying attention to what hunter-gatherers are telling us, this is just what we should be questioning, and in doing so laying down a challenge not only to cultural anthropology but to ecological science as well. We may admit that humans are, indeed, just like other animals; not, however, insofar as they exist as organisms rather than persons, as constituent entities in an objective world of nature presented as a spectacle to detached scientific observation, but by virtue of their mutual involvement, as undivided centers of action and awareness, within a continuous life process. In this process, the relations that human beings have with one another form just one part of the total field of relations embracing all living things.[62]

There can, then, be no radical break between social and ecological relations; rather, the former constitute a *subset* of the latter. What this suggests is the possibility of a new kind of ecological anthropology, one that would take as its starting point the active, perceptual engagement of human beings with the constituents of their world—for it is only from a position of such engagement that they can launch their imaginative speculations concerning what the world

is like. The first step in the establishment of this ecological anthropology
would be to recognize that the relations with which it deals, between human
beings and their environments, are not confined to a domain of "nature" separate from and given independently of the domain in which they lead their lives
as persons. For hunter-gatherers as for the rest of us, life is given in engagement, not in disengagement, and in that very engagement the real world at
once ceases to be "nature" and is revealed to us as an environment for people.
Environments are constituted in life, not just in thought, and it is only because
we live in an environment that we can think at all.

Notes

1. Shweder 1990:2.
2. Sahlins 1976:209.
3. Rappaport 1968:237–241; Ellen 1982, chapter 9; cf. Ingold 1992a:47–48.
4. Sahlins 1976:210.
5. Shweder 1990:24.
6. MacCormack 1980:6.
7. Hastrup 1989:7.
8. Ingold 1996:117.
9. Turnbull 1965:19.
10. Subsequent ethnographic work among the Mbuti has, it should be noted, cast
considerable doubt on the authenticity of Turnbull's somewhat "romantic" account. Thus,
Grinker (1992) fails to find indigenous conceptions that would correspond to the feeling
for the forest that Turnbull imputes to the Mbuti. And Ichikawa (1992) observes that
Mbuti attitudes toward the forest are, in reality, decidedly ambivalent: the forest is held to
be the home of destructive as well as benevolent powers. But such ambivalence is equally
characteristic of intimate relations in the human domain, which also have their undercur-
rent of negativity. However, by addressing the forest as "Father," Ichikawa states, Mbuti
"are appealing to it for the benevolence normally expected from a parent" (1992:41).
11. Endicott 1979:82.
12. Bird-David 1990:190.
13. Bird-David 1990.
14. Bird-David 1992a.
15. Lakoff and Johnson 1980.
16. Bird-David 1992a:31; Bird-David 1990:190 (emphasis added).
17. Gudeman 1986.
18. Gudeman 1986:37.
19. Gudeman 1986:38.
20. Gudeman 1986:43–44.

21. Cf. Price 1975; Ingold 1986:116–117.

22. In responding to the criticisms of Abramson (1992) and myself (Ingold 1992b), Bird-David significantly softens this contrast. Following Gudeman (1992), she stresses the pragmatic—as against the cognitive—aspect of modeling, regarding it in the first place as a kind of activity or performance. Through performance, the model is actualized as lived experience. Considering the example "a dog is a friend," she points out that by bestowing the affection due to a human familiar upon her dog—to which the dog evidently responds by showing every sign of affection for her—it actually becomes a friend and is not merely "thought of" as such (Bird-David 1992a:44). To refer to the dog as her friend is thus to draw attention to an underlying quality of relationship that can subsist just as well in gestures toward nonhuman as toward human familiars. This argument, though it comes close to agreement with that advanced in this chapter, by the same token departs significantly from the approach of Lakoff and Johnson (1980).

23. Sahlins 1976:100.

24. Gudeman 1986:154.

25. Sahlins 1972:186, footnote 1.

26. See Ingold 1988a:275.

27. Bird-David 1992a:29–30.

28. Bird-David 1992a:30.

29. Bird-David 1992b:39.

30. Willis 1990:11–12.

31. Trevarthen and Logotheti 1989:167.

32. Feit 1973:116.

33. Scott 1989:204.

34. Tanner 1979:136.

35. Ingold 1988b:6.

36. Feit 1973:116.

37. Tanner 1979:137–138.

38. Scott 1989:195.

39. Tanner 1979:137.

40. Tanner 1979:137.

41. Gudeman 1986:148–149, citing Tanner 1979:138, 148–150.

42. Scott 1989:197.

43. Scott 1989:195.

44. Lakoff and Johnson 1980:5.

45. Jackson 1983:132. As Bird-David puts it, in connection with the friendliness of her dog (see note 22), the dog is not merely "like" a friend, "it *is* a friend" (1992a:44).

46. Tanner 1979:136.

47. Scott 1989:198.

48. Griffin 1976, 1984; see Ingold 1988c.

49. Scott 1989:195.

50. Scott 1989:195.

51. Scott 1989:195.

52. Tanner 1979:136–137.

53. Scott 1989:195.

54. Scott 1989:202.

55. Scott 1989:199.

56. Schutz 1970:163.

57. See, for example, Binford 1983:339–346; Ingold 1986:82–87.

58. Winterhalder and Smith 1981:x.

59. Winterhalder 1981b:16.

60. Bird-David 1992b:40.

61. For example, Bird-David 1992b:38.

62. Ingold 1990:220.

References

Abramson, A. 1992. Comment on Nurit Bird-David, "Beyond 'The Original Affluent Society.'" *Current Anthropology* 33, no. 1: 34–35.

Binford, L. R. 1983. *Working at Archaeology*. London: Academic Press.

Bird-David, N. 1990. "The Giving Environment: Another Perspective on the Economic System of Gatherer-Hunters." *Current Anthropology* 31:189–196.

——. 1992a. "Beyond 'The Original Affluent Society': A Culturalist Reformulation." *Current Anthropology* 33:25–47.

——. 1992b. "Beyond 'The Hunting and Gathering Mode of Subsistence': Culture-Sensitive Observations on the Nayaka and Other Modern Hunter-Gatherers." *Man* (N.S.) 27:19–44.

Ellen, R. F. 1982. *Environment, Subsistence and System*. Cambridge: Cambridge University Press.

Endicott, K. 1979. *Batek Negrito Religion*. Oxford: Clarendon Press.

Feit, H. 1973. "The Ethno-Ecology of the Waswanipi Cree: Or How Hunters Can Manage Their Resources." In *Cultural Ecology: Readings on the Canadian Indians and Eskimos*, ed. B. Cox, 115–125. Toronto: McClelland and Stewart.

Gibson, J. J. 1979. *The Ecological Approach to Visual Perception*. Boston: Houghton Mifflin.

Griffin, D. R. 1976. *The Question of Animal Awareness*. New York: Rockefeller University Press.

——. 1984. *Animal Thinking*. Cambridge, MA: Harvard University Press.

Grinker, R. R. 1992. Comment on Nurit Bird-David, "Beyond 'The Original Affluent Society.'" *Current Anthropology* 33, no. 1: 39.

Gudeman, S. 1986. *Economics as Culture*. London: Routledge and Kegan Paul.

——. 1992. Comment on Nurit Bird-David, "Beyond 'The Original Affluent Society.'" *Current Anthropology* 33, no. 1: 39–40.

Hastrup, K. 1989. "Nature as Historical Space." *Folk* 31:5–20.

Ichikawa, M. 1992. Comment on Nurit Bird-David, "Beyond 'The Original Affluent Society.'" *Current Anthropology* 33, no. 1: 40–41.

Ingold, T. 1986. *The Appropriation of Nature*. Manchester: Manchester University Press.

——. 1988a. "Notes on the Foraging Mode of Production." In *Hunters and Gatherers (1): History, Evolution and Social Change*, ed. T. Ingold, D. Riches, and J. Woodburn, 269–285. Oxford: Berg.

——. 1988b. "Introduction." In *What Is an Animal?*, ed. T. Ingold, 1–16. London: Unwin Hyman.

——. 1988c. "The Animal in the Study of Humanity." In *What Is an Animal?*, ed. T. Ingold, 84–99. London: Unwin Hyman.

——. 1990. "An Anthropologist Looks at Biology." *Man* (N.S.) 25:208–229.

——. 1992a. "Culture and the Perception of the Environment." In *Bush Base, Forest Farm: Culture, Environment and Development*, ed. E. Croll and D. Parkin, 39–56. London: Routledge.

——. 1992b. Comment on Nurit Bird-David, "Beyond 'The Original Affluent Society.'" *Current Anthropology* 33, no. 1: 41–42.

——. 1996. "Human Worlds Are Culturally Constructed: Against the Motion (I)." In *Key Debates in Anthropology*, ed. T. Ingold, 112–118. London: Routledge.

Jackson, M. 1983. "Thinking Through the Body: An Essay on Understanding Metaphor." *Social Analysis* 14:127–148.

Lakoff, G. and M. Johnson. 1980. *Metaphors We Live By*. Chicago: University of Chicago Press.

MacCormack, C. 1980. "Nature, Culture and Gender: A Critique." In *Nature, Culture and Gender*, ed. C. MacCormack and M. Strathern, 1–24. Cambridge: Cambridge University Press.

Price, J. A. 1975. "Sharing: The Integration of Intimate Economies." *Anthropologica* 17:3–27.

Rappaport, R. A. 1968. *Pigs for the Ancestors*. New Haven, CT: Yale University Press.

Sahlins, M. D. 1972. *Stone Age Economics*. London: Tavistock.

——. 1976. *Culture and Practical Reason*. Chicago: University of Chicago Press.

Schutz, A. 1970. *On Phenomenology and Social Relations*. Ed. H. R. Wagner. Chicago: University of Chicago Press.

Scott, C. 1989. "Knowledge Construction Among Cree Hunters: Metaphors and Literal Understanding." *Journal de la Société des Americanistes* 75:193–208.

Shweder, R. 1990. "Cultural Psychology—What Is It?" In *Cultural Psychology: Essays on Comparative Human Development*, ed. J. W. Stigler, R. A. Shweder, and G. Herdt, 1–43. Cambridge: Cambridge University Press.

Tanner, A. 1979. *Bringing Home Animals*. London: Hurst.

Trevarthen, C. and K. Logotheti. 1989. "Child in Society, Society in Children: The Nature of Basic Trust." In *Societies at Peace*, ed. S. Howell and R. Willis, 165–186. London: Routledge.

Turnbull, C. M. 1965. *Wayward Servants: The Two Worlds of the African Pygmies*. London: Eyre and Spottiswoode.

Wagner, R. 1986. *Symbols That Stand for Themselves*. Chicago: University of Chicago Press.

Willis, R. 1990. "Introduction." In *Signifying Animals: Human Meaning in the Natural World*, ed. R. Willis, 1–24. London: Unwin Hyman.

Winterhalder, B. 1981. "Optimal Foraging Strategies and Hunter-Gatherer Research in Anthropology: Theory and Models." In *Hunter-Gatherer Foraging Strategies*, ed. B. Winterhalder and E. A. Smith, 13–35. Chicago: University of Chicago Press.

Winterhalder, B. and E. A. Smith. 1981. "Preface." In *Hunter-Gatherer Foraging Strategies*, ed. B. Winterhalder and E. A. Smith, ix–x. Chicago: University of Chicago Press.

two

On Yeti and Being Just

Carving the Borders of Humanity in Early Modern China

Carla Nappi

THE MOUNTAINS AND FORESTS OF THE SOUTH WERE THICK WITH wild women.

These hairy she-beasts were lewd, dangerous, and possessed ravenous appetites. Many people who had seen wild women (*yenü* 野女) compared them to naked, barefoot apes wearing the barest strips of leather to cover their loins. They stalked the forests looking for human men, dragging away unlucky captives and forcing them to mate. Just once, according to a popular report, one of these men fought back.[1] After killing his captor, the man cut her open and was astonished by what he found: the wild woman's heart looked just like a piece of lustrous jade, apparently covered in some sort of writing.

What, exactly, had this man just cut into—a fierce woman run wild or a beast with inhuman lusts? How scholars and doctors made sense of this tale is

Portions of this essay have been adapted and reprinted by permission of the publisher from *The Monkey and the Inkpot: Natural History and Its Transformations in Early Modern China* by Carla Nappi, pp. 121–135 (Cambridge, MA: Harvard University Press), Copyright © 2009 by the President and Fellows of Harvard College.

part of a much larger question that occupied early modern naturalists in China: what distinguished humans, beasts, and things? And why did it matter?

Seeing Things

> A person is not simply a person; what person is not also a thing? A thing is not simply a thing; what thing is not also a person? Moreover, where is there a person who is not also a thing? I am a special thing, imbued with spirit. Things are in some small sense imbued with me, are combined with me. Familiarity has made us forgetful, and we don't understand the relationship between things and people.
> —Lü Kun 呂坤 (1536–1618), 1580 preface to *Jian Wu* 見物 [Seeing Things][2]

Early Chinese writings had been full of reflections on the relationship of heaven, earth, and man, the great conceptual triumvirate. Though he was ultimately a thing (*wu* 物) like the other creatures in the universe, man was the ultimate perfected form of a thing, embodying and recapitulating the structure of heaven itself.[3] In the early modern period, a trend toward naturalization of the exalted reignited scholarly debate of this issue. Lü Kun was one of many late Ming dynasty (1368–1644) scholars whose writings sought to ground an understanding of man's qualities and nature within a more general notion of material objects in the universe: "The Maker's single bellows fires the creation of ten-thousand kinds, breathing into each an aspect of person and of thing. Can these aspects then be separated in two? Man himself built the fences and walls between them."[4] This question of naturalizing man was taken up quite explicitly in *materia medica* and natural history texts in the late sixteenth century: Were people things? Were they beasts? In either case, how ought one understand and draw the boundaries of humanity? Naturalists turned to wild women, Bigfoot-like beings, and monsters to address these questions.

Human Oddities

Li Shizhen 李時珍 (1518–1593) knew a thing or two about monsters. The doctor and naturalist, famous today as a founding father of modern science and medicine in China, was in his own time centrally preoccupied with understanding the metamorphoses of the natural world.[5] In his *Bencao gangmu* 本草綱目

(*Systematic* Materia Medica, hereafter *Bencao*), a massive compendium of information about medical substances and directions for their use, Li classified the stones, plants, animals, and other objects in nature into a hierarchical system that began with the most basic (waters, fires, earths, and stones) and culminated with mankind.[6] Li was most fascinated with the entities that occupied the borders between categories and the metamorphoses that engendered them, and he devoted a significant part of his encyclopedia of *materia medica* to puzzling over things (*wu*) that were difficult to classify. For Li, humans were among the most problematic entities in nature.

Starting from some of the same premises as his contemporary Lü Kun, Li came to a very different conclusion. People and things were indeed different, according to Li.[7] However, when something went wrong with the universal *qi* 氣, the vital organizing life-force that permeated the entire cosmos, boundaries became more fluid. In a special section on "Human Oddities" (*rengui* 人傀) in the *Bencao*, Li enumerated a host of cases of unusually shaped humans that he felt could be understood within the context of the transformative processes of the universe at large. The changes of men, however, sometimes fell outside what was typical and expected.[8] Any scholar of broad learning or doctor charged with protecting another's life was obligated to know about such changes, Li urged, and he thus justified his inclusion of a section on "human oddities" at the end of his text.

There were women who were sterile or androgynous, men who were likewise ambiguously gendered,[9] and people who split the month between acting like a man and a woman: these were all people (*ren* 人), but they were strange. They had a form, but no reproductive function.[10] Women in tribal communities gave birth after anywhere from six months to three years. Some people were born from a mother's rib, from her head, or from her back if the normal channels of *qi* in the womb were disturbed.[11] Kings had been born in extraordinary circumstances, from pustular sores or swollen ribs. Histories include stories of women conceiving by stepping in the footprints of a giant or by swallowing birds' eggs and of men getting pregnant, producing milk, and nursing their young.[12] Spontaneous sex changes were not unheard of. In all of these cases, there was a common thread: though these odd occurrences were strange and thus worthy of noting in historical records, the subjects discussed were nonetheless all people, in fact some were kings, and they were formed from unusual behavior of the normal forces and material of the universe.

After recounting records of people giving birth to worms and hatching from eggs or lumps of meat, however, Li made a telling statement. In remote, wild, and border areas,[13] people were born in the environment of such unusual *qi* that they might have three heads, tails, or the faces of birds.[14] These odd folk were included in the People category of the *Bencao*'s classification of the natural world. As people, however, they were more like "birds and beasts" than Li would like; he found them *so* unlike his fellows of common descent (*tongbao zhi min* 同胞之民),[15] that he placed them at the very end of the People category and indeed of the entire *Bencao*.

Upon closer examination this seemingly straightforward classification looks quite a bit more complicated. The boundary group that closes the section on Beasts and immediately precedes the section on People reveals the tensions underlying both categories.[16] The *yulei* 寓類 or *guailei* 怪類, the "strange and unusual" beasts, included monkeys, monkey-men, corpse-eaters, Bigfoot-like creatures, and voracious wild-women.

Ming Sasquatch: On Yeti and Being Just

> It is not that a poem or a painting or a palm tree or a person is "true," but rather that it ignites the desire for truth by giving us, with an electric brightness shared by almost no other uninvited, freely arriving perceptual event, the experience of conviction and the experience, as well, of error. . . . It comes to us, with no work of our own; then leaves us prepared to undergo a giant labor.
> —Elaine Scarry, *On Beauty and Being Just*[17]

Oddly shaped anthropoid figures had appeared in Chinese literature for most of its history. The distinction between apes and men was relatively fluid before the late Ming, and authors frequently attributed human-like characteristics to creatures that would now be classified as nonhuman primates. Much as the contemplation of wild men and Bigfoot in contemporary American society provides a medium for working out social and cultural anxieties, the study of humanoid creatures was also a study of the idea of humanity itself.[18]

According to Elaine Scarry, beauty "ignites the desire for truth" by providing the dual experiences both of certainty and of error. The experience of beauty, for Scarry, entails what Alexander Nehamas has called a "radical decentering" that makes us rethink our conceptions and beliefs.[19] The contemplation of wild women and Yeti-like beasts required a similar reconceptualization for sixteenth-century thinkers like Li. As the contemplation of beauty remakes one's experience of truth, the contemplation of wild men and humanoid beasts similarly shaped Li's conception of mankind. These beasts were, at the same time, both human and utterly nonhuman. The effort to decide which way to understand them came from a need to know where to place them in his categorization of nature. Li Shizhen described many of the most famous examples of the borderline beasts in his *materia medica*.

According to an early dictionary, said Li Shizhen, the mihou 獼猴[20] beast (see figure 2.1) looked like a person of Hu 胡 descent and even had a special name (maliuyun 馬留云) in the Hu dialect.[21] The mihou was one of many "unusual" beasts in the Bencao who occupied a southern natural habitat, and many of the animals in this category were believed to dwell in the mountains or forests of southern China. Li himself went on to embellish the account given by the Shuowen by adding that the mihou's eyes were like that of a worried Hu person.

This similarity to humans was further detailed: The *mihou*'s appearance, its hands and feet, its walk, its gestation, and the sounds it made were all humanoid. It washed its face and could be tamed. According to the *Majing* 馬經 [Horse Classic],[22] people kept these creatures in stables to keep horses from getting sick: the menstrual blood of the *mihou* was spread over the horse fodder each month and kept disease away.[23] This was an important example of the role of gender in Li's drug descriptions. The *mihou* is one of the only beasts whose menstrual blood is prescribed as a drug in the *Bencao*, further underscoring its place as a boundary being between animals and men. People in the South and in the Yue and Bajiao regions reportedly liked to eat the heads and flesh of *mihou* as a delicacy.

The *mihou* beast underwent several transformations over the course of its potentially lengthy life: after 800 years it metamorphosed into a *yuan* 猿; after 1,000 years it became a toad. Before these changes, when the *mihou* was only 500 years old it became a different kind of creature known as *jue* 玃 (see figure 2.2).[24] The *jue* was another southern humanoid—though this Sichuan native looked like a *yuan* monkey, it walked like a person and had a habit of taking human consorts.[25] Known from several texts to live in communities of strictly males or females, the *jue* frequently stole into houses to kidnap girls or men, took them home, and forced them to mate. People living in the South ate the heads of these beasts, according to Li.

The *guoran* 果然 liked to hang itself in trees with its tail shoved up its nose. This behavior became an identifying trait of the creature, and illustrators typically depicted the *guoran* with its tail stuffed in a nostril (see figure 2.3).[26] The

猴　　獼

FIGURE 2.1. The *mihou*. From Li Shizhen, *Bencao gangmu*, in *Wenyuange Siku quanshu*, Zhong-guo kexue jishu dianji tonghui, vol. 6, pt. 1 (Zhengzhou: Henan jiaoyu chubanshe, 1994), 310. Reproduction of 1778 edition.

FIGURE 2.2. The *jue*. From *Gujin tushu jicheng* [Compendium of Images and Texts, Ancient and Modern], vol. 522 (Shanghai: Zhonghua shuju, 1934), 20b. Early eighteenth century.

texts that Li cited (an assortment of poems, classical works, and tales) largely concurred in their claims that the *guoran* traveled together (with the aged in front and the young in the rear) and demonstrated qualities of kindness, filiality, respect, and wisdom. They were generous with food, lived peacefully, and could be counted on to rescue one another if attacked. Some early authors claimed that the *guoran* could call out his own name.[27] According to the *Bencao* discussion, the term *guoran* was often used as a nickname for suspicious people due to the reportedly suspicious nature of the beast. A rhapsody on the *guoran* by Zhong Yu 鍾毓[28] and the early encyclopedic work *Lüshi chunqiu* 呂氏春秋

FIGURE 2.3. The *guoran*. From Li Shizhen, *Bencao gangmu*, vol. 1 (Beijing: Zhongguo shudian chubanshe, 1988), 102. Reproduction of 1885 edition.

[Master Lü's Spring and Autumn Annals][29] provided accounts of the delectability of the flesh of these southern mountain-dwellers and their kin.

The *xingxing* 猩猩 could predict the future.[30] This beast, mentioned in several classical texts, generated no small amount of debate: though its hair and ears resembled those of a monkey and pig, its face and legs were quite human-looking, and it cried like a human baby (see figure 2.4).[31] Local people in Fenxi (an area that today is just north of Vietnam) would catch the beast by placing wine and straw sandals on the roadside. The *xingxing* would come to the spot, call out the names of the ancestors of the people who placed the things on the road, drink the wine, and try on the sandals. While the beasts were thus distracted, the locals caged them and kept them for meat. The fattest ones would be chosen first, and reportedly wept just before being killed. They were bled to dye fabric, in a rather cruel procedure that involved flogging the creatures while asking them how many times they'd like to be beaten. Several texts claimed the *xingxing* could speak, though this was debated among the authors Li cited.[32]

So what kind of thing was this *xingxing*? Li claimed it had the shape of a person but perhaps ought to be grouped with the beasts like the *mihou* we saw above. The classification of the *xingxing* was a difficult question for him. According to one of the main texts he cited, the *Erya yi*, the creature was very much like a naked, barefoot woman with long hair and no knees, and it traveled in groups.[33] Many people called them "wild people" (*yeren* 野人). According to this account, said Li, it seems that this might be the same thing as the "wild woman" (*yenü* 野女 or *yepo* 野婆), which was described next in the *Bencao*.

The story of the wild woman should now be a familiar one—this is the creature whose inscribed heart was examined at the beginning of this chapter. Li was fascinated by the apparent language of the wild woman's viscera; he knew that Chinese characters in seal script were also found on the eggs of male mice, and on a mirror-like image under the wing of a certain *zhiniao* 治鳥 bird.[34]

Since these two other cases existed, Li surmised that the case of the wild woman was not strange (*feiyi* 非異), and he classified the wild woman as a subcategory of *xingxing*. By drawing an analogy between the writing on the wild woman's heart and cases of seal characters found in beasts, and by extension comparing the wild woman to an animal, Li classified her as subhuman and grouped her along with beasts. Conceiving the wild woman as an animal was itself an innovation: The wild woman, or *yenü*, was typically treated alongside foreign and minority peoples in scholarly texts. To help prove all of this, Li reminded readers of the long anec-

FIGURE 2.4. The *xingxing*. From *Gujin tushu jicheng* [Compendium of Images and Texts, Ancient and Modern], vol. 522 (Shanghai: Zhonghua shuju, 1934), 22a. Early eighteenth century.

dote about catching, killing, and eating this beast. He went on to cite at least three other texts that described how delicious the meat of this *xingxing*, or wild woman, was and how it made one more intelligent, live a longer life, and walk more surely. The lips were particularly tasty.

The *feifei* 狒狒 (see figure 2.5) skulked throughout early texts and other natural histories that Li cited. Alternate names for this creature included "man-bear" (*renxiong* 人熊) and "wild man."[35] It lived in the Southwest and both resembled and had a habit of eating people. Immediately before it attacked, it apparently started to laugh so hard that its upper lip covered its eyes.[36] The varied qualities of the beasts included their ability to predict the future, their ability to speak somewhat like humans, and their tendency to launch into hysterics and flap their lower lip around before eating a person.[37] The last bit reportedly made it easier to catch the *feifei*: while the beast was laughing, hunters would take advantage of its distraction and nail the creature's lip to its forehead. After it was captured, its hair could be used to make wigs, its blood made an excellent dye, and eating its flesh allowed a person to see spirits.[38] In his description of the *feifei* Li provided several accounts of people eating its paws and hide.

Finally, before the corpse-eaters that ate the brains and livers of dead people, Li listed a number of mountain-dwelling monsters.[39] Previous and later works grouped these with spirits and demons or described them in completely different

FIGURE 2.5. The *feifei*. From Li Shizhen, *Bencao gangmu*, in *Wenyuange Siku quanshu*, Zhongguo kexue jishu dianji tonghui, vol. 6, pt. 1 (Zhengzhou: Henan jiaoyu chubanshe, 1994), 311. Reproduction of 1778 edition.

terms from plants and animals, but Li decided instead to categorize them with beasts (as a subcategory of *feifei*) and place the group almost immediately prior to People. (Recall that Li's classification system for the *Bencao* to a large extent was determined by likeness, so if he placed two animals next to each other in his classification it usually indicated some kind of relationship.) These mountain monsters all were described as being or looking like people, though many had one leg, reversed feet, or very short stature. A number of them spoke like people, some buried their dead like people, and some even traded in special ghost-markets with people.[40] They used stones to catch shellfish, roasted them over a fire, and ate them.[41] The "mountain husband" and "mountain auntie," a southern set of beasts who had only one foot (attached backwards), were known to knock on doors at night to beg for things.[42] These creatures might sneak into houses at night and have sex with women, causing and spreading disease. They could be banished from houses by calling out their names, by finding a thousand-year-old toad to munch them to death, or simply by behaving virtuously.[43] Like the previous monkey-like creatures, many of these monsters were said to live in the South, and their flesh could be cooked and eaten. (Li provided a recipe.)

To sum up, discussions of these creatures centered on a few major tropes. First, ethical behavior plays an important role in the classification process and is one site where these unusual creatures appear similar to humans: many were filial and polite. Also notable was the analogy to humans in their appearance and habits. Some traded in markets with humans. They spoke and acted like people, they mated with people, and many were characterized by human-like gender roles. Monkeys and Sasquatch-like beings were some of the only animals in the *Bencao* whose menstruation was discussed and whose menstrual blood was prescribed for its medicinal and magical effects. Many of these man-beasts mated with humans, and sex, reproduction, and the gendering of medical drugs played important roles in the Human Oddities discussion.

These two issues (ethics and analogy) also took center stage in the next section of the *Bencao*, the category of People.

A third concern also bound these sections and the debates within them—the importance of eating.

Eating the "Two-Legged Sheep"

Li Shizhen was particularly concerned with eating.[44] He used culinary preferences to differentiate communities, to determine what was "normal," and to distinguish between more and less civilized people and beasts. Eating habits served on numerous occasions as evidence supporting a claim that on the surface would seem to have little to do with food or consumption.[45]

The wild women and other beasts discussed above all looked and acted like people and, according to some authors, were nearly indistinguishable from foreign peoples or people born with deformities. According to Li, however, these boundary beasts were not properly human. Li's decision stemmed in part from the fact that they ate human flesh, but also in part from the claims of several authors in varied genres that men ate the flesh of these creatures and cited the various medical and gustatory benefits of doing so. Although most accounts of cannibalism acting as a boundary-making device between proper men and some "other" emphasize the importance of eating human flesh as an act that makes one less human,[46] here we have a reversal of that logic. For Li, it was instead *being eaten* that, by analogy with the act of eating animal flesh, made one into a beast. The People section of the *Bencao* was the critical stage on which Li worked out this issue.[47]

Modern accounts of Chinese cannibalism tend to generalize the practice of eating human body parts as somehow typical of "traditional" Chinese medicine, but the practice was hotly debated among naturalists and medical scholars in early modernity.[48] If both eating human flesh and being eaten, as in the case of the wild men, proved that one was somehow less than human, then why was it permissible to consume human body parts that might confer significant health benefits? Anthropophagy was an active issue in late Ming scholarly society. Many Ming novels contained accounts of cannibalism, famously epitomized by a fictionalized inn that served dumplings filled with human meat in the *Shuihu zhuan* 水滸傳 [Water Margin]. The issue of human-meat-filled dumplings is prominent in four sections of the novel, but the real action starts in section 27. In this scene, the hero Wu Song enters the inn and argues with the proprietress over the contents of the meat-filled buns she serves. When he asks if they were filled with human or dog flesh, she slyly answers that they were made with high-grade beef (*huangniu*). The truth eventually comes out, of course. (It's people! The buns are made of people!)[49] A plethora of late Imperial Confucian and Buddhist texts extolled the benefits of stewing up one's flesh or internal organs to serve up as medicine to sick parents, touting the miraculous healing effects that resulted. Such acts of filiality were rewarded by merciful goddesses like Guanyin.[50]

The issue of consuming human flesh played an increasingly important role in the medical literature of the late Ming.[51] The only human-derived drug that had been included in the earliest known *materia medica*, the *Shennong bencao jing* 神農本草經 (*Divine Husbandman's* Materia Medica, hereafter *Bencao jing*), was human hair. In his preface to the People category of his own work, Li cited this paucity of human-derived drugs as evidence of an important difference between people and the rest of the things of the world.[52] He claimed to record in detail only those human parts whose use did not "harm" (*hai* 害) his sense of human justice and propriety (*yi* 義).[53] Li noted that adepts justified their use of all manner of human parts (including bones, flesh, gallbladder, and blood) by calling them "medicine" (*yao* 藥), and he found this practice to be utterly inhumane. The arrangement of the objects listed in the People category reveals Li's apprehension about its contents. The arrangement of items in any category of the *Bencao* was usually from the most mundane or common to the most strange or problematic. In the People category, Li placed human flesh almost at the end of the entire section, followed only by "human mummy confection" (*munaiyi* 木乃伊), a general description of geographic differences among people, and "human oddities."

Despite his misgivings, however, the preceding few hundred years of *bencao* work demanded that Li expand on the *Bencao jing*'s treatment and add his own commentary. The use of human body parts as medicine had been recorded and advised by one of the *bencao* authors Li cited most prolifically, doctor and military official Chen Cangqi 陳藏器 (fl. eighth century), perhaps the first author to include so many human drugs in a medical text. Categorizing them within the "beasts and birds," Chen suggested the medical use of such materials as human saliva, blood, flesh, organs, facial hair, and corpse parts.[54] Though he did not provide much description or commentary to supplement his indication of the illness each drug cured, Chen's innovation and his work were cited in many later Song and Ming compendia of *materia medica*, and given this precedent Li seems to have felt compelled to weigh in on the issue. In contrast to Chen, Li repeatedly denounced the use of several human body parts in medicine and had harsh words for the doctors who advocated their use. Indeed, eating some human parts was definitely not permissible. But where to draw the line?

Chen Cangqi had recommended the use of human skeletal remains, but Li was skeptical: after all, he urged, even dogs did not eat the bones of other dogs.[55] Human skulls were typically not eaten by a gentleman, but in cases where it was the only thing available then Li judged it permissible to use a skull in medicine if it had been buried for a very long time.[56] Human placenta had not been frequently used until the Ming, when a famous doctor included it in a life-prolonging pill that reportedly enjoyed wide distribution.[57] Some texts recorded women from Liuqiu (*liuqiu guo* 琉球國) eating the placenta after a baby was born.[58] Ferocious people from the Bagui 八桂 region served up the placenta of newborn male children with Chinese five-spice.[59] The consumption of human placenta raised a question for Li, and it was left open in the *Bencao*: there was much proof that this drug invigorated people, but was it right for people to eat parts of others or did it violate the rules of morality? Li seems to have had no problem with using placental fluid in medicine. The umbilical cord, as well, was fine: Li compared its drying and falling off to that of a "ripe melon falling off a vine," an act of botanical analogy that rhetorically made the consumption of placenta permissible.[60]

Human gallbladders presented an interesting case. The use of human bile by soldiers on the northern borders to heal wounds during battle was described by Li as a remedy that should only be used in emergencies.[61] However, gallbladders that were gathered up and dried made a perfectly good drug that did not offend against ritual or morality. Li drew the line at the behavior of bandits who killed a person, ripped out his gallbladder, and ate it with wine.[62]

Human flesh was a major issue for Li. Chen Cangqi had written that taking human flesh could help cure wasting disease and apparently this idea, along with the widespread Confucian and Buddhist anecdotes about the miraculous medical effects of cooking one's own flesh and serving it up to one's parents, had prompted much of the consumption of human meat, livers, gallbladders, and the like to treat illness. Li protested that this practice was extremely unfilial, supporting his position with an anecdote about the first Ming emperor criticizing such behavior as improper, against morality and ritual, and worthy of being banned.[63] He then repeated a passage from the jottings of fourteenth-century author, Tao Zongyi 陶宗儀 (fl. 1360–1368), who provided lengthy and somewhat pornographic accounts of the eating of human flesh. Tao described soldiers and people in dire circumstances preparing human flesh in various ways, including a sort of people-jerky. That of young children was supposedly tastiest.

The above examples (bone, placenta, gallbladder, flesh) provoked varying degrees of moral questioning for Li. At the same time, however, there were some parts of people the medical use of which Li treated as unproblematic, and for which he provided long and detailed prescriptions in the *Bencao*. Human hair,[64] dandruff, earwax, toenails, and teeth were all permissible. Newborn baby feces could be used to remove tattoos from a criminal's face.[65] Li provided more than forty ways to use urine (especially that of young boys), including to quench thirst, to treat headaches, and to maintain a youthful appearance. He recommended a sure-fire cure for sudden cramps in the abdomen: the patient should have someone sit on him and urinate into his navel. (This was also apparently a good way to wake up a traveler suffering from heatstroke).[66]

Li also included *pishi* 癖石 [Obsession Stone], a kind of concretion that was thought to form in a person's body when he or she was extremely devoted to something.[67] Li provided several accounts of bodies that were cremated but whose hearts refused to burn, were cut open afterward and revealed various kinds of obsession-stone inside: a mini-landscape in a woman who had loved staring at landscape paintings when alive; an image of the goddess Guanyin in the heart of a Buddhist monk. Eating these was a way to dissolve hard masses.

Chen Cangqi had recommended a method for extracting human blood by piercing the skin and drinking the stuff while it was fresh and hot. Li did not endorse this vampirish technique: "Those who began this practice of prescribing [fresh blood] are inhumane. Will this not have consequences? Brutal soldiers and savage evildoers also drink human blood with wine. These people should be slain by heaven, so that evil shall be rewarded with evil."[68] Li did, however, permit the use of human blood that had been collected in what he considered to be a humane manner. He went on to encourage the use of underwear stained with menstrual blood, an excellent remedy for bloody wounds and poisons because the stuff itself was so foul and filthy that it killed evil spirits.

Taken together, these examples indicate is that there was nothing taboo about a body part just because it came from a human. Rather, the parts of people the use of which was most vociferously denounced were those parts that were regularly removed from animals and used in medicine: flesh, gallbladders, organs. The problem with eating human flesh can in part be understood as a problem of an act of consumption that analogized men to animals and thereby destabilized that which ostensibly made humans unique. In contrast to some of his contemporaries, Li did want to make men into something special, both a part of nature and somehow above it. More than a century later, Zhao Xuemin 趙學敏 (1719–1805), the most well-known commentator on the *Bencao*, went even further and denounced Li Shizhen for including a human drug section at all, a move which Zhao deemed "unethical." Zhao's commentary (the *Bencao gangmu shiyi* 本草綱目拾遺 [Correction of Omissions in the *Bencao gangmu*]) recapitulated the structure of Li's work except that he left out the People section altogether.

Ugly Custard: Steps Toward a History of Euphemism

The issue of consuming human flesh is particularly interesting both because the act was rationalized by analogy to animals and because it lent itself to the prolific use of euphemism in writings that discussed cannibalism. Terms for human meat appeared in many Ming texts, and the source that the vast majority of these works cited for accounts of cannibalism was the twelfth-century *Jilebian* 雞肋編 [Chicken-Rib Stories]. The *Jilebian* included many terms for consumed human flesh. There were general names as well as more specific ways to refer to meat from particular folk. The meat of pretty teenage women was called "Ugly custard" (*bumeigeng* 不美羹) or "Won't miss mutton" (*buciyang* 不羨羊, the meat being so tasty that it was better than mutton), depending on which edition of the text the reader had at hand.[69] The meat of children was called "Cooked with bones" (*hegulan* 和骨爛, ostensibly because the meat was so tender, bones were added to the pot to keep the flesh from melting straight away). The flesh of old, emaciated men who died of hunger or cold was dubbed something roughly translatable as "Intense fire" (*raobahuo* 饒把火, indicating the extra-hot cooking conditions under which the tough meat that came off these thin men was stewed).[70] The *Jilebian* also provided a general term for consumed human flesh as a whole: "Two-legged sheep" (*liangjiaoyang* 兩腳羊). Tao Zongyi included all of these in the *Chuogenglu* 輟耕錄 [Notes Made on a Rest from Ploughing] and supplemented them with his own contribution, a general term used by soldiers to apply to all kinds of human meat: "Thinking meat" (*xiangrou* 想肉).[71]

By the time Li Shizhen used the *Chuogenglu* in the People section of his own work, he further transformed this parade of euphemisms. Omitting all of the specific terms from the *Jilebian* that Tao had cited, Li included only two terms for human flesh: "Thinking meat" and "Two-legged sheep," attributing both terms to evildoers.[72] This was a significant deviation from the *Chuogenglu* itself and was consistent with Li's interest in demonizing the consumption of human meat and his general tendency to denigrate soldiers and bandits in the *Bencao*. Eating and naming human flesh were practices Li attributed largely to military men and rascals: "This is done by thieves and evildoers devoid of human nature—putting them to death would not be punishment enough!"[73] At the same time, he did not attribute cannibalistic behavior to foreigners, as had many Song and Ming accounts of people living outside or on the boundaries of the empire. These earlier texts provided occasionally graphic descriptions of foreigners or ethnic minorities consuming human meat. The *Taiping yulan*, for example, had included discussions of human meat used in yearly sacrifices to gods in the land of *Zhenla* 真臘 (Kampuchea); *Hu* people and hermits using human flesh from corpses to make medicine; soldiers in the land of *Jianguo* 兼國 cutting off the heads of people, eating their flesh, and drinking their blood; and a city in Chengdu where human meat was sold in street markets.[74] Li's choice to attribute this practice to bandits and soldiers and not to mention it in his description of foreigners or of *fangmin* is a fascinating deviation from the prevailing norm of his time.

This brief chronicle of the discourses that surrounded the consumption of human meat through the Song, Yuan, and Ming periods allows some concluding thoughts in this preliminary step toward a history of how the borders between humanity and animality shifted in early modern China. It also provides a window into the significance of analogy and euphemism to knowledge-making in the *Bencao*. Unlike Li, later authors seemed to prefer using euphemisms for cannibalism that related men to animals. Ming and later editions of the *Jilebian* used different forms of the euphemism for the meat of pretty young girls that almost all included "sheep" (*yang*) in the name. In a further analogy, the stuff was often compared to dog and pig meat, as were some of the slaughtering techniques used to prepare human flesh for consumption. It was just this comparison and analogy to an animal that was supposed to make a cannibal inhuman. However, by continually juxtaposing man or man flesh and animal vocabulary, just the opposite occurred: over the course of the early modern period, man became more of an animal through a kind of naturalization via analogy.

What was it to be human in the late Ming? The answer for Li Shizhen, as we've seen, was rooted in an understanding of man's place in nature that made humans and human-derived drugs both part of the natural world and above it. Though a gentleman and fellow countryman was *not* an animal, once he consumed part of a human that could be analogized to that of an animal he compromised his ethics and humanity. The act effectively dropped both the eater and the eaten (city man or wild man) down into the realm of the boundary-creatures and the subhuman. Later authors such as Zhao drew this line at any human part whatsoever—but in the sixteenth century, the boundary was still being drawn.

Notes

1. Account taken from Li Shizhen 李時珍, *Bencao gangmu* 本草綱目 (*Systematic* Materia Medica).

2. Li Su 李蘇 1985, Lü Kun's preface: 133. Lü was a scholar-official from Ningling, Hunan. Translations in this essay are mine unless otherwise noted.

3. See Sterckx 2002, esp. 17–18, for a brief discussion of the term *wu* with respect to understanding the general concept (or lack thereof) of "animal" in Warring States and Han China.

4. Li Su 1985, Lü Kun preface: 133.

5. The *Bencao gangmu* was first published in 1596 and is still known to most educated people in China today. For much more background on Li Shizhen and his work, see Nappi 2009. The term "natural world" is not a direct translation of a Chinese concept, but rather my own shorthand for discussing an object of study that included the living beings (and occasionally also materials like stone and fabric) in the universe.

6. A *bencao* 本草 text typically includes information about drug materials used in Chinese medical prescriptions, including the categorization of the drug by qualities such as flavor (*wei* 味), toxicity (presence of *du* 毒), presence of heat, and appearance, as well as a discussion of the derivation and alternate names of the substance. *Bencao* texts could also include discussions of the textual and natural history of each drug.

7. *Bencao gangmu*, *juan* 52, *ren bu* 人部 [People], *rengui* 人傀 [Human Oddities], 1943. I will hereafter use this format to reference quotations and sections of the *Bencao gangmu*: *Bencao gangmu*, *juan* [Chapter], *bu* [Major category, followed by an English translation of the category name], *tiao* [General entry cited, followed by an English translation of the name of the object], subsection of the entry (if there is one), page number. The page numbers correspond to Liu Hengru and Liu Shanyong edition.

8. *Bencao gangmu*, *juan* 52, *ren bu* 人部 [People], *rengui* 人傀 [Human Oddities], 1941. On reproductive oddities in the sixteenth and seventeenth centuries, see Furth 1988: 1–31.

9. *Bencao gangmu*, *juan* 52, *ren bu* 人部 [People], *rengui* 人傀, 1942. Among many examples, Li lists the five nonfemale women (*wu bunu* 五不女) and the five nonmale men (*wu bunan* 五不男).

10. *Bencao gangmu*, *juan* 52, *ren bu* 人部 [People], *rengui* 人傀 [Human Oddities], 1942.

11. A litany of examples is provided in *Bencao gangmu*, *juan* 52, *ren bu* 人部 [People], *rengui* 人傀, 1942.

12. *Bencao gangmu*, *juan* 52, *ren bu* 人部 [People], *rengui* 人傀 [Human Oddities], 1943. One example among many: 唐書云: 元德秀兄弟襁褓喪親, 德秀自乳之, 數日乳中渾流, 能食乃止。(According to the *Tangshu*: Yuan Dexiu's brother lost his wife while their baby was still in swaddling clothes. Dexiu nursed the child himself. After several days his breasts flowed with milk and didn't stop until the child could eat [food].)

13. The phrase Li uses is *huangyi zhiwai* 荒裔之外, literally, "beyond the border/periphery," i.e., beyond the borders of the empire. *Bencao gangmu*, *juan* 52, *ren bu* 人部 [People], *rengui* 人傀 [Human Oddities], 1944.

14. Any similar exotic cases appeared in daily-use encyclopedias and illustrated editions of the *Shanhaijing* 山海經 [Classic of Mountains and Seas] printed in the late Ming. In these texts, descriptions of animals and accounts of odd foreigners living outside the boundaries of the dynasty were typically juxtaposed both on a single page (creating a kind of explicit visual comparison) and occasionally in the descriptions of foreign peoples themselves. See, for example, Xu Qilong 徐企龍 2001a, 2001b.

15. *Bencao gangmu*, *juan* 52, *ren bu* 人部 [People], *rengui* 人傀, 1944.

16. *Bencao gangmu*, *juan* 50, *shou bu* 獸部 [Beasts], 1906. These form a section called *shou zhi san*: *yulei, guailei* 獸之三: 寓類, 怪類 [Beasts Section Four: Strange and Unusual Beasts]. This was one category—though Li provided two names, the *yu* and *guai* were not separated in the text; neither were the individual beasts classified as one or the other.

17. Scarry 1999:52–53.

18. The most lucid accounts of the study of wild men in America that I have found are Blu Buhs 2009; Coleman 2003; and Meldrum 2006. On popular accounts of hairy *yeren* (wild men) in modern China, see Schmalzer 2008:210–245. For an anthropological account of the same topic, see Dikötter 1998:51–74.

19. See also Nehamas 2000:394.

20. *Bencao gangmu*, *juan* 51, *shou bu* 獸部 [Beasts], *mihou* 獼猴, 1906–1907. In modern Chinese, *mihou* is frequently translated as "macaque." Though the remaking of early modern animals into modern beasts *via* translation is a common phenomenon, the character of the *mihou* and the other beasts we will see in this chapter did not necessarily occupy the same epistemological space as the renderings that have been used to make sense of them in modern science and medicine. Incidentally, the *mihou* was often depicted in illustrations with a fruit in its hand, and this was likely a means of representing the *mihou tao* 獼猴桃, or "peach of the *mihou*," now identified as a kiwi. The *mihou* was often paired with another apelike beast, the *yuan* 猿, defined as a gibbon in Robert van Gulik's *The Gibbon in China: An Essay in Chinese Animal Lore* (1967).

21. *Bencao gangmu*, *juan* 51, *shou bu* 獸部 [Beasts], *mihou* 獼猴, *shiming*, 1906. Li also includes a Sanskrit name: *mosi* 摩斯. *Hu* was often used to refer broadly to the people of Central Asia that came into contact with or resided in the western or northwestern borders of China.

22. The provenance of the *Majing* that Li used is uncertain. Li provides no indication of the date or authorship of the text.

23. *Bencao gangmu*, *juan* 51, *shou bu* 獸部 [Beasts], *mihou* 獼猴, *jijie*, 1906.

24. *Bencao gangmu*, *juan* 51, *shou bu* 獸部 [Beasts], *mihou* 獼猴, *jijie*, 1906. This is sometimes also pronounced "*que.*"

25. *Bencao gangmu*, *juan* 51, *shou bu* 獸部 [Beasts], *mihou* 獼猴, *fulu* 附录, *jue* 玃, 1907.

26. *Bencao gangmu, juan* 51, *shou bu* 獸部 [Beasts], *guoran* 果然, 1908.

27. *Bencao gangmu, juan* 51, *shou bu* 獸部 [Beasts], *guoran* 果然, *jijie*, 1908.

28. Zhong Yu was an author of *fu* 賦 poetry active during the Wei period (220–265) of the Three Kingdoms (220–280). Li listed this *fu* as an independent entry in the nonmedical texts section of his bibliography.

29. The previous quotation from the *Guoran fu* had claimed that the flesh of *guoran* was not especially tasty and that the beast was good only for its hide. Li offered this tidbit from the *Lüshi chunqiu* as a way of raising a question—because the *guoran* and the two beasts mentioned in the *Lüshi chunqiu* were alike, how could it be that the flesh of the *guoran* was not tasty as well?

30. *Bencao gangmu, juan* 51, *shou bu* 獸部 [Beasts], *xingxing* 猩猩, *shiming*, 1908. The *xingxing*'s abilities to call out its own name and foretell the future (*zhilai* 知來) are provided as justification for the beast's moniker: *xingxing* 惺惺 means "wise." *Xingxing* is often translated as "orangutan" today.

31. The claims related in this paragraph are found in *Bencao gangmu, juan* 51, *shou bu* 獸部 [Beasts], *xingxing* 猩猩, *jijie*, 1908.

32. Medieval travel writer William of Rubruck included a version of the *xingxing* story in the accounts of his travels to China. See van Ruysbroeck 1900:199–200. Different versions of this story appear relatively frequently in Chinese literature. For a translation of the *Shanhaijing* account, see Strassberg 2002:189.

33. *Bencao gangmu, juan* 51, *shou bu* 獸部 [Beasts], *xingxing* 猩猩, *jijie*, 1909.

34. *Bencao gangmu, juan* 51, *shou bu* 獸部 [Beasts], *xingxing* 猩猩, *fulu* 附錄, *yenü* 野女 [Wild Women], 1909. See also *Bencao gangmu, juan* 49, *qin bu* 禽部 [Birds], *zhiniao* 治鳥, *jijie*, 1765. Elsewhere in the *Bencao* Li reported additional cases of printed or otherwise marked concretions in human bodies, including a petrified heart with a landscape formed inside it and a monk's heart whose center was found to contain a miniature statue of the Buddha. Some of these cases are discussed in Zeitlin 1991:1–26.

35. *Bencao gangmu, juan* 51, *shou bu* 獸部 [Beasts], *feifei* 狒狒, 1909–1911. Today this is commonly translated as "baboon."

36. *Bencao gangmu, juan* 51, *shou bu* 獸部 [Beasts], *feifei* 狒狒, *jijie*, 1909.

37. *Bencao gangmu, juan* 51, *shou bu* 獸部 [Beasts], *feifei* 狒狒, *jijie*, 1910.

38. *Bencao gangmu, juan* 51, *shou bu* 獸部 [Beasts], *feifei* 狒狒, *jijie*, 1910.

39. *Bencao gangmu, juan* 51, *shou bu* 獸部 [Beasts], *feifei* 狒狒, *fulu* 附錄, 1910–1911.

40. See, for example, *Bencao gangmu, juan* 51, *shou bu* 獸部 [Beasts], *feifei* 狒狒, *fulu* 附錄, *muke* 木客, 1910.

41. *Bencao gangmu, juan* 51, *shou bu* 獸部 [Beasts], *feifei* 狒狒, *fulu* 附錄, *shanxiao* 山臊, 1910.

42. *Bencao gangmu, juan* 51, *shou bu* 獸部 [Beasts], *feifei* 狒狒, *fulu* 附錄, *shanxiao* 山臊, 1910.

43. All of these remedies are prescribed by Li in *Bencao gangmu, juan* 51, *shou bu* 獸部 [Beasts], *feifei* 狒狒, *fulu* 附錄, 1910–1911.

44. Vivienne Lo has written extensively on the connection between medicine and the culinary arts in China. See, for example, Lo and Barrett 2005:395–422; and Lo 2005:163–185.

45. Eating habits were also used to justify naming practices, especially with regard to insects. See, for example, *Bencao gangmu*, *juan* 41, *chong bu* 蟲部 [Bugs], *feilian* 蜚蠊 [Cockroach], *shiming*, 1550. Here, Li explains that three bugs (the *feilian*, the *xingye* 行夜 [a kind of beetle, sometimes translated as "bombardier beetle"], and the *fuzhong* 阜螽 [grasshopper]) were different creatures that had been conflated and considered to be the same because a minority group ate all three, calling them by the same name.

46. Modern accounts of cannibalism in China include the journalistic Yi Zheng *Scarlet Memorial: Tales of Cannibalism in Modern China* (1996). On cannibalism in Chinese literary history, see Yue 1999. The use of human body parts in traditional Chinese medical recipes has also been a popular topic in modern and contemporary Chinese fiction. Some examples include Yan 1995:172–181; Xun 1990a:29–41; Xun 1990b:49–58.

47. See *Bencao gangmu*, *juan* 52, *ren bu* 人部 [People], 1912–1944.

48. On cannibalism and the consumption of mummies and "corpse-medicine" in early modern Europe, see Sugg 2006:225–240.

49. See Shi Nai'an 施耐庵, *Shuihu zhuan* 水滸傳 [Water Margin] (Hong Kong: Zhonghua shuju, 2002), 327.

50. Li discusses the issue of *gegu* 割股 ("cutting the thigh/flesh") in *Bencao gangmu*, *juan* 52, *ren bu* 人部 [People], *renrou* 人肉 [Human Flesh], *faming*, 1939–1940. He criticizes folk who engage in this practice as "foolish people" (*yumin* 愚民). For an example of the *gegu* literary tradition, see de Bary and Bloom 1999:532–534. The selection, "Guanyin and Cutting One's Body (*Gegu*)," contains selections from *Guanyin jingzhou linggan huiyao* and the *Gujin tushu jicheng*. For an exhaustive discussion of cannibalistic practices in Chinese dynastic histories, see Pettersson, 1999:73–182. Pettersson includes a discussion of *gegu* and other piety-related forms of cannibalism.

51. For a classic treatment of the use of human body parts as drugs, especially with regard to correlations with modern bio-medicine, see Cooper and Sivin 1973: 203–272.

52. *Bencao gangmu*, *juan* 52, *ren bu* 人部 [People], *mulu*, 1912. For Li's comments on the moral questions regarding the use of human flesh in medicine, see *Bencao gangmu*, *juan* 52, *ren bu* 人部 [People], *renrou* 人肉 [Human Flesh], *faming*, 1939–1940.

53. *Bencao gangmu*, *juan* 52, *ren bu* 人部 [People], *mulu*, 1912. The 37 major drugs listed in the People section, in order, were: *fabi* 髮髲 (wig of hair), *luanfa* 亂髮 (hair in disarray), *tougou* 頭垢 (dandruff), *ersai* 耳塞 (earwax), *xitougou* 膝頭垢 (dirt on the knee, "knee dandruff"), *zhaojia* 爪甲 (fingernails and toenails), *yachi* 牙齒 (teeth), *renshi* 人屎 (excrement), *xiao'er taishi* 小兒胎屎 (excrement of a newborn), *renniao* 人尿 (urine), *nibaiyin* 溺白垽 (white urinary sediment), *qiushi* 秋石 (processed urinary sediment, "Autumn stone"), *linshi* 淋石 (urinary stone), *pishi* 癖石 (obsession stone), *ruzhi* 乳汁 (milk), *furen yueshui* 婦人月水 (menstrual blood), *renxue* 人血 (blood), *renjing* 人

精 (semen, "human essence"), *koujintuo* 口津唾 (saliva), *chiyin* 齒垽 (sediment on the teeth), *renhan* 人汗 (sweat), *yanlei* 眼淚 (tears), *renqi* 人氣 (human *qi*), *renpo* 人魄 (human *po*), *cixu* 髭鬚 (beard and moustache), *yinmao* 陰毛 (pubic hair), *rengu* 人骨 (bone), *tianlinggai* 天靈蓋 (skullcap), *renbao* 人胞 (placenta), *baoyishui* 胞衣水 (placental fluid), *chusheng qidai* 初生臍帶 (umbilical cord), *renshi* 人勢 (penis), *rendan* 人膽 (gall bladder), *renrou* 人肉 (human flesh), *munaiyi* 木乃伊 (human mummy confection), *fangmin* 方民 (humans from different locations), *rengui* 人傀 (human oddities).

54. See Unschuld 1986: 50–52 on Chen Cangqi and his prescription of the use of human drugs.

55. *Bencao gangmu*, juan 52, *ren bu* 人部 [People], *rengu* 人骨 [Human Bones], *faming*, 1935.

56. *Bencao gangmu*, juan 52, *ren bu* 人部 [People], *tianlinggai* 天靈蓋 [Human Skullcap], *faming*, 1936.

57. This was according to Li. See *Bencao gangmu*, juan 52, *ren bu* 人部 [People], *renbao* 人胞 [Human Placenta], *faming*, 1937; and *baoyi shui* 胞衣水 [Placental Fluid], 1938–1939.

58. The region *Liuqiu guo* 琉球國 described in Sui Dynasty (581–619) sources has been identified variously as Taiwan or Ryukyu. For other accounts of cannibalism in *Liuqiu* from the *Suishu*, see Pettersson 1999:127.

59. *Bencao gangmu*, juan 52, *ren bu* 人部 [People], *renbao* 人胞 [Human Placenta], *faming*, 1937. The term I translate here as "ferocious" (*liao* 獠) can also be interpreted as an alternate form of the term *liao* 僚, indicating an ethnic minority from southern China. See *Hanyu da cidian suoyinben* 漢語大詞典縮印本 [Major Dictionary of the Chinese Language, Compact Edition] (Shanghai: Hanyu da cidian chubanshe, 2002), 2:2779c.

60. See *Bencao gangmu*, juan 52, *ren bu* 人部 [People], *chusheng qidai* 初生臍帶 [Umbilical Cord], *shiming*, 1939.

61. *Bencao gangmu*, juan 52, *ren bu* 人部 [People], *rendan* 人膽 [Human Gall Bladder], *faming*, 1939.

62. See Zheng 1996 for very similar descriptions recapitulated in stories about cannibalism during the Cultural Revolution, stories that often invoked the medical and tonic benefits of such practices. Recall that Li claimed he was *not* including recipes for human drugs that he judged to be immoral or inhumane, though he included prescriptions for each of the three aforementioned drugs: bone, placenta, and even fresh gallbladder.

63. *Bencao gangmu*, juan 52, *ren bu* 人部 [People], *renrou* 人肉 [Human Flesh], *faming*, 1939–1940.

64. In no small part because of the *locus classicus* of its discussion in the *Shennong bencao jing*, hair became an important topic of discussion in *bencao* literature. Many authors had credited this seemingly mundane stuff with powers of miraculous transformation, and its importance to medical theory was underlined by the widespread claim in medical texts that hair was one form of human blood.

65. Li included a number of prescriptions from previously published formularies that recommended the use of feces to counteract arrowhead and other poisons. See *Bencao gangmu, juan* 52, *ren bu* 人部 [People], *renshi* 人屎 [Human Excrement], *fufang*, 1921–1923. This prescription (for *xiao'er taishi* 小兒胎屎, or newborn feces) was culled from Chen Cangqi. See *Bencao gangmu, juan* 52, *ren bu* 人部 [People], *xiao'er taishi* 小兒 胎屎 [Newborn Baby Feces], *zhuzhi*, 1923.

66. *Bencao gangmu, juan* 52, *ren bu* 人部 [People], *renniao* 人尿 [Human Urine], *fufang*, 1923–1925. Another interesting urine-derived drug discussed in this literature was *qiushi* 秋石, now understood to be a kind of processed urinary sediment. Li relates that wealthy customers had long been known to refuse to use urine in medicine, believing it to be unclean, which prompted "adepts" to manufacture (or fake) this stuff as a more appealing alternative. This case is interesting in illuminating what seems to have been a difference in drug markets among wealthy and lower-class patients.

67. See Zeitlin 1991 for an excellent treatment of the relationship between *pishi* and literature on obsession. See also *Bencao gangmu, juan* 52, *ren bu* 人部 [People], *pishi* 癖石 [Obsession Stone]. This was a human version of petrified animal concretions like bezoars.

68. *Bencao gangmu, juan* 52, *ren bu* 人部 [People], *renxue* 人血 [Human Blood], *faming*, 1932.

69. The *Gujin tushu jicheng* edition of the *Jilebian* reads "Ugly Custard" 不美羹, whereas the *Siku quanshu* reads "The Unenviable Sheep" 不羨羊. It is clear that a transcribing mistake could generate these differences, and copying mistakes seem responsible for the transformation of these terms in later texts, which include versions like "The Sheep That Goes Into the Custard" 下羹羊 (in a Yuan edition of the *Chuogenglu*) or "The Ugly Sheep" 為美羊 (in a citation of the *Jilebian* included in the *Siku quanshu* edition of the Ming text *Yuzhitang tanhui* 玉芝堂談薈 [Gatherings at Jade Mushroom Hall]).

70. In his citation of the *Jilebian*, Tao Zongyi attributed this name to both old, thin men *and* women.

71. See Tao Zongyi, *Chuogenglu* 輟耕録 [Notes Made on a Rest from Ploughing] (Beijing: Zhonghua shuju, 1980), 123–124 [想肉]. Euphemistic analogy also occurs elsewhere in the *Bencao*, where the edible flesh of the frog (thought by many to be a foul creature) was called the "Field-chicken" and rats were deemed "House Deer." This dialogue somewhat resembles the Daoist and Buddhist proscriptions against eating beef, a practice that also encouraged the creation of euphemisms. See Kieschnick 2005:186–212.

72. *Bencao gangmu, juan* 52, *ren bu* 人部 [People], *renrou* 人肉 [Human Flesh], *faming*, 1939–1940.

73. *Bencao gangmu, juan* 52, *ren bu* 人部 [People], *renrou* 人肉 [Human Flesh], *faming*, 1940.

74. See *Taiping yulan* [Imperial Digest of the Taiping Era] (Beijing: Zhonghua

shuju, 1998), vol. 4, *juan* 786, *Zhenla*, 3483; vol. 3, *juan* 549, *shi* [Corpses], 2485; vol. 3, *juan* 506, *yimin* [Recluses] 6, 2308; vol. 2, *juan* 339, *xubinqi* [Soldiers' Weapons], 1555; and vol. 4, *juan* 828, *maimai* [Selling and Buying], 3693. For examples of foreign cannibalism in dynastic histories, see Pettersson 1999:126–128.

References

Blu Buhs, Joshua. 2009. *Bigfoot: The Life and Times of a Legend*. Chicago: University of Chicago Press.

Coleman, Loren. 2003. *Bigfoot! The True Story of Apes in America*. New York: Paraview Pocket Books.

Cooper, William and Nathan Sivin. 1973. "Man as Medicine: Pharmacological and Ritual Aspects of Traditional Therapy Using Drugs Derived from the Human Body." In *Chinese Science: Explorations of an Ancient Tradition*, ed. S. Nakayama and N. Sivin, 203–272. Cambridge, MA: MIT Press.

de Bary, William Theodore and Irene Bloom, comps. 1999. *Sources of Chinese Tradition*, vol. 1. New York: Columbia University Press.

Dikötter, Frank. 1998. "Hairy Barbarians, Furry Primates, and Wild Men: Medical Science and Cultural Representations of Hair in China." In *Hair: Its Power and Meaning in Asian Cultures*, ed. Barbara Diane Miller and Alf Hiltebeitel, 51–73. Albany: State University of New York Press.

Furth, Charlotte. 1988. "Androgynous Males and Deficient Females: Biology and Gender Boundaries in Sixteenth and Seventeenth Century China." *Late Imperial China* 9, no. 2: 1–31.

Kieschnick, John. 2005. "Buddhist Vegetarianism in China." In *Of Tripod and Palate*, ed. Roel Sterckx, 186–212. New York: Palgrave Macmillan.

Li Su 李蘇. 1985. *Jian Wu* 見物 [Seeing Things]. *Congshu jicheng xinbian* edition, vol. 44. Taipei: Xinwenfeng.

Lo, Vivienne. 2005. "Pleasure, Prohibition, and Pain: Food and Medicine in Traditional China." In *Of Tripod and Palate*, ed. Roel Sterckx, 163–185. New York: Palgrave Macmillan.

Lo, Vivienne and Penelope Barrett. 2005. "Cooking Up Fine Remedies: On the Culinary Aesthetic in a Sixteenth-Century Chinese *Materia Medica*." *Medical History* 49:395–422.

Meldrum, Jeff. 2006 *Sasquatch: Legend Meets Science*. New York: Forge Books.

Nappi, Carla. 2009. *The Monkey and the Inkpot: Natural History and Its Transformations in Early Modern China*. Cambridge, MA: Harvard University Press.

Nehamas, Alexander. 2000. "The Return of the Beautiful: Morality, Pleasure, and the Value of Uncertainty." *Journal of Aesthetics and Art Criticism* 58, no. 4: 394.

Pettersson, Bengt. 1999. "Cannibalism in the Dynastic Histories." *Bulletin of the Museum of Far Eastern Antiquities* 71:73–182.

Scarry, Elaine. 1999. *On Beauty and Being Just*. Princeton, NJ: Princeton University Press.

Schmalzer, Sigrid. 2008. *The People's Peking Man: Popular Science and Human Identity in Twentieth-Century China*. Chicago: University of Chicago Press.

Sterckx, Roel. 2002. *The Animal and the Daemon in Early China*. Albany, NY: SUNY Press.

Strassberg, Richard E. 2002. *A Chinese Bestiary: Strange Creatures from the Guideways Through Mountains and Seas*. Berkeley: University of California Press.

Sugg, Richard. 2006. "'Good Physic but Bad Food': Early Modern Attitudes to Medicinal Cannibalism and Its Suppliers." *Social History of Medicine* 19, no. 2: 225–240.

Unschuld, Paul. 1986. *Medicine in China: A History of Pharmaceutics*. Berkeley: University of California Press.

van Gulik, Robert. 1967. *The Gibbon in China: An Essay in Chinese Animal Lore*. Leiden, the Netherlands: Brill.

van Ruysbroeck, Willem. 1900. *The Journey of William of Rubruck to the Eastern Parts of the World*. London: Hakluyt Society.

Xu Qilong 徐企龍. 2001a. *Wanshu yuanhai* 萬書淵海 [A Deep Sea of Ten Thousand Works]. Tokyo: Kyuko Shoin, reprint of 1610 woodblock ed.

——. 2001b. *Wuche wanbao quanshu* 五車萬寶全書 [Five Cartsful of Treasures]. Tokyo: Kyuko Shoin, reprint of 1614 woodblock ed.

Xun, Lu. 1990a. "Diary of a Madman." In *Diary of a Madman and Other Stories*, trans. William Lyell, 29–41. Honolulu: University of Hawaii Press.

——. 1990b. "Medicine." In *Diary of a Madman and Other Stories*, trans. William Lyell, 49–58. Honolulu: University of Hawaii Press.

Yan, Mo. 1995. "The Cure." In *Chairman Mao Would Not Be Amused: Fiction from Today's China*, ed. Howard Goldblatt, 172–181. New York: Grove Press.

Yue, Gang. 1999. *The Mouth That Begs: Hunger, Cannibalism, and the Politics of Eating in Modern China*. Durham, NC: Duke University Press.

Zeitlin, Judith. 1991. "The Petrified Heart: Obsession in Chinese Literature, Art, and Medicine." *Late Imperial China* 12, no. 1: 1–26.

Zheng, Yi. 1996. *Scarlet Memorial: Tales of Cannibalism in Modern China*. Boulder, CO: Westview Press.

three

Pastoral Power in the Postcolony

On the Biopolitics of the Criminal Animal in South India

Anand Pandian

EARLY ONE MORNING IN OCTOBER 2001, I WADED ACROSS THE
swollen river toward the wide plain of paddy fields at the heart of the Cumbum
Valley, a lush agricultural region in the south Indian state of Tamil Nadu.
Clambering up onto a narrow rise above the water, I spotted a young herdsman named Surya following behind his small herd of black water buffalo. I
tried to engage him in a conversation about these animals, but Surya wanted
to speak instead about the moral shortcomings of the people of this village.
"They do not know how they ought to live," he complained—they stole from
orchards to satisfy their hunger, they plotted and schemed to bring each other
down. "You should teach them how to live well," he told me, and embarrassed,
I tried to shift the subject back to his animals. They had been crossing the
swift waters of a narrow canal one by one as we spoke, making for the grassy
cover of a coconut orchard just beyond the banks. Suddenly, a young calf with
an injured leg began to slip downstream, unable to handle the current fed by
recent rains. Surya stripped off his *lungi* and dashed into the water to hold the
calf and guide it to safety. Grazing needed such vigilance, he returned to tell
me: a close and careful watch not only against the perils of the environment,

but also against the meandering impulses of the animals themselves. He pointed out the "thievish" way that one of the buffaloes too had stolen off to search for better grass, before rushing again to give the animal a quick blow of his staff and bring it back into line with the others. Notwithstanding the conduct of his own neighbors, Surya was clearly teaching these creatures how they ought to live.

Although these were no more than the daily trials of a rural livelihood, I was struck by the casual way in which this young herdsman had bound together the moral government of his animals with the moral self-conduct of his peers. He seemed to imply that the people of his village too were in need of a little "grazing." To those familiar with the ruminations of Western intellectuals, these associations may betray a startling resemblance to what Michel Foucault[1] had described as "pastoral" power: the government of a population modeled on the relationship between a figurative shepherd and the individual members of a flock. Foucault had dwelt upon this long-standing Western image of power as a means of grappling with the tension between individualizing care and totalizing control in modern forms of biopolitics. But what is striking about this fragment of rural south Indian life is the way in which the government of animal nature here drew both care and control together into a particular form of intimacy. I contend in this article that attending to such practices and the circumstances of their exercise offers a way of pluralizing our understanding of what is at stake in the modern government of life. Specifically, I argue that a close examination of the government of animals *by* humans is vital for an anthropology of biopolitics: for an understanding, that is, of the many ways in which humans themselves have been governed *as* animals in modern times.

In recent years, numerous scholars have sought to take the very "human" lodged at the heart of anthropology's disciplinary concerns as a problem for critical thought.[2] In one influential intervention, for example, Giorgio Agamben[3] sketched an animalization of human being in modern times: the violent dehumanization and extermination of that "bare life" deemed as obstacle to collective welfare. This argument, like the work of Foucault[4] it sought to develop further, was based upon a particular genealogy of political thought and state practice in the West. My aim in this article is to work toward a way of theorizing biopolitics in milieus beyond the modern West. I suggest that we may do so by examining other histories, practices, and idioms of government through which distinctions between the human and the animal emerge as essential problems of politics elsewhere. Relying upon materials from south India, I call attention to three domains of local difference: the particular con-

FIGURE 3.1. A ploughman carefully tends to his bull after a morning of labor. Working oxen are cherished animals in the rural Cumbum Valley, but such affections are earned most readily by animals that embody the moral virtue of restraint. In this sense, their conduct and its government are not altogether dissimilar from that of the human inhabitants of the region. Photo by the author.

ditions of modernity that constitute certain human lives as animal objects of government; the quotidian practices of care and struggle through which animal natures are governed in moral terms; and the cultural idioms through which these lives become visible and intelligible as appropriate sites for the exercise of both power and resistance. In making these arguments, I draw particular inspiration from two bodies of critical thought: efforts to rethink the human in relation to the conceptual and practical challenges raised by living animals,[5] as well as efforts to rethink the modern in relation to the constitutive alterity of colonial and postcolonial experience in India.[6]

In the Cumbum Valley, for example, Surya's complaints may be taken as a veiled comment upon the animal stakes of a regional problem in moral government. This was a lush vale tucked between the mountain forests of the Western Ghats and the dry plains of Tamil Nadu, its irrigated fields and orchards sustaining a market-oriented agrarian economy. Surya's village, like most others in the valley, was dominated by households of the Piramalai Kallar caste, one of the most prominent communities of southern Tamil Nadu. State officials and ordinary citizens alike insisted that the recent prosperity of Kallar households here depended upon their collective pursuit of "crooked paths" such as theft, smuggling, and other illicit trades rather than agrarian toil. Such assertions built upon long-standing antagonisms between the caste and other cultivating communities in the region, but also more recent colonial histories. Blamed for habitual cattle theft, blackmail, and highway robbery by British officials throughout the nineteenth century, the Piramalai Kallar caste was designated a "criminal tribe" in 1918. Until Indian independence nearly three decades later, all Piramalai Kallar men were fingerprinted, prohibited from leaving their villages without written permission, and subjected to a profound range of official reform measures, whether or not they had been convicted of any crime. These agrarian politics and colonial histories continue to shape how men and women of the caste seek to make themselves into moral subjects today.[7]

In what follows, the government of animal nature provides the lens through which I examine these histories and their ironic legacies in the postcolonial present. The article begins by discussing how the Criminal Tribes Act governed Kallars and other native subjects in India as organisms of impulsive, habitual, and instinctual criminality. It turns then to the echoes of these colonial histories of policing in the everyday practices through which ploughmen, herdsmen, and cultivators seek to govern the "thievish" conduct of domesticated animals in the region. These agrarian practices also inform, I argue, a vernacular imagination of government in rural south India as an enterprise of "grazing" those beings—either human or animal—deemed incapable of controlling themselves. I briefly chart a cultural genealogy of this agrarian conception of good government, and then sketch its salience for the contemporary management of human beings in rural south India. All of these materials testify to various forms of coexistence between practices of care and techniques of control in the pastoral engagement of an animal nature. But they also support a way of engaging biopolitics in relation to the empirical specificity of particular places and histories—a way of pluralizing, that is, the forms of welfare, modes of right conduct, and kinds of living being at stake in the modern government of collective life.

Our trail begins with the notion of a "pastoral" power and its flock of guided beasts—the traces of the nonhuman animal with a theory of modern life and its government.

On the Politics of the Living Animal

There is something deeply and harshly ironic in the politics of life in modern times, as living beings have become subject to unprecedented forces of both meticulous improvement and total annihilation. "Modern man is an animal whose politics places his existence as a living being in question," Foucault has written.[8] He had sought to understand how this had happened, how it was that life itself—"the indispensable, the useful, and the superfluous"—had become the object and terrain of modern government.[9] Foucault identified the emergence of a particular kind of power responsible for the state management of collective life in the West, a "strange technology of power" in which certain individuals and institutions assumed responsibility for the lives and welfare of many others. He called this a "pastoral" power, for it treated "the vast majority of men as a flock with a few as shepherds."[10] This was a form of power that was both individualizing and totalizing, carefully ensuring the distinct and particular welfare of each one within a population of subjects while submitting all of them to greater degrees of discipline and control. Although this may appear paradoxical from a certain standpoint—this coexistence of individual freedom and total power, of indulgent care and stern control—Foucault had argued that there was no real impasse here. Power and freedom always coexisted in a "complicated interplay."[11]

The play of power and freedom has been widely shown to orient the lives of many kinds of human beings: women, children, colonial subjects, putative criminals, classificatory lunatics, and many others in varied circumstances have found that the promise of freedom from power is conditioned upon submission to it.[12] One class of living beings has only recently begun to gain such scholarly attention, however, and that is a class at the very heart of a specifically "pastoral" form of power. The model to which Foucault had turned to understand what he described as the modern "government of men by men"—that of the shepherd and the flock—concerned in fact the government by men of animals. Foucault had suggested, as a mode of engaging critically with this and other forms of power, the posing of a certain question: "how are such relations of power rationalized?"[13] Here, however, Foucault himself might have examined more closely the ways in which ideas of animality and practical relations with animals may have served to rationalize this particular kind of power. Foucault's work has played a vital role in challenging celebratory accounts of the human individual as a locus of autonomous identity and subjectivity. But this anti-humanist orientation, one might argue, is most fully realized when we also consider the place of the animal within the body of theory itself.[14] Would a closer consideration of the relations with animals evoked by the notion of pastoral power aid in grasping what is at stake in the tension between care and control? Let us take a closer look at the politics of pasturage as a means of addressing this question.

In his 1980 "Tanner Lectures," Foucault ventured an explanation of why modern states sought to govern the lives of their individual subjects so meticulously and indeed so dangerously. Here it was not sufficient to consider the paradoxes of Enlightenment reason, he argued: "We have to refer to much more remote processes if we want to understand how we have been trapped in our own history."[15] The "remote processes" at stake here involved what Foucault described as a "pastoral modality of power": "the idea of the deity, or the king, or the leader, as a shepherd followed by a flock of sheep." In this early theory of power—which Foucault traced back to the "ancient Oriental societies" of Egypt, Assyria, and especially Judaea—the shepherd was expected to direct a "constant, individualized, and final kindness" toward each of the beings in his flock.[16] Although Greek thinkers largely dismissed this image of power, it was taken up in early Christian theology as a way of conceiving the personal and willful obedience sought by Christian pastors from their individual wards. Foucault argues that the modern practice of government elaborated beginning in the seventeenth century—and in particular, the doctrine of a "police"[17] meant to secure the moral well-being of a population through a close supervision of its conditions of life—borrowed from these Christian instruments of power. "That people survive, live and even do better than just that, is what the police has to ensure": the means by which it attains these ends—in families, schools, workplaces, hospitals, and so on—are pastoral in their nature.[18]

Foucault's work here is deeply illuminating and provocative. But there is also a way in which this genealogical account excises practical relations with animals from its narrative economy, reducing pasturage to nothing more than a political metaphor for most of Western history. With respect to the Hebraic texts, for example, Foucault insists on the metaphorical status of the Shepherd-God. "They're just themes," he suggests. "In no way do I claim that that is effectively how political power was wielded in Hebrew society before the fall of Jerusalem."[19] Turning to the dismissal of the shepherd as "political metaphor" among the Greeks, Foucault argues similarly that the task of the politician is to assure the unity of a city rather than to foster the life of each person.[20] And again in the many centuries of medieval Christian Europe, Foucault identifies a series of reasons as to why pastoral power failed to emerge at this time as an "effective, practical government of men": "The pastorate of souls is an especially urban experience, difficult to reconcile with the poor and extensive rural economy at the beginning of the Middle Ages . . . the pastorate is a complicated technique which demands a certain level of culture, not only on the part of the pastor but also among his flock."[21]

Ironically enough, pastoral power was least effective within the rural milieu that lent it a name. This foreclosure, like each of the others, served Foucault a particular explanatory purpose. It is only in modern times, he argued, that pastoral power came to guide political practice at the level of the state. However, this argument also affects a complete break between pastoral models of politics and practical histories of pastoral engagement with animals. We are left again with a simple, yet crucial question: what, if anything, might the government of animal life by human beings tell us about the government of human life in the West?

This is a difficult question that I can only address elliptically and speculatively here. One might call attention, for example, to the practice of shepherding in the ancient Near East as political tactic as well as metaphor: the kingly city designed and constructed as "cattle-pen" and "sheepfold" in the Sumerian literary compositions of southern Mesopotamia,[22] for example. Or one might suggest that the dismissal of such metaphors in classical Greece may have had at least something to do with the political distinction between freemen and slaves in polis society, as herds were grazed primarily by slaves and low-status hired freemen while agrarian husbandry enjoyed much greater repute as a primary cause of civilization.[23] Whereas early Christians such as Chrysostom challenged the image of Christ as pastor by contrasting his style of leadership with that of living shepherds—"Actually shepherds do the opposite and follow their sheep from behind"—late medieval Christian preachers like the Englishman John Bromyard challenged in their sermons both the heresies of figurative shepherd-pastors as well as the real dangers of disease to living sheep.[24] Lastly, in early modern Europe, we may consider the import of works such as Stefano di Stefano's *Pastoral Rationale* (1731), a treatise on the sheep-owners guild as the paradigmatic "political body" of the predominantly rural Kingdom of Naples—penned by a pastoral poet and longtime officer in the Neapolitan Royal Sheep Customshouse.[25]

Admittedly, these are only fragmentary bits of evidence.[26] But however episodic, these intersections between pastoral image and pastoral practice suggest that material engagements with nonhuman beings in rural settings may constitute an important domain of the "unthought" within Foucault's own conceptualization of pastoral power. Relations between shepherds and flocks rely upon a radical difference in kind between pastors and the populations in their care. Flocks are made up of beings that would scatter, starve, suffer, die, or simply lose their way without the careful attention of someone else with better judgment. It is for this reason that the pastoral care of such beings is intimately bound up with their close control: any apparent contradiction between power and freedom is dulled under such conditions by the judgment that they are incapable of acting effectively on their own. Among human beings as well, attributions of animality support numerous ways in which stern control may be rationalized as the most appropriate form of care. Distinctions between the human and the animal, in other words, yield some of the most effective ways in which certain individuals and institutions seize responsibility for the welfare of others. It is not altogether surprising that Kant had celebrated the moral virtue of those for whom "reason holds the *reins* of government in its own hands."[27] Pastoral restraint was most fitting for those incapable of restraining themselves.

These are abstract claims made at a precarious level of generality. How might we defend them in a manner consonant with anthropology's commitment to the specificity of forms of life, history, and cultural imagination? Let us return for a moment to one of Foucault's most potent claims concerning the biological life of modern individuals: "Modern man is an animal whose politics places his existence as a living being in question."[28] What would an anthropological engagement with this claim concerning the human animal entail? One might ask about the particular conditions of modernity that orient this life whose existence is placed in question. One might ask about the practices of interaction, struggle, and care through which such existence emerges as a political problem of government. And one might ask about the kind of existence as a living being that is at stake under these conditions and in relation to these practices: what forms of life in particular milieus—human, animal, and otherwise—are subject to such power? Each of these problems or arenas of investigation yields a distinctive way of pluralizing and particularizing our understanding of biopolitics. Each also offers, more specifically, a way of grappling with particular forms of animal life as loci of power and subjection.

Take the first problem concerning modernity, for example. Although often occluded in the political history of the West, the government of humans *as* animals has been a prominent feature in the management of Europe's colonies. "The terms the settler uses when he mentions the native are zoological terms," wrote Frantz Fanon, for example.[29] European colonial power worked explicitly on beings beyond the threshold of the fully human, as this line was drawn in Enlightenment thought and the techniques of government that put its expectations into the practice. Subjects of colonial rule throughout Europe's empires struggled against the dictates of a biopolitics of difference whose horizons of possibility were framed by a difficult double bind. The not-quite-human either had to submit themselves to ambitious projects of training, discipline, and domestication—assuming the status of "an object of experimentation"—or had to endure the racial violence of an exclusionary humanism.[30] An abundant anthropological and historical literature has mapped the constitutive difference and postcolonial afterlife of "colonial modernity" in India, Asia, and elsewhere,[31] with respect to matters as varied as liberal politics,[32] panoptic authority,[33] and the status of civil society.[34] Similarly, reflecting on the animalization of colonial subjects offers a way of grappling with the specificity of postcolonial biopolitics and its paradoxical forms of care.

The problem of practice leads in a slightly different direction. Donna Haraway has reminded us that animals are not only good to think with—as Claude Levi-Strauss had famously suggested—but also "here to live with."[35] Her work suggests that bestial images and metaphors are best understood in relation to embodied practices of engagement, labor, and struggle between our species and others. Such practices of animal care and control may continue to matter in subtle, yet significant ways even when transmuted into figurative tropes such as that of the pastorate. Raymond Williams has pointed out, for example, that even the prosaic word "manage"—so central to the rhetoric of modern governmental rationality—came into English from the Latin *maneggiare*: "to handle, and especially to handle or train horses."[36] Kant's "reins" of government gain an unexpected resonance in this light.[37] In grappling with such practices of animal engagement, one must pay close attention to the kinds of animal life they engage: to be governed as a pet within the protective confines

of a domestic environment is of course rather different from being governed as
a wild creature found beyond its fringes, and different yet again from the treatment of working animals in agrarian and other settings. Is this a creature fit
for indulgence, extermination, or careful discipline? Each of these modes of
relation may be taken as a route of "traffic" between the human and the animal: the practical conduct of animal conduct as a model of and for human
conduct, and the conduct of human conduct as a way of imagining and exercising the government of animal life.[38]

Lastly, we may also examine the ideas of life and living being at stake in
particular social, cultural, and historical milieus. The very distinction between
the human and the animal, for example, may be taken as a means of tracing
rival forms of subjection to power. This has long been a shifting and slippery
line in the West—as Agamben has shown, for example, modernity has entailed
a certain bestialization of the human as "bare life" with deep antecedents in
classical thought.[39] If this is the archive in relation to which modern biopolitics is articulated in the West, parallel forms of distinction and exclusion may
be identified in other places, each with their own traditions and histories of
constituting subordinate forms of life as objects of both violence and care.
Consider, for example, the political engagement of Manchu tribal leaders as
"barbarian" animals in Qing imperial China,[40] the rearing of Hutu peasants as
beings akin to domestic beasts in the Burundian refugee narratives recorded
by Liisa Malkki,[41] and the use of customary idioms of hunting and butchering
in the Colombian political massacres of the 1950s.[42] Modernity has not eliminated these local cultural forms of care, control, and extermination of animal
being, nor is biopolitics in such places reducible to the exercise of colonial and
modern forms of government. Rather, what we find in postcolonial milieus
throughout the globe are various kinds of articulation between existing idioms
and practices, and the legacies of modern governmental intervention. Through
such articulations, biopolitics beyond the West emerges as a terrain of encounter between rival ways of governing life.

The sections that follow are meant to lend flesh to each of these successive
arguments. Let us begin with the animal reason of colonial power in rural
south India.

Descent of Criminal Man

News of the fallen World Trade Center flooded the Tamil-language television
and print media of south India in September 2001, as it did in much of the rest

of the world. I was immersed in fieldwork in the Cumbum Valley at the time, and countless people asked to make sure that the parents of this American visitor were safe from the carnage. Although they marveled at the scale of destruction broadcast relentlessly on the television, I found to my surprise that many situated this jarring event quite easily within a local history of power, morality, and defiance. Watching yet another rerun of grainy black-and-white video footage within the living room of a rural family I knew quite well, I was startled to hear a kinswoman of theirs call out a pair of words at the sight of the crashing planes: "thieving fellows!" Another elder grandfather in the family pulled me aside on the street later that day, murmuring laments over and over again about the "jealousy" that must have prompted these unknown men to attack a prosperous and powerful America. Two months later, a retired police superintendent in the village ranted loudly to me about the moral hazards of wealth and rivalry. As with Osama bin Laden, he insisted, excessive desire could lead a man who held the "form" of a human being to behave nonetheless "like a bloody animal." These assessments betrayed the force of the colonial past and older agrarian histories on the moral life of the postcolonial present. This was a village dominated by Piramalai Kallar castefolk, and these attributions of thievishness, overweening desire, and bestial tendency presented a strong echo of the colonial policing of this community's conduct in animal terms.

In economic and political as well as numerical terms, Kallars constitute one of the dominant castes of southern Tamil Nadu. Although most Kallars today work as cultivators, laborers, and small traders, the name "Kallar" itself means "thief" in Tamil, and it is widely held in places like the Cumbum Valley that many have relied upon "crooked paths" to advance themselves. Kallars began to settle here in large numbers in the late nineteenth century, fleeing famine in their native tracts to the east. Some tended herds of cattle and cleared woods to cultivate dry grains. Many others worked as watchmen for the established landholding castes—Gounders, Chettiars, Vellalas, and others—of the region, looking after their standing crops, harvested grain, livestock, and household gates. In many of these villages today, Kallars have far surpassed these other castes in property holdings, economic wealth, and political influence. In the village of KG Patti—where the reactions to September 11 narrated above took place—their advancement had depended upon their willingness to poach and pilfer timber, cane, sandalwood, ivory, and other valuables from the well-guarded state forests ringing the valley. But here and elsewhere in earlier decades, some Kallar households had also made a living taking from the ripening crops, domestic goods, and cultivated landholdings of other less forthright castes—often out of desperate need, but sometimes also with a proud sense of entitlement.

These practices of depredation were grounded historically in struggles between Kallars and other cultivating castes over political sovereignty in the southern Tamil countryside. For centuries, hereditary warrior communities like the Kallars had established themselves as chieftains and watchmen in the dry plains of the region. Their authority was closely bound up with their feudatory right to protect these localities from attack and plunder, but also with their ability to submit them to similar violence if that authority was not recognized by their inhabitants. This uneasy intimacy of protection and predation led colonial British administrators in the nineteenth century to decry the character and conduct of Kallar watchmen. Colonial law criminalized the Kallar watch as a ritual form of blackmail, a protection racket forcing cultivators to pay tithes to the very thieves who would otherwise make off with their cattle and crops.[43] In this tussle between rival forms of government in the countryside, Kallar conduct was identified in official terms as a species of "terrorism."[44] In 1918, the Piramalai Kallars—an endogamous subcaste most notably defiant of the Pax Brittanica—were declared as criminal by nature under the terms of the Criminal Tribes Act.

This particular instrument of colonial law in India governed its subjects as heirs of a stubbornly animal disposition. The 1871 act authorized the classification of populations demonstrably "*addicted* to the systematic commission of non-bailable offenses" as criminal communities.[45] Its language of addiction attributed repeated entanglements with the state to the irresistible compulsions of untutored desire, among groups who lived in and preyed from the margins of rural society. Nocturnal highway robbery was described, for example, as a favored "pastime" among men of the Kallar caste, a "principal recreation" and a source of "natural excitement" for Kallar youths nursing a "love of adventure."[46] These naïve pleasures were seen as the residues of an underdeveloped nature among the most defiant of colonial wards. One District and Sessions judge, for example, asserted the following about Kallars and other warrior communities in the southern Tamil countryside: "In my opinion you could no more eradicate this hereditary instinct of theft from these men than you could from a magpie."[47] The Criminal Tribes Act was predicated upon the assumption that such bodily impulses could indeed be redirected through an appropriate form of handling by the state.

The new criminology of nineteenth-century Europe had invested the criminal self with a hitherto unexplored topography of internal drives, pressures, and instincts, as Foucault has written.[48] Properly trained and exercised, these forces could be endowed with virtuous habits and tendencies; governed improperly, they careened toward ruin.[49] At stake here was the moral conscience as an emblem of the fully human: as a compulsion born of social life, cultivated through instruction and example, and ideally capable of restraining the momentary tugs of lower instincts.[50] Criminals, like animals, savages, and children, were widely imagined by late Victorian observers as reckless and impulsive creatures largely insensible to such moral persuasions. To thinkers and social planners wrestling then with the implications of evolutionary science, the criminal heart betrayed an atavistic and retrogressive animal nature.[51] But the notion of criminal heredity was itself poised at the crossroads of two modes of evolutionary reasoning, creditable to the workings of innate disposition on the one hand and the noxious influence of social contagion on the other.[52] Delinquent tendencies were seen as incubated most quickly in a social milieu of vice and degeneracy.

Conceived in this intellectual environment, India's Criminal Tribes Act of 1871 singled out a number of groups of itinerant traders, forest dwellers, and putatively professional thieves in north India for special surveillance, spatial constraint, and rigid controls.[53] The act was extended to the Madras Presidency of south India in 1911 and applied to the Piramalai Kallars in 1918. Each adult Kallar male in nearly 900 villages was fingerprinted and registered as a "possibly active criminal," whether or not he had been convicted, imprisoned, or even fined for previous infractions.[54] Fresh names were added annually to police station rolls, and a small number were removed each year on evidence of "good conduct." The number of registered Kallars peaked at 39,056 in 1932, representing well over half of those subject to the Criminal Tribes Act throughout the Madras Presidency.[55] Those registered under section 10(1)(b) of the act could not leave their villages for any reason between sunrise and sunset without first acquiring a written passport, be it to work, trade, or simply visit relatives. A much smaller number registered in addition under section 10(1)(a) were required to report for a roll call every night at the nearest police station at both 11:00 p.m. and 3:00 a.m.—most of these men likely spent each night sleeping as best they could in stationhouse doorways rather than trekking several miles twice nightly. Those who violated these spatial constraints risked imprisonment.

Measures such as these worked upon the animal nature or biological being of suspected criminals: they sought to govern instinctual tendency by controlling the movement of bodies through space. But this is not the only way in which the Criminal Tribes Act may be understood as an exercise of "pastoral" power. The act was held *in terrorem* over Kallar villages, to use the Latin phrasing of a district official central to the endeavor.[56] Its most restrictive provisions were reserved as a threat to be imposed on the men of uncooperative or recalcitrant villages. The prospect of reform was therefore absolutely central to the operation of the act, and this prospect of "weaning" Kallars from crime was put into play through strategies of care as well as tactics of control. The police post of "Kallar Special Officer" was created in 1920 with a portfolio of responsibilities vastly outstripping the duties of ordinary policemen. These officers went on to form local panchayats, or village councils, in Kallar villages, open compulsory elementary schools and boarding hostels for Kallar children, supervise the disbursal of agricultural loans and lands, establish rural centers for cottage industry and cooperative production, and even organize Boy Scout and Girl Guide corps for Kallar youths.[57] One district official described these measures as a "giving of the benefits" combined with a "shaking of the big stick," echoing the carrots and canes with which proverbial mules are goaded.[58]

The threat of compulsion hovered over all of these multifarious ventures in moral tutelage. If the Kallar Special Officer served as "nurse" to the population, as one District Collector wrote, this was a care that had exacted its dues in fear.[59] Police officials expected that the instruments necessary at the outset to force the prospect of "Kallar Reclamation" would ultimately give way to conditions supporting an autonomous exercise of moral judgment among these subjects. "It is hoped that in course of time the whole thing will be quite voluntarily done without exception," noted the first of the Kallar Special Officers in 1923.[60] With that horizon still distant, however, Kallars had no choice but to be governed as beings incapable of governing themselves: as beings intrinsically likely to stray, regardless of whether there was any evidence that particular individuals among them had done so. Like others subjected to the Criminal Tribes Act elsewhere in India, members of this caste were policed in a manner that tested the limits of the "humanizing influences" of British rule.[61] The animal rationality of these interventions is essential to understanding their peculiar blend of control and care.

Despite the rhetoric of improvement that justified these stringent measures, Kallar caste leaders and community representatives repeatedly complained of rampant extortion, degradation, and abuse at the hands of police personnel.[62] On the eve of Indian independence in 1947, native delegates to the Madras Legislative Assembly repealed the Criminal Tribes Act: not for having successfully humanized its targets and achieving its intentions, but rather for having reduced the state and its own officials to the "monstrous" and "inhuman" cruelty of animals.[63] Even today, descendants of those subjected to the act recall its strictures with a profound degree of ambivalence: they are remembered both as necessarily harsh measures intended to make "good men" of their "savage" forebears and as cruel devices that restrained their subjects in the manner of captive beasts.

I want to shift now to some of the contemporary legacies of these colonial instruments, seen from a particular and perhaps even peculiar vantage point: the pastoral practices by which domestic animals are managed in the agrarian economy of the region today. Here we find some surprising echoes of the way in which human beings were once policed. But we also find another cultural terrain in which the pastoral government of humans as animals may be imagined, exercised, and resisted—a local counterpoint to colonial biopolitics.

Thieving Bulls: Care, Restraint, Rebellion

One afternoon in 2002, I sought out Mokkarasu Thevar—a ninety-one-year-old Kallar man known for his nationalist activism during the Indian struggle against colonial rule—in his native village in the Cumbum Valley. As we sat on his cot chatting about this history, a high fan above us lazily deflecting the midday heat, the elder man unexpectedly likened the Criminal Tribes Act to a particular tool of bovine discipline. "The Criminal Tribes Act was like a nose-rope," he said to describe the law that even he had lived under as a young man. This "nose-rope" was a basic means of guiding and restraining plough bulls in the region, a thick braided cord passed through the nostrils of the animal and capable of inflicting a flash of pain when sharply tugged. Startled by this comparison between humans and bulls, I asked Mokkarasu Thevar what he meant by it. "With the nose-rope, an ox will obey in fear of pain," he replied. "The white man tried to do the same with the Thevars. But their valor cannot be controlled so easily. It will not change. It will not soften." This image of colonial official as cowherd presented a close echo of the notion of pastoral power as a mode of rule. Here it appeared, however, that a problem of defiant will drew together the policing of men and bulls alike. With this likeness in mind, let us explore the care of oxen in south India as a rural practice of government.

Working oxen are cherished animals in the rural reaches of south India. Respect for these creatures among the cultivators, herdsmen, and ploughmen of the region goes far beyond the anthropological image of "sacred" Indian cows, for it derives less from the purity that they may lend to human rituals and more from the moral virtues exercised by these animals themselves.[64] Oxen are widely understood to have a "heart" capable of feeling all that humans do. Ploughmen recounted the capacity for memory that these animals shared with human beings—oxen would remember even those who had sold them off, I was told, sometimes pausing for a moment at the threshold of former homes on their way back from a day in the fields. Folktales celebrated as well the loyalty of oxen as a species: oxen are said to have lost their original ability to speak only because a pair of bulls had once taught their owner how to cheat the god of death. In my many months in the Cumbum Valley, I was always struck by the patient care with which ploughmen bathed their bulls in the river after a long morning of labors, painstakingly wiping away every clump of caking soil from their legs and flanks. Every January with the Tamil *Pongal* festival, cultivators would brightly decorate the bodies of their plough bulls for ritual prayers and the promise of a day's rest to these toiling creatures.

These sentiments persist even as the place of oxen within the agrarian economy of the region continues to evolve. Many of the upland reaches of the Cumbum Valley were first settled in the nineteenth century by migratory herdsmen of various castes, including Kallars. The mountain forests, scrub thickets, and dry fallow fields of the region sustained large herds and flocks of hundreds of cattle, goats, and sheep, which would roam over this terrain with scant supervision. Farmers relied upon oxen in particular for ploughing, leveling, manuring, and irrigating fields. Much of this has changed with the rise of

FIGURE 3.2. Ploughmen and plough bulls at work in the wetland paddy fields of the Cumbum Valley. Although mechanical tractors have largely displaced these animals in environments such as the uplands in the distant background of this image, farmers in the region insist that bulls remain necessary for more subtle operations in the cultivated lowlands. Photo by the author.

a market-oriented orchard economy here in the last three decades. The undu-
lating and once-open uplands of the valley have been steadily fenced for closely
managed commercial crops of coconuts, grapes, bananas, cabbage, onions,
beets, and other vegetables. Large itinerant herds of cattle have been almost
fully displaced by these developments, with plough bulls and hybrid dairy animals now grazed largely within the restricted spaces of riverbanks, roadsides,
and private orchards or stall-reared on special diets within domestic courtyards.
Chemical fertilizers and tractors fitted out with disc and rotor blades have also
dislodged most oxen from their niches in the agrarian economy. Pastoral care
of such animals here is now much less a matter of flocks, herds, and populations
and more a domain of individualized attention.

Nevertheless, for those who still own, tend, hire, and work with such animals, their management remains a compelling arena of both practical struggle
and reflection. In speaking with these men and women about their efforts to
manage these animals, I also came to see more of what was at stake in the
moral government of their human peers. I learned that with oxen, as with humans too under many circumstances here, restraint was the price of affection:
not simply being restrained, that is, but being willing to submit oneself to restraint. Those susceptible to restraint were more likely to enjoy the good favor
of those who tended them. And those that were not—in spite of anything one
might say about the sacral character of bovine life in Hindu India—were readily driven for sale to the butcher shops and beef markets in the nearby hills of
Kerala. It was through this moral distinction between good and bad animals—
between those capable of control and therefore deserving of care, and those incapable of control and therefore condemned—that the government of bovine
life in the valley intersected with that of its human inhabitants. Specifically, that
is, the legacies of the Criminal Tribes Act and its action upon a locally dominant caste surfaced too as a way of making sense of bovine indiscipline.

Slightly after dawn one cool October morning in 2002, for example, I
found cultivator Logandurai driving his pair of plough bulls along the main
road in the Cumbum Valley village of KG Patti. He had joined a long train of
bullock teams trundling toward the paddy fields to the distant southwest: the
transplantation season was under way, and the ploughmen had been hired to
blend and level the wet mire of the fields for tender seedlings of rice. As we followed behind his pair of bulls, Logandurai taught me some of the calls with
which he spoke to these animals: *tluk tluk* for them to walk, *adiyee!* to drive
them forward quickly, *haa!* for them to stop. Oxen would not respond to such
commands to work, he told me, unless they had the will to do so. A good ox
could be described as just that: "good." But like other cultivators and ploughmen

in the region, my friend reserved for a bad ox the startling epithet *kalavaani*, or "thievish." Thievish oxen were lazy animals that wished to eat without toil, he explained. A thievish bovine might steal into a field or orchard to nibble at ripening crops rather than ambling as far as a forest or pasture. And on the ploughing fields, a thievish ox would toss its neck repeatedly to shake off its yoke, Logandurai told me, or just lie immobile in the mud without getting up to pull.

I was intrigued by this image of criminal oxen, which I learned was ubiquitous among those who handled these animals in the region. It depicted animal misconduct in moral terms as a problem of government, one that identified bovine indiscipline with the mode of conduct at issue in the region's most distinctive colonial history: thievery. And it presented the agrarian landscape as one of varied temptations—ripe crops close at hand, cool wet mud, the comfort of a body at rest, and so on—toward which working animals might stray. Most interesting perhaps about this characterization was the way in which it distinguished between animals able and unable to restrain themselves in the face of such lures. "If a vehicle has no brake, we must fix the brake. If we don't, it will go wrong, no?" one grazer explained to me, reaching for an analogy to explain this need even among animals for a faculty capable of controlling desire. Ploughmen, grazers, and cultivators working with cattle certainly had means at their disposal to restrain those animals that would not restrain themselves. The nose rope was one such ordinary device, but one could also light a fire to the hindquarters of a lazy animal that refused to move, I was told, or even restrain cattle that roamed willfully with a *konti kattai*: a stick dangling between the forelegs from a wooden block around the neck of the animal, discouraging it from running quickly. These, however, were exceptional measures. As Logandurai had insisted that October morning, thievishness in an ox was largely a matter of habit: "Some men will just let their cattle graze on the crops of others. But my oxen never act thievishly."

Like many others I knew in the Cumbum Valley, Logandurai cared deeply for his plough bulls. I had once seen him glum and listless for days because one of these oxen had been refusing to eat and none of his own remedies had worked. A veterinarian had finally diagnosed the problem as an impacted rumen, and the animal recovered in some time. For Logandurai, the moral conduct of his animals grew out of such close and ongoing practices of care. One could punish these oxen for behaving in particular ways, but they would ultimately do only what they were accustomed to doing. Most effective in "conducting" their conduct was the careful cultivation of particular inclinations and dispositions.[65] Like human beings, Logandurai and other ploughmen assured me, for example, bulls too would refuse to work only if they had been left idle for a very long time. Accustomed to moving and acting in particular ways over time, they would not need to be controlled too violently, for they would move and act in a controlled fashion of their own accord. Such claims emphasized that everyday modulations of careful attention and stern discipline were essential to the moral subjection of these animals. Some would certainly present stubborn limits to such engagement, and their owners would have no choice but to sell them to the slaughter markets. But for the most part, these were effective practices: among these populations of animals, they yielded moral subjects.

"Pastoral care" on the agrarian terrain of the Cumbum Valley yields a way of moralizing animal subjects through a particular regime of power. These practices of animal management also gesture more specifically here, however, toward the moral character of the humans too that inhabit this terrain. It is no accident that bad bulls earn the epithet *kalavaani*, or "thief": Kallar thievery and its control have long been some of the most stubborn problems of collective politics in the region. Gounders, Vellalars, Chettiars, and other established cultivating communities here had struggled for decades to guard their fields against the nocturnal raids of those landless and desperate Kallar men and women willing to take from ripening fields and grain heaps. As Kallar households themselves began to attain a certain degree of numerical predominance, economic prosperity, and political authority in the region, such crop depredations also surfaced as a deliberate tactic of social struggle. I heard numerous accounts of herds of livestock purposefully unleashed on the ripening fields of others in the event of personal feuds or episodes of collective violence between rival castes and clans. When Logandurai—a Gounder and an affine of the headman's lineage in his village of KG Patti—spoke of certain individuals willing to let their animals graze on the fields of others, he gestured obliquely toward such histories. Thieving bulls testified to a defiance of the rural moral order by the humans too that tended them.

This quality of defiance that may be shared by men and bulls alike underscores the fact that the pastoral tending of such animals—like the pastoral tending of such men—is in fact a power relation rather than a scenario of total control: a relationship of mutual and "permanent provocation" as Foucault has written.[66] It is this ongoing tension between the adamant nature of a resistant will and the moral force of government that explains how the image of the thieving bull circulates in the Cumbum Valley today: not only as a sketch of bovine excess, but also as an essential emblem of Kallar resistance to the historical strictures of the Criminal Tribes Act as well as more contemporary forms of policing. Local narratives describe inveterate Kallar rogues of the colonial era as *cantiyar maatu*: "obstinate bulls" that would not bow to the will or yoke of another. When Mokkarasu Thevar described the "valor" of those Kallars who refused to yield to the "nose-rope" of colonial law, he had called upon this association. And another younger kinsman from his village of Anaipatti—especially notorious throughout the valley to this day for the willful and unrepentant depredations of many of its Kallar households—pointedly asked me the following: "If you suddenly tie up an ox that has been grazing on cultivated fields all its life, what will it do?" The thieving bull in such statements is far more than an analogy, turn of phrase, or purely symbolic likeness between man and beast.[67] It conveys instead the common defiance of a form of power to which humans and animals alike have been submitted: it reveals "grazing," that is, as a vernacular mode of governing humans too in south India. I want to sketch now the place of this mode of power in the genealogy of biopolitics in the region.

"Grazing" as a Practice of Rule

The Indian Penal Code of 1860 laid the foundations for the operation of law in modern India. The exercise of power in postcolonial India still owes much to the categories, structures, and predilections of colonial rule; nevertheless, other earlier forms of power and authority continue to surface in durable, if unexpected ways. I sat on a front stoop with a number of middle-aged Kallar men one afternoon in the village of KG Patti, talking about the Criminal Tribes Act and its work upon their forebears. A man named Karuppu said that his own father had perished of diarrhea in a local jail, imprisoned for failing to send his sons regularly to the Kallar Reclamation school. Another, named Muthu, described how colonial officers had given his father a grant of land to cultivate, which he had held onto for a few years before losing it for good. Muthu himself worked as a field watchman, or *kaaval*, for other cultivators, and I turned to ask his brother Perumal—a retired police constable—whether there was anything that agrarian watchmen and constables had in common, given that they were both denominated in Tamil by the same word, *kaaval*. Perumal's reply took me completely by surprise. "Aren't the police those who graze men?" he quipped with a mischievous smile. Karuppu broke in to explain this terse remark with a proverbial utterance: "A teacher educates speech, a policeman educates conduct." The didactic formalism of his saying gestured toward its modern derivation. But was there anything else at stake in Perumal's image of police

officers "grazing" their citizens? Could this be taken as an Indian variant, ana-
logue, or antecedent of pastoral power?

Earlier in this article, I suggested that the pastoral metaphor of the shepherd and the flock had intersected with various forms of pastoral practice in
the history of the West, intersections that may have been essential to its salience as an image of good government. I want to argue now that a political
idiom of "grazing" has circulated in a similar fashion in south India as a long-
standing means of imagining effective rule. In a grammatical sense, the verbal
root *meey* in Tamil accommodates both transitive and intransitive acts of
"grazing." *Meeythal* is to graze upon, feed on, or prey upon, whereas *meeyth-
thal* is to lead birds, beasts, and other creatures in acts of grazing or feeding.
The *Tamil Lexicon* notes that the latter verb bears an additional colloquial
sense: "to govern," as in "to restrain and rule over."[68] Indeed, the term is often
used in everyday expression to refer to the management of subordinate human
flocks of various sorts. Teachers could "graze" their students, I learned in my
months in the Cumbum Valley, just as overseers grazed their field laborers,
parents their children, and police constables the criminals and crowds in their
jurisdiction. At work in these practices of grazing is a form of power founded
on the careful supervision and bodily restraint of those beings deemed incapable of restraining their own desires and impulses. How might we sketch its
genealogy?[69]

Literary materials attest to various ways in which subjects of authority in
India have been governed as if populations of animals in earlier times. Classical Sanskrit evocations of *danda*, for example—the figurative rod or scepter of
royal righteousness enforced by the threat of punishment—bear pastoral reso-
nances of goading and driving.[70] Sketched at its moment of creation in the canonical *Laws of Manu*, *danda* is identified as "Law" and "protector of all beings": protector of a people construed here as a herd of *go*, or cattle.[71] Although
this might appear to us in retrospect as an instrument of violence rather than
care, it is important to emphasize that its exercise was often construed as a
necessary means of guidance for those subjects unable to distinguish between
superior and inferior ends of existence on their own.[72] The presence or absence
of such a faculty of discrimination among rival modes and ends of worldly life,
in fact, has for centuries served as one of the most durable ways in which the
properly human is distinguished from the merely animal in Indian literary and
philosophical tradition.[73] Virtuous self-conduct among proper human beings,
in other words, is widely understood in Indian moral and cultural life as a
practice of controlling sensual impulse. Religious texts in particular sketch

restraint from without as a way of cultivating those beings as yet unable to restrain their own desires: the deity Siva, for example, as a "grazer" subjecting the "milk cows" of the senses to stern pastoral guidance, in order to enable the moral perfection of the devotee within whose heart they wander.[74]

Various forms of historical traffic would have drawn such ideas beyond the domain of elite literary culture and into contact with the cultural lives and material practices of ordinary people. Take, for example, the way in which a low-caste rural laborer proclaims his religious devotion in the *Mukkutal Pallu*,[75] an eighteenth-century Tamil dramatization of agrarian life performed in both courtly venues and local temple festivals:[76]

> Those who spurn and do not bow
> toward the 108 places of [the deity] Perumal—
> I will bind their fiendish legs
> and yoke them to the plough!
> Those who do not know [the devotional verses of] *Tiruvaymozhi*
> I will make into two-legged oxen
> and "*thi thi*!" with my ploughing staff
> I will drive them Lord!

Presented with the colloquial rural language and ribald humor of the Tamil literary genre from which it is derived, there is no doubt a parodic quality to this laborer's assertion that he will yoke and drive those who remain ignorant and indifferent to his faith through the fields as "two-legged oxen." And yet, the moral authority of this ploughing staff bears the unmistakable traces of a form of power founded on the need to restrain and guide an animal—specifically bovine—nature incapable of acting virtuously on its own. Here is another species of what Foucault might have called "pastoral" power: one in which the animal qualities of the tended body are absolutely essential to the control exercised in the name of its care.

In the agrarian traditions of the Cumbum Valley—a little more than a hundred kilometers to the north of the setting for this play—subordinate individuals had been subjected in many ways to the plough as instrument of moral and political ordering. A ritual veneration of the headman's plough, for example, took place annually in each village of the valley. Before harnessing his own plough for the cultivating season, every farmer was expected to pray before and lead once around a field a plough that the headman had harnessed and kept ready. The ritual publicly affirmed the necessity of the headman to bring prosperity, rain, and a bountiful harvest. "Only he was fit to support and protect," an elder Kallar cultivator in the village of KG Patti explained to me. Agrarian and domestic workers dependent upon the care of the headman and other leading cultivators would have had their subordinate status marked by other practices as well. As recently as a few decades ago, for example, Kallars working as watchmen and farm laborers for higher-caste cultivators in the region were served their rice and water in iron winnows and tins—vessels kept aside for such use only within the cattle sheds, I was told, of respectable households. The aging Gounder headman of KG Patti likely had this hierarchical economy of relations in mind when he told me an apocryphal tale of a British official inviting his father to "graze all the villains" inhabiting his village in exchange for a grant of state land. When I asked why he insisted that such reform measures had failed, he spluttered out a single word with as much force as he could muster from toothless lips: "Animal!"

Much of the old headman's ire stemmed from his inability now to guard his tamarind trees in the distant uplands of the valley from pilfering by others. The field of power here has been greatly recomposed in the last fifty-odd years: Kallars in this and other local villages have risen to an unparalleled local dominance, and village leaders must now negotiate the scope of their authority with the numerous servants of a postcolonial bureaucracy. Despite such shifts, grazing remains a vernacular idiom of government in the region, one that marks the continued salience of certain practices of collective handling. Techniques of physical pursuit and harness are essential to state police work in the Cumbum Valley, for example: regular beat patrols, recurrent raids in problem villages, pursuit of suspected criminals on foot and by jeep, preventive as well as punitive confinement in both village and stationhouse spaces, and so on. We may find an evocation of such practices in retired constable Perumal's claim that policing was no more than a matter of grazing human beings. But we may also find the kind of power at stake here clarified by the ways in which such officers themselves distinguish between the human and the animal qualities of those in their care. "They are without human quality—they will never ever reform," another senior Cumbum Valley constable once insisted to me concerning the Kallar population of his jurisdiction. A stubborn and irredeemable animal nature was the moral condition that demanded a close and continuous regime of supervision and control.

We ought to recall at the same time, however, that the verb for "grazing" in Tamil bears two distinctive senses: leading in grazing, but also grazing or preying *upon*. In the Cumbum Valley today, as in much of the rest of India, police hold little in the way of moral authority, as officers of the law are deemed more likely to prey upon their own wards for bribes, gifts, and other favors than they are to lead them toward any superior means of livelihood. The very proverb that I cited earlier concerning the educative role of teachers and police officers, for example, is typically slurred and bent to suit the times these days in a far more ironic register: "A teacher is one who lacks good speech, a policeman is one who lacks good conduct."[77] In light of such judgments, lawbreaking itself is easily admired by some for its defiance. Many of the Kallar men and women that I knew, for example, denounced police constables as "thieves" in their own right, proudly recounting the many occasions the animal vigor with which they had outrun these putative pastoral guardians. "We would wander about like unyoked oxen," a former ganja trafficker in the village of KG Patti told me, fondly reminiscing about his younger days of willful insurrection. And a much younger sandalwood smuggler in the same village bragged in similar fashion with a drunken laugh one evening: "I run so fast that even the police cannot catch me." His friends celebrate his speed with the nickname Kalairasu—"royal bull."

It is worth lingering on such boasts—which I often heard from Kallar men dwelling on the margins of the agrarian economy—for they challenge the *telos* of moral subjection implicit in the many forms of pastoral care that I have sketched here. To be sure, policing is imagined in south India as a task of domesticating animal tendencies and fashioning proper human beings. But even within these humanizing selves, the inherited strains of animal character remain: elements to be celebrated, excused, or further trained depending upon the moral dispositions of particular subjects. The "becoming-animal" of delinquent Kallars both echoes and displaces the moralizing premises of pastoral government.[78] Such confounding trajectories reveal once again the hybrid nature of the biopolitical body in postcolonial India, indebted to the persistence in the present of multiple forms of subjection from the past.[79] The thieving bull is a being fashioned at the intimate interstices of rival forms of pastoral power, depredation, and care—a not-quite-domestic animal, both subject and rebel simultaneously. From the vantage point of such beings, postcolonial freedom may ultimately appear less as a path to becoming human in any one given sense and more as a possibility of inhabiting the animal—in multiple, overlapping, and inconsistent ways.

Conclusions

For biopolitical subjects in the contemporary United States, Hurricane Katrina proved to be one of the most troubling reminders in recent times of the harsh limits to pastoral care and attention here. And yet what is striking about much of the public discourse in the wake of the disaster is the extent to which victims and observers alike turned to the image of livestock to make sense of the government's callous response. "We were herded over there like cattle," one of hundreds moved to the Mississippi Coliseum complained on September 5, 2005, while a reporter for the Associated Press described the "human cattle yards" into which New Orleans refugees crowded, struggling to somehow survive. Some found echoes here of earlier forms of bestialization, such as the writer of a bluegrass parody in which the condition of those who'd been "put in the arena an' kept herded there like cattle" was underscored by juxtaposed drawings of a slaving ship and the infamous Louisiana Superdome. To be treated like an animal in such accounts was to be denied the care due to a proper human being. Others, however, challenged the very premise of such complaints. "I don't think I've ever seen an evacuation or disaster relief effort where people were not treated like cattle," one blogger wrote, "because the best way to **save** the most people is to act in mass." And a team of doctors described the horror they felt in branding the foreheads of the most desperate victims to be evacuated from a flooded medical center: "It's just very hard to go and start marking people like cattle." Yet this is exactly what they reported having to do, wielding a "marks-a-lot" pen in the name of triage, even as the practice reminded at least of one them of Auschwitz.[80]

Why are some people herded and driven as animals rather than cared for as proper human beings? What I have sought to do in this article is to query the terms of such a contrast by examining modes of human government deeply indebted to forms of animal care. Pastoral power may appear paradoxical if one opposes sympathetic care to brutal control, domains of freedom to domains of power, or nurturing conditions in which one may act autonomously to the situation of being herded, driven, and compelled against one's will. But these oppositions quickly collapse if and when the subjects of such power are judged and governed as animal beings. In south India, I have tried to show that this was the case in British colonial struggles to police and reform putatively criminal instinct; in quotidian efforts to govern the moral conduct of stubborn livestock; and in vernacular idioms of government that authorize the restraint of those deemed incapable of restraining themselves. To address the animal as a moral problem of government is to confront the borders of a persistent humanism that still often frames both prevailing understandings of and intellectual investigations into the nature of modern life. Focusing closely on the virtues and vices attributed to animal subjects, I have argued, may also help deepen our understanding of the basic premises and limits of human government as well.

It is insufficient, however, to make such arguments in the abstract alone. "How . . . might one begin to mark out the specificity of our contemporary biopolitics," Nikolas Rose has asked, a question essential to any anthropology of the biopolitical.[81] Building here on accounts of the constitutive difference of colonial and postcolonial modernities, I have sought to take the very premise of that common "our" as an invitation for critical inquiry. Conversations on life and its qualities in the Cumbum Valley of south India certainly do at times invoke genes, chromosomes, and other related entities, as do such conversations in many other parts of the world today. But other ways of imagining, engaging, and governing living beings and their natures continue to matter in this eminently modern milieu. The contemporary here is therefore shot through with the traces of other moments and prior forms of biopolitical government, both Western and non-Western, and each with their own genealogies both distinctive and intertwining. Ideas of moral life among humans and animals alike are unintelligible in the region today except in relation to the legacies of the colonial past—but this colonial past too, however, is itself understood and recollected in the terms of a much older cultural imagination of good government in the region. I have sought to bring into focus the afterlife of these multiple biopolitical pasts in the postcolonial present, as a means of suggesting that the government of life in any milieu must be understood in relation to its specific history. These materials support an anthropology of biopolitics that begins with the specific ways in which life may enter politics in particular places, and the practices through which it may come to serve as an arena for the exercise of power.

This is not meant, however, as a plea for specificity alone: claims made in relation to such cultural histories and practices should also be capable of attaining a level of generality beyond the scope of the empirical materials that constitute their grounds. I have pursued such generality here in a particular manner. The politics of living being, like any politics, involves practical relations of power whose impetus and character can only be grasped in relation to the everyday deeds of living beings. The traces of such engagement, however, may also be found at work within our own language of abstraction. It is for this reason that I have tried to take the pasturage implicit in a theory of "pastoral" power seriously, for here we have both a theory of power and a marker for material practices of governing life engaged elsewhere. By tracing the pastoral back and forth between these two domains of theory and practice, I have paid heed not only to the practical government of animal life but also to the complex ways in which that life itself has struggled into and beyond the domain of our own forms of knowledge. Such traffic points to a way of material-izing theory itself—to a way of lending flesh, substance, and the obstinate force of embodied existence to our own instruments of understanding.

Notes

1. Foucault 1981.

2. Rabinow 2003; Petryna 2002; Biehl 2005.

3. Agamben 1998.

4. Foucault 1978.

5. Haraway 1989; Rothfels 2002; Wolfe 2003; Daston and Mitman 2005.

6. Guha 1997; Chakrabarty 2000; Gupta 1998; Sivaramakrishnan and Agrawal 2003.

7. Pandian, 2009.

8. Foucault 1978:143.

9. Foucault 1981:250.

10. Foucault 1981:231.

11. Foucault 1983:342.

12. Mahmood 2005; Mehta 1999; Mbembe 2001; Foucault 2000.

13. Foucault 1981:254.

14. Fudge 2002.

15. Foucault 1981:226.

16. Foucault 1981:227.

17. By the term "police" Foucault does not solely refer here to the restricted domain of law enforcement as it is understood today, but rather to the emergence of myriad public offices in seventeenth-century Europe—public health, statistics, economic planning, the scientific management of natural resources, and so on—dedicated to securing the moral well-being of populations through the close supervision of their conditions of life.

18. Foucault 1981:250.

19. Foucault 1981:230.

20. Foucault 1981:235.

21. Foucault 1981:240.

22. Harmansah 2004.

23. Hodkinson 1988.

24. Hill 1993:51–52.

25. Marino 1986.

26. "The idea of the shepherd-king may seem to emerge as neither archetypal myth nor cultural image, more a history of fragments and chance meetings" (Murray 1990:13).

27. Baxley 2007.

28. Foucault 1978:143.

29. Fanon 2004:42.

30. Mbembe 2001:27.

31. Barlow 1997; Gaonkar 2001.

32. Mehta 1999.

33. Kaplan 1995.

34. Chatterjee 2004.

35. Haraway 2003:5.

36. Williams 1976.

37. For a thoughtful reflection on the language of command and the relations of government at work in the training of horses, see Patton (2003).

38. Haraway 1989.

39. Agamben 1998.

40. Zarrow 2004.

41. Malkki 1995.

42. Uribe 2004.

43. Pandian 2005.

44. Cardew to Price, December 3, 1895, G.O. No. 473 Judicial, March 31, 1897, Tamil Nadu State Archives (hereafter TNSA).

45. Emphasis added. Amendments made in 1896 enabled the application of the 1871 Criminal Tribes Act to any section of any group. In 1911, the act's reach was extended to the Madras Presidency in south India.

46. Francis 1906; Paddison to Judicial Secretary, April 27, 1918, G.O. No. 1331 Home (Judicial), June 5, 1918, TNSA; Mullaly 1892; Loveluck, "The Kallar problem in South India," G.O. No. 596 Law (General), June 16, 1921, TNSA.

47. Davies to Price, September 30, 1895, G.O. No. 473 Judicial, March 31, 1897, TNSA.

48. Foucault 2000.

49. See Collini 1991.

50. For Darwin (1872), for example, it was the "moral sense" among human beings that worked against this brutal imprint. Conscience was a compulsion born of social life, cultivated and passed onward through instruction and example, habit and reflection, to be turned against the momentary tugs of lower instincts and impulses.

51. Atavism formed the kernel of the criminal anthropology propounded by Italian physician Cesare Lombroso beginning in the 1860s. His "Natural History of the Criminal" pinned innate delinquency to the outlines of a brutish and retrogressive physiognomy: apish arms and jutting jaws, noses hooked like birds of prey, and so on (Lombroso-Ferrero 1911). English Victorian writers throughout the nineteenth century repeatedly sketched the bestial and animal nature of born delinquents (Leps 1992).

52. On the tension between these contrary forms of evolutionary reasoning, see Moore, Pandian, and Kosek (2003).

53. Interestingly enough, however, the object of notification under the Criminal Tribes Act in India was never a criminal "caste" as such, but always a criminal "tribe,

gang or class." Late nineteenth-century designations of collective criminality were provisional and contradictory wherever applied, argues Freitag (1991), often sacrificing the subtleties of native self-identification to the necessities of police administration.

54. Loveluck, "The Kallar problem," G.O. No. 596 Law (General), June 16, 1921, TNSA.

55. G.O. No. 436 Public (Police), August 18, 1933, TNSA. Aside from Kallars, there were a total of 36,471 others registered as criminal tribe members that year, of whom 4,901 were women. At no point were Piramalai Kallar women registered under the act. On the controversy surrounding women of other communities registered under the act, see Radhakrishna (2001:60–64).

56. Paddison to Legislative Council, August 28, 1915. Judicial Department. G.O. No. 1649, June 27, 1916, TNSA.

57. Hall to Marjoribanks, May 17, 1924, G.O. No. 541 Judicial (Poli), October 29, 1924, TNSA.

58. J. F. Hall to IGP, April 6, 1931, GO No. 485 Public (Police) September 12, 1931, TNSA.

59. Hall to Marjoribanks, May 17, 1924, G.O. No. 541 Judicial (Poli), October 29, 1924, TNSA.

60. 1922 Administration Report, G.O. No. 2683 Law (General) Misc., November 8, 1923, TNSA.

61. O'Farrell to Chief Secretary, G.O. No. 473 Judicial, March 31, 1897, Tamil Nadu State Archives.

62. Mukkulathor Sangham petition to the Governor of Madras, G.O. No. 920 Home, March 23, 1945, TNSA.

63. *Legislative Assembly Debates*, Second Session of the Second Legislative Assembly, Government of Madras, Vol. V, Nos. 1–14, 557–581, TNSA.

64. For more on virtues as cultivated dispositions of moral conduct in rural south India, see Pandian 2009.

65. This is akin to the "rehearsed" forms of spontaneous moral conduct discussed by Mahmood (2005), suggesting yet again that moral practices of virtue are at stake in such animal care.

66. Foucault 1983:342.

67. "Becoming-animal" is *real*, Deleuze and Guattari (1987) argue. Ploughing expeditions, oxen races, and *jallikattu* contests, a popular sport in which young men compete to bring down bucking bulls and seize the bundles of coins fastened to their horns, serve as arenas in which rural men may "become-bull." Several wildly popular Tamil films—such as the 1980 *Murattu Kaalai* (*Rough Bull*) starring action hero Rajnikanth—match the virility of those who engage in *jallikattu* contests with the indiscipline of the bulls they tame. Historically in this part of Tamil Nadu, these contests have been identified most closely with Piramalai Kallar men.

68. *Tamil Lexicon* 1982:3353.

69. On the difference between Tamil ideas of moral restraint and the Kantian notion of virtue itself as a capacity for self-restraint, briefly alluded to earlier, see Pandian 2009.

70. Scharfe 1989.

71. See Olivelle 2004: Section 7.14.

72. Glucklich 1988.

73. The fifth-century Tamil grammar *Tolkappiyam*, for example, identifies the *manasu*, the internal discriminating faculty of heart and mind, as the sixth sense distinguishing humans from other forms of life. Lest we conceive this as a matter solely of physiology, the text goes on to class *maakkal*—men without the quality of "discrimination"—among the beasts and other beings whose senses numbered no more than five (Murugan 2000:630–632).

74. Varadarajan 1988:99.

75. Kesikan 1960.

76. Peterson 1996.

77. From *vaakkai kattravan vaaththiyaar, pookkai kattravan poolisaar* to *vaakkillaathavan vaaththiyaar, pookkillaathavan poolisaar* in spoken Tamil.

78. Deleuze and Guattari 1987.

79. My use of the polyvalent term "hybrid" is guided most closely by the work of Guha (1997), on the braiding of colonial governmental strategies with Indian rationalities of rule.

80. These materials were culled from the following Web pages in successive order: http://www.wwltv.com/local/stories/WWLBLOG.ac3fcea.html; http://www.wwltv.com /sharedcontent/nationworld/katrina/stories/090205ccwcKatrinaWalkthru.1bc07ce2 .html; http://folksong.org.nz/new_orleans/index.html; http://www.beheardblog.com /blog/_archives/2005/8/31/1185667.html#comments; http://www.msnbc.msn.com/id /14516700/page/4/. Boldface in original.

81. Rose 2001: 5.

References

Agamben, Giorgio. 1998. *Homo Sacer: Sovereign Power and Bare Life*. Stanford, CA: Stanford University Press.

Barlow, Tani, ed. 1997. *Formations of Colonial Modernity in East Asia*. Durham, NC: Duke University Press.

Baxley, Anne M. 2007. "Kantian Virtue." *Philosophy Compass* 2, no. 3: 396–410.

Biehl, Joao. 2005. *Vita: Life in a Zone of Social Abandonment*. Berkeley: University of California Press.

Chakrabarty, Dipesh. 2000. *Provincializing Europe: Postcolonial Thought and Historical Difference*. Princeton, NJ: Princeton University Press.

Chatterjee, Partha. 2004. *Politics of the Governed: Reflections on Popular Politics in Most of the World*. New York: Columbia University Press.

Collini, Stefan. 1991. "The Idea of Character: Private Habits and Public Virtues." In *Public Moralists: Political Thought and Intellectual Life in Britain 1850–1930*, 91–118. Oxford: Clarendon Press.

Darwin, Charles. 1872. *The Descent of Man and Selection in Relation to Sex*. New York: D. Appleton and Company.

Daston, Lorraine and Gregg Mitman, eds. 2005. *Thinking with Animals: New Perspectives on Anthropomorphism*. New York: Columbia University Press.

Deleuze, Gilles and Felix Guattari. 1987. *A Thousand Plateaus: Capitalism and Schizophrenia*. Minneapolis: University of Minnesota Press.

Fanon, Frantz. 2004. *Wretched of the Earth*. New York: Grove Press.

Foucault, Michel. 1978. *History of Sexuality*, vol. 1: *An Introduction*. New York: Pantheon Books.

——. 1981. "Omnes et Singulatim: Towards a Criticism of 'Political Reason.'" In *The Tanner Lectures on Human Values*, vol. 2. Salt Lake City: University of Utah Press.

——. 1983. "The Subject and Power." In *Michel Foucault: Beyond Structuralism and Hermeneutics*, ed. Hubert Dreyfus and Paul Rabinow, 208–226. Chicago: University of Chicago Press.

——. 2000. "About the Concept of the 'Dangerous Individual' in Nineteenth-Century Legal Psychiatry." In *Power*, ed. James D. Faubion, 176–200. New York: New Press.

Francis, W. 1906. *Madura District Gazetteer*. Madras, India: Government Press.

Freitag, Sandria B. 1991. "Crime in the Social Order of Colonial North India." *Modern Asian Studies* 25, no. 2: 227–261.

Fudge, Erica. 2002. "A Left-Handed Blow: Writing the History of Animals." In *Representing Animals*, ed. Nigel Rothfels, 3–18. Bloomington: Indiana University Press.

Gaonkar, Dilip, ed. 2001. *Alternative Modernities*. Durham, NC: Duke University Press.

Glucklich, Ariel. 1988. "The Royal Scepter as Legal Punishment and Sacred Symbol." *History of Religions* 28, no. 2: 97–122.

Guha, Ranajit. 1997. "Colonialism in South Asia: A Dominance Without Hegemony and Its Historiography." In *Dominance Without Hegemony*, 1–99. Cambridge, MA: Harvard University Press.

Gupta, Akhil. 1998. *Postcolonial Developments: Agriculture in the Making of Modern India*. Durham, NC: Duke University Press.

Haraway, Donna. 1989. *Primate Visions: Gender, Race and Nature in the World of Modern Science*. New York: Routledge, Chapman and Hall.

——. 2003. *The Companion Species Manifesto: Dogs, People, and Significant Otherness*. Chicago: Prickly Paradigm.

Harmansah, Omur. 2004. "The Shepherd, the Cattle-Pen and the Cedar Forest: Ideals of Divine Kingship, Mythical City and Fecund Landscapes in Early Mesopotamian Literature." Paper presented at the Suspending (Dis)Belief Conference, University of Pennsylvania. Philadelphia, March 27.

Hill, Ordelle G. 1993. *The Manor, the Plowman, and the Shepherd: Agrarian Themes and Imagery in Late Medieval and Early Renaissance English Literature*. Toronto: Associated University Presses.

Hodkinson, Stephen. 1988. "Animal Husbandry in the Greek Polis." In *Pastoral Economies in Classical Antiquity*, ed. C. R. Whittaker, 35–74. Cambridge, MA: Cambridge Philological Society.

Kaplan, Martha. 1995. "Panopticon in Poona: An Essay on Foucault and Colonialism." *Cultural Anthropology* 10, no. 1: 85–98.

Kesikan, Puliyur, ed. 1960. *Mukkutal Pallu*. Chennai, India: Pari Nilaiyam.

Leps, Marie-Christine. 1992. *Apprehending the Criminal: The Production of Deviance in Nineteenth Century Discourse*. Durham, NC: Duke University Press.

Lombroso-Ferrero, Gina. 1911. *Criminal Man, According to the Classification of Cesare Lombroso*. New York: G.. P. Putnam.

Mahmood, Saba. 2005. *Politics of Piety: The Islamic Revival and the Feminist Subject*. Princeton, NJ: Princeton University Press.

Malkki, Liisa. 1995. *Purity and Exile*. Chicago: University of Chicago Press.

Marino, John A. 1986. "The State and the Shepherds in Pre-Enlightenment Naples." *Journal of Modern History* 58, no. 1: 125–142.

Mbembe, Achille. 2001. *On the Postcolony*. Berkeley: University of California Press.

Mehta, Uday S. 1999. *Liberalism and Empire: A Study in Nineteenth-Century British Liberal Thought*. Chicago: University of Chicago Press.

Moore, Donald S., Anand Pandian, and Jake Kosek. 2003. "The Cultural Politics of Race and Nature: Terrains of Power and Practice." In *Race, Nature, and the Politics of Difference*, eds. Donald S. Moore, Jake Kosek, and Anand Pandian, 1–70. Durham, NC: Duke University Press.

Mullaly, Frederick S. 1892. *Notes on Criminal Classes of the Madras Presidency*. Madras, India: Government Press.

Murray, Oswyn. 1990. "The Idea of the Shepherd King from Cyrus to Charlemagne." In *Latin Poetry and the Classical Tradition*, ed. Peter Godman and Oswyn Murray, 1–14. Oxford: Clarendon Press.

Murugan, V., trans. 2000. *Tolkappiyam in English*. Chennai, India: Institute of Asian Studies.

Olivelle, Patrick. 2004. *Manu's Code of Law*. New York: Oxford University Press.

Pandian, Anand. 2005. "Securing the Rural Citizen: The Anti-Kallar Movement of 1896." *Indian Economic and Social History Review* 42, no. 1: 1–39.

——. 2009. *Crooked Stalks: Cultivating Virtue in South India*. Durham, NC: Duke University Press.

Patton, Paul. 2003. "Language, Power, and the Training of Horses." In *Zoontologies: The Question of the Animal*, ed. Cary Wolfe, 83–99. Minneapolis: University of Minnesota Press.

Peterson, Indira. 1996. "The Fortune-Teller (Kuravanci) Plays of 18th Century Tamil

Nadu: The Social History of an Indian Literary Genre." Paper presented at the 14th European Modern South Asia Conference, Copenhagen, August 21–24.

Petryna, Adriana. 2002. *Life Exposed: Biological Citizens after Chernobyl.* Princeton, NJ: Princeton University Press.

Rabinow, Paul. 2003. *Anthropos Today: Reflections on Modern Equipment.* Princeton, NJ: Princeton University Press.

Radhakrishna, Meera. 2001. *Dishonoured by History: "Criminal Tribes" and British Colonial Policy.* New Delhi: Orient Longman.

Rose, Nikolas. 2001. "The Politics of Life Itself." *Theory, Culture & Society* 18, no. 6: 1–30.

Rothfels, Nigel, ed. 2002. *Representing Animals.* Bloomington: Indiana University Press.

Scharfe, Hartmut. 1989. *The State in Indian Tradition.* Leiden, the Netherlands: E. J. Brill.

Sivaramakrishnan, K. and Arun Agrawal, eds. 2003. *Regional Modernities: The Cultural Politics of Development in India.* New York: Oxford University Press.

Tamil Lexicon. 1982. Madras, India: University of Madras.

Uribe, Maria. 2004. "Dismembering and Expelling: Semantics of Political Terror in Colombia." *Public Culture* 16, no. 1: 79–95.

Varadarajan, M. 1988. *A History of Tamil Literature.* New Delhi: Sahitya Akademi.

Williams, Raymond. 1976. *Keywords.* Oxford: Oxford University Press.

Wolfe, Cary, ed. 2003. *Zoontologies: The Question of the Animal.* Minneapolis: University of Minnesota Press.

Zarrow, Peter. 2004. "Historical Trauma: Anti-Manchuism and Memories of Atrocity in Late Qing China." *History and Memory* 16, no. 2: 67–107.

PART II

Animal Matters

Human/Animal and the Contemporary West

MELFORD SPIRO ONCE FAMOUSLY WROTE THAT THE TASK OF anthropology is to make "the strange familiar, and the familiar strange."[1] In many ways, the essays in part II of this volume do just that. They especially allow us to see the "familiar" in a new light, making it cast unfamiliar shadows, revealing areas of culturally informed invisibility, and forcing us to confront the habitual as strange. Given that so many of our relationships with and thinking about nonhuman animals falls in a taken-for-granted category, these excavation-type undertakings represent a crucial starting point in our efforts to better understand the ethical contours of our engagements with animals and the role they play in human self-conception.

The reach of capitalist industrialism knows no bounds; the world and its inhabitants are all construed as resources and managed for maximum profit. In "Discipline and Distancing: Confined Pigs in the Factory Farm Gulag" (chapter 4), Joel Novek argues for examining the treatment of animals, on the one hand, and humans, on the other, as parallel phenomena within contemporary techno-industrial society; both humans and animals are rationalized according to an ideology of commodification.

Novek fruitfully engages with sociological theory to reveal its applicability to the question of the animal. Arguing that modern techno-industrial society operates via a double logic of "discipline" and "distance"—without which the present social order would collapse under the weight of its own contradictions— Novek reveals the extent to which modern industrial agriculture is grounded in these logics. Beginning with the concept of "discipline," he employs labor process theory to demonstrate how capitalism's exploitation of productivity operates in essentially the same way on animals as it does on humans: both are subject to its rule of mechanization and rationalization of production, division of work, and deskilling. Further, both humans and animals have their basic needs for social interaction restricted or denied and their productive capacities colonized by "machines and managers." Novek stresses, however, that with non-human animals, it is primarily their reproductive capacities (mating, breeding, gestation, birth, nurturing their young) that are the focus of subjugation and discipline, and here he draws on Michel Foucault's notions of bio-power to understand the ways in which the vitality of bodies (both human and animal) is harnessed and transformed, through disciplinary techniques and surveil-lance, into docile and productive subjects in the interest of (social) power. Novek shows how post-humanism further extends Foucault's insight into the vigorous, diffuse, and ubiquitous reach of power by taking seriously the hybrid nature of contemporary social systems, composed as they are of networks of animate and inanimate nature, all of which are integrated into continuous production systems. Arguing that modern agriculture serves as an apt example of a hybrid system in which humans, animals, and technology function as as-semblages aimed at maximizing industrial production, Novek nevertheless warns that an overemphasis on hybridity undercuts important distinctions that must be retained between sentient beings and nonsentient machines.

"Distancing" is a key concept in sociological thought because it describes an essential strategy of modern societies to displace, but never disrupt, institu-tions that are problematic but vital for the maintenance of the social order. Much sociological work concerns itself with the phenomenon of distancing in the management of prisoners, the mentally ill, the dying, and so on, and Novek avails of it to analyze the social consequences of the dramatic shift in modern agriculture away from the family farm and barnyard to the industrial-ized and concealed animal factory. Philosopher David Hume's assertion that distancing produces a "weaker and more imperfect" moral connection (between actors and actions) informs Novek's discussion of how spatial distancing re-sults in a rupture of consumers from the moral, ecological, and economic consequences of their choices.

Novek's analysis of the ways in which deep-seated moral contradictions are maintained through the rationalization and sequestration of experience, although sober, is not entirely bleak. When contradictions become too great or when they are no longer economically justifiable, change does occur. Just as the gulag system of the former Soviet Union eventually collapsed under the weight of its own economic and moral corruption, the modern industrial farm now finds itself in a defensive position, confronted with a growing chorus of critics highlighting its economic, ecological, health, and moral shortcomings.

Novek's focus on the modern hog farm can be read as a critique of industrialized agriculture more generally and of the economic instrumentalism that underpins it. The declining legitimacy of the factory farm, therefore, also suggests that the mechanistic and instrumental view of life, which has so dominated modern society, may itself be starting to give way.

Humor is most compelling when it succeeds at forcing us to look at ourselves in a new light, revealing aspects of ourselves that we might otherwise not see, or ever even consider. Sometimes it is cultural proclivities that are uncovered, other times humor has the potential to expose the fragility, and vicissitudes, of the human condition. But when humor flirts with the frontier that separates humanity from animality, moving back and forth across it, the gag reflex is as likely to be provoked as the funny bone tickled. In "Boys Gone Wild: The Animal and the Abject" (chapter 5), Cynthia Chris explores humor that deliberately disrupts the species boundary, rousing disgust as often as delight.

Chris's analysis focuses on *Wildboyz*, MTV's genre-blurring wildlife series that purposefully toys with the species-transgressing abject to provoke reaction from its television audience. The abject, Julia Kristeva tells us, "confronts us . . . with those fragile states where man strays on the territories of *animal*."[2] Straying on the territories of animal, and dallying there long enough to be discomfited and debased, is what the Wildboyz are all about.

Chris traces the development of wildlife filmmaking from its late nineteenth-century beginnings through to the emergence of the classical genre in the postwar period and, at the close of the century, to the rise of so-called reality variants, of which *Wildboyz* is a part.

Although *Wildboyz* makes use of many of the conventions of classical wildlife television programming and film, in most ways it represents a dramatic departure from the genre. For instance, whereas traditional wildlife television programming relies on the presence of a detached and knowledgeable observer to guide the viewer through the exotic and unpeopled world of wild animals, the "boyz" blunder their way into chaotic and intimate encounters that more often than not leave them bruised, scratched, and bitten. Ill-prepared and openly bewildered, their unchoreographed interspecies boundary-testing engagements are characterized more by shrieking and laughter than by the transmission of knowledge.

Chris asks how we are to understand the Wildboyz and queries whether the program merely captures the market for silliness in our multichannel universe. Is it merely juvenile horseplay? scatological travelogue? purposefully offensive cultural critique, replete with "bad taste, buggery, and bestiality"? Or, she submits, "are the Wildboyz up to something serious?"

The Wildboyz engage in performances that reveal frontiers to be powerful sites of provocation. Humor and abjection are sparked at the borders: slippage from animal to human rouses mirth that is "benign," whereas slippage from human to animal incites disgust and "mirthless laughter." Humor is the rupture or disjuncture between the categories of human and animal, and, we are to infer, if slippage were more absolute, there would be no laughter at all. The boundary-testing performances of the Wildboyz are funny, therefore, precisely because they are such spectacular failures.

Chris's analysis reveals humor to be serious business: it has the potential not only to expose the fragility of the human condition, but to mark its limit.

In "Animal Heroes and Transforming Substances: Canine Characters in Contemporary Children's Literature" (chapter 6), Michelle Superle immerses us in the imaginative world of children's literature, where animals have long played central roles. Superle's study focuses on the dog story genre as a contemporary mythological narrative in which dogs are depicted as "superior beings" and catalysts for change who help humans to achieve their full humanity. Straddling the binary between wildness and civility, dogs represent mythical heroes who effectuate a spiritual breakthrough and transformation in their human companions.

Whereas dogs have long played central roles in children's literature, their heroism before the mid-twentieth century was, in the main, conceived within a realistic genre. Animals were depicted as "physical saviors," celebrated for rescuing humans from bodily danger. The phenomenon of animals as spiritual saviors first emerged in the 1960s and is connected with the growing cultural disillusionment with technocratic society. Superle argues that animals' association with nature and, in particular, domesticated animals' liminal status between the domestic and the wild make them ideal mediators in children's literature, capable of bridging the nature-culture divide.

Contemporary children's literature now regularly conveys the message that domesticated animals, dogs especially, are "transforming substances" that have the power to heal and profoundly change lives. The relationship between children and dogs is treated as a privileged one, superior to other human relationships, and free of artifice. Where adult characters routinely reject dogs, perceiving them as disruptive "others," children work to integrate them into the family, helping them shed some of their wildness. The process highlights children's connection with the natural world and parallels their own move toward greater integration within the family and community and toward a new balance between their humanity and animality. In this way, Superle argues, dogs enable children to become more fully human.

From villain to hero, the wolf has served as a potent symbol through which Americans have understood themselves and their relationship to the land. Indeed, so powerful is the symbol that in "The Making of a Wilderness Icon: Green Fire, Charismatic Species, and the Changing Status of Wolves in the United States" (chapter 7), Gavin Van Horn suggests "icon" as the more appropriate term, conveying as it does a sense of profound emotional and imaginative associations at work in directing and focusing thought. Popular conceptions of the wolf have moved a great distance over the past century, from zealous vilification (leading to the wolf's effective extermination in the early years of the twentieth century) to their quasi-deification as symbols of freedom. Van Horn traces this history and its intimate connection with the nation's evolving idea of itself.

The wolf, as a symbol of wild and dangerous "otherness" antithetical to human civilization and decency, had an important place in the imagination of the early settlers in North America, much as it had in the European lands from which it came. Steeped in an ideology of progress, in which social Darwinism and manifest destiny played key roles, the American landscape was transformed to conform to human interests. This zeal formed the basis of the settlers' "domesticating missiology," which aimed to make the land secure for domestic animals and promote maximum productivity of desirable game species.

Van Horn explains how, by the early twentieth century, the resultant deterioration of wildlife caused a shift in popular sentiment and a reevaluation of old policies. The public's growing interest in the conservation of wild species did not, however, initially extend to include predator animals. The wolf, in particular, as immoral, dangerous, and violent, was an enemy of civilization and remained a target for extermination. It was only when the landscape was devoid of the wolf that Americans, in ever increasing numbers, began to question the wisdom of an ideology that sought to create a predator-free nation.

A new set of values gradually took root in response to the rapidly urbanizing American landscape. Van Horn documents the emergence, following the Second World War, of an ecological movement that espoused a radically distinct vision of the human place in the natural world. Aldo Leopold became a spokesperson for this new outlook, which saw the human not as a conqueror, but as a "plain member and citizen" of the biotic community. But Leopold's attitude was hard won: only after gleefully hunting a mother wolf and her cubs did he find himself awed as he stood watching the animal die, the "green fire" in her eyes growing dim.

Leopold's spiritual journey from "conqueror to citizen" was a microcosm of the changes that were occurring in the broader society at conflict with itself and powerfully captured the changing sentiments of the nation. Suddenly, the wolf—ever associated with the wild—now came to symbolize loss.

Van Horn's essay documents how the change in the iconographic status of wolves over the period of a century reflects a major shift in public perceptions of wild animals and of nature more generally. By the late twentieth century, the wolf became an icon of all that was good and right in the world—an icon of freedom, authenticity, and wildness that needed to be preserved. Just as the wolf's early demise came to be viewed as an egregious display of human arrogance and immorality, its gradual return to the land (through successful reintroduction programs) offered the possibility of spiritual and ecological redemption. The multiple and paradoxical images associated with the wolf reveal, Van Horn argues, the often contradictory relationships humans have with the land and the large degree to which human identity is grounded in these relationships.

Ron Broglio begins chapter 8, "Thinking with Surfaces: Animals and Contemporary Art," with an assertion of the importance of surfaces: "That which is most animal, including the biological element of animale rationale, lives on the surface of things." Broglio understands animality to refer to the active becoming of existence, that dimension of life that is rooted in transient flesh and routinely disavowed in our understandings of ourselves. Just as our retreat into the privileged interiority of an "I" is a denial of the importance of the outside world, through art, economy, politics, and religion we attempt to transcend our surface. Broglio endeavors to take surfaces seriously and to reveal them as sites of meaningfulness. He does so through an exploration of the surface of animal bodies and the surface of the artist's canvas on which animal bodies are represented.

Broglio begins with a discussion of eighteenth-century animal portraiture, a genre that depicted sheep, cattle, horses, hogs, and dogs as specimens of exemplary domestication, with the primary function of advertising a breed. This genre communicated an understanding of the animal's surface as its real meaning, malleable and open to human improvement. Preconceived images of what an ideal animal should look like played a central role in determining which traits should be inherited, and therefore which animals to breed. Broglio reveals the central role that art played, not only in depicting, but also in transforming the natural world. Graziers, for instance, for whom the cattle's surface is read as cuts of meat, used animal portraiture to build and establish cattle breeds. Because animals were evaluated by their lines and surfaces, artists held a privileged position in the promotion of breeds, depicting the cattle's corpulence as an object, viewed at a distance, for human consumption.

Broglio contrasts the "enframed" animal of animal portraiture with the work of the contemporary collaborative British artists known as Olly Suzi, for whom canvas surfaces offer an opportunity for unframed animals to leave their marks and provide glimpses of their worlds. Olly Suzi shun the security of the artist's studio and work in the animal's own territory, often in extreme environments far outside human dominion. They don't steer clear of danger nor do they try to neutralize it through shielding measures, when it exists (e.g., in their work with sharks and polar bears). The anxiety they experience is part of the artistic engagement in that it keeps them "in contact with the surface," preventing them from being lulled into adopting a position of the detached observer. As such, they acquire new gestures, as well as a heightened and different awareness of themselves as "surfaces"—as bodies engaging with other bodies. The canvas becomes the contact zone on which the bodies of humans and animals create, and the product is the outcome of a negotiation of its space.

Decidedly unlike cattle portraits of the eighteenth century, which denied animals a space outside our human understanding, the canvases of Olly Suzi reveal the very limits of our knowing. The marks left by animal bodies hint at a world to which we have little access, a world that can never be fully captured by the human other.

Anne Vallely

Notes

1. Spiro 1990.
2. Kristeva 1982:12 (emphasis in original).

References

Kristeva, Julia. 1982. *Powers of Horror: An Essay on Abjection*. New York: Columbia University Press.

Spiro, M. E. 1990. "On the Strange and the Familiar in Recent Anthropological Thought." In *Cultural Psychology*, ed. J. W. Stigler, R. H. Shweder, and G. Herdt, 47–61. New York: Cambridge University Press.

four

Discipline and Distancing

Confined Pigs in the Factory Farm Gulag

Joel Novek

> This is an economy and in fact a culture of the one night stand. "I had a good time," says the industrial lover, "but don't ask me my last name." "Just so," the industrial eater says to the svelte industrial hog, "We'll be together at breakfast. I don't want to see you before then, and I won't care to remember you afterwards."
>
> —Wendell Berry, *Citizenship Papers*, 2002

PIGS USED TO BE EVERYWHERE IN RURAL CANADA. THEY ROAMED in pastures and barnyards and sheltered in barns and huts during the long, cold winters. In the early 1950s, half a million Canadian farms raised hogs, making them the most widely produced form of livestock in the country.[1] They were a staple of the mixed arable livestock systems, combining grain and meat production, that dominated the rural landscape. What a difference a half century makes. By the new millennium, Canada's pig population had more than doubled, to over 14 million, but the number of hog farms had dropped below 13,000, representing just 6 percent of all farms.[2] The average number of pigs per farm is now more than 900 head,[3] and the largest 7 percent of hog farms account for one half of Canada's swine herd.[4]

The Canadian case illustrates a profound transformation in animal agriculture globally. Intensive farming—that is, large-scale, industrialized farming methods that confine animals indoors—has largely replaced smaller scale, husbandry-driven "extensive farming" in the poultry, dairy, and swine industries.[5] Animal production has moved out of pastures and barnyards and indoors into climate-controlled structures.[6] Mechanization of animal handling, feeding, and waste disposal has substantially reduced the need for human labor. Animals are kept indoors and confined in cages or pens through the various stages of their lives with little opportunity to move around.[7] Intensive operations have become all-year continuous production systems, replacing the seasonal or batch production characteristic of extensive agriculture. They are also capital intensive and provide cost advantages to the largest operations, which are better able to take advantage of volume output.[8]

Social scientists have not ignored animal production systems. They have examined the agro-industrial complex characterized by mechanization, economic concentration, monocultural animal production, complex supply and marketing chains, and global trade.[9] Some have looked at the environmental impact of factory farms with their accumulation of livestock manure and its threat to air, water, and soil quality.[10] Other researchers have stressed socioeconomic polarization and a loss of viable rural communities resulting from concentration in the livestock sector and a steep decline in the number of small family farms.[11]

But social scientists also need to address the impact of industrialized animal production on the relations between humans and nonhuman farm animals. Humans have subjected farm animals to extreme forms of regulation, surveillance, and control. What strategies, techniques, and technologies have humans employed to manage the livestock under their responsibility? Have these strategies been "successful" or have they provoked dysfunctions and systemic problems? Intensive confinement reinforces the "otherness" of farm animals who are isolated and hidden from human gaze, off limits to the public. Their reproduction and growth, in oppressive conditions, takes place substantially beyond the boundaries of human awareness. How does this marginalization affect our cultural understanding of the farm animals whose flesh most of us consume on a daily basis? And what, if anything, does our treatment of farm animals tell us, reflexively, about the structure and institutions of industrial society in the twenty-first century? These questions, along with efforts to answer them from a sociological perspective, will be the focus of this chapter.

Many of these issues have been addressed from an animal welfare perspective.[12] Social scientists, and sociologists in particular, have no special expertise in this area. They can, however, draw parallels between the institutional regulation of humans and of nonhuman animals. Livestock, like humans, are sentient beings that have been subject to various techniques of surveillance and control. Techniques for the management of humans have long been the object of sociological analysis, and some of these insights can be applied to understanding the management of livestock. As Bruno Latour states, "Whenever we learn something about the management of humans we shift that knowledge to nonhumans and endow them with more and more organizational properties."[13] Reflexively, we can also apply knowledge about the management of nonhumans to the examination of human institutions in industrial society.

Discipline and Distancing

Two concepts drawn from sociological theory, discipline and distancing, can help us trace the parallels between the management of humans in industrial society and the management of livestock under intensive confinement. Both concepts represent processes of modernity that are mutually reinforcing and supporting. Discipline, especially the disciplinary techniques of factories, prisons, and hospitals, refers to the ensemble of techniques that comprise what John O'Neill (1992) has termed "the disciplinary society." The goal of social organization in this society is the efficient regimentation of docile bodies, which, in the industrial sector, allows for continuous production under management control. In industrial societies, discipline tends to be increasingly technical in nature. This means that discipline is imposed on subjects through technical controls embedded in machinery, structures, and technological processes.[14] If we apply this concept to livestock agriculture, we can advance the argument that intensive confinement operations represent a new phase in the domestication of farm animals, marked by the imposition of large-scale industrial discipline.

The concept of discipline to be applied in this analysis derives from three sources: labor process theory, Michel Foucault's notions of bio-power, and post-humanist perspectives on the integration of humans and nonhumans. Labor process theory looks at the two-way interaction between the creative working human being and the natural world.[15] It examines the process by which work is transformed by organization and technology and the powers of nature are deployed to produce the goods that humans want. Bio-power, according to Foucault, represents the reproductive and developmental potential of living bodies harnessed to the service of power.[16] Bodies are transformed into docile and productive subjects through the agency of power. The post-humanist perspective as developed by Donna Haraway (1991) and Bruno Latour (1999) sees modern social organizations as hybrids, composed of networks of humans, technical artifacts, and nature. Livestock agriculture is a social construction designed to exploit the reproductive power of animals (Latour 1999), who possess the status of actants within the networks.

The disciplining of farm animals does not take place transparently; rather, it is carried out "at distance," behind enclosures, in locations shielded from scrutiny.[17] Distancing refers to processes of modernity and globalization in which the idea of space is bent, stretched, and compressed. Industrial and commercial activities are "lifted out" from their local contexts and concentrated elsewhere, which interposes the "friction of distance" between transactional parties.[18] This allows morally troubling acts, such as the disciplining of livestock, to proceed relatively free of public observation. One strand of distancing theory derives from "the political economy of consumption."[19] Global commerce separates resource production from consumption, breaking informational and feedback loops and isolating consumers from the consequences of their actions. Social geography contributes the concept of the appropriation of space for specific activities, some of which are considered degrading and disreputable.[20] This enables the friction of distance, mentioned above, to reinforce patterns of segregation and act as a barrier to human interaction. Finally, Anthony Giddens bases his notion of high modernity on what he terms the "sequestration of experience."[21] He argues that humans achieve ontological security by establishing institutions to conceal morally contentious activities—the control of the sick, the criminal, the insane, and the natural world—from the regularities of day-to-day life. These ideas will be developed further in the section on sociological perspectives.

This chapter focuses on discipline and distancing as strategies used by humans to regulate the commercial swine herd and advances our understanding of social science concepts as lenses for viewing the treatment of animals in intensive animal agriculture. The Canadian swine industry serves as an excellent case study of the transition to intensive production. Hog production in Canada has grown more rapidly than any other form of livestock over the past thirty years and has undergone a massive shift from pasture and barnyard to intensive confinement systems, along with a concomitant increase in economic concentration. Indoor confinement systems have proven especially popular for raising hogs, given Canada's northern, and often inclement, climate. The practice, of course, reinforces the segregation and concealment of hog production from the everyday social world.

The Industrialization of Canadian Hog Production

At mid-twentieth century, Canadian hog farming was generally batch production on a small scale as an adjunct to grain production.[22] Pigs were raised in pastures and open feedlots with access to bedded shelters. Structures for housing pigs were small and primitive by today's standards—often open-ended shelters or portable huts. Sows were confined to pens during the farrowing (birthing) process. Otherwise they had, in comparison with today, considerable freedom to move about.[23] The weaning period for young pigs lasted eight to ten weeks. Sows would be rebred when weather conditions and farm labor availability permitted.[24] The biggest problem facing this outdoor extensive system, and the reason it could not grow beyond a form of batch production, was the inability to farrow, or give birth, to new piglets during the long cold winter months. Young pigs could simply not survive outdoors, or even in primitive shelters, under Canadian winter conditions.[25] Producers could only farrow their sows at certain times during the year—most commonly in spring.

Indoor pig production had been advocated as a solution for some time, but had faced powerful obstacles. Chief among them was the difficulty of providing adequate nutrition for pigs without access to pasture and the threat of diseases spreading in cramped indoor conditions. Research conducted in the 1940s and early 1950s at the Canadian federal experimental farm at Lacombe, Alberta, demonstrated that pigs confined indoors in sanitary feeding pens and fed a mixture of grain and protein supplements made faster and more economical gains than those raised on pasture.[26] Vitamin B_{12} had been isolated as an active ingredient in animal protein supplements. It was most effective when combined with antibiotics such as penicillin as a feed supplement to assure a rapid rate of gain. Antibiotics held a second advantage for indoor pig production. Researchers believed they were essential for limiting the spread of communicable illnesses that inevitably occurs in indoor confinement.[27]

The development of commercially available feeds and feed supplements meant that hogs could be successfully raised all year round. Farmers were no longer restricted to their own grain and pasture in raising their herds.[28] Pig farms could become larger and more specialized by raising hogs indoors and purchasing grain and feed supplements to give them greater production capacity. Other obstacles to larger scale pig production remained to be overcome. One was the loss of many young pigs to "overlaying," or crushing by the sow during nursing.[29] A second problem was the labor-intensive nature of swine raising. Efforts to find a technical solution to these problems contributed to both the industrialization of hog farming and the subjection of the pigs, especially the breeding herd, to much tighter industrial discipline.

One area subject to confinement was the farrowing process. Sows began to be bred year-round to assure a continuous supply of piglets. To speed up the process the weaning period was reduced to four weeks, allowing farms to rebreed the sow more quickly.[30] Since the gestation period is about four months, sows can now average more than two litters a year.[31] To solve the problem of crushing during nursing, producers began to confine sows in farrowing stalls.[32] These stalls provide minimal space for sows, usually less than 20 square feet. The sows cannot walk or turn around. Along the sides, bars or rails provide a protected zone called a creep, where the piglet is supposedly protected from crushing by the sow. When farrowing stalls were first introduced, they were used only for a few days.[33] Producers began to leave sows in the stalls for longer and longer periods until they encompassed the entire lactation cycle. These stalls represented a form of technical control designed to reduce the need for human labor in animal handling, to save space, and to allow more pigs to be crammed into the barns.

The same dynamic of intensified discipline and isolation through the widespread dissemination of a technical solution can be seen with the common use of gestation stalls. "Function creep" is a term used to describe the tendency of a technological innovation to find new applications.[34] This applies to gestation stalls, which were first introduced to control sows' feeding during the critical breeding and gestation period.[35] Under confined conditions, there is competition among sows for feed. This would be less of a problem in more spacious conditions where the sows would be able to establish natural hierarchies of dominance and submission. In confinement, however, competition and aggression are intensified, and the dominant or "boss" sows may get more than their share of feed, leaving the subordinate animals undernourished.[36]

The technical solution to this problem was individual feeding stalls about two feet wide and six feet long.[37] This restricted fighting and guaranteed more accurate feeding. What was first introduced mainly for feeding soon became the normalized mode of sow confinement during the entire four-month gestation period. Breeding sows are now subject to rigid confinement through virtually all stages of their lives. The nursing period was reduced and sows are quickly rebred, so there is almost no time when they are not in production. Producers have achieved a remarkable time-space compression of the hog breeding process. More pigs are crammed into confined spaces and the breeding cycle has been speeded up so that the average sow produces 2.3 or even 2.6 litters per year.[38] Young pigs move though nursing, weaning, and finishing in about 190 days. Production is conceptualized as a series of cycles, or "pig flows." One for the breeding sows to be continuously bred, farrowed, and rebred, and another for the market hogs to progress from nursing to weaning to finishing.

Perhaps the most significant change is that production has moved into specially designed differentiated and segregated units. Pigs have been confined to a vast, concentrated factory farm Gulag, where their exploitation takes place in sealed enclosures: windowless, heated and air conditioned, and restricted. While pigs are less and less visible, the economic significance of hog farming has grown. In my home province of Manitoba, hogs now rival wheat and canola as the biggest agricultural revenue generator. Driving through the summer fields of wheat, barley, canola, and flax, with nary a pig in site, this fact seems hard to believe. Only the glimpse of distant enclosures, and the foul odours emanating from them if the wind is blowing in your direction, might lead you to believe otherwise.

The Industrial Paradigm and Its Contradictions

The industrial paradigm has been the dominant perspective used to explain and justify the development of the factory system of animal production. The industrial paradigm assumes that the industrialization of agriculture mimics the organization of capital, labor, and technology, which has occurred in other sectors of advanced economies: "Animal agriculture is undergoing a process of reorganization and technological transformation parallel to processes that occurred much earlier for other sectors of the economy."[39] Proponents argue that current changes in agriculture are progressive because they increase human capacity to provide more abundant food and a higher quality of life for a greater number of people.[40] According to economic theory, industrialization is based on increasing specialization, a more acute division of labor, and the substitution of machines for human effort in order to increase efficiency.[41] When this paradigm is applied to animal agriculture, the animals themselves must be socially constructed as resources and subjected to a regime that is intensely mechanistic, reductionist, and manipulative.

The reductionist approach to animals, especially farm animals, has ideological and ethical dimensions. Vandana Shiva writes: "When organisms are treated as if they are machines, an ethical shift takes place—life is seen as having instrumental rather than intrinsic value. . . . The reductionist machine view of animals removes all barriers of ethical concern for how animals are treated to maximize production."[42] Carolyn Merchant makes a similar, if broader point in relation to the colonization of nature by industry: "Because nature was now viewed as a system of dead, inert particles moved by external, rather than inherent forces, the mechanical framework itself could legitimate the manipulation of nature."[43] If we believe that nature, including animal nature, is devoid of sentience and open to human manipulation, then any objections we may raise against such manipulation for human benefit can be put aside.

Although the industrial paradigm remains the dominant perspective through which our society views animal agriculture, it is highly problematic. It suffers serious deficiencies in two interrelated areas—one, functional, the other, cultural. From a functional perspective there is growing evidence that factory farm techniques have failed to effectively control farm animal behavior and to take full advantage of the latter's potential for growth and reproduction. A clear illustration of the failure of technique under intensive confinement has been the prevalence of the physiological and behavioral disorders called stereotypies, which are common in the confined hog industry.[44] These are abnormal, repetitive, and, apparently, meaningless behaviors, such as gnawing, bar biting, and tail biting, which may go on for several hours each day.[45] One industry response has been tail "docking," cutting off the tails of young piglets without any pain killers to reduce injuries. Similar to debeaking in the poultry sector, this practice further victimizes the victims of factory farming. There is also evidence that confined breeding sows "burn out" and lose their reproductive abilities much more quickly than they would under less intensive forms of production. Sow mortality is increasing despite years of selecting pigs for adaptability to cages and slatted floors. About half of sow mortality occurs in the first three weeks after giving birth.[46] These failures of technique have demonstrated that livestock are not mechanical objects, but living creatures who suffer profoundly from stress and cruelty in factory farms.[47] They also refute ideological claims by the factory farming industry that their industrial operations are progressive and efficient, producing contented as well as highly productive animals.

A second problem with the industrial paradigm is cultural. As David Fraser (2001) points out, there has been a general cultural trend in the late twentieth and early twenty-first centuries in which the older notion of human uniqueness vis-à-vis nonhuman animals is losing force. The physiological and behavioral connections between humans and other animals are now widely accepted.[48] A more sentimental view of animals, with its roots in critical scholarship, popular literature, and scientific research, has challenged the commercial agricultural view of animals as commodities to be produced, processed, and traded.[49] In terms of critical scholarship, the work of Peter Singer (1991) and Tom Regan (1985) has been influential in the area of animal rights and in opposing the assumption that animals are resources for human exploitation. These points have also been made by popular writers who have drawn public attention to systemic animal abuse in factory farming.[50] Fraser believes that the most significant contribution has come from modern science, which has established the fundamental similarities between humans and other animal species in terms of anatomy and evolutionary theory.[51] Led by the primatologists, scientists now study animals in ways that illustrate the intelligence, resourcefulness, and complex lives of specific animal subjects.[52] Academic and scientific opinion as well as popular culture have contested the instrumentalist and reductionist view of animals, leading to a contrary social construction of animals as much closer to humans in biology and behavior.

These observations have clear implications for animal agriculture. As early as 1965, the Brambell Commission in Great Britain, acting in response to Ruth Harrison's (1964) exposé of animal abuse, recommended a bill of rights for farm animals.[53] This included such basic rights as the right to stand up and turn around, rights that are still routinely denied to millions of pregnant sows in North America confined to gestation crates. Evidence of animal distress has reinforced public perceptions that confined pigs are sentient creatures whose suffering would be mitigated under more humane conditions. European research on domesticated pigs released into seminatural environments called "pig parks" has provided support for the view that pigs are highly intelligent and sociable.[54] In this environment, scientists observed that pigs communicated with each other in a variety of vocalizations and that they are also clean animals, dunging far away from feeding and nesting areas. Marlene Halverson states, "In the pig parks, scientists observed that pigs were very active in the day, foraging, socializing, and exploring their environment. They maintained social organization and built nests for night rest. Sows isolated themselves, gathered material, and built nests before giving birth."[55] This research, based on the emerging discipline of animal welfare science, established a deeper appreciation of the suffering of pigs in confined environments, where so many of their most powerful inclinations, such as rooting, nest building, and socializing, cannot be carried out.[56] The sympathetic portrayal of the social life of sows is part of the general cultural shift, favoring what philosopher David Hume called "gentle usage," rather than raw exploitation, of nonhuman animals.[57]

Ray Murphy has provided a framework that advances our understanding of the relationship between the natural world and human cultural perceptions of nature.[58] In his framework, human conceptions are influenced by "prompts" from "nature's actants." In this paper, nature's actants are animal actants—confined pigs on factory farms that are sentient creatures and capable of at least a limited amount of agency. Prompts could refer to the prevalence of animal stereotypies, which, mediated through accounts in popular literature and the press, have provided the public with representations of the physical and behavioral abnormalities of confined pigs.[59] The effect of these prompts has been to stimulate a sense of cultural uneasiness with animal confinements. It has not, however, caused the majority of consumers to seek out meat from animals outside the factory farm system or to abandon meat-eating for vegetarianism.[60] The declining legitimacy of the industrial paradigm of animal production has left us with a cultural disconnect between the product (meat), which we continue to consume, and the process (factory farming), which arouses moral disquiet and conflicted sentiments.

Discipline

The declining legitimacy of the mechanistic and instrumental view of farm animals lends an opportunity for sociological theory to offer suggestions as to the kinds of social relationships that prevail between humans and domesticated livestock. Our interest as sociologists is to examine the connections between human organizational techniques and those applied to nonhuman animals. The concept of discipline is central to this examination since it refers to that ensemble of techniques that aims to transform living creatures into docile and productive bodies. Since there is a well-established sociological literature on the labor process, which analyzes the deployment and subordination of human workers under capitalism, and since our understanding of the connectedness of human and animal behavior is deepening, it makes sense to start there, taking the connection one step further.

Labor Process: Animals as Subordinate Workers

A number of writers make the analogy between domesticated farm animals and human slaves or subordinate workers.[61] They reject the functionalist view of symbiosis between agricultural producers and farm animals.[62] Domesticated livestock is seen as exploited for human consumption in a system for which the livestock receives no benefits beyond the survival of the breed. Barbara Noske (1997) views farm animal exploitation from a Marxist perspective and provides the most sociologically relevant account. She argues that capitalism has fully incorporated animals into its production technology. Drawing on labor process theory, she states that modern animal agriculture is characterized by mechanization and rationalization of production, a detailed division of work, and, most interestingly, a deskilling of animal capacities, such as a mother pig's ability to care for her offspring.[63] Confinement systems are not only designed to crowd many animals into a limited space and manipulate them to greater productivity, they are also designed to subdivide animal skills and bodies to better control them according to principles of industrial engineering: "The animals' natural capacity for movement, play, preening, social interaction, and contact with the natural environment is almost felt to be subversive: much animal behavior is referred to as 'unbusinesslike.' Like the human worker's creativity it has to be kept under control or better still done away with. All animal activity must be directed towards cheap and rapid production of human wanted things."[64] Animal agriculture engages in the colonization of animal reproductive cycles in which control has passed from animals to machines and managers. The sphere of reproduction—mating, breeding, gestation, and birth—is converted into "working time."[65] She argues that this process parallels the alienation and loss of control experienced by human workers under capitalism. This is an important insight. Livestock are neither inert objects nor machines; rather they are living beings with productive and reproductive capacities that have been repressed, controlled, and narrowly channelled in the interest of productivity and profit. Innovations in technology and work organization, which have reduced the need for human skills in animal husbandry, have also been imposed at the expense of animal skills and capacity.

For example, modern factory farming has virtually dispensed with the sow's role in suckling and nurturing her piglets. The weaning period was reduced from eight to ten to four weeks, speeding up the rate at which sows could be rebred to produce new litters. Now, segregated early weaning (SEW) separates pigs from their mothers at between five and fifteen days and transports them to special sterilized nurseries. Sows can be rebred even sooner, but their maternal role, after farrowing, is no longer needed. Despite the fact that factory discipline dispenses with animal skills, Noske raises the possibility of social change by imparting agency to animals. Just as human workers can benefit from improvements in quality of work life, farm animals could also benefit—through reduced stress and stereotypic disorders—from significant reforms in the way animal production units are organized.

The analogy between farm animals and human workers has important limits. The labor process model that Noske employs is based on workers in an economically dependent relationship to their employer.[66] Critical aspects of this model deal with the relative bargaining power of labor and capital, and thus have only limited application to animals in confined production. Perhaps most significantly, intensive animal agriculture is concerned much more with the reproductive than the productive activities of livestock. The reproductive power of animals—to reproduce and grow—is colonized, rather than their labor power. This suggests that other perspectives, which deal more specifically with bodies, sexuality, health, and reproduction, might provide more insight on the discipline of farm animals. The notion of bio-power, developed by Foucault to describe the harnessing of human bodies to the interests of social power, is promising in this regard.

Bio-Power: Animals as Productive Bodies

Whereas labor process theory views power as concentrated in the capitalist mode of production, Foucault sees it as omnipresent, coursing through the myriad nodal points and capillaries of society. Foucault describes bio-power as a series of techniques or "disciplines" designed to manipulate human bodies and transform them into docile and productive subjects.[67] These disciplinary techniques were perfected in the major institutions of emerging industrial societies such as factories, prisons, hospitals, and barracks.[68] The consequence was the insertion of disciplined and orderly bodies into the machinery of production. The emphasis on disciplining human bodies and sexuality in the interests of power makes the Foucauldian notion of bio-power a useful perspective to be applied to animal agriculture. If human bodies can be colonized for their vitality and reproductive power, then similar techniques can be applied to the discipline of animal bodies. The goal is to forge "a docile body that may be subjected, used, transformed, and improved."[69]

In the Foucauldian perspective, bodies are subdivided into their constituent parts for purposes of discipline, control, and retraining.[70] In order to achieve the goal of total docility, control must be carefully exercised over space, time, and motion. This means that bodies must be organized into specific enclosures of space that are partitioned into regular units like slots on a grid: "Each individual has a place and each place has an individual."[71] The slots are designed to facilitate bodily discipline. Other Foucauldian principles include surveillance, hierarchical observation, individualization, and normalization.[72] Power is exercised by separating individual bodies and subjecting them to surveillance. Normalizing judgment is facilitated by careful accounting and the compilation of dossiers on the progress and performance of each body.[73] These observations shed light on the Canadian intensive hog industry in which sows are separated from their fellow pigs and confined to individualized gestation crates, ensuring maximum surveillance and control of hog bodies in space and time. Simultaneously, normalizing judgment is brought about by careful record keeping of the weight and health of each pig and its stage in the reproductive cycle.

Foucault provides examples from prisons, barracks, hospitals, and factories.

The hospital analogy is especially important for swine production, in which confinement systems—especially those based on the "all in, all out" principle—are organized much like hospitals with regard to the practice of segregation, isolation, and sterilization in order to reduce the risk of disease under crowded conditions.[74] Specialized farrowing rooms, nurseries, and finishing rooms segregate pigs at different stages of their life cycles. They are filled with pigs, then emptied, cleaned, and sterilized before being filled again by the next batch of animals. The notion of bio-power gives us insights into the physical disciplining and control of bodies in the interest of human society.

Foucault's approach does not allow much scope for agency or resistance to develop in the face of industrial-scale discipline. There is no obvious way that social control, as represented by the panopticon, can be overcome. The danger of one-dimensionality is a dilemma for any understanding of human society, but it also applies to animal production.[75] Surveillance and discipline can and do break down. Animals are sentient beings subjected to considerable stress under the regime of intensive production. Behavioral stereotypies in the intensive swine industry, such as bar biting and tail biting, have led to additional efforts at control, from tail docking to the reliance on crates to maintain order by confining sows. Pigs, it seems, have not been fully socialized to accept the disciplinary techniques that have been imposed on them.

Post-Humanism: Animals as Actants

In his analysis of the production of human subjects, Foucault emphasizes the role played by social institutions as it relates to the comparative neglect of the role played by advanced technology and nonhuman nature. Post-humanism addresses this problem by bringing both technical artifacts and nature into its analysis. Post-humanism sees modern society as constructed of networks of humans and nonhumans organized into hybrids.[76] Nonhumans may be plants, animals, or technical artifacts. Technologies are employed to manage the assemblages of humans and nonhumans, which are integrated into continuous production systems.[77] An important aspect of modern society, as Latour makes clear, is the extension of social relations to nonhumans. The premise of post-humanism is radically anti-essentialist in that the taken-for-granted distinctions usually made between humans and nonhumans are leveled.[78] Both categories possess the status of actants and are subject to reorganization and reconfiguration in order to maximize industrial productivity.[79]

Latour characterizes modern agriculture as "internalized ecology" based on the "intense socialization, re-education, and reconfiguration of plants and animals."[80] Technology plays a crucial role in this ongoing reconfiguration. It replaces human labor, animal labor, and even nature in animal agriculture. On intensive hog farms, feeding systems, which mechanically bring flows of feed to pigs, and waste disposal systems, which hydraulically move flows of manure out of the barns, reduce the need for effort on the part of both pigs and human workers. They also reduce the need for pasture, which formerly served as a source of feed and an outlet for waste. The emphasis on technical artifacts facilitates the analysis of such key aspects of modern animal agriculture as genetics, nutrition, and pharmaceuticals, as well as sow housing and waste disposal. The strength of post-humanism is that it allows us to view modern animal agriculture as a hybrid, encompassing humans, animals, and technology. The radical anti-essentialism has, however, been criticized for assuming a plasticity that obliterates any moral boundaries distinguishing human and nonhuman animals from machines.[81] If we posit an interchangeability between sentient beings and machines, both merely actants in the assemblages in which they are embedded, the danger of a return to a mechanistic and reductionist perspective increases. There is little room for animal agency and sentience.

This is a difficult problem to unravel. Nonhumans as actants are capable of some degree of independent action, rather than serving only as a plastic and malleable resource. They can "strike back" against efforts to control them.[82] This raises a question about the behavioral stereotypies that have bedeviled the intensive hog industry. Are they expressions of pig nature that have so far resisted complete human control? Do pigs strike back? Or do they represent a dysfunction in the technological assemblage, possibly amenable to technical fixes? The concept of animal agriculture as human-animal-technical hybrid contains the potential for instability, even conflict.

Distancing

There is a problem with the concept of discipline that goes beyond the issue of animal agency and possible resistance to human control. This is the cultural dilemma mentioned above: the change of cultural sensibilities in favor of "gentle usage" of nonhuman animals, and thus unfavorable to the kind of discipline that factory farming demands. Yet we continue to consume meat that overwhelmingly comes from factory farms. How do we reconcile this contradiction? A common strategy is to avert our eyes.[83] In the modern world, this strategy can be reasonably effective. The distancing effects of modernity ensure that more and more of the products we consume come from far away, often leaving consumers with little knowledge of their origin and context.[84] Hence, modernity facilitates distancing between the point of origin and the point of consumption. Although the phenomenon of distancing is salient to modern social science, it forms a key component of David Hume's (1964) moral philosophy. Hume distinguished between two kinds of objects, the contiguous and the remote, and argued in support of a greater concern for, and connection to, those persons, objects, and events contiguous to us in time-space. Distancing, from Hume's point of view, would produce a "weaker and more imperfect" moral connection.[85] A weakened moral concern, reinforced by the friction of distance, underlies much of the contemporary discussion of distancing.

Political Economy of Consumption

The political economy of consumption provides a description of distancing that is highly relevant to the cultural dilemma surrounding the consumption of meat.[86] Distancing refers to commercial patterns, such as long distance trade and complex commodity chains, which bring about the separation of production and consumption decisions.[87] This separation insulates consumers from the consequences—moral, ecological, and economic—of their choices. It also interrupts the informational and feedback loops that would normally link producers with consumers and would sensitize each group to the other. Distancing is thus "the severing of ecological and social feedback as decision points along the [commodity] chain are increasingly separated."[88] The rupture is both social and spatial. Consumers are often ignorant of the social, cultural, and ecological contexts in which the products they consume originated. This results in more narrowly self-interested consumption decisions.[89]

Jaffe and Gertler (2006) have applied this perspective specifically to food consumption. They argue that "consumers become progressively less 'skilled,' in absolute and relative terms, as they become increasingly distanced in time and space and experience from the sites and processes of production."[90] They also see a rupture in communications flow and feedback between producers and ultimate consumers. "The growing distance and separation between producer and consumer means that farmer-producers receive information on what the consumer demands only via food processors, manufacturers, and retailers. This filter biases information flowing in both directions."[91]

They identify agro-industry, especially food processors, manufacturers, wholesalers, and retailers, as the party responsible for the fact that consumers encounter food in standardized, processed, packaged, and portion-controlled form. Food products appear disembodied, detached from place and any real agricultural context.[92] Meat is represented by various portions of packaged, processed, or frozen parts of beef, poultry, and pork, bearing virtually no relationship to any identifiable animal. Contemporary supermarkets expunge all images of live (or dead) animals subjected to the discipline of factory farm or slaughterhouse. Noelie Vialles comments, "The urban consumer is never, in terms of his daily alimentary experience, brought face to face with the animal— for him, the origin of that meat is entirely hidden from view."[93] Little wonder that the consumer's sense of moral connection to the food products they buy, including the animals they eat, is one of "low involvement."[94]

The political economy of consumption makes an important contribution to our understanding of the consumers' experience, especially their sense of detachment—their "weaker and more imperfect" connection—with the animals that are the ultimate source of their precooked bacon strips and chicken nuggets. However, by focusing on consumption as the point of analysis, it tends to reify production and consumption as separate spheres of action. It does not deal with the ways that producer and retailer interests and legislative processes have deliberately engineered distancing through the social and spatial separation of animal confinement operations, not only from consumption but also from other activities. This must now be addressed.

Social Geography: Appropriation and Domination of Space

A key task of social geography, especially in an era of expanding global trade and a complex international division of labor, is to examine the processes by which spaces and places are constructed, appropriated, and divided for specific activities.[95] The implementation of new technologies, and of new forms of industrial, commercial, and residential development, requires innovations in the built environment and new land use patterns. The construction of a freeway, a housing subdivision, or a factory farm demands that particular spaces be occupied—appropriated—and cordoned off from other activities. The appropriation of space, however, is often contested and becomes a struggle for the domination of space as a place reserved for a particular project.[96] Powerful groups dominate the organization and control of space to ensure the success of the developments they promote. The contestation becomes particularly fierce if citizens judge the proposed developments to be harmful, threatening, disreputable, or disturbing to persons, property, or the local community.

When that happens, David Harvey (1989) suggests that private and state actors may interpose the "friction of distance" between the controversial activity, on the one hand, and local citizens and communities, on the other. Their aim is to protect their favored projects from opposition. This could be through "state and administrative divisions of space; exclusionary zoning; forbidden spaces; hierarchies; spaces of fear; and spaces of repression."[97] Affluent and powerful citizens and communities are able to say "not in my backyard" and can also impose the friction of distance between themselves and threatening or disturbing activities. Lower status citizens are less able to resist incursions into their places. Developers often site polluting industrial and resource projects, waste processing units, and other activities that are disreputable or potentially harmful in communities of low income and of color.[98]

Vialles (1994) observed that in nineteenth-century France, government ordinances banished abattoirs to sites outside city limits. Urban dwellers could no longer view the spectacle of animals being killed as part of their daily routine. She makes the connection between discipline and distancing. The distancing of abattoirs from population centers permitted the slaughter to continue without arousing public concern—in her words, "concealing the killing in order not to give people ideas."[99] The ideas she is referring to are new public attitudes about violence and death and growing concern for animal suffering. She goes on, "The exiling of the abattoir, by confining slaughtering to an enclosed space, simultaneously satisfied the need to monitor, control, and if necessary, punish (to take up once again the themes developed by Michel Foucault)."[100]

Industrial animal production is following a similar path. Business decisions, public pressure, and government regulations are moving livestock confinement operations further away from population centers. Over the past twenty years, the province of Manitoba has become one of the largest industrial hog producers in North America. At the same time, disputes about where hog confinement operations can be located are now a routine fixture of Manitoba rural and small town politics. Citizens have objected to the odor, the dust, the noise, and the polluting of soil and water from manure, as well as to the harsh discipline imposed on the pigs. But the hog industry is economically and politically potent and has continued to build new or expanded operations. The solution, supported by provincial and municipal authorities, and tacitly supported by industry, is zoning bylaws that require greater separation distances between hog confinements and residential areas. Recommended separation distances vary according to the size of the confinement operation and the number of residences in the vicinity. For example, separation distances are four times greater from designated residential areas than from a single residence.[101] Large confinements, with more than 12,800 animal units, must maintain a distance of 2,670 meters from residential areas, versus 530 meters for smaller ones of 100 animal units or less. The further removed the confinements from where people live, the less likely they are "to give people ideas."

Social geography views distancing as the outcome of conflicts over the appropriation and domination of space. Business interests, political factions, citizen and community groups, and other actors are parties to the process. The result is an exiling of factory farms, like slaughterhouses, from population centers, both rural and urban. This temporarily resolves some land use conflicts at the expense of weakening people's sense of moral connection to the animals housed in these distant enclosures. The question remains: is distancing the somewhat random outcome of land use conflicts or, at a deeper level, is it related to a central moral dilemma of modern society? How do we deal with our continued dependence on certain activities that we culturally judge to be disreputable and disturbing?

Modernity: The Sequestration of Experience

Giddens (1990, 1991), perhaps more than any other social theorist, addresses the linkage between modernity and distancing. He argues that the institutional process of concealment, which he terms the "sequestration of experience," is precisely the mechanism by which modern society copes with the moral challenge of dealing with conditions or actions that are threatening or disturbing.[102] We gain "ontological security" by removing basic, but unpalatable, aspects of experience from our daily routines. Madness, criminality, sickness and death, and extrinsic nature are all parts of our experience that we seek to conceal from ordinary life and subject to institutional control: "The ontological security which modernity has purchased, on the level of day to day routines, depends upon an institutional seclusion of social life from fundamental existential issues which raise central moral dilemmas for human beings."[103]

Giddens further asserts that the sequestration of experience is part of the modernization process whereby people came to see the social and natural worlds as transformable. Modern societies constructed prisons, hospitals, mental asylums, and built environments as institutions for the correction and socialization of criminals, the sick, the emotionally deranged, and extrinsic nature, respectively. Achieving "ontological security" requires correcting those who threaten the social order and excluding disturbing modes of behavior from daily life experience. Although Giddens disputes Foucault's claim that the emergence of institutions of sequestration relates to broader processes of discipline in society, there is a strong parallel between his notion of ontological security and Foucault's conception of normalization.[104] In both cases, the "normal" can only exist because political authority subjects the abnormal and the deviant to procedures of correction and control.

Where Giddens differs is in the application of the principle of sequestration to the socialization of raw, or extrinsic, nonhuman nature. Nature, for Giddens, no longer exists as a domain that is truly separate from human society. He argues that humans increasingly live in built environments—like cities—sequestered from nature. This sequestration allows humans to intervene to bring extrinsic nature under control, to socialize it. In Giddens's words, "Becoming socialized, nature is drawn into the colonization of the future and the partly unpredictable arenas of risk created by modern institutions."[105] Giddens's idea of a "socialized" nature inseparable from human society has much in common with the post-humanist position, which also stresses the pervasiveness of the socialization of nature and the proliferation of hybrid environments that incorporate both natural and human-made objects.

When we examine the socialization of nature as it applies it to factory farming, we see that the strategy of sequestration is problematic as a mechanism to achieve ontological security. Socialization occurs when the objects of socialization undergo a process of conformity and internalize new attitudes and patterns of behavior. As the problem of stereotypies has shown, factory hog farms do not in fact socialize pigs; rather, they subject them to oppressive and highly imperfect forms of discipline. If factory farming seems to be a socially stable institution, it is because its disciplinary processes are sequestered and carried out at a distance from an increasingly uneasy public and not because of the success of factory farming in socializing pigs to conform to human will. Concealment of morally contentious activities, like industrial animal production, is effective as a means of deflecting public concern for a time. It is, however, an unlikely foundation for the ontological security that Giddens views as necessary for the smooth functioning of society.

Discussion and Conclusions

History is dotted with major civilizations that engaged in disturbing and disreputable practices that were in conflict with their stated ideals but integral to their continued operation. Ancient Athenian and eighteenth-century American democracy were constructed on foundations of slavery. The advanced European societies of the Enlightenment built great colonial empires that oppressed, exploited, dispossessed, and, when necessary, slaughtered Aboriginal people on five continents. In the twentieth century, the Soviet Union, which presented itself as an egalitarian and socially progressive alternative to capitalism, erected an enormous network of slave labor camps, the Gulags, where millions of prisoners were put to work building the Soviet economy under extremely oppressive conditions.[106] The majority of the camps were located in the Far East and Far North, away from the major population centers, and their workings were largely concealed from Soviet citizens.

We in contemporary North America have our own Gulag system where instead of humans, millions of pigs, fowl, and dairy cattle are maintained under cruel discipline and isolated from sunlight, the outdoors, and public scrutiny. The analogy I am drawing between the Gulag system and industrial farming is not meant to suggest moral equivalence or support a comparison between the abuses of factory farming and Hitler's death camps.[107] We should exercise caution before equating intensive animal agriculture with the planned extermination of human populations. Hateful depictions of despised minorities (Jews, Gypsies, homosexuals) were central to Nazi racial ideology. There is no similar ideological basis to industrial animal production: farm animals are more often depicted sympathetically, usually in pastoral settings. By contrast, the Gulag analogy draws our attention to the fact that contemporary industrial societies tolerate the development of huge animal confinement complexes, on which they depend economically, yet which contradict some of their most deeply held cultural values. These values include the extension of basic rights to new groups and social categories; concern for the environment; growing appreciation of the behavioral and biological sophistication of nonhuman animals; and increasing demands for the "gentle usage" of animals, rather than their exploitation or harsh treatment. An all too common means of dealing with this contradiction, even for those who consider themselves deeply concerned about moral issues, is to look the other way and declare, "I don't want to know."[108]

The Gulag analogy and sociological theory help us understand that there are reasons we have tolerated the harsh discipline of factory farming despite the growing cultural importance of animal welfare. If we behave indifferently to the plight of factory farm animals, this is not simply because we are indifferent to their suffering. One reason for our toleration is the symmetry between techniques of discipline applied to human and nonhuman animals. Following Latour, we can cross the culture/nature divide and recognize in factory farms techniques that are distorted, yet still familiar, disseminations from institutions for human confinement, such as factories, schools, prisons, and hospitals. Modern animal confinement systems borrow important principles from these institutions. They are assemblages of human, technological, and natural actants organized to ensure continuous production. As in assembly lines, control is embedded in physical structures and the production process itself. The pigs who are subjected to power have been cut off from their natural sociability, isolated in individual units, and placed under surveillance.

At the same time, we can discern a reciprocal relationship between factory farming and the control of human bodies and behavior. This is exemplified by Ritzer's notion of McDonaldization.[109] Factory farming makes possible the standardized production of meat portions and other inputs that enable the fast food industry to flourish. The industry, in turn, imposes tight controls over its human workers, subject to massive deskilling, and its consumers, whose choices are limited and whose feeding takes place in a rigidly industrialized manner. Ritzer extends his notion of the rationalization of experience to what he terms the "colonization of life and death."[110] Human birthing and dying now take place in institutionalized confinements under highly routinized medical procedures. The birth, maintenance, and disposition of human bodies are fully industrialized. Factory farming can thus be related, in a reflexive manner, to more general processes of discipline, regulation, and control in modern society.

A second reason is that factory farming has been distanced from the life experiences of most citizens. As consumers, they gain an economic advantage from their ready access to relatively cheap and abundant supplies of meat. The meat they encounter comes in packaged and processed form, unrecognizable as any animal they can identify. Corporate supply chains, long distance trade, environmental and land use regulations, and citizen opposition have resulted in the exile of factory farms to regions far away from population centers. The confinement of animals is largely carried out behind closed doors and sequestered from public view. Citizens may sense some unease about the oppressive discipline imposed on the animals they consume, but the "weaker and more imperfect" moral connection they feel toward the latter, reinforced by the friction of distance, makes it difficult to translate this unease into concrete opposition to factory farming.

Regimes of disciplinary confinement are rarely carved in stone; nor are they impervious to decline or even collapse. Giddens comments, "The frontiers of sequestered experience are fault lines, full of tensions and poorly mastered forces, or, to shift the metaphor, they are battlegrounds."[111] The confinement of persons suffering from mental disorders is much less practiced in modern society, and many institutions for the mentally and emotionally disturbed have been closed. The enormous Gulag system of forced labor camps, symbol of an omnipotent regime, is now a relic of the former Soviet Union. In her important book on the subject, Anne Applebaum provides two major reasons the Gulag system collapsed fairly swiftly following the death of Stalin. One was the loss of legitimacy; people no longer saw the Gulag as fulfilling any morally justifiable purpose. The second was the decline of its economic rationale as the cost of maintaining it mounted relative to any benefits.

The disciplinary regime of the modern factory farm is problematic for both of these reasons. Cultural changes have eroded its legitimacy. The industrial paradigm legitimated factory farming with its reductionist and mechanistic ideology that viewed farm animals as little more than machines. As this paper has suggested, the ideological support for the intensive confinement system of animal agriculture is declining. The public in affluent societies appears to be less comfortable with instrumental conceptions of farm animals than formerly. In both scientific and popular culture, there is a growing body of opinion supporting the connection between humans and animals at the emotional and physiological levels.[112] These popular and scientific prompts have encouraged an attitudinal shift. Farm animals, though neither the companion animals of popular culture nor the wild animals championed by environmentalists, have benefited from the trend to view nonhuman animals as sentient creatures that can suffer.[113] Concern for the welfare of farm animals is gradually breaking down the friction of distance, which has been shielding the abusive discipline of factory farming from the public's gaze. Popular literature, the media, and political activists have made us aware of the animals concealed behind walls and confined to crates and pens. They are more familiar, less "other" than they used to be.

Also, the costs of the industrial mode of animal production, relative to its benefits, are becoming evident. Disciplining animals is an imperfect process, subject to instabilities and uncontrollable factors. Disciplinary technologies imposed on livestock under intensive confinement do not abolish nature in the form of animal behavior; rather they redeploy it and internalize its effects for maximum benefit to humans. Factory farms are human social constructions that recombine "nature's dynamics to accomplish particular goals."[114] These goals are not always realized. Nature—in this case animal bodies and activities—cannot be assumed to be malleable and easily subject to human agency; it has an agency all its own. High levels of stress and related health and behavioral problems among confined pigs highlight the imperfections of the disciplinary process they endure. Despite decades of subjection to confinement, pigs continue to show evidence of distress, misery, and even resistance. This is illustrated by aggression and the prevalence of stereotypies, such as bar biting and repetitive pacing. These problems impose costs: on the health of the pigs; on the producers who are forced to invest in more capital-intensive technical controls, such as crates and isolation chambers, putting many smaller farmers out of business; and on human beings in the form of environmental and public health concerns.

When we factor in the environmental and human health costs of industrial animal production, it turns out to be very costly indeed. According to a report released by the United Nations Food and Agriculture Organization, industrial livestock production constitutes a major threat to the environment.[115] The livestock sector generates more greenhouse gas emissions, as measured by CO_2 equivalent, than transport. Most of this comes from manure. Concentrations of manure, antibiotics, hormones, heavy metals, and chemicals from industrial animal production have had a damaging impact on the earth's increasingly scarce water resources. Livestock production is also the single largest anthropogenic user of land, accounting for about 30 percent of the earth's land surface.[116] Human health has suffered from the ingestion of contaminated water and overexposure to antibiotics leading to their reduced effectiveness. These environmental and health costs, externalities that industrial animal production has imposed on human communities, are mounting. Similar findings were repeated in a subsequent study released by the Pew Commission.[117]

Applebaum (2003) identified a turning point in the early 1950s when a majority of the Soviet leadership became aware that the costs of the Gulag system far exceeded its benefits. We may be reaching that point with respect to industrial agriculture. The factory farming colossus is starting to yield to changing cultural and political realities. In 2001 the European Union, acting in response to public pressure, restricted the use of sow stalls effective in 2013. Under the new regulations, pregnant sows can be kept in stalls only for four weeks and then must be moved to group housing. A growing number of

American states, California among them, have banned or restricted gestation crates. Perhaps the distance between industrial hog and industrial eater is beginning to shrink.

Notes

1. Wilson, Stothart, and DeLong 1951:5.
2. Statistics Canada 2001a.
3. Statistics Canada 2001a.
4. Statistics Canada 2001b.
5. Kunkel 2000.
6. Fraser, Mench, and Millman 2001.
7. Mason and Singer 1980.
8. Halverson 2000:16; Van Arsdell and Nelson 1984.
9. Friedman 1998; Bonanno and Constance 2001.
10. Bell 1998; Novek 2003.
11. Thu and Durrenberger 1994; Thu 1996; Edwards and Ladd 2000.
12. Harrison 1964; Mason and Singer 1980; Singer 1991; Fraser et al. 2001; Regan 1985; Halverson 2000; Halverson 2001.
13. Latour 1999:207.
14. Edwards 1979.
15. Dickens 2002.
16. Dreyfus and Rabinow 1983; Rabinow 1984.
17. Giddens 1991:21.
18. Giddens 1990:21; Harvey 1989:189.
19. Princen, Maniates, and Conca 2002; Davidson and Hatt 2005.
20. Harvey 1989; Soja 1989; Sassen 2001.
21. Giddens 1991:149.
22. Wilson, Stothart, and DeLong 1951:5.
23. Wilson, Stothart, and DeLong 1951:20.
24. National Research Council 1980:331.
25. Turnbull and Bird 1981:5.
26. Wilson, Stothart, and DeLong 1951:42.
27. National Research Council 1980:331.
28. Van Arsdell and Nelson 1984:34.
29. Deyoe and Krider 1952:265.
30. Halverson 2001:169.
31. Singer 1991:125.
32. Halverson 2001:163–166.
33. Phillips and Fraser 1993:51n.
34. Winner 1977.

35. Halverson 2001:160.

36. Halverson 2001:157.

37. Singer 1991:126.

38. Turnbull and Bird 1981:6.

39. Thompson 2001:199.

40. Rhodes 1995; Stricklin and Swanson 1993.

41. Piore and Sable 1984.

42. Shiva 1997:32.

43. Merchant 1980:193.

44. Singer 1991:127–128; Baxter 1989:2349.

45. Halverson 2001:162.

46. Halverson 2000:101.

47. Rollin 2001.

48. Coppinger and Smith 1983.

49. Jasper and Nelkin 1992.

50. Masson 2003.

51. Fraser 2001:178–179; Rachels 1990.

52. Goodall 1971; Fossey 1983.

53. Halverson 2000:97.

54. Halverson 2000:97–98.

55. Halverson 2000:98.

56. Fraser, Mench, and Millman 2001.

57. Hume 1975:190.

58. Murphy 2004:254.

59. Adcock and Finelli 1996.

60. Singer and Mason 2006.

61. Clutton-Brock 1994; Halverson 2001; Noske 1997.

62. Coppinger and Smith 1983.

63. Noske 1997:19.

64. Noske 1997:15.

65. Noske 1997:17.

66. Braverman 1974.

67. Foucault 1978:139.

68. Dreyfuss and Rabinow 1983:135.

69. Foucault 1979:136.

70. Dreyfuss and Rabinow 1983:153–154.

71. Foucault 1979:143.

72. Rabinow 1984:191–197.

73. Rabinow 1984:202–203.

74. Dreyfuss and Rabinow 1983:155.

75. Feenberg 2002:69.

76. Haraway 1991; Latour 1992; Latour 1999.

77. Latour 1999:202.

78. Feenberg 2002:28–29.

79. Latour 1999:207.

80. Latour 1999:208.

81. Feenberg 2002:30–31.

82. Latour 2000.

83. Scully 2005.

84. Princen et al. 2002.

85. Hume 1964:139.

86. Princen, Maniates, and Conca 2002; Davidson and Hatt 2005.

87. Friedman 1993.

88. Princen, Maniates, and Conca 2002:16.

89. Princen 2002:116.

90. Jaffe and Gertler 2006:143.

91. Jaffe and Gertler 2006:145.

92. Jaffe and Gertler 2006:154.

93. Vialles 1994:28.

94. Jaffe and Gertler 2006:152.

95. Soja 1989; Sassen 2001.

96. Harvey 1989.

97. Harvey 1989: table 3.1.

98. Bullard 1994.

99. Vialles 1994:19.

100. Vialles 1994:22.

101. Manitoba Agriculture 2001.

102. Giddens 1991:149.

103. Giddens 1991:156.

104. Giddens 1991:160.

105. Giddens 1991:166.

106. Applebaum 2003.

107. Regenstein n.d.; Smith 2006.

108. Scully 2005:2.

109. Ritzer 1993, 1996.

110. Ritzer 1996:300.

111. Giddens 1991:168.

112. Kaufman 2003.

113. Humane Society of the United States 2001.

114. Murphy 2004:252.

115. Steinfeld et al. 2006.

116. Steinfeld et al. 2006.

117. Pew 2008.

References

Adcock, M. and M. Finelli. 1996. "Against Nature: The Sensitive Pig Versus the Hostile Environment of the Modern Pig Farm." *HSUS News*, Spring:34–38.

Applebaum, Anne. 2003. *Gulag: A History*. New York: Doubleday.

Baxter, M. R. 1989. "Intensive Housing: The Last Straw for Pigs." *Journal of Animal Science* 67, no. 9: 2433–2440.

Bell, M. 1998. *An Invitation to Environmental Sociology*. Thousand Oaks, CA: Pine Forge Press.

Bonanno, Alessandro and Douglas Constance. 2001. "Corporate Strategies in the Global Era: The Case of Mega-Hog Farms in the Texas Panhandle Region." *International Journal of Sociology of Agriculture and Food* 9, no. 1: 5–28.

Braverman, H. 1974. *Labor and Monopoly Capital*. New York: Monthly Review Press.

Bullard, Robert. 1994. *Dumping in Dixie*. Boulder, CO: Westview Press.

Clutton-Brock, Juliet. 1994. "The Unnatural World: Behavioral Aspects of Humans and Animals in the Process of Domestication." In *Animals and Human Society*, ed. Aubrey Manning and James Serpell, 23–35. London: Routledge.

Coppinger, R. and C. Smith. 1983. "The Domestication of Evolution." *Environmental Conservation* 10:283–292.

Davidson, D. and K. Hatt, eds. 2005. *Consuming Sustainability*. Halifax, Nova Scotia: Fernwood Publishing.

Deyoe, G. P. and J. L. Krider. 1952. *Raising Swine*. New York: McGraw Hill.

Dickens, Peter. 2002. "A Green Marxism? Processes, Alienation, and the Division of Labor." In *Sociological Theory and the Environment*, ed. Riley Dunlap, Frederick Buttel, Peter Dickens, and August Gijswijt, 51–72. Lanham, MD: Rowman and Littlefield.

Dreyfuss, Hubert and Paul Rabinow. 1983. *Michel Foucault: Beyond Structuralism and Hermeneutics*. Chicago: University of Chicago Press.

Edwards, B. and A. Ladd. 2000. "Environmental Justice, Swine Production and Farm Loss in North Carolina." *Sociological Spectrum* 20:263–290.

Edwards, Richard. 1979. *Contested Terrain*. New York: Basic Books.

Feenberg, Andrew. 2002. *Transforming Technology: Critical Theory Revisited*. Oxford: Oxford University Press.

Fossey, D. 1983. *Gorillas in the Mist*. Boston: Houghton Mifflin.

Foucault, Michel. 1978. *The Will to Knowledge*. Vol. 1 of *The History of Sexuality*. Trans. Robert Hurley. New York: Pantheon Books.

——. 1979. *Discipline and Punish: The Birth of the Prison*. Trans. Alan Sheridan. New York: Vintage Books.

Fraser, David. 2001. "Farm Animal Production: Changing Agriculture in a Changing Culture." *Journal of Applied Animal Welfare Science* 4, no. 3: 175–190.

Fraser, David, Joy Mench, and Suzanne Millman. 2001. "Farm Animals and Their Welfare 2000." In *The State of the Animals, 2001*, ed. Deborah Salem and Andrew Rowland, 87–99. Washington, DC: Humane Society Press.

Friedman, H. 1993. "After Midas' Feast: Alternative Food Regimes for the Future." In *Food for the Future: Conditions and Contradictions of Sustainability*, ed. P. Allen, 213–233. New York: John Wiley and Sons.

——. 1998. "A Sustainable World Food Economy." In *Political Ecology: Global and Local*, ed. R. Kell, D. Bell, P. Penz, and L. Faucett, 87–101. London: Routledge.

Giddens, A. 1990. *The Consequences of Modernity*. Stanford, CA: Stanford University Press.

——. 1991. *Modernity and Self-Identity: Self and Society in the Late Modern Age*. Stanford, CA: Stanford University Press.

Goodall, J. 1971. *In the Shadow of Man*. London: William Collins.

Halverson, Marlene. 2000. *The Price We Pay for Corporate Hogs*. Minneapolis, MN: Institute for Agriculture and Trade Policy.

——. 2001. *Farm Animal Health and Well Being*. Minnesota Planning Agency, Environmental Quality Board. Posted April 23. http://www.eqb.state.mn.us/geis/TWP _AnimalHealth.pdf (accessed October 21, 2010).

Haraway, D. 1991. *Simians, Cyborgs, and Women: The Reinvention of Nature*. New York: Routledge.

Harrison, Ruth. 1964. *Animal Machines: The New Factory Farming Industry*. London: Vincent Stuart Publishers.

Harvey, David. 1989. *The Condition of Post Modernity*. Oxford: Basil Blackwell.

Humane Society of the United States. 2001. "Factory Hog Farming Called Inhumane." Posted March 31. http://www.hsus.org/programs/farm/halthogfactories /index.html (accessed September 23, 2001).

Hume, David. 1964. *A Treatise of Human Nature*, vol. 2. London: Dent.

——. 1975. *Enquiries Concerning Human Understanding and Concerning the Principles of Morals*, 3rd ed., ed. L. A. Selby-Bigge. Oxford: Clarendon Press.

Jaffe, J. and M. Gertler. 2006. "Victual Vicissitudes: Consumer Deskilling and the (Gendered) Transformation of Food Systems." *Agriculture and Human Values* 23:143–162.

Jasper, James and Dorothy Nelkin. 1992. *The Animal Rights Crusade*. New York: Free Press.

Kaufman, Frederik. 2003. *Foundations of Environmental Philosophy*. New York: McGraw-Hill. See especially chapter 5, "The Moral Status of Animals," 141–193.

Kunkel, H. O. 2000. *Human Issues in Animal Agriculture*. College Station: Texas A&M University Press.

Latour, Bruno. 1992. "Where Are the Missing Masses?" In *Shaping Technology/Building Society*, ed. Wiebe Bijker and John Law, 225–258. Cambridge, MA: MIT Press.

——. 1999. *Pandora's Hope: Essays on the Reality of Science Studies*. Cambridge, MA: Harvard University Press.

——. 2000. "When Things Strike Back." *British Journal of Sociology* 57, no. 1: 107–123.

Manitoba Agriculture, Food and Rural Initiatives. 2001. *Farm Practices Guidelines for*

Hog Producers in Manitoba, May. http://www.gov.mb.ca/agriculture/livestock/pork/swine/bahoo500.html (accessed January 6, 2007).

Mason, Jim and Peter Singer. 1980. *Animal Factories*. New York: Crown Publishers.

Masson, Jeffrey M. 2003. *The Pig Who Sang to the Moon: The Emotional World of Farm Animals*. New York: Ballantine Books.

Merchant, C. 1980. *The Death of Nature: Women, Ecology and the Scientific Revolution*. San Francisco: Harper and Row.

Murphy, Ray. 2004. "Disaster or Sustainability: The Dance of Human Agents with Nature's Actants." *Canadian Review of Sociology and Anthropology* 41, no. 3: 249–266.

National Research Council. 1980. *The Effects on Human Health of Subtherapeutic Use of Antimicrobials in Animal Feeds*. Washington, DC: National Academy of Sciences, Office of Publications.

Noske, Barbara. 1997. *Beyond Boundaries, Humans and Animals*. Montreal: Black Rose Books.

Novek, J. 2003. "Intensive Livestock Operations, Disembedding, and Community Polarization in Manitoba." *Society and Natural Resources* 16:567–581.

O'Neill, John. 1992. "The Disciplinary Society: From Weber to Foucault." In *Critical Thought Series 2: Critical Essays on Michel Foucault*, ed. Peter Burke, 157–173. Aldershot, UK: Scolar Press. Originally published in *British Journal of Sociology* 37 (1986): 42–60.

Pew Commission on Industrial Animal Production. 2008. *Putting Meat on the Table: Industrial Farm Animal Production in America*. Baltimore, MD: The Pew Charitable Trusts, Johns Hopkins Bloomberg School of Public Health.

Phillips, P. A. and D. Fraser. 1993. "Developments in Farrowing Housing for Sows and Litters." *Pig News and Information* 14, no. 1: 51n–55n.

Piore, M. and C. Sabel. 1984. *The Second Industrial Divide: Possibilities for Prosperity*. New York: Basic Books.

Princen, T. 2002. "Distancing: Consumption and the Severing of Feedback." In *Confronting Consumption*, ed. T. Princen, M. Maniates, and K. Conca, 103–131. Cambridge, MA: MIT Press.

Princen, T., M. Maniates, and K. Conca. 2002. "Confronting Consumption." In *Confronting Consumption*, ed. T. Princen, M. Maniates, and K. Conca, 1–20. Cambridge, MA: MIT Press.

Rabinow, Paul, ed. 1984. *The Foucault Reader*. New York: Pantheon Books.

Rachels, J. 1990. *Created from Animals: The Moral Implications of Darwinism*. New York: Oxford University Press.

Regan, T. 1985. "The Case for Animal Rights." In *Defence of Animals*, ed. P. Singer, 13–26. London: Blackwell Publishers.

Regenstein, Lewis. n.d. "Holocaust on Your Plate." *PETA Living*, 1–3. http://peta.org/Living/commentary_listing.aspx?id-85 (accessed January 24, 2007).

Rhodes, V. James. 1995. "The Industrialization of Hog Production." *Review of Agricultural Economics* 17:107–118.

Ritzer, G. 1993. *The McDonaldization of Society.* Thousand Oaks, CA: Pine Forge Press.

——. 1996. "The McDonaldization Thesis: Is Expansion Inevitable?" *International Sociology* 11, no. 3: 291–308.

Rollin, Bernard. 2001. "Farm Factories." *Christian Century* 19, no. 26: 26–29.

Sassen, Saskia. 2001. *The Global City,* 2nd ed. Princeton, NJ: Princeton University Press.

Scully, Matthew. 2005. "Fear Factories: The Case for Compassionate Conservatism—For Animals." *The American Conservative* May 23:1–14. http://www.mathewscully.com/fear_factories.htm (accessed January 5, 2007).

Shiva, Vandana. 1997. *Biopiracy.* Toronto: Between the Lines.

Singer, Peter. 1991. *Animal Liberation,* 2nd ed. New York: Avon Books.

Singer, Peter and Jim Mason. 2006. *The Way We Eat: Why Our Food Choices Matter.* Emmaus, PA: Rodale Books.

Smith, Justin. 2006. "The Animal Holocaust? Why Factory Farming Is a Serious Problem." *Animal Concerns,* December 12, 1–2. http://www.animalconcerns.org/resource.html?itemid-200612114 (accessed January 24, 2007).

Soja, Edward. 1989. *Postmodern Geographies: The Reassertion of Space in Critical Social Theory.* London: Verso.

Statistics Canada. 2001a. "Livestock Statistics." *Catalogue # 23–603-UPE.* Ottawa: Minister of Supply and Services.

——. 2001b. "Livestock Statistics." *Catalogue # 23–603-XPE.* Ottawa: Minister of Supply and Services.

Steinfeld, H., P. Gerber, T. Wassenaar, V. Castel, M. Rosales, and C. de Haan. 2006. *Livestock's Long Shadow: Environmental Issues and Options.* United Nations Food and Agricultural Organization. http://www.virtualcentre.org/en/library/key_pub/longshad/A0701E00.htm (accessed January 17, 2007).

Stricklin, W. Ray and Janice Swanson. 1993. "Technology and Animal Agriculture." *Journal of Agricultural and Environmental Ethics* 6, Special Supplement 1: 67–80.

Thompson, Paul. 2001. "Animal Welfare and Livestock Production in a Postindustrial Milieu." *Journal of Applied Animal Welfare Science* 4, no. 3: 191–205.

Thu, K. 1996. "Piggeries and Politics: Rural Development and Iowa's Multibillion Dollar Swine Industry." *Culture and Agriculture* 53:19–23.

Thu, K. and G. P. Durrenberger. 1994. "North Carolina's Hog Industry: The Rest of the Story." *Culture and Agriculture* 49:20–23.

Turnbull, J. E. and N. A. Bird. 1981. *Confinement Swine Housing.* Ottawa: Agriculture Canada.

Van Arsdell, Roy and Kenneth Nelson. 1984. *US Hog Industry.* Washington, DC: United States Department of Agriculture, Agricultural Economics Report #511.

Vialles, Noelie. 1994. *Animal to Edible*. Trans. J. A. Underwood. Cambridge: Cambridge University Press.

Wilson, H. E., J. G. Stothart, and G. E. DeLong. 1951. *Swine Production*. Ottawa: Department of Agriculture.

Winner, Langdon. 1977. *Autonomous Technology: Technics Out of Control as a Theme in Human Thought*. Cambridge, MA: MIT Press.

five

Boys Gone Wild

The Animal and the Abject

Cynthia Chris

We have this huge debate going on right now about same-sex marriage. There are people who are against it and people who are for it, and the people who are against it—some people say, "marriage is a union between a man and a woman and it's always been that way and it should always remain that way and if we change it and it's between two people of the same sex, then what's next? Someone could marry an animal." That's where they go to right away. These people scare me. And they think we're weird? I don't want to marry a goat. I really don't. I can't imagine marrying a goat. I can't even imagine dating a goat, getting to the point that you're that serious to make that kind of commitment.

—Ellen DeGeneres, in *Ellen DeGeneres: The Beginning* (2000)

IN A STAND-UP PERFORMANCE RECORDED FOR HBO IN 2000, Ellen DeGeneres addressed simmering election-year debates over gay marriage by calling out opponents for their absurd fretting that the expansion of civil rights to gay men and lesbians would inevitably lead to legal and social tolerance for an array of sexual behaviors long held to be despicable, including bestiality.[1] What's funny about the monologue is, of course, DeGeneres's flirtation, however fleeting, with the very idea that she has just declared unimaginable, an out-of-bounds scare tactic of hatemongers, the exclusively perverse purview of

The author is indebted to Phil Gardner, research assistant, and to Sarah Banet-Weiser, Jonathan Burt, Paula Chakravartty, Una Chaudhuri, Tarleton Gillespie, Lisa Henderson, Akira Mizuta Lippit, Tara Mateik, Michael Mandiberg, Nic Sammond, Julia Steinmetz, and Michael Wenyon for feedback, suggestions, and opportunities to present previous versions of this work as lectures.

the opposition. In one characteristically breathless run-on swoop, DeGeneres sidles toward abject territory, first dismissing the idea that sexual congress might breach the stalwart species barrier and then taking the idea seriously. The monologue continues with a meandering consideration of what it might actually be like to date a goat, to introduce the animal to one's parents, to wake up with a creature more likely to consume the morning paper than read it.

Ultimately DeGeneres sidesteps true abjection, exiting the segment smiling and chuckling as if to remind herself—and signal her audience—that it's only a joke. But in the joke—which is less a joke than an absurdly alternative universe described in all too plausible detail—DeGeneres employs a kind of humor that enables us to look at ourselves in new (if sometimes twisted) light, exposing and renegotiating aspects of the human condition and its vicissitudes that we might otherwise overlook. Sometimes, according to Simon Critchley, this kind of "humour explores what it means to be human by moving back and forth across the frontier that separates humanity from animality."[2] Delving into such material, the humorist patches a gaping hole in the fence that marks such a separation, but not until she has savored a good long look through it. Critchley finds similar slippages across the species divide in a handful of anonymous jokes and in a wide range of literature from Aesop's fables dating to the sixth century B.C., to the early eighteenth-century *Gulliver's Travels*, by Jonathan Swift, to Will Self's 1992 novel *Great Apes*, among others. Responding to their species-mixing humors, Critchley observes that "when the animal becomes human" (when we imagine the goat spiffed up to meet the folks?), "the effect is pleasingly benign and we laugh out loud . . . But when the human becomes animal" (when DeGeneres asks us to imagine her holding Billy's cloven hoof in her hand?) "the effect is disgusting and if we laugh at all then it is what Beckett calls 'the mirthless laugh,' which laughs at that which is unhappy."[3] The mirthlessness of the laugh reminds us that the routine is at least half serious, routing us back to the hatefully absurd equation of homosexuality and bestiality, returning us to the point that motivated the monologue.

Is this mirthless laugh inevitable whenever the usually reliable species barrier is breached? Failure to guard that boundary seems to tickle the funny bone as well as the gag reflex, melding in one response mirthful glee and mirth-killing disgust. The revulsion elicited by the transformation of human into animal, or vice versa, is alleviated by comic twists in *Wildboyz* (2003–2006), MTV's genre-blurring attempt to restage a *Jackass* spin-off in settings typical to wildlife and ethnographic filmmaking.[4] The series, in mockumentary style, riffs on both the traditions and the historic excesses of the genre, which have perhaps been most famously typified in recent years by the late Steve "Crocodile

Hunter" Irwin. But instead of looking at the animal—the object of the gaze in most wildlife film and television programs—the hosts of *Wildboyz* immerse themselves in it. Where other wildlife film and television hosts disappear behind the camera, *Wildboyz* performers Chris Pontius and Steve-O (Stephen Glover) mug and moon. Where others seek to avoid animal attack, the Wildboyz bring it on, subjecting themselves to bites, scratches, and stings. Others strive for control, presenting themselves and their bodies as intact, impenetrable, and implacable; the Wildboyz renounce control, bleeding, swelling, shrieking, and laughing. Others maintain a tidy distance between themselves and animal Others; the Wildboyz, in contrast, toy with animal excrement and indulge in bestial flirtations. They may not want to marry animals, but they are not averse to occasionally making out with them, seeking a sometimes perverse proximity. In doing so, Pontius and Steve-O turn their bodies into porous surfaces, displacing the genre's typical masculinist control with a boundary-less chaos that not only tests the species barrier, but also destabilizes presumptive heterosexual subject positions by means of homoerotic play. They become abject in the sense that Julia Kristeva uses the word: "The abject confronts us, on the one hand, with those fragile states where man strays on the territories of *animal*," where the animal might represent unrestrained sexuality and violence.[5] In that fragile state, the boys laugh, and we might laugh at them.

Is it the mirthless laugh that is provoked by *Wildboyz*? How is it that *Wildboyz* stunts so readily elicit laughter, mirthless or otherwise, from both its performers and its viewers? Is that all there is, a discomforted giggle, when all manner of body and species borders are crossed? And how can we account for the emergence of a series that so flagrantly flaunts the conventions of a venerable genre from which it derives many of its features? To begin to answer these questions, I sketch a brief history of the wildlife genre, tracing some of its varieties toward their conflation with what has come to be known as reality or reality-based television.[6] Then, examining select *Wildboyz* programs, I consider the kinds of meanings constructed by, in the language of the show's performers, this "stunty" version of the genre. Despite the many disavowals—of knowledge, of authority, of bodily integrity—that structure the show, I argue that its performers traffic productively in the delineation of human and animal subjectivities by skittering up to, and sometimes over, presumed boundaries between us and them. They renounce human society and common sense, seeking to return to a precivilized animal otherness, to become animal, not only for the sake of guffaws, but also within a meaningful project of making sense of what it means to be human.

Wildlife on TV: Where the Boys Are

Animals have been represented in nonfiction cinema since its earliest days, frequently and famously, in actualities and travelogues peppered with violent confrontations. As early as 1894, animals are pitted against one another, as in Thomas Alva Edison's *Cockfight* films, or less brutally in *The Boxing Cats (Prof. Welton's)*. But frequently, those confrontations take place between humans and animals. For example, for the infamous short *Electrocuting an Elephant* (1903), Edison not only filmed the death of the elephant—a resident of Coney Island's Luna Park who had killed an abusive keeper—but also acted as executioner. Edison rigged the contraption that delivered the fatal jolt using his competitor George Westinghouse's alternating-current electrical technology, in (unfulfilled) hopes of promoting his own direct-current model as the safer system. Animals appeared frequently as hunting quarry in short films and as early as 1912 in features such as *Paul Rainey's African Hunt*. Eventually, "camera-hunting"—expeditions with photography or filmmaking as their primary purpose—marked a nascently conservationist shift, but the genre was far from reconstructed. In the feature-length *Simba* (1928), prolific husband-and-wife filmmaking team Martin and Osa Johnson provoke rhino, elephant, and lion to charge their camera so that the footage boasts maximum proximity and maximum action. Inserted cutaways staged later imply that Martin continues to crank the film as Osa (or, more likely, an off-camera sharpshooter) fells the oncoming animal. *Simba* is typical of a steady flow of expedition films that found their way to theaters in the late 1910s and throughout the 1920s, featuring wealthy (or, as in the Johnsons' case, well-funded), white American or European adventurers, usually in East Africa or the South Pacific, assisted by indigenous bearers and guides as they gathered footage of lands, animals, and peoples approached as little-known, exotic spoils of the colonial legacy, ripe for consumption by mass audiences back home.

Only in the postwar period did wildlife filmmaking's "classic" mode fully emerge. In classic wildlife filmmaking, filmmakers gather footage of apparently free-roaming animals, which is edited to take the shape of narratives about animal life in a particular ecosystem (as in Disney's True-Life Adventure *The Living Desert*, 1953) or among a particular species (as in the recent and stunningly successful *March of the Penguins* by Luc Jacquet for National Geographic Feature Films, 2005).[7] These films forgo hunting themes in favor of conservationist ethos. The heroic hunter-protagonists and the frequently offensive depictions of indigenous peoples found in prewar expedition films give way to an almost absolute absence of human subjects. The classic style seeks to mask the presence of humans, save for explanatory voiceovers and musical scores, representing wildlife and wilderness as largely separate from human society, the sprawl of our built world, the impact of our industrial activities on the environment, and the mediations of our modes of representation.

In a commonplace variation from the unpeopled classic style, a presenter/host leads a virtual tour of a given environment, showing and telling the viewer about the animals he (these naturalist-performers are usually male) encounters. Sir David Attenborough has served as presenter/host of countless wildlife programs for British Broadcasting Corporation (BBC) since the mid-1950s. Many (*Life on Earth*, 1982; *The Living Planet*, 1985) reached American audiences on PBS, alongside the much-admired *Nature* (1982–) series and *National Geographic Specials*.[8] Others premiered on commercial American television: *The Trials of Life* (which Attenborough wrote and hosted) on TBS in 1991 and *Planet Earth* (2006), for which he earned another writing credit and narrated the version released in the United Kingdom. Attenborough generally took a hands-off approach, explaining the physiology and behavior of animals from a discrete distance if on-screen, and often in voiceover, but always with polite, but unassailable authority. But the interactions of some hosts and the wildlife they encounter have been emphatically hands-*on*. In many episodes of *Mutual of Omaha's Wild Kingdom* (a weekly primetime nonfiction wildlife series on NBC, 1963–1971, and part of an FCC-mandated syndication boom, 1971–1988), Marlin Perkins and sidekicks actively intervened in animal life, capturing, subduing, and tagging animals for research purposes.

Alternatively, wildlife filmmakers may drop in on established research sites, where a scientist at the site mediates the encounter between viewer and animal. In contrast to other modes of wildlife filmmaking, these interlocutors are frequently (but by no means exclusively) female.[9] Perhaps most famously, Jane Goodall's pioneering work in primatology was introduced to the public in National Geographic Specials, including *Miss Jane Goodall and the Wild Chimpanzees* (1965), filmed by Hugo van Lawick. Likewise, Cynthia Moss's research on elephants at Amboseli National Park in Kenya is documented by Martyn Colbeak in a series of films, beginning with *Echo of the Elephants* (1992). In these cases, the dedication and discoveries of the research scientist are as much the filmmaker's subject as are the animals that she studies.

In the early 1980s, most nature programming in all these forms on American television found its airtime on PBS, but the cable boom of the 1980s whetted television's appetite for nonfiction of all kinds, resulting in growing markets for news, music video, sports, documentary, and the relatively inexpensive "reality," how-to, travel, science, and nature genres. Many upstart cable channels couldn't afford to produce much original programming, especially in the more expensive dramatic genres. As the broadcast networks lost viewers—and therefore ad revenue—to cable, even they displaced some big-budget sitcoms and dramas for "unscripted" entertainment. The prominent use of wildlife by the Discovery Channel after its launch in 1985 and the success of Attenborough's *The Trials of Life* reinforced the new commercial marketability of the genre. A host of concurrent changes throughout global television markets and a trend toward narrowly niched channels, such as Animal Planet and the National Geographic Channel, continued to create new opportunities for the genre in the 1990s.

Gaping stretches of programming hours had to be filled on these new channels. A number of personality-driven wildlife shows developed around charismatic presenter hosts, such as Steve Irwin of *The Crocodile Hunter* (1999–2004) and Jeff Corwin of *The Jeff Corwin Experience* (2000–2003), both on Animal Planet, and the Kratt Brothers of *Be the Creature* on the National Geographic Channel (2003–2004). Each embodies the exuberant masculinity and daredevilry that is traditional to the genre, and in an approach that is anything but camera-shy, each displays apparently sincere environmental ethos as motivation to pursue, approach, handle, and show off animals to the presumed audience. As a group, they are more hands-on Perkins than hands-off Attenborough, with more emphasis than either grandfatherly predecessor on good looks, coupled with charmingly sensitive streaks and occasional bursts of humor. Irwin was as likely to make a joke about his wife's driving or shrug off a bloody wound ("Outlaws of the Outback," 2000), as he was to coo over the birth of his children or make nearly tearful pleas for animal protection ("Steve's Story," 1999). He died in 2006 as a result of an injury sustained while filming segments for a new series to be co-hosted by his young daughter: a stingray's barb punctured his chest. Martin Kratt might express both disgust and glee when getting close to the animal: in one case, scent-marked by a mongoose in a 2003 episode, he quickly removed his damp shirt, but also exclaimed, "Now I'm really one of them," pridefully reminding viewers (and perhaps himself) that he has been treated as a member of the pack. In these cases the chase brings the human close to the animal, not just to look, but also, sometimes, via a mediating expert-host, to touch and be touched, however fleetingly, however threateningly.

As the genre turned in television's competitive markets toward these ever-more audacious hosts, animals also cropped up in generic variations and hybrids, such as the talent-cum-game show *Pet Star* (2002–2005); the telepathic-talk phenomenon *Pet Psychic* (2002–2004); and the anti-cruelty *Animal Precinct* (2001–2008) and *Animal Cops* (2002–). Each of these has been found, predictably, on Animal Planet. But animals on television would not be confined to expected outlets: channels usually devoted to other kinds of programming would also dabble in animal genres. For example, the Fox broadcast network knitted together home video clips for the reality specials *When Animals Attack* (1996 1997); pitted animals against humans in footraces, lifting contests, and tug-of-war in the special *Man vs. Beast* (2003); and elicited from National Geographic a tongue-in-check tract on the mating behaviors of species, including humans, in *When Animals Attract* (aired on the eve of Valentine's Day, February 13, 2004). Explicit parallels between animals and humans also comprise the series *The Most Extreme* (2002–2007), which is produced by Natural History New Zealand for Animal Planet. Each episode of the series comprises a top-ten list relative to some physiological or behavioral theme ("Builders," "Jumpers," "Gluttons," "Cheats"), juxtaposing footage of animals and humans for each entry on the list. In 2005, Animal Planet found a surprise hit in *Meerkat Manor*, an Oxford Scientific Films project documenting scenes from the daily life of a meerkat mob in South Africa's Kalahari Desert, flecked with soap-opera flourishes, and garnering some of the channel's highest ratings to date. And although many of these series draw more heavily on reality-television tropes than on the wildlife genre's conventions, the high-end classic form also persists, forgoing a central presenter-host, in projects such as a revitalized *Mutual of Omaha's Wild Kingdom*, relaunched by Animal Planet in 2003, and the BBC's *Planet Earth* (2006), aired by Discovery in 2007.

Where the Wild Boys Go

At the end of the twentieth century and beginning of the twenty-first, wildlife television plunged evermore intrepidly into animal territory and incorporated human behaviors into its terrain, with increasingly rough-and-tumble hosts leading the way. In 2003, MTV got in on the animal act with *Wildboyz*. MTV long ago abandoned an all-music format for a schedule heavy with so-called unscripted entertainment like *The Real World* (1992–), the travelogue *Road Rules* (1995–2004), the stunt-driven *Jackass* (2000–2002), and Ashton Kutcher's celebrity-pranking *Punk'd* (2003–2007). The *Jackass* television series, created by Spike Jonze, Jeff Tremaine, and Johnny Knoxville, became phenomenon enough to spawn a feature film, *Jackass: The Movie* (2002), which was produced for a modest $5 million and earned some $64 million in its North

American theatrical release. A sequel, *Jackass: Number Two* (2006), cost $11.5 million and took in nearly $73 million at the domestic box office, and a more costly follow-up, *Jackass 3D* (2010), grossed more than $50 million in just its opening weekend. Between the first two features, MTV added another *Jackass* spin-off, *Wildboyz*, to its television lineup.[10] In its first season, MTV slotted *Wildboyz* as part of its "Sunday Stew," reaching a target audience of 12- to 34-year-olds sometimes numbering upwards of two million and skewing only slightly male ("a 55–45 split," according to MTV executive Brian Graden).[11]

Wildboyz melds the travel, prank, and stunt motifs common to many reality series (including some of its MTV predecessors), with the gross-out challenges of *Fear Factor* (2001–2006, NBC), which also, at times, stages encounters between humans and the animals (spiders and other insects, snakes, rats) that seem to scare us most. *Wildboyz* reunited Jonze, Tremaine, and two regular *Jackass* performers, Chris Pontius and Steve-O.[12] Wildlife expert Manny Puig joined the *Wildboyz* cast in a dozen episodes, following from his specials *Extreme Contact* (2000, Animal Planet) and *Diary of a Sharkman* (aired during Shark Week on the Discovery Channel, 2003), and a few *Jackass* appearances. Snake handler David Weathers and *Jackass* alumni Knoxville and Jason "Wee Man" Acuña also appear as occasional *Wildboyz* guests. And whereas *Jackass* utilized urban and suburban American settings for stunts involving skateboards, shopping carts, and portable toilets, *Wildboyz* takes its cast and crew to foreign lands where they undertake exercises of controlled risk and willing abjection culled from both culture and nature. In four seasons, each consisting of eight new episodes, *Wildboyz* traversed much of the globe, visiting and revisiting locations in Africa (including South Africa and Kenya), Central America (Belize and Costa Rica), South America (Argentina and Brazil), the South Pacific (Australia, New Zealand, and Indonesia), and North America (Mexico as well as locations in the United States from Alaska to Florida).

The show does touch base with recognizable genre conventions in its choice of settings and subjects and in the educational on-screen notation of animals' common and binomial Latin names. The settings may be familiar, but it is a flaunting of any of these common themes that defines *Wildboyz*. In a typical half-hour episode, such as one set in Kenya, Steve-O, Pontius and Wee Man engage in about ten stunts. Most involve interactions with animals, but in a few, they sample local customs, especially food and drink. First, Wee Man and the prop master test the reaction of bathing hippos to a motorized, life-sized blow-up doll directed in the water via remote control. Samburu tribesmen cut and dye Steve-O's hair in the local, nearly shorn, bright-red style. Steve-O, Pontius, and Wee Man allow themselves to be stung by bees and then by army ants, as the Samburu look on. Afterward, one of the local men shares a beer made from honey with his guests. Changing settings, Pontius, Steve-O, and Wee Man wrestle in a muddy pond they claim to be an "elephant toilet" while several baby elephants scamper nearby. They track a rhino, coming close enough for Wee Man to stroke its horn and for Steve-O to cop a quick feel of its penis. Pontius and Steve-O place two dung beetles on tabletop-sized soccer field, where the insects compete for control of a ball of shit. Eventually, the winner falls with "the ball" into one of the goals, just as it would push the thing into an underground burrow. The *Wildboyz* crew drains a concrete pool of water containing live, captive crocodiles so that the "boyz" can skateboard among the animals. Finally, the episode concludes by returning to footage shot with the Samburu, who share a ritual mixture of cow's blood and milk. Sitting in a tight, chummy circle with their hosts, Pontius, Steve-O, and Wee Man try the drink. All three vomit, leaning just a little away from the Samburu and a little closer to the camera.

Despite the eccentricities, *Wildboyz* does draw on familiar aspects of wildlife film and television. For instance, after the title sequence, each episode begins with a graphic image of a spinning topographical globe that zooms in on the country (or state) that the show is visiting. Launching an episode from a globe or map is a convention found throughout the genre for decades: in Paul L. Hoefler's feature-length (and partly faked) travelogue *Africa Speaks* (1930), the more educational theatrical short *Private Life of the Gannet* (1934, written by Julian Huxley and produced by Alexander Korda), Disney's True-Life Adventures, and at least some episodes of the original *Wild Kingdom*. Most conventional references, however, are parodic. In some segments of the Kenya episode, Steve-O, Pontius, and Wee Man wear oversized khaki safari suits and pith helmets. Occasional voiceovers are provided with plummy, faux-British profundity. But Steve-O and Pontius toss in only a few vague statements about the animals they encounter, displaying their knowledge with the likes of "black rhinos kill people," a warning gleaned from their Kenyan guide, James Koskei, who is introduced as a local rhino expert. They occasionally jokingly refer to themselves as "scientists" or refer to an upcoming animal encounter as "research." In Brazil, preparing to be shocked by a large electric eel, Pontius declares, "We're going to have to go study him." But they are usually more honest: in Florida, Steve-O prepares to kiss a batfish's toad-like mouth by declaring, "I'd better do a stunt." In Brazil, their lack of naturalist expertise is clear: kneeling by a large leaf on which they find a monkey spider, Pontius reveals, "I read about these guys on the Internet, and I didn't like what I found out." (He doesn't say why.) Steve-O's knowledge is even thinner: "All I know about spiders is that when one

of them is hairier than your scrotum, it's not a good idea to mess with them."
Beginning the stunt, Pontius instructs Steve-O to lie down on his back ("lay
down or I'm going to hit you!"). Steve-O, unshirted, complains and shivers as
the spider crawls from his navel to his chest, then clambers to the ground via
his armpit. Pontius picks it up again and surreptitiously slips it onto a cameraman's shoulder.

Some *Wildboyz* segments place Pontius and Steve-O among people, where
they witness or experience challenging or exoticized and unexplained cultural
practices. In Australia and Florida episodes, *Wildboyz* cast and crew are sometimes escorted into animal territory by local animal experts—keepers of private zoos, for example—but every stunt involves an animal. Perhaps tellingly,
Pontius and Steve-O don't regularly try to reproduce local customs in these
First World, English-speaking settings. (Louisiana is an exception. Saying that
despite having been around the world, they've never felt so far from home,
Pontius and Steve-O mingle as much with voodoo and Cajun culture, with
rap artists in New Orleans and trailer-park nudists in Slidell, as they do with
skunks, possums, and alligators.)[13] In India, often bare-chested, showing off
tattoos, clad in dhoti and turbans while many of the Indian men they encounter wear jeans and button-down shirts, Pontius and Steve-O firewalk, lie on a
bed of nails, pierce Steve-O's cheek, and lick the bare feet of strangers, an act
they proclaim to be a gesture of respect, which is surely mitigated by Steve-O's
revolted retching. Sometimes, Steve-O's acrobatic skill hints at his professional
clown training, but more often, both he and Pontius grimace and scurry
though feats that are more elegantly performed by their more-practiced new
acquaintances.

The show is largely promoted as the "boyz'" adventures in nature, even as
humans are present during many of the animal encounters. In India among
snake charmers, Steve-O cowers in a corner. Pontius cackles joyfully at first
sight of the snakes, but calls for the scene to end when a cobra strikes at the
flute he tries to play. They wrestle sloth bears until Steve-O's torso is striped
with claw marks. They join elephant polo teams, but disrupt play when Steve-O
throws fresh elephant excrement, collected in his bare hands before it has even
fallen to the ground, at Pontius. To conclude the episode, Steve-O crouches
beneath an elephant and waits for it to urinate. Soaked, he tackles the show's
director and then gags in disgust; this is the third time he vomits or nearly
vomits in a half-hour episode.

A trip to South Africa includes a brief visit to a Zulu village, where Pontius
and Steve-O are introduced to local smoking, dance, and marriage traditions,
but most of the episode is spent among animals. Frequently, they masquerade

as—perhaps more accurately, *become*—prey to expose themselves to animal attacks. Dressed in a two-man zebra costume, Pontius and Steve-O are attacked by a lion that trots off with the cloth zebra head while they retreat. In another scene, Pontius holds scorpions in place to sting Steve-O's buttocks, a favored target of *Wildboyz* stunts generally (in other episodes, his bare butt is offered as a target for a stinging centipede, the claws of a stone crab, and the bite of a water python, among other creatures; see figures 5.1 and 5.2). While more traditional wildlife-television counterparts strive to present *impervious* bodies, ever in control of themselves and of nature (and, like Steve "Crocodile Hunter" Irwin, downplaying real injuries that do occur when control is lost), Pontius and Steve-O are exhibitionists constantly testing their own abject *perviousness*, albeit staged and temporary: they are regularly pelted with excrement, gashed open, bloodied by animal claws, and otherwise injured. Their bodies, often nearly naked, come into intimate contact with one another. They are scrutinized in extreme close-up by the camera and penetrated by objects. And sometimes they engage in explicitly sexual behaviors.

In South Africa, Steve-O stands on stilts to coax a giraffe to lick and "kiss" him on the mouth while Pontius photographs its genitals. In Belize, Pontius, feminized by wearing a bright red flower over his left ear, introduces a kinkajou as it licks his nipple, which is smeared with a substance that glistens like honey. With the left side of his face shown in profile, eyes closed and open-mouthed, he allows the animal to lick his chin, lips, and tongue, groaning softly over a romantic musical cue (see figure 5.3). In the next shot, Pontius has turned away from the scene and walks with the right side of his body to the camera in medium shot so that the flower in his hair is no longer visible. He addresses the camera with chagrin: "I feel kinda' weird. I don't know if it's because I made out with an animal or because I made out with a *male* animal," then grins mischievously and laughs to end the scene. Pontius's encounter with the kinkajou has rendered the performer (temporarily) abject: first, by broaching taboo cross-species sexual behavior and, second, by challenging his assumed heterosexual identity. Pontius recognizes his performance as both bestial and homosexual. Rather than a masochistic act on his body, he sees the performance chipping away at his self-representation as presumptively heterosexual.

Pontius's contact with the animal produces a kind of woozy revulsion that is marked as traumatic more because it constitutes a same-sexual contact than because it constitutes cross-species sexual contact. His response nears a version of "homosexual panic," the sudden urge to disavow oneself from implication in a same-sex desire, sometimes turning violent, in what Eve Kosofsky Sedgwick calls "a socially sanctioned . . . condition of male heterosexual entitlement."[14]

FIGURE 5.1. Steve-O and Chris Pontius, wearing a zebra costume, entice lions to attack, in *Wildboyz*, "South Africa II," first aired November 23, 2003 (season 1, episode 5).

FIGURE 5.2. Chris Pontius positions a scorpion to sting Steve-O, in *Wildboyz*, "South Africa II," first aired November 23, 2003 (season 1, episode 5).

But of course it is not always the animal that induces such a panic. In Brazil, Steve-O and Pontius visit a research center specializing in electric fish and eels. After expert Chris Aadland shows them some smaller specimens in aquariums, they ask to meet a six-foot-long eel housed in an outdoor pond. Standing in nearly waist-high water, they hold hands to experience its 600 volts, as Steve-O declares, "If one of us gets shocked, we both do." Pontius's hand brushes the eel as it slinks by, sending a painful charge through both their bodies.

Afterward, on land, recounting the experience, Pontius and Steve-O, perhaps unconsciously, reenact (see figure 5.4). Steve-O suddenly realizes that he and Pontius have rejoined hands. His free right hand points to the clasped left, his facial expression turns to disdain, and he withdraws his hand, steps away from Pontius, and folds his arms across his chest. Pontius jumps up and down, laughing at their affectionate gaffe, and covers his face with his hands for a moment. Their reactions are disavowing gestures of self-protection and shame.

FIGURE 5.3. Steve-O, on stilts, uses bananas to tempt a giraffe to "kiss" him, in *Wildboyz*, "South Africa II," first aired November 23, 2003 (season 1, episode 5).

FIGURE 5.4. Steve-O and Chris Pontius hold hands while recalling the shock of an electric eel, in *Wildboyz*, "Brazil," first aired May 2, 2004 (season 2, episode 2).

Nevertheless, in the very next scene, they court rather than accidentally veer into similar identity-confusing territory. When Steve-O places a large rubber condom on his head (after trying to place it on an anaconda) Pontius bends over and cries, "Give it to me in the butt!" Steve-O obliges, charging headfirst into his back end, a collision that brings on laughter. Of course, as Leo Bersani has pointed out, a glimpse of—even a parodic gesture toward—the homosexual Other does not precisely incorporate the boys as queer: "Their security as males with power may very well not be threatened at all by that scarcely traumatic sight."[15] In fact, their heterosexuality is emphatically reinforced by their renunciation, in laughter, of the homoeroticism of the scenes they have staged.

These events are typical of the series, each an exercise in subjecting one's own body to pain or the grotesque, relieved by the capacity to walk away from too-arduous rituals or uncomfortable new subject positions. To have an experience is enough; to comprehend it is not required. In Brazil, facing a ritual practiced among indigenous Indians to mark a boy's passage to manhood, Pontius and Steve-O explain that they will become men by wearing an ornately feathered glove that contains biting ants for as long as they can bear. Steve-O asks, "Why is it that things that make you a man tend to be such dumb things to do?" But he does it anyway. In turn, they shout and writhe in pain and later they pay a visit to an emergency room for treatment. But usually the "boyz" flirt with danger only until the threat of serious injury, beyond a scrape or burn or bite that will heal, becomes too real. If, as John Berger claims, most contact with "the wild" has been lost in modern daily experience,[16] in *Wildboyz* it is a voraciously consumed and becomes a disposable backdrop for an exhibition of power that echoes the genre's colonial roots: white, masculine physical prowess and cultural mobility.[17]

Are the interspecies performances on *Wildboyz* only evidence of the chimeric slapdashery of television genres in the fiercely competitive, heavily niched, multichannel universe: one part juvenile horseplay professionalized as dumb and dumber stunt work, one part speeded-up cultural immersion project, one part sex tourism transposed to perversely "wrong" settings? Is *Wildboyz* just a fully conscious frat-boyish fuck-you to what Mary Douglas would call a "symbolic system" that censures, in varying degrees, bad taste, buggery, and bestiality?[18] Is it simply a comically and purposefully offensive scatological travelogue or are the *Wildboyz* up to something serious?

To be sure, to a great extent the show is simply yet another variation on familiar reality and wildlife themes. The inter-genre marriage doesn't even require much of an imagination: *Wildboyz* could have been quite obviously pitched as *Jackass* meets *The Crocodile Hunter*, or as the *Boston Herald* once

suggested, "Jacques Cousteau meets *Beavis and Butthead.*" Some high concept.[19] But the thing is more than the sum of its transparent parts, for the animals engaged in *Wildboyz* antics are not simply props or objects of human action. Instead, they are participants in boundary-testing performances that
make sense and make meaning in an era rife with reformulations of how we—
humans—and other animals are like and unlike. As performers, most of the
animals appearing in *Wildboyz* stunts are unwitting, or at least half-witting,
though this undoubtedly varies from species to species. It is also, perhaps, beside the point if we accept the idea of Erving Goffman, Richard Schechner,
and others that all kinds of behaviors are performance if they are framed as
such for distribution and consumption—regardless of how knowing or not-
knowing the performer.[20] The animal may, then, perform, but does it get its
own jokes? Critchley, citing Aristotle, holds that humor is exclusively human.[21] He might just as easily have returned to Bergson, who also claimed
that "the comic does not exist outside the pale of what is strictly *human.*"[22] The
joke may be ours and ours alone, but it may also be on us.

Who Laughs Last?

Classic wildlife filmmaking generally takes a serious tone, as it warns gravely
of the inevitable extinctions brought on by habitat destruction, poaching, pes-
ticides, and other perils. The likes of Irwin, Corwin, and the Kratts may use
humor now and then, but they are earnestly awed by their animal subjects and
gravely aware of just how dangerous nearby animals might be as they strive for
photogenic proximity without actually stepping into harm's way. *Wildboyz*
adopts a different tone, expressed in all manner of outbursts. Pontius giggles,
Steve-O gags, they yelp as they experience sensations—scrapes, burns, pokes,
smells, tastes—both painful and pleasurable. They render themselves the (often
literal) butt of jokes as they invite rather than try to sidestep animals' defenses,
their claws, jaws, stings, and excrement. They place themselves in an animal's
shoes, so to speak, situating themselves as prey. And such abject antics are
funny: funny to them and funny to us, even if revulsion is mixed with the
laughs. According to Simon Critchley, it is, perhaps, the fact of border-crossing that produces both responses:

> If humour is human, then it also, curiously, marks the limit of the
> human. . . . Humour is precisely the exploration of the break between

nature and culture, which reveals the human to be not so much a category by itself as a negotiation between categories. We might even define
the human as a dynamic process produced by a series of identifications
and misidentifications with animals. Thus, what makes us laugh is the
reduction of the human to the animal or the elevation of the animal to
the human.[23]

But why is revulsion mixed in the laughs? Why are the gag reflex and the
funny bone tickled at the same time? Thinking of the Yahoos of Jonathan
Swift's *Gulliver's Travels* and the primates that people Will Self's *Great Apes*,
Critchley reminds us that there is pathos in the comic performance:

> What becoming an animal confirms is the fact that humans are incapable
> of becoming animals. For, the sad truth is that in humour humans show
> themselves to be useless animals; hopeless, incompetent, outlandish ani-
> mals, shitting from trees and grunting like great apes. There is some-
> thing charming about an animal become human, but when the human
> becomes animal, then the effect is disgusting.[24]

Indeed. If the slippage across species barriers is fleeting, incomplete, if it is
only vaguely entertainingly disgusting to us, it is, at times, specific, spasm-
inducing disgust that seizes the "boyz." Steve-O, especially, is willing to do or
touch or taste almost anything, at least once, even if the tastes and smells, human and animal, raise his gorge. He wretches (twice) after licking the feet of
men he meets in India, and he throws up after sampling the blood-and-milk
drink of the Samburu in Kenya and a fermented-fruit liquor produced by Indians indigenous to the Amazon river basin in Brazil. He gags after placing himself in a shower of elephant urine in India and after, crouching behind a rhino
in Kenya, he catches its flatulent wind. In Australia, he pukes voluminously out
the window of an enclosed chairlift, after Pontius, seated next to him, farts. In
Jackass: Number Two, Pontius sips semen freshly ejaculated by a stallion—and it
is Steve-O, observing nearby, who vomits.

Pontius and Steve-O challenge one another, repeatedly, to endure some
pain or another (in Kenya, for example, the pinch of an army ant placed on a
nipple) in a macho silence they find impossible to achieve. They scream, they
grimace, and they shimmy, as the Samburu look on, laughing at the "boyz'"
abject failure to endure, even for a second, an entirely voluntary pain. The
"boyz" laugh at their own failure and extend it to others by holding a bee in

place to sting the tip of Wee Man's nose and sneaking up with bee in hand so that it stings a cameraman on the back of his neck. They are, in Critchley's words, "useless . . . hopeless . . . outlandish." Perhaps their failures, as Kristeva suggests, are inevitable. Kristeva describes the not-fully-doable work of abjection by explaining that "there looms, within abjection, one of those violent, dark revolts of being, directed against a threat that seems to emanate from an exorbitant outside or inside, ejected beyond the scope of the possible, the tolerable, the thinkable. It lies there, quite close, but it cannot be assimilated."[25] Yet they repeat their failed feats in episode after episode, in new settings, among new species and new people. The animal lies close, but remains threateningly Other: impossible, intolerable, unthinkable.

And yet the animal returns. For all their brashness, *Wildboyz*'s interspecies encounters—what Jane Desmond has called border crossings—are not unique.[26] They are also found in animal performances such as the elaborate fun-for-the-whole-family productions put on at Sea World, especially those involving killer whales/orcas and known as the Shamu show. For Susan G. Davis, the humor—"impishness," even—displayed in acts undertaken by orcas in these exhibitions constitutes a choreographed anthropomorphization—or "humanization"—of the animal.[27] Using reinforcement techniques, trainers adapt natural "animal behaviors to get animals to act like humans."[28] The orca obeys (and sometimes disobeys or is trained to pretend to disobey) commands to perform acrobatics. It splashes the audience. It waves goodbye. In doing so, "the orca is now gathered within the image of the human—it is now participating with us, acting like us, copying us, tricking us."[29]

But the animal is not the only participant whose identity is destabilized and restructured in the performance. To Desmond, performances in which trainers swim, communicate, and for all practical purposes dance with whales are those in which "animal and human are one."[30] Such a border-crossing, a momentary merger, "facilitates the absorption of the human into the whale's aqueous world. The whale is aestheticized while the human is transformed into a marine mammal partner, equally at home in the water as the whale. The natural is culturalized while the cultural is naturalized, and the transformative process is framed as art."[31] In *Wildboyz*, the human proves moronic in his world or that of any Other. And laughter, in all forms, from giggles to guffaws, may be Pontius and Steve-O's most frequent response to the abject failure to become animal as they stage and restage. Is it Beckett's mirthless laughter? Yes, in that they laugh in response to an unhappy, abject state. But it is worth remembering that it is, invariably, themselves that the Wildboyz laugh at. They laugh at the ordeals they have put themselves through. DeGeneres laughs at the ordeal she imagines herself in when she comes too close to the goat. Critchley's notion that the mirthless laugh is consoling, rather than cruel or condemning, comes through his glance at Freud's 1928 essay "Humour," a kind of after-thought to his 1905 book on jokes.[32] In humor, according to Freud, we recognize ourselves—our boundaries, our attempts to breach them, our failures to do so—as ridiculous. To do so is not to condemn or resign ourselves to failure. Rather, according to Freud, "Humor has in it a liberating element."[33] It is the superego that assents to humor, a "repudiation of the possibility of suffering," that provides balm to an ego that may be bruised, battered, or bewildered: "humor is not resigned; it is rebellious. It signifies the triumph of not only the ego, but also of the pleasure principle, which is strong enough to assert itself here in the face of the adverse real circumstances."[34] In recognizing our failures, in salving them with laughter, we repair the self and the self's boundaries. This kind of laughter, in terms of a Freudian economy of the self, is a for-giving laugh, a productive laugh. The Wildboyz, again and again, misidentify with the animal, fail to become animal, and laugh at their failures. In laughing they comfort the self that has confronted in abjection the territory of the animal and found that the animal, like the self, remains not fully knowable.

Notes

1. Former Pennsylvania Senator Rick Santorum lumped together homosexuality, pedophilia, and bestiality as deviancies from which the institution of marriage must be protected: "In every society, the definition of marriage has not ever to my knowledge included homosexuality. That's not to pick on homosexuality. It's not, you know, man on child, man on dog, or whatever the case may be. It is one thing." See Associated Press 2003. Likewise, the late Reverend Jerry Falwell condemned the expansion of gay rights by raising the specter of bestiality: "So here we have now same-sex marriage. What's next, polygamy? . . . Why not? And why not bestiality?" (CNN 2004). See also "Bill O'Reilly's Continuing Obsession with Inter-Species Marriages" (Media Matters 2005).

2. Critchley 2002:29.

3. Critchley 2002:33. Actual bestiality has been treated by other authors as well as in the docudrama *Zoo* (2007), based on a true story of a group of men in Washington State who engaged in sexual activities with horses, leading to the death of one of the men. Robinson Devor directed the film as a series of highly aestheticized reenactments of events leading up to and following the fatal act. On a lighter note, consider "plushie" or "furry" fans and fetishists, who may don animal costumes, sometimes as part of sexual activity; see Savage 2002. A *CSI* episode based on the phenomenon, "Fur and Loathing" (first aired by CBS, October 30, 2003), is controversial within the Web-based

furry community, some of whom found its emphasis on orgiastic behavior sensational-
izing. I leave both kinds of human-animal encounters aside here.

4. In most episodes of *Wildboyz*, most stunts involve nonhuman animals. However,
in some episodes, the *Wildboyz* interact with indigenous people in the locations they
visit. Given the context for which this essay is written, the kind of cultural tourism they
perform merits further consideration in a separate analysis.

5. Kristeva 1982:12 (emphasis in original). She continues, "The abject confronts us,
on the other hand, and this time within our personal archeology, with our earliest attempts to release the hold of *maternal* entity even before existing outside of her, thanks
to the autonomy of language. It is a violent, clumsy breaking away, with the constant
risk of falling back under the sway of a power as securing as it is stifling" (13; emphasis
in original).

6. This history draws on and elaborates on the author's own *Watching Wildlife*
(2006). See also three excellent works on the wildlife genre: Bousé 2000, Burt 2002,
and Mitman 1999.

7. For more on classic wildlife film style, see Bousé 2000:127–151. On the True-Life
adventures, see also Sammond 2005:195–246, 247–299. Both *The Living Desert* and
March of the Penguins were landmarks in the genre. *The Living Desert* earned as much as
$5 million in its theatrical release, some twentyfold its production budget, proving to
the Walt Disney Company that feature-length nonfiction wildlife films could deliver
audiences at low cost. *March of the Penguins* earned $70 million in North America alone
within three months of its release (by National Geographic Feature Films and Warner
Independent Pictures), impressive returns on a $2 million production, far outpacing
other recent attempts to replicate in conventional cinemas the success of wildlife programming on television and in the IMAX format. For comparison, note *Winged Mi-
gration* (2002), with domestic box office earnings of just under $11 million.

8. The *National Geographic Specials* first ran, four per year, on CBS (1964–1973) and
ABC (1973–1975). *National Geographic* moved to PBS in 1975 and stayed there through
1994. In 1995, the *Specials* returned for a time to NBC, and in 1997, National Geographic launched its own channel, first in the United Kingdom, then throughout
global markets, including the United States, in 2001. Co-owned by NBC and News
Corporation, the channel competes with Animal Planet, a Discovery Channel spin-off
and joint venture with the BBC, launched in 1996.

9. See Haraway 1989:133–185.

10. The experiences of the *Wildboyz* cast and crew appeared to influence the first
Jackass sequel. Whereas in the first movie, only seven stunts (just over 10 percent of the
total) used live animals, *Number Two* featured fifteen stunts (about a third) using live
animals.

11. Werts 2004:F7.

12. Meanwhile, *Jackass* alumni dispersed to other projects—for example, actor
Johnny Knoxville, to the movies, starring in John Waters's *A Dirty Shame* (2004) and

The Dukes of Hazzard remake (2005); professional skateboarder Bam Margera, to his own MTV reality series, *Viva la Bam* (2003–2005), and *Bam's Unholy Union* (2007); and Steve-O, to the shortlived series *Dr. Steve-O* on USA Network (2007) and several episodes of ABC's *Dancing with the Stars* (2009).

13. The *Wildboyz* distancing comments are rendered poignant in the post-Katrina Gulf Coast. Although it is still possible in New Orleans to spot the occasional bumper sticker that makes a similar joke ("Third World and Proud of It!"), one was also likely to see, at post-Katrina political rallies, signs imploring inclusion ("Mr. Bush, Are We Part of the United States? Then Help!"). Thanks to Joy Van Fuqua for insights into the Louisiana episode and for pointing out these signs.

14. Kosofsky Sedgwick 1990:20, 185.

15. Bersani 1987:207.

16. Berger 1980:1–26. First published in three parts: "Animals as Metaphor," *New Society* 39 (March 10, 1977): 504–505; "Vanishing Animals," *New Society* 39 (March 31, 1977): 664–665; and "Why Zoos Disappoint," *New Society* 40 (April 21, 1977): 122–123.

17. This section is expanded from Chris 2006:118–120.

18. Douglas 2002.

19. Wedge 2003:E35. According to Justin Wyatt, a "high concept" Hollywood film (or television program) is one for which the premise can be summed up in one short sentence, often in reference to previous films. It also sports at least one bankable star, presumable mass-market appeal, and potential for merchandising. See Wyatt 1994.

20. Schechner 1988:257.

21. Critchley 2002:25–29.

22. Bergson 1911:3.

23. Critchley 2002:29.

24. Critchley 2002:34

25. Kristeva 1982:1.

26. Desmond 1995:230.

27. Davis 1997:216.

28. Davis 1997:216.

29. Davis 1997:217.

30. Desmond 1995:228.

31. Desmond 1995:224–225. Desmond identifies "the mobility of a crossing of the species (hence, nature/culture) border" as one of two primary themes that pervade the Shamu shows at Sea World, the other being familial relationships (1995:230; see also Davis 1997:219–226). Compare Kristeva's claim that primal repression the making of the differentiated self-subject—takes as its object, on one hand, the animal; on the other, the maternal (1982:12–13).

32. Freud 1963; Freud 1960.

33. Freud 1963:265.

34. Freud 1963:265.

References

Associated Press. 2003. "Sen. Rick Santorum's Comments on Homosexuality in an AP Interview." *San Francisco Chronicle*, April 22. http://www.sfgate.com/cgibin/article .cgi?file=/news/archive/2003/04/22/national1737EDT0668.DTL (accessed July 13, 2005).

Berger, John. 1980. "Why Look at Animals?" In *About Looking*, 1–26. New York: Pantheon.

Bergson, Henri. 1911. "Laughter: An Essay on the Meaning of the Comic." Trans. Cloudesley Brereton and Fred Rothwell. Project Gutenberg, 2003, http://www .gutenberg.org/etext/4352 (accessed June 8, 2007).

Bersani, Leo. 1987. "Is the Rectum a Grave?" *October* 43 (Winter 1987): 207.

Bousé, Derek. 2000. *Wildlife Films*. Philadelphia: University of Pennsylvania Press.

Burt, Jonathan. 2002. *Animals in Film*. London: Reaktion.

Chris, Cynthia. 2006. *Watching Wildlife*. Minneapolis: University of Minnesota Press.

CNN. Wolf Blitzer Reports. 2004. February 24. http://transcripts.cnn.com/TRAN SCRIPTS/0402/24/wbr.00.html (accessed June 15, 2007).

Critchley, Simon. 2002. *On Humour*. London: Routledge.

Davis, Susan G. 1997. *Spectacular Nature: Corporate Culture and the Sea World Experience*. Berkeley: University of California Press.

Desmond, Jane C. 1995. "Performing 'Nature': Shamu at Sea World." In *Cruising the Performative: Interventions into the Representation of Ethnicity, Nationality, and Sexuality*, ed. Sue-Ellen Case, Philip Brett and Susan Leigh-Foster, 217–236. Bloomington: Indiana University Press.

Douglas, Mary. 2002. *Purity and Danger*. New York: Routledge. First published in 1966.

Freud, Sigmund. 1960. *Jokes and Their Relation to the Unconscious*. Trans. James Strachey. New York: W. W. Norton.

——. 1963. "Humour." In *Character and Culture*. New York: Collier.

Haraway, Donna. 1989. *Primate Visions: Gender, Race, and Nature in the World of Modern Science*. New York: Routledge.

Kosofsky Sedgwick, Eve. 1990. *Epistemology of the Closet*. Berkeley: University of California Press.

Kristeva, Julia. 1982. *Powers of Horror: An Essay on Abjection*. New York: Columbia University Press.

Media Matters. 2005. "Bill O'Reilly's Continuing Obsession with Inter-Species Marriages." September 16. http://mediamatters.org/mmtv/200509160009 (accessed October 29, 2010).

Mitman, Gregg. 1999. *Reel Nature: America's Romance with Wildlife on Film*. Cambridge, MA: Harvard University Press.

Sammond, Nicholas. 2005. *Babes in Tomorrowland: Walt Disney and the Making of the American Child, 1930–1960*. Durham, NC: Duke University Press.

Savage, Dan. 2002. "Savage Love: Furry Friends." *The Portland Mercury* 3, no. 10, August 8–14. http://portlandmercury.com/2002-08-08/savage.html (accessed July 27, 2005). [Link no longer active; article can now be found at http://www.thestranger.com/seattle/SavageLove?oid=11570.]

Schechner, Richard. 1988. "Magnitudes of Performance." In *Performance Theory*, rev. ed., 290–232. New York: Routledge.

Wedge, David. 2003. "Sons of 'Jackass.'" *Boston Herald*, October 24, E35.

Werts, Diane. 2004. "Teenage Males Lap Up MTV's Outrageous 'Sunday Stew.'" *Seattle Times*, May 5, F7.

Wyatt, Justin. 1994. *High Concept: Movies and Marketing in Hollywood*. Austin: University of Texas Press.

six

Animal Heroes and Transforming Substances

Canine Characters in Contemporary

Children's Literature

Michelle Superle

A certain old Seneca chief is quoted as saying: "It is true that whenever a
person loves a dog he derives great power from it."
—Maria Leach, *God Had a Dog*[1]

AN ANALYSIS OF NEARLY A HUNDRED ENGLISH-LANGUAGE
children's dog stories (see the appendix at the end of this chapter) reveals not
only the great prevalence of the "dog story" subgenre[2] but also some striking
patterns. In dog stories from the latter half of the twentieth century onward,
dogs are depicted as superior beings capable of effecting psychological transformations through which child protagonists and their families achieve
growth. These late twentieth-century hero dogs allow a kind of rebirth for
child characters and their families. Dogs become *transforming substances*—both
agents and catalysts that enable families to achieve a fuller humanity.

Considering "myth" in a manner indebted to the influential historian of
religions Mircea Eliade, I argue that children's dog stories constitute a mythological narrative in the sense that they (a) are an account of creation or rebirth

This research was supported by the University of New Brunswick's Eileen Wallace
Fellowship in Children's Literature.

(b) accomplished with the aid of heroic beings superior to ordinary humans (in this case, dogs) that (c) facilitate a breakthrough of "the sacred" (often connected in these stories with childhood, nature, and wildness) in which (d) human beings achieve their full humanity.[3]

In order to accomplish this function, children's dog stories utilize binary oppositions such as wildness versus civility and childhood versus adulthood.[4] Dogs and children (but not adults) span these extremes, possessing the remarkable capacity to move back and forth between them.

Equally important in dog stories is the widespread literary construction of canine characters as benevolent, helping creatures. They ultimately assist the humans they touch to achieve a fuller human identity. In the dog stories I surveyed—from nineteenth-century texts such as *Beautiful Joe* to mid-twentieth-century cultural icons such as *Lassie Come-Home,* through early twenty-first-century texts like *Star in the Storm*—dogs have most often been portrayed as benevolent helpers.

In *Picturing the Beast: Animals, Identity, and Representation*, Steve Baker observes that various animals come to represent something simple and easily recognizable to humans—"the cute cat, the lucky cow, the white horse as the 'very image of freedom.'"[5] As benevolent creatures that can straddle the distance between binary oppositions such as wildness and civility, I contend that dogs represent mythical heroes.

In her analysis of animal heroes in children's realistic animal fiction, Lori Jo Oswald argues:

> As the twentieth century progressed, the definition of animal hero in realistic animal fiction generally changed from wild animals that were heroic for surviving against all odds to domesticated animals that were heroic for rescuing humans from wild beasts. . . .
>
> The heroic dog usually shows no fear [of] . . . wild animal[s]. The dog hero always values human life—at least its beloved master's or mistress's life—above its own. It is the dog's duty and function to protect humans, even if it must die in doing so.[6]

Oswald's focus on the physical role and function of dog heroes is too narrow in its determined exclusion of the role dogs play in promoting psychological and social well-being.

Canine characters begin to "save" child characters psychologically with the rise of increasingly realistic children's fiction in the 1960s. In earlier children's literature from the mid-nineteenth through the early twentieth centuries, the dog's role was, as Oswald points out, as physical savior, rescuing both children and adults from bodily danger. During this period children's literature was deeply infused with the Romantic vision of the child in which childhood was set against adulthood as a time of innocence when imagination and creativity reigned, largely due to the child's perceived connection with "nature." Children themselves were frequently portrayed as saviors of adults through their ability to inspire transformation, growth, and rebirth as a result of their innocence and closeness to nature.

After 1960 it is canine characters that become agents of transformation and rebirth in children's dog stories. In this portrayal there is a discernible despair over the inability of adults to help children and even of humans to help humans while a connection with and reliance on the natural world, bridged by domesticated canines, is celebrated as a source of power.

Just as the Romantic child enacted positive change in the lives of adult characters in earlier children's literature, canine characters, as heroes, enact positive change in lives of child protagonists and their families. Perhaps drawing on folktale sources that symbolically portray dogs as catalysts for change,[7] dogs come to figure in children's literature as agents of transformation that bridge the nature-culture divide. As Jungian psychologist Eleanora Woloy eloquently states: "the dog [is] a threshold animal. . . . In this position at the crossroads, the dog transmutes instinct into spirit, thus bringing rebirth. Jung states that 'because of its rich symbolic context the dog is an apt synonym for the transforming substance.'"[8]

Consider this passage from Pam Houston's *Sight Hound* (2005), a rare contemporary "dog story" for adults:

> Dr. Theo calls me an object (though he won't dare say it while I'm lying on the floor of his office, drinking water out of his proffered little Tupperware and making his job, I might add, easier by half). He says I'm the object she [Rae] created so she could learn to love herself.
>
> Aren't the humans perfectly marvelous creatures? Doesn't it make you double over with laughter the way they remain committed to the idea that they're the only species that feels deeply, because—what—they have words to talk about their feelings? Has it not occurred to them that perhaps the reason they need so many words, the reason their words consistently fail them, is that they are so much poorer at interpreting their emotions than we are, that interpretation, per se, is a step that in the dog world we just skip?[9]

The voice belongs to the central canine character Dante, and his observations capture human discomfort with the limits of our own communication, as well as our current societal reluctance to admit the possibility of a transformative connection with an animal companion.

In spite of these cultural constraints, *Sight Hound* offers a convincing portrayal of a canine hero that transforms the life of those around him. Dante helps to heal his "mom," Rae, by integrating both her personality and her personal relationships; he allows her to grow emotionally whole enough to love both herself and others. A tall order for a mere dog? Perhaps so, and the need for skepticism from adult human characters in this novel portrays the widespread cultural belief that there is something suspect or hokey about this healing process, no matter how earnestly and zealously the author shapes her story. But then, this is a novel for grownups.

We tell the children something quite different. We tell them, in hundreds of dog stories, that dogs *can* help to heal them, *can* integrate their relationships, *can* transform their lives and help them to realize their full humanity. In this different positioning of the human-canine connection, childhood is linked with all that we romanticize about the natural world. Dogs and children are paired in a relationship that simultaneously excludes adults and, unexpectedly, allows for greater connectivity between adults and children. The canine character's status as a mythical hero rests on its ability to bridge the natural and human worlds, thus allowing child protagonists and their families to be reborn into a fuller humanity.

For the purposes of this discussion, "dog stories" will be classified as works of longer fiction (novels) that are either about a dog or feature a dog character in a central role and are intended for readers aged eight to twelve. The ninety-eight dog stories in my sample were identified primarily from the subject guide of the University of British Columbia catalog and supplemented from the Eileen Wallace Children's Literature Special Collection at the University of New Brunswick. Picture books, young adult fiction, and easy chapter books, such as the excellent *Henry and Mudge* series by Cynthia Rylant, have been excluded for brevity and consistency of analysis. There is a range of genres within the dog story: I have identified them broadly as the dog biography, the boy and his dog story, the fantasy dog story, the problem novel dog story, and the domestic dog story.

Wildness and Civility: Kids and Dogs Together
Against the Grownups

Dogs' powerful status is closely related to the place they hold on the threshold of an imagined nature/culture, wildness/civility divide. Although children's literature is often used as a vehicle of social indoctrination, it can equally be a subversive force against hegemonic values.[10] In dog stories, writers create a textual space that validates the relationship between animals and children as not only positive, but also superior to other human relationships and capable of benefiting them in unique ways. Although it may initially appear in dog stories that children and animals are being linked together as inferior, uncivilized beings who require reform, canine characters are, perhaps subversively, set up as heroes that free children from the expectations of civility and reconnect them with nature.

Almost universally in the genre, adult characters in dog stories perceive canine characters as "other," as threats that can range from nuisance-level to serious hazards. The dogs are most often initially rejected by adult characters because of the hassle the dogs (could) cause, the dirt they carry, or the potential danger they represent. Their "wildness" is frequently at the center of parental concern. Similarly, parental characters often object to their children's behavior, complaining that they are messy, lazy, and irresponsible. The children, like the dogs, have not yet been fully tamed by socialization or "growing up." Developmental psychologist Gail Melson neatly summarizes this link between dogs and children in children's literature by noting:

> The association of children and pets has strong historical and intellectual underpinnings. . . . In a worldview that radically separates humans from nonhumans, and rationality from animality, both children and pets straddle this great divide. Each is seen as not quite human and not quite animal. Pets are the humanized animals. . . . Children are the animal human, the instinctual, untamed substrate. . . . Children's essential animality has sometimes been viewed as problematic; at other times the animal nature of children has been idealized.[11]

Many pastoral classics infused with the Romantic view of childhood, such as *The Secret Garden* (1911), show the connection between childhood and nature as wholly positive; however, the portrayal in dog stories is slightly more ambivalent (although the conclusions of both kinds of stories—integrated relationships and healed spirits—are the same). Paul Shepard offers an explanation for this ambivalence when he notes that although today dogs are beloved pets:

> We must realize that throughout most of its history of at least ten thousand years, dogs have seldom fared as well as they do now. . . . the inverse dog is the spoiler of human graves and eater of corpses, the keeper of hell's gates, the carrier of rabies. . . . The antitype of the dependable servant at the doorstep is the untamed, bastardized outsider, all those hangdogs who have circled human settlements for millennia, wolfing scraps, harassing livestock.[12]

Shepard further argues:

> [Dogs are] everywhere the most liminal of animals because of the tension between [their] civilized associations and [their] degraded state in the wild. . . . On the one hand the dog is "man's best friend," valorized as . . . companion. . . .
>
> On the other hand the dog is the alien monster and hypocrite, fallen and hateful, the most corrupt of animals. . . . Dogs seem to go over from ambiguity to duality, their gross bestiality representing all that is opposed to humanity and civilization.[13]

In the views of many parental figures in dog stories, children share this duality and ambiguity. Children, too, have one foot in the wildness of instinct and gratification and the other in civility and social acceptability. This duality generally is considered problematic by adults, but canine characters, fraught with duality themselves, allow child characters to mediate between both states. Children find a new balance between their humanity and animality, between their civility and wildness, while simultaneously garnering adult acceptance, thus integrating their family and community. This positive resolution highlights the natural world as a source of power, even while nature may seem threatening to adult characters.

Most protagonists in these dog stories are aged ten to twelve, and thus they inhabit an even further fractured middle ground. They are too old for their behavior to be under constant parental control, but too young to take on the autonomy and responsibility usually associated with adolescence. It seems appropriate, then, that child characters feel a strong connection with the dogs and share none of the adults' concern.

On the contrary, child characters foil adults by offering unconditional acceptance to dogs. Even the most unpleasant aspects of their pet dogs' physicality do not deter children's unconditional love. An excellent example of this occurs in *Dolphin Luck*, Hilary McKay's sequel to *Dog Friday*. When the Robinson children's geriatric, senile, and very ill dog, Old Blanket, is dying, they accept everything about him: "Perry reached out and drew Old Blanket . . . toward him . . . and from Old Blanket there came a revolting noise and a fresh and terrible smell. '*Darling* Old Blanket,' said Ant."[14] Later, when missing Old Blanket after his death, Ant is still forgiving of Old Blanket's shortcomings: "I *liked* the way Old Blanket smelled!"[15] This unconditional love and acceptance highlights the fact that children are in some ways closer, in their "dual citizenship," to the world of canines than to that of adult humans. When considering children's literature specifically, Melson observes:

> [There is] a recurring theme in animal stories—children as allies and often saviors of vulnerable animals against an unfeeling, cruel adult world. The child and animal form a bond, share a common language. . . . Both child and animal are outsiders in the adult world, marginal to its rules but subject to their arbitrariness. . . . In the process of saving the animal, the child grows stronger.[16]

Melson does not consider in this equation the ways in which dogs save children. In most dog stories, there is a rescue scenario: through the early twentieth century, the dog was usually the rescuer, but from the mid-twentieth century on—my area of focus in this paper—child characters more often rescue stray, abandoned, or abused dogs. Interestingly, even though in later twentieth-century dog stories the canine characters are more often *rescued*, they still maintain the hero status established so convincingly through earlier literature such as Ballantyne's *The Dog Crusoe* (1861), London's *The Call of the Wild* (1903), DeJong's *Dirk's Dog, Bello* (1939), and Gipson's *Old Yeller* (1956) when they were the *rescuers*. These new dog heroes simply perform psychological rather than physical rescue.

It is this role as psychological rescuers that I have in mind when calling dogs transforming substances. Dogs allow child characters to integrate themselves psychologically and to harmonize their social relationships—in sum, to become more fully human.

A particularly strong example of the dog character's role as transforming substance is found in *The Promise* (1999) by Jackie French Koller. Protagonist Matt, along with his father and younger brother, is "trying to make the best of" the "first Christmas after Ma died."[17] While outside feeding the birds at night on Christmas Eve, Matt and his dog, Sara, are chased by a bear. They become hopelessly lost in the woods, and Sara is badly injured when she fights the bear to protect Matt. Later, the boy falls asleep in the cold, but he is awakened by the dog speaking to him:

> It sounded like . . . Ma! But Ma was . . . "Matt," the voice called again. I looked up at the sky. "Ma?" I said. "Here, Matt." I looked down again. The voice was coming from right in front of me. From . . . no. It couldn't be. Sara's eyes were open, her head was up, and she was looking at me. "Sara?" I said. The voice came again. "You've got to go for help," it said.[18]

The dog, channeling Matt's mother's voice, guides the boy back home to get help. After this miraculous assistance from Sara, Matt then becomes the physical rescuer when he returns to the woods as soon as he can, ensuring Sara's survival. When the dog awakens completely healthy on Christmas Day, Matt's younger brother exclaims that "Ma sent us a Christmas miracle!"[19] Christmas Day is a happy celebration after all, and the dog has brought about this transformation.

The Dog as Superior Being and Social Integrator: A Literary Exploration of *A Dog on Barkham Street*, *To Catch a Tartar*, and *Sable*

In describing dogs as playing the role of hero in a contemporary myth I have insisted, perhaps counter-intuitively and against other scholars such as Oswald,[20] that dogs are portrayed as superior to ordinary humans. A more detailed literary exploration of three boy and his dog stories and three problem novel dog stories will illustrate this subtle canine superiority—this imagined ability of dogs to bridge the nature-culture divide and transform lives. In the boy and his dog genre, canine characters are shown as heroes that promote acceptance and social integration in both communities and, more often, families. Here, integration provides the ultimate conclusion to the dog's arrival, healing whatever rift divided the family or community at the outset of the text and allowing for rebirth. Dogs can accomplish what no human being can do and, paradoxically, while at one level outside of human community, dogs prove decisive to the proper functioning of human relationships.

In the earliest work of this examination, *A Dog on Barkham Street* (1960) by Mary Stolz, the family rift is relatively benign: protagonist Edward desperately wants a dog but his mother will not let him have one. His problem is essentially due to the power hierarchy in his household: in spite of Edward's perseverance in asking for a dog and promising to care for it, his parents forbid it because they believe he is not responsible enough. Further, Edward feels displaced in his community because his neighbor continually bullies him. The problem is more complex in *To Catch a Tartar* (1973) by Lynn Hall. Protagonist Duncan is isolated from both his family and his entire community by his antisocial behavior. In a portrayal rare in children's literature, the bully's side of the story is empathetically presented through Duncan's perspective: he is aware of how problematic his behavior is: "He was disgusted with himself and with the things he did. . . . He could not bear to think of what kind of person he was becoming."[21]

In a much later boy and his dog story, gender equality infiltrates the subgenre; the protagonist of *Sable* (1994) by Karen Hesse, is Tate, a girl who feels voiceless and disempowered within her family because her distant mother will not allow her to get a dog and, equally frustrating, her father will not allow her to help him in his carpentry workshop.

In each of these stories, a fairly consistent structural pattern unfolds after the initial rift is revealed. This pattern is astutely identified by Edward in *A Dog on Barkham Street* in a moment of unusual and amusing metafiction: "There were no end of stories in which a boy wanted a dog but didn't get one until a wonderful dog came along and selected *him*. In the stories these dogs were either stray ones, or the people who owned them saw how the boy and the dog loved each other and gave the dog up. In the stories the parents agreed to keep the dog, even if they'd been very much against the idea before."[22]

So, first comes the unexpected arrival of the dog and the initial parental rejection. Significantly, as agents that have a powerful connection with nature and wildness, the canine characters frequently emerge from natural settings: Argess is wandering in the Grand Canyon, and Tartar and Sable emerge from wooded areas. In *A Dog on Barkham Street*, Argess's arrival is marked by Edward's mother's sighs and protest—"I might have known. Animals. . . . I don't suppose there's anything I can do about it."[23]

The dog in *To Catch a Tartar* is a stray and has been rejected from several families and communities due to his perceived violent behavior (he is actually only being loving and playful). Arriving at Duncan's school, the dog has been alone for "nearly a year" and his "loneliness [is] heavy," so he "settle[s] into the underbrush at the edge of the playground" to watch the children.[24] Immediately, he notices Duncan and "something about the boy [draws] The Tartar's attention."[25] When Duncan brings the dog home, his mother's rejection of the stray is primarily financial. The family is desperately poor, and they can't afford a dog.

In *Sable,* Tate's mother's deep fear of dogs (the result of a dog attack in her childhood) means that she "would not hear about having a dog. She didn't like them, none of them."[26] In all of these scenarios, parental control is absolute until the dog arrives, but once the animal establishes a clawhold on the scene, the children find a way to allow their beloved new pets to stay in spite of parental rejection. In each case the dog is other in the mothers' eyes: Argess a nuisance, Tartar "rigwoody," and Sable frightening. The mothers seem to be objecting to the wildness within the animals. However, the dogs' wildness, their connection to the natural world, is also a source of power.

The child character's absolute acceptance of dogs upon their arrival, regardless of their myriad shortcomings, is almost universal in the genre. This widespread lack of criticism—here showcased in quick acceptance of dogs—is positioned as binary to adult skepticism—here of canines, but also encompassing other humans, including certain qualities in the adult characters' own children. The children love the dogs immediately and wholeheartedly, and simply because they are dogs, not because there is anything special about them. Childhood openness is portrayed as superior to adult fear and skepticism. For example, immediately upon interacting with Argess, Edward is taken with her. Duncan's acceptance of Tartar is just as immediate: after interacting with the stray for only a few moments, Duncan begins to feel that there is "a bond between" them, and almost immediately the dog becomes "more important to him than all the kids in the world."[27]

However, the acceptance from a family member who holds no power is not particularly effective. Thus, though canine characters win a tenuous place in new homes because of children's quick acceptance and subsequent tenacity, dogs—a threatening other—must modify their behavior to comply with adult standards in order to maintain their newfound security. Straddling the civilized, social world of adults and the wild, sensual world of canines, it is the children's job to bring about the dogs' behavioral modification.

In *A Dog on Barkham Street,* Argess is not allowed to wander free because of the local bylaw prohibiting dogs at large and because dogs allegedly "destroy people's gardens, they frighten small children, sometimes they bite."[28] Within Edward's household, his mother subscribes to the same views, defending the bylaw: "We live in a very *nice* community . . . which I happen to like and want to live it. Peacefully. Without violating the rules. Argess can't run loose."[29] Edward, then, becomes the dog's keeper—responsible for her behavior in the neighborhood as well as in his own home.

The pattern is at its most dramatic in *Sable*. A (former) stray, Sable is in the habit of stealing, and having a secure home does nothing to eradicate her ways. Summing up the liminal position of both children and dogs, Tate explains the situation to her dog: "If you're not perfect, absolutely perfect, I don't know what [Mam] will do. . . . you've got to be good."[30] The children's role is to train dogs to shed some of their otherness, their wildness. In this way, the canine characters come one step closer to securing a place in the human world, and child characters connect with the natural world through the dogs. As the child protagonists work to integrate the dogs into human society, canine characters effect a transformation that brings the children one step closer to securing productive, harmonious relationships within their social, human spheres.

However, before parents will finally accept the dog, there is some sort of crisis. Often, the child protagonist runs away from home or faces some kind of danger. Only after the crisis passes are the parents able to see the value and importance of the dog's presence within the family—something that has been clear to the children from the moment of the dog's arrival. In their eventual welcome of the dog into their home, the parents seem finally to prioritize the health, safety, and happiness of their children above the perceived threat of the dog. At a deeper level, though, they have tacitly acknowledged and accepted the wildness in their children by accepting the beloved animal. Perhaps it is this acceptance that finally allows the families to relate to one another harmoniously.

The ultimate resolution of boy and his dog stories—the establishment of a secure position within the family for the dog—ensures an integration of the family or community for the protagonist. Quite clearly, at the outset of the story, the families and/or communities were incomplete. With the addition of a dog, a link to the nonhuman world, they become complete. By the end of the story the unsettling rift that existed at its outset is made harmonious. In *A Dog on Barkham Street,* Edward's problems with his neighbor the bully are resolved with Argess's help. Even more importantly, he and his parents achieve a new harmony. When his parents allow him to keep the dog, Edward immediately reciprocates by enacting the kind of responsible behavior they have been demanding of him: "Suddenly, to everyone's surprise, Edward said, 'I think I'll take a bath.' He whistled to his dog and they went upstairs together."[31] As bathing was Edward's least favorite chore ("I hate taking baths because they *make* me"[32]), his voluntary and independent move to take a bath is a significant behavioral change that also signals his willingness to comply with socially acceptable norms.

Whereas the initial rift in *A Dog on Barkham Street* is minor, the situation is far more dire in *To Catch a Tartar*. On the one hand, in finding a way to keep the stray Tartar, Duncan risks both his place in his family and his ultimate standing in the community, as many children are afraid of the dog (and of Duncan), and if the boy and his dog should cause harm to any member of the community, Duncan would be completely ostracized. On the other hand, he stands to gain respect and acceptance within his community should he be successful. When he trains the dog to behave in a safe and trustworthy manner, a small child who was once terrified of Duncan rewards the former bully and makes clear his future standing in the community by smiling and saying, "I'm not scared of you anymore."[33] Now that both he and his dog can interact with the community in a positive way, Duncan feels satisfied: "For the first time in years he felt completely good. For the first time in years he liked himself."[34] Duncan symbolically marks the moment by changing his dog's name from Tartar—ferocious opponent—to "Fere"—trusted companion.[35]

In these three stories and many others in the boy and his dog genre, the dog's arrival is a catalyst that sets off a chain of events ultimately resulting in harmoniously integrated relationships for the protagonist and his or her family and community. The dog is a hero that provides a psychological rescue for child protagonists, and this in turn allows for rebirth in her or his social sphere. As Vikram Seth notes in his (adult) novel *An Equal Music*, a dog's "presence makes the family inviolate."[36] By interacting with canine characters, children in dog stories find a productive, secure place in their families and communities. They can begin to live a new life of social harmony. Where humans fail, the extraordinary ability of dogs to give and elicit benevolent concern and bridge the fractures of human families establishes canines as possessing a power superior to any found among ordinary humans.

Of course, there are many fractured and highly dysfunctional real-life families that include a dog in their number—these stories aren't taken by anyone to portray a literal reality. Still, there is an earnestness and seriousness in these stories. They constitute a mythologically true lore about what it means to be a community, a human, and a family. As Marjorie Garber writes in *Dog Love*:

> Dog stories find a place in our ongoing folklore as the real embodiment of what we would like to think were "family values" among human beings. . . . In default of any consensus about social policy, family planning, even what constitutes "the family," in a populace increasingly weary of economic struggle and social divisiveness, "family values," like

other values, are—it is fascinating to note—now often passed on in pop-ular culture not through human stories, but through stories of, and love for, dogs.[37]

The Dog as an Agent of Emotional Transformation: A Literary Exploration of *Lost and Found*, *Dog Friday*, and *Because of Winn-Dixie*

The problem novel genre typically depicts more intense child-dog relationships. Here, canine characters remain heroes that enable transformation and pro-mote social integration as in the boy and his dog genre. However, this role is superseded by dogs' central position as heroes that provide emotional rescue to child characters. Here, dogs come into children's lives at a crucial stage, often a transitional period, and act as guides that enable child characters to achieve an emotional transformation and experience a new wholeness that was absent at the outset of the story.

Problem novel dog stories generally tend to be the most resonant of all dog stories: here dogs are celebrated for their ability to provide nurture to child char-acters within the texts. The reciprocal affection and communication between children and dogs makes their relationship unique and gives dogs a powerful place in human communities.

Despite other differences, some basic patterns do emerge in this sample of stories, and my focus here is on these commonalities. Some of the most salient features particular to the problem novel dog story are: the acquisition of the dog, communication with the dog, the pattern of dependence between the protagonist and the dog, the way the dog transforms relationships in the pro-tagonist's life, and the way the dog benefits the protagonist psychologically. Examining these features in *Lost and Found* (1985), a Canadian dog story by Jean Little, *Dog Friday* (1994), a British dog story by Hilary McKay, and *Be-cause of Winn-Dixie* (2000), an American dog story by Kate DiCamillo, will show these similarities and meaning. This examination will also challenge the idea of a condescending, negative othering of dogs and argue that it is in fact adulthood that is other and marked with a negative valence. Dogs are cast in the superior role of heroes that enable transformation and growth, ultimately affecting a symbolic rebirth for child protagonists.

In most realistic fiction dog stories, the dog is acquired within the story, very often near its beginning (often in this genre as well, dogs emerge from nature—for example, Friday is mired in sand and seaweed on the beach). In this way, the dog is assured its transforming role as the one variable in the protagonist's life that changes. Because of this change, a whole series of other changes is sparked. Usually the characters have been struggling with difficult adjustments prior to the dog's arrival, but these efforts lack traction until the dog arrives. These child protagonists are depicted as struggling with difficult social and emotional problems (as opposed to situations of physical danger) and as seeking a way to regain their "innocence." This transformation is ultimately achieved by reconnecting with the natural world through canine characters.

For example, in *Lost and Found*, Lucy moves to a new town, where she feels "lost."[38] At the beginning of the second chapter, she finds a little dog she believes "must be lost," whom she names Trouble.[39] In *Dog Friday,* Robin is adjusting to the presence of a new family of next-door neighbors. He has also recently become the target of a bully. These situations are punctuated by his rescue of a nearly dead stray dog about a third of the way into the book. The subsequent action in the story concerns whether the dog, Friday, is truly a stray or if his former owners might take him away from Robin, as well as the growing friendship between Robin and his former nemesis, Dan, sparked through Friday. In *Because of Winn-Dixie*, Opal has also recently moved to a new town. While coping with loneliness and boredom, she finds a stray dog in the grocery store (from which Winn-Dixie acquires his unusual name) in the first chapter and pretends he belongs to her in order to take him home. Opal neatly summarizes Winn-Dixie's role as catalyst in her life—the same role that most dogs in problem novels play—when she says that "just about everything that happened . . . that summer happened because of Winn-Dixie."[40]

Crucially, all three child characters are beyond the help of their parents and other adults around them. Further, their parents refuse to acknowledge the emotional seriousness of the children's situations. When her mother asks, "What's wrong, Lucy?," the girl refuses to answer because "she did not want her mother to see how sad she was."[41] However, when Lucy does admit that she feels bored and lonely, her mother immediately scoffs at and dismisses her feelings, saying, "That's just plain silly."[42] This impasse of communication and respect between child and adult is difficult for Lucy, and she retreats from the situation by going outside, where she finds Trouble. In contrast with Lucy's mother, Trouble "listen[s] hard" when Lucy speaks and responds positively to the girl by wagging his tail and "lick[ing] her chin."[43] Lucy feels connected to Trouble; rather than retreating, as she did from her mother, Lucy "put her arms right around the dog and gave him a hug."[44]

In a similar situation, Robin is shown to be beyond the reach and help of the adults in *Dog Friday*. The principal of his school is unable to stop Dan's bullying behavior, and Robin's mother's (admittedly weak) attempt to "cure" his dog phobia is ineffectual. When she notes that "there are dogs in the world. You have to face it," Robin is forced to agree (although this does nothing to solve his problem), but when he tries to explain the basis of his fear—"'It's their breathing' . . . Mrs. Brogan does not seem to think this was a reasonable explanation."[45] Robin is on his own—until Friday's arrival. And in *Because of Winn-Dixie*, Opal's father is emotionally absent, leaving her no avenue to connect with him: "My daddy is a good preacher and a nice man, but sometimes it's hard for me to think about him as my daddy, because he spends so much time preaching or thinking about preaching or getting ready to preach."[46]

In sharp contrast to this rift between adults and children, dogs and children relate to one another openly and in a reciprocally respectful way, which is portrayed as natural and positive. This way of relating is a significant feature of the realistic fiction dog story: dog-human communication is characterized by child protagonists speaking to the dogs just as though they were people. Whereas in other dog stories, especially in the boy and his dog genre, protagonists may address dogs only in command form, highlighting human mastery of animals, in this genre the dogs' elevated role—one of equality—is mirrored by the way human characters communicate respectfully and interactively with the dogs. Significantly, dog-human communication is also highlighted by the dog's response. In realistic fiction, when a protagonist talks to a dog, the dog "talks" back physically (wagging, extending a paw), thus deepening the relationship. Some stories, including *Lost and Found*, show the communication at yet a higher level: the protagonist tells the dog her thoughts and feelings. Lucy feels better when she talks to Trouble: "'If you were mine, then neither of us would feel lost. I'd be your friend and you'd be mine.' The dog began to wag his tail. Then he got up on his hind legs and licked her chin. Lucy thought she would burst."[47]

Similarly, in *Because of Winn-Dixie*, Opal speaks to the dog as to a human and also shares her thoughts and feelings with him in a comforting way: "I told him how we were alike. 'See,' I said, 'you don't have any family and neither do I. I've got the preacher, of course. But I don't have a mama. I mean I have one, but I don't know where she is. . . . I can't hardly remember her. . . . So we're almost like orphans.'"[48] Unlike Opal's father's retreat from attempted communication, "Winn-Dixie looked straight at me when I said that to him, like he was feeling relieved to finally have somebody understand his situation."[49] Of course, it is really Opal who feels relieved to have a living being with whom to share her innermost feelings in a nonthreatening way.

This dog-child communication suggests a connection between the natural and human worlds—at least at their fringes. Canine characters communicate physically and thus pull the children into a wordless, more natural way of being. Child characters communicate with language, pulling the dogs into their human way of being. Each one responds to the other openly and without judgment, though in different ways. The bridge between the natural world and the human world is imagined as a clear, open pathway that can be traversed in either direction.

Not surprisingly, parents either engage in no direct speech with dogs at all or, at best, offer a brief and perfunctory initial greeting, thereby highlighting the children's different approach. The elevated level of communication between canine and child characters reflects the respect protagonists feel for their dogs, as well as the dogs' elevated status in the stories, a sort of "non-othering" by children in contrast to adults' othering of both children and dogs. In contrast to children's failed communication with adults, the dogs respond in the manner the children solicit. The dog's spontaneous, natural approach to the child's problems proves superior to any adult approach.

In almost all dog stories of realistic fiction, most especially in the problem novels, there is an interesting relationship of dependence. On the surface, the dogs seem most dependent on the humans. Often the dogs have been rescued from unsatisfactory or even dangerous circumstances, and the protagonist physically cares for the dog by providing food and shelter. This situation allows the child to act as an agent, to provide care for a living being rather than receiving care from an adult. This guardianship has the capacity to mask the fact (from the child) that in every case it is the protagonist who truly relies on the dog psychologically: the child needs the dog as much as or more than the dog needs the child. The child character has the empowering feeling of acting as savior, but the canine character is the actual hero, bringing the power of the natural world to transform the child and facilitate a kind of rebirth.

For example, when Trouble goes back to his old home in *Lost and Found,* he has no difficulty leaving Lucy: "Then Lucy could not hold onto Trouble. He struggled to get loose. His tail whacked against her. He gave little yips of joy. Lucy had to let him go . . . Lucy did not want to believe it."[50] Even though she "rescued" the dog, Lucy depended on Trouble psychologically in an ultimately more profound manner. The children's dependence reflects the integral way in which canine characters provide emotional and psychological support to child protagonists. The dogs are relatively independent, emphasizing their heroic status.

On the whole, however, interdependence is a more accurate designation for the dog-child relationship. Within this interdependence, there is a significant absence of struggle for or hierarchy of power (this is not the case in other genres). This is an important difference from the way children relate to adults.

Adults alienate children by refusing to communicate and interact with them, often because they are trying to control the child's behavior or to socialize the child into "appropriate" emotional states. Ultimately, although they may administer as much power as they possess, adults actually are powerless to change a child's state of psychological well-being: Lucy's mother cannot make her less lonely, and Robin's mother cannot cure his fear of dogs. It is perhaps this uncomfortable, unacknowledged lack of power that causes the adult characters to lack patience and empathy with children in dog stories.

By contrast, other than their need for pack leadership, dogs are portrayed as uninterested in pursuing power struggles. Dog characters agitate to obtain commodities they consider valuable, such as food, space, or exercise but are not bent on dominance. If the child protagonist provides basic leadership and care for the dog, the dog accepts the child as the leader and ignores other power struggles. This freedom from tension and unrealistic expectations creates a space where dogs can relate with children as equals, positioning canines in direct contrast to adults who distance themselves from children through a rigidly imposed hierarchy in which the children have little power.

The dog's ability to communicate and live in a symbiotic interdependence with children works synergistically in problem novel dog stories and ultimately the dog functions as an emotional catalyst that transforms central relationships in the protagonist's life. In this way, canine characters provide psychological rescue, when adults and indeed no other humans can, and become the unexpected heroes of the narrative.

In *Lost and Found*, Trouble helps Lucy become friends with her next-door neighbor, Nan. Lucy has been worried that she will not make friends in her new town, but because of Trouble, she does. At the end of the book, Missy, the dog Lucy ultimately adopts from the local shelter, is the catalyst that helps Lucy start a friendship with another girl, Barbara, as well: "Lucy . . . lifted Missy up into her arms. She smiled at Barbara over the top of the little dog's head."[51]

In *Because of Winn-Dixie*, the dog functions in the same way. Like Lucy, Opal has just moved to a new town and has not yet made friends. Only after she befriends Winn-Dixie and they begin to go everywhere together (because he cannot bear to be left alone) does Opal meet people and make friends. As Opal says of one prospective friend, "She might like Winn-Dixie . . . almost everybody does."[52] Interestingly, Winn-Dixie's role as "social glue" is depicted as allowing Opal to make friends of different ages, races, sexes, and backgrounds.

Although dogs in problem novel dog stories are essential in changing relationships in the protagonist's life, they are even more important as a transforming substance in the protagonist's own psyche. When a canine character helps a protagonist to achieve emotional growth—a fuller measure of humanity—the dog functions in perhaps its most iconic role. This growth can take many forms. For example, in *Lost and Found*, first Trouble and then Missy help Lucy to feel settled and secure in her new town; by the end of the novel, Lucy affirms that "now everything was different."[53]

In *Because of Winn-Dixie*, the dog plays an even more important role. Winn-Dixie helps Opal realize that she and her father are a satisfactory self-sufficient unit. The dog's presence helps both she and her father come to the revelation that they are whole, even without her mother:

> We stood there hugging and rocking back and forth, and after a while the preacher stopped shaking and I still held on to him. . . .
>
> "We'll keep looking [for Winn-Dixie]," said the preacher. "The two of us will keep looking for him. But do you know what? I just realized something, India Opal. When I told you your mama took everything with her, I forgot one thing, one very important thing that she left behind."
>
> "What?" I asked.
>
> "You," he said. "Thank God your mama left me you." And he hugged me tighter.
>
> "I'm glad I've got you, too." I told him. And I meant it.[54]

Further, the dog gives Opal a sense of security that helps her feel settled in her new town and her life. When he returns after running away in the thunderstorm, Opal revels in her newfound friends at a birthday party: "I looked around the room at all the different faces, and I felt my heart swell up inside me with pure happiness."[55] This scene contrasts dramatically with the beginning of the story, when Opal felt lonely and saddened by her mother's absence and her lack of friends. As in other stories of this genre, Winn-Dixie ultimately effects an emotional transformation, allowing Opal to become more whole.

In many dog stories of the problem novel format, adults are portrayed as preoccupied with forcing socially desirable behavior on their children and unable to productively communicate with children. In these ways, adults in dog stories function as others to the norm of the child.

Dogs, by contrast, belong with children and form a symbiotic relationship with them. Dogs communicate in a "natural" way that allows them to be heard. Further, dogs aid social and emotional growth in child protagonists by allowing them a natural space free of constructed social obligations in which to heal. In these ways, dogs act as transforming substances. Dogs are the heroes of these stories.

Conclusion

The Nobel Prize–winning author Anatole France observed, "Until one has loved an animal, a part of one's soul remains unawakened."[56] This awakening— what I have described as transformation and rebirth—is precisely what child characters in dog stories experience. In children's literature, the dog's persistent role is to help, protect, and save children on a social and emotional level. Dogs, through their connection with the natural world, become heroes that effect miraculous transformations in children's lives. Dogs' potency as heroes flows from their ability to bridge the gap between wildness and civility, between childhood and adulthood, and between nature and culture. In children's literature, both canines and children are separate from adults, with one foot in the untamed wilderness of self-gratification and the other in the domestic civility of productive social interaction. Canine characters help children in dog stories negotiate a productive balance between these two states.

Literary critic Karla Armbruster believes that in many stories about dogs, the inevitable socialization of the dog is a cultural expression of the overlap between nature and culture and a valorization of human domination over nature. In her article "'Good Dog': The Stories We Tell About Our Canine Companions and What They Mean for Humans and Other Animals," she argues: "For many writers and thinkers today, the dog's perceived position on the nature/culture boundary promises modern humans a connection to nature that has otherwise largely been lost. . . . In fact, in order to prove itself a good dog as defined by its human caretakers, the dog must do no less than conclusively demonstrate its loyalty to culture over nature, usually to the extreme of placing human interests above self-interest."[57]

Interestingly, Armbruster makes no distinction in her discussion between works originally published for a child audience and those directed toward adults, nor does she acknowledge that children in many dog stories make much the same sacrifice as dogs. Due to their powerlessness, and in order to maintain a relationship with the dogs they love so much, with which they feel such a strong connection, children must shape their behavior according to adult expectations and norms, as well as coaxing their animal companions into the same behavior. Dogs and children alike must place societal interests above self-interest.

Concluding her analysis, Armbruster urges that instead of justifying or celebrating human dominance over dogs, we should "instead 'feel with' the dogs and other domestic animals we encounter and find some common ground on which we can establish a mutually beneficial and satisfactory relationship."[58] I maintain that this is precisely what most child characters in dog stories attempt to do, only to be thwarted by the adult power figures in their lives.

In children's stories the presence of canine characters allows for common ground between parents and children, promoting adults' acceptance of the children's wild nature, even as the children begin to take initiative for their own taming. Canine characters enact transformation and allow healing and wholeness for child protagonists and their families by bridging the divide between the disparate states of childhood and adulthood, between nature and culture, even while their presence draws attention to the distance between these two worlds.

In these ways, dogs in dog stories make a statement about animals and humanity; they suggest that humans are flawed creatures who need animals' help. Whereas Armbruster contends that "a great deal of the contemporary human relationship with dogs revolves around our need from them to affirm the rightness and value of human culture,"[59] I believe that contemporary dog stories more clearly show the value of the nonhuman. By acting as agents of integration in dog stories, canine characters do affirm the rightness of human culture, but they also suggest a kind of animal superiority.

Melson argues that "animal stories and symbols guide children into deeper understanding of what it means to have a *human* self."[60] Indeed, canine characters in children's literature showcase a fascinating cultural belief that animals can help us to become more human. Perhaps, as Paul Shepard speculates, "the human species emerged enacting, dreaming, and thinking animals and cannot be fully itself without them."[61] In this sense dog stories are a kind of contemporary creation myth, showcasing the birth of a new world in which, with the direct intervention of dogs, humans find emotional healing and social integration.

What dog stories suggest is that we need animals in our lives to be fully human. A tall order for a mere dog story? Surely—but dog stories are not only stories. We live with both dog *and* dog story: the dog as a symbol and the dog as a biological individual interact. Dog stories reflect, shape, and are shaped by actual human relationships with dogs. Dog stories, however true or idealized they ring, are stories about a very real relationship between families and their animal companions. Perhaps the patterns in dog stories are so prolific because they offer a wisdom that we are determined to pass along to our children.

APPENDIX: Children's Dog Stories Analyzed

Title	Author	Year of Publication	Genre	Country	Human Protagonist's Gender	Dog Character's Gender
The Biography of a Spaniel	Anon.	1804	Bio	B	–	M
The Dog Crusoe	Ballantyne	1861	Bio	C	M	M
A Dog of Flanders	Ouida	1870	B & D	E	M	M
Beautiful Joe	Saunders	1894	Bio	C	F	M
Beautiful Joe's Paradise	Saunders	1902	Fant	C	M	M
Call of the Wild	London	1903	Bio	A	M	M
Jock of the Bushveld	Fitzpatrick	1907	Bio	B	M	M
Greyfriars Bobby	Atkinson	1913	Bio	B	M	M
Treve	Terhune	1924	Bio	A	M	M
A Dog Named Chips	Terhune	1931	Bio	A	–	M→F
Rusty, a Cocker Spaniel	Meek	1938	Bio	A	M	M
Dirk's Dog, Bello	DeJong	1939	B & D	A	M	M
Panuck: Eskimo Sled Dog	Machetanz	1939	Bio	A	M	M
Lassie Come-Home	Knight	1940	Bio	B	M	F
Big Red	Kjelgaard	1945	B & D	A	M	M
Quest in the Desert	Andrews	1950	B & D/Bio	A	M	M
Toyon, a Dog of the North and His People	Kalashnikoff	1950	RF	A	M	M
Ginger Pye	Estes	1951	RF	A	M	M

Title	Author	Year	Genre			
Hurry Home, Candy	De Jong	1953	Bio	A	—	M
The Dog That Could Swim Underwater	Selden	1956	Bio	A	—	F
101 Dalmatians	Smith	1956	Bio/Fant	B	M, F	M, F
Old Yeller	Gipson	1956	B & D	A	M	M
The Dog Who Wouldn't Be	Mowat	1957	B & D	C	M	M
The Tide Won't Wait	Bannon	1957	B & D	C	M	M
Along Came a Dog	DeJong	1958	Bio	A	M	M
A Dog on Barkham St	Stolz	1960	RF	A	M	F
The Dog Who Came to Stay	Borland	1961	Bio	A	M	M
The Incredible Journey	Burnford	1961	Bio	C	—	M, M
Silver Chief: Dog of the North	O'Brien	1961	Bio	C	M	M
Where the Red Fern Grows	Rawls	1961	B & D	A	M	M, F
The Dog in the Tapestry Garden	Lathrop	1962	Fant	A	F	F
A Dog So Small	Pearce	1962	RF	B	M	M
Mishmash	Cone	1962	B & D	A	M	M
Windigo	Annixter	1963	B & D	C	M	F
Daddles: The Story of a Plain Hound Dog	Sawyer	1964	B & D	A	M, F	M
Ribsy	Cleary	1964	Bio	A	M	M
A Dog Like No Other	MacKellar	1965	B & D	A	M	M
Eddie the Dog Holder	Haywood	1966	RF	A	M	—
Molly: The Dog Who Wouldn't Quit	Perkins	1966	B & D	C	M	F

APPENDIX (continued)

Title	Author	Year of Publication	Genre	Country	Human Protagonist's Gender	Dog Character's Gender
Sailor's Choice	Carlson	1966	RF	C	M	M
The Shy Ones	Hall	1967	RF	A	F	F
The Starlight Barking	Smith	1967	Fant	B	–	M, F
Kavik the Wolf Dog	Morey	1968	B & D	A	M	M
Big Ben	Walker	1969	RF	A	M	M
Rex of Larkbarrow	Chipperfield	1969	Bio	B	M	M
Tarr of Belway Smith	Agle	1969	Bio	A	–	M
Inky: Seeing Eye Dog	Heppner	1971	HF	A	M	F
Yankee Boy	Scholefield	1971	RF	A	M	F
Cockleburr Quarters	Baker	1972	RF	A	M	F
A Dog Named Wolf	Munsterhjelm	1972	Bio	A	–	M
The Ghost of Grannoch Moor	Mackellar	1973	B & D	B	M	F
Riff, Remember	Hall	1973	Bio/B & D	A	M	M
To Catch a Tartar	Hall	1973	Bio	A	M	M
Just a Dog	Griffiths	1974	Bio	B	–	F
Rufus, Red Rufus	Beaty	1975	Bio	A	M	M
Shadows	Hall	1977	RF	A	F	M
A Dog Called Houdini	Palmer	1978	Bio	C	M	M
Dog Detective Ranjha	Sharma	1978	Bio	I	M	M
Misty and Me	Girion	1979	RF	A	F	F
The Trouble with Tuck	Taylor	1981	RF	A	F	M

Title	Author	Year	Genre			
Howliday Inn	Howe	1982	Fant	A	—	M
Irma and Jerry	Selden	1982	Bio	A	—	M
The Wicked Stepdog	Benjamin	1982	RF	A	F	M
Lost and Found	Little	1985	RF	C	F	F, F
Selby: Adventures of a Talking Dog	Ball	1985	Fant	A	—	M
Different Dragons	Little	1986	RF	C	F	M
Woof!	Ahlberg	1986	Fant	B	M	M
Shiloh	Naylor	1991	RF	A	M	M
Tuck Triumphant	Taylor	1991	RF	A	M	F, M
Wanted . . . Mud Blossom	Byars	1991	RF	A	M, F	M
Jim Ugly	Fleischman	1992	B & D	A	M	M
Red Dirt Jessie	Myers	1992	RF/HF	A	F	M
The Soul of the Silver Dog	Hall	1992	RF	A	F	M
A Dog Called You	Prince	1993	Bio	B	—	M
Bringing Up Beauty	McNicoll	1994	RF	C	F	F
Dog Friday	McKay	1994	RF	B	M	M
The Latchkey Dog	Auch	1994	RF	A	M	F
Gooseberry Park	Rylant	1995	Fant	A	—	M
Protecting Marie	Henkes	1995	RF	A	F	F
Chuck and Danielle	Dickinson	1996	RF	B	F	F
Eliza's Dog	Hearne	1996	RF	A	F	F
Stay! Keeper's Story	Lowry	1997	Bio	A	—	M
Jan and Patch	Hughes	1998	RF	C	F	M

APPENDIX (continued)

Title	Author	Year of Publication	Genre	Country	Human Protagonist's Gender	Dog Character's Gender
The Promise	Koller	1999	Fant	A	M	F
TtuM	Jam	1999	RF	C	F	F
Because of Winn-Dixie	DiCamillo	2000	RF	A	F	M
My Dog, Cat	Crisp	2000	RF	A	M	M
Nothing Wrong with a Three-Legged Dog	McNamee	2000	RF	A	M	M
Star in the Storm	Harlow	2000	RF/HF	C/A	F	M
The Carved Box	Chan	2001	Fant	C	M	F
Berta: A Remarkable Dog	Lottridge	2002	RF	C	F	F
The Boy Who Spoke Dog	Morgan	2003	Fant	A	M	F
Dog Days	McCaughrean	2003	HF	B	M, M	F
The Last Dog on Earth	Ehrenhaft	2003	Fant	A	M	F
Silky: The Dog that Saved the Day	Innis-Weiss-eneder	2004	HF	C	F	M
Dog House Blues	Pearce	2005	RF	C	F	M, M, F
A Dog's Life	Martin	2005	Bio	A	—	F

Key to "Genre" codes: B & D = boy and his dog story; Bio = dog biography or autobiography; Fant = fantasy, talking dog; HF = historical fiction; RF = realistic fiction of child and family life. Key to "Country" codes: A = American; B = British; C = Canadian; E = European; I = Indian. Key to "Dog's Gender" codes: M → F = dog is initially believed to be male but ultimately revealed to be female.

Notes

1. Leach 1961:293.

2. The use of dogs in literature for children began as soon as the first stories to amuse and educate children were written down in seventeenth-century battledores. When extended literary works such as novels were developed for children, dogs were there: R. M. Ballantyne's 1861 novel *Dog Crusoe* is an early example. From that time to the present day, hundreds of dog stories have been created for children. Dog characters are also frequently included in popular children's books. For example, J. K. Rowling includes dogs as important figures in the *Harry Potter* series: consider Fang, Fluffy, and Sirius Black. Similarly, in several of Enid Blyton's best-selling adventure series, a dog always accompanies the children on their adventures.

3. In *Myth and Reality*, Mircea Eliade defined myth as (a) "an account of 'creation'" (b) about what "*really happened*" (emphasis in original) (c) to "Supernatural Beings . . . known . . . by what they did in the transcendent times of the beginnings" in which (d) "dramatic breakthroughs of the sacred" occurred and (e) the Supernatural Beings intervene to make "man himself . . . what he is today" (1964:6). My definition differs significantly from Eliade on two points: contrary to Eliade's understanding of myth, the dog stories I have considered are overtly portrayed as fictional and are not about "the transcendent times of the beginnings." However, even given this departure from Eliade, I maintain that the stories achieve a similar mythological status. The children's dog stories I have considered are positioned as teaching lessons about "real life," and although they don't take place in "the times of the beginning," they do speak to a "beginning" of another sort—childhood—that is perhaps just as primordial. And as in Eliade's understanding of myth, I will show that dog stories provide "exemplary models" (1964:8) of what it means to be fully human (emotionally whole in a harmonious society), and, if we consider that these stories are often read to children in the intimacy of their homes by their parents, one might even argue that there is a "ritual" context for children's dog stories.

4. Children's literature in general draws heavily upon binaries to shape narratives and develop themes, as Nodelman has persuasively argued in *The Pleasures of Children's Literature* (2003:198–203). In dog stories, the binaries are both ancient—wildness versus civility—and much more modern—childhood versus adulthood. These particular binaries are at work widely within children's literature and not exclusive to dog stories. One explanation for this is society's paradoxical view of children: "The concept of the child, from adult culture's point of view, is difficult to pin down. On the one hand a child is innocent, pure, and possesses innate wisdom. On the other hand, a child is, at the same time, wild, voracious, primitive, and in need of instruction: the tenets of Romanticism and Puritanism persist and coexist" (Daniel 2006:12).

5. Baker 1993:28.

6. Oswald 1995:136–138. Oswald unfortunately does not define children's realistic animal fiction, nor her parameters of analysis, so it is difficult to know precisely which body of literature she is analyzing.

7. Hausman 1999:1.

8. Woloy 1990:37.

9. Houston 2005:282.

10. Reynolds 2007:5.

11. Melson 2001:55.

12. Shepard 1996:62.

13. Shepard 1996:63–64.

14. McKay 1998:5.

15. McKay 1998:58 (emphasis in original).

16. Melson 2001:154.

17. French Koller 1999:1.

18. French Koller 1999:41–42.

19. French Koller 1999:71.

20. Oswald argues that in children's realistic animal stories about dogs there is "a devaluing of animal life, or a valuing of human life above animal life," which she believes is the result of "the frequent occurrence of animal deaths and the infrequent occurrence of human deaths" (Oswald 1995:139). I argue that upon closer examination of dog stories, the canine characters are actually portrayed as superior to humans, both in the estimate of child characters and by the portrayal of adult authors.

21. Hall 1973:49.

22. Stolz 1960:18.

23. Stolz 1960:73.

24. Hall 1973:44–45.

25. Hall 1973:45.

26. Hesse 1994:3.

27. Hesse 1994:60–62.

28. Stolz 1960:81.

29. Stolz 1960:81 (emphasis in original).

30. Hesse 1994:32.

31. Stolz 1960:184.

32. Stolz 1960:133 (emphasis in original).

33. Hall 1973:90–91.

34. Hall 1973:91.

35. Hall 1973:78, 91.

36. Seth 1999:177.

37. Garber 1996:15.

38. Little 1985:1.

39. Little 1985:6.

40. DiCamillo 2000:60.

41. Little 1985:1.

42. Little 1985:2.

43. Little 1985:8.

44. Little 1985:8.
45. McKay 1994:11.
46. DiCamillo 2000:13.
47. Little 1985:8.
48. DiCamillo 2000:21.
49. DiCamillo 2000:21.
50. Little 1985:62.
51. Little 1985:82.
52. McKay 1994:55.
53. Little 1985:82.
54. DiCamillo 2000:166–168.
55. DiCamillo 2000:176.
56. Wolfelt 2004:73.
57. Armbruster 2002:353–354.
58. Armbruster 2002:375–376.
59. Armbruster 2002:375–376
60. Melson 2001:150 (emphasis in original).
61. Shepard 1996:4.

References

Armbruster, Karla. 2002. "'Good Dog': The Stories We Tell About Our Canine Companions and What They Mean for Humans and Other Animals." *Papers on Language and Literature* 38, no. 4 (Fall): 351–377.

Baker, Steve. 1993. *Picturing the Beast: Animals, Identity, and Representation.* Manchester and New York: Manchester University Press and St. Martin's Press.

Daniel, Carolyn. 2006. *Voracious Children: Who Eats Whom in Children's Literature.* New York: Routledge.

DiCamillo, Kate. 2000. *Because of Winn-Dixie.* Cambridge, MA: Candlewick.

Eliade, Mircea. 1964. *Shamanism: Archaic Techniques of Ecstasy.* Princeton, NJ: Princeton University Press.

French Koller, Jackie. 1999. *The Promise.* New York: Scholastic.

Garber, Marjorie. 1996. *Dog Love.* New York: Simon & Schuster.

Hall, Lynn. 1973. *To Catch a Tartar.* Chicago: Follet.

Hausman, Gerald and Loretta Hausman. 1999. *Dogs of Myth: Tales from Around the World.* New York: Simon and Schuster.

Hesse, Karen. 1994. *Sable.* New York: Scholastic.

Houston, Pam. 2005. *Sight Hound.* New York: W. W. Norton.

Leach, Maria. 1961. *God Had a Dog: Folklore of the Dog.* New Brunswick, NJ: Rutgers University Press.

Little, Jean. 1985. *Lost and Found.* Toronto: Viking.

McKay, Hilary. 1994. *Dog Friday.* London: Aladdin.

——. 1998. *Dolphin Luck*. New York: Margaret McElderry Books.

Melson, Gail. 2001. *Why the Wild Things Are: Animals in the Lives of Children*. Cambridge, MA: Harvard University Press.

Nodelman, Perry and Mavis Reimer. 2003. *The Pleasures of Children's Literature*, 3rd ed. Boston: Allyn and Bacon.

Oswald, Lori Jo. 1995. "Heroes and Victims: The Stereotyping of Animal Characters in Children's Realistic Animal Fiction." *Children's Literature in Education* 26, no. 2: 135–149.

Reynolds, Kimberley. 2007. *Radical Children's Literature: Future Visions and Aesthetic Transformations in Juvenile Fiction*. London: Palgrave.

Seth, Vikram. 1999. *An Equal Music*. Toronto: McArthur & Co.

Shepard, Paul. 1996. *The Others: How Animals Made Us Human*. Washington, DC: Island Press.

Stolz, Mary. 1960. *A Dog on Barkham Street*. New York: Harper & Row.

Wolfelt, Alan. 2004. *When Your Pet Dies: A Guide to Mourning, Remembering and Healing*. Fort Collins, CO: Companion Press.

Woloy, Eleanora M. 1990. *The Symbol of the Dog in the Human Psyche: A Study of the Human-Dog Bond*. Wilmette, IL: Chiron.

seven

The Making of a Wilderness Icon

Green Fire, Charismatic Species, and the Changing Status

of Wolves in the United States

Gavin Van Horn

JUST WEEKS BEFORE VOTERS WENT TO THE POLLS IN OCTOBER 2004, they were presented with a presidentially approved advertisement that was notable for its use of animal imagery. The advertisement opened with a bird's-eye view of dense woods, then quickly cut to a series of images with wolves shifting furtively in the undergrowth as a female voiceover intoned, "In an increasingly dangerous world, even after the first terrorist attack on America, John Kerry and the liberals in Congress voted to slash America's intelligence operations." The penultimate camera shot—before President Bush was shown on the phone giving his approval for the advertisement—included a group of wolves at the forest's edge who rose and moved toward the viewer while the disembodied voice concluded, "And weakness attracts those who are waiting to do America harm."[1]

Had the advertisement been aired during Dwight Eisenhower's campaign, when television first became a popular medium for presidential advertisements, it would have raised few eyebrows. However, in the span of fifty years the status and iconographic significance of wolves had changed dramatically, making this advertisement objectionable to many.[2] Relying upon wolves to symbolically embody the threat of terrorism is no longer as simple as it was in the past, when popular labels for wolves included terms like "outlaws," "bootleggers," "cattle rustlers," or low-caste "varmints."[3]

By way of contrast, a very different image of wolves achieved some notoriety in January 1998 when a snapshot was taken of a wolf that had just been released into the Apache National Forest of eastern Arizona (figure 7.1). This release initiated the federal reintroduction of Mexican gray wolves (*Canis lupus baileyi*), a subspecies of gray wolf that had come perilously close to extinction. For those who supported reintroduction efforts, the wolf in this photograph— called the "posterwolf" because of the wide distribution and popularity of the image—represented the fruits of a twenty-year effort.[4] For some, including Bobbie Holaday, the founder of the Arizona-based wolf advocacy group Preserve Arizona's Wolves (P.A.W.S.), the experience was more than one of ecological import; it was also confirmation of a renewed ontological order. She described the moment as "one of those times when you just want to exclaim, 'God's in His Heaven; all's right with the world.'"[5]

The Bush "Wolves" advertisement and the posterwolf call attention to the

FIGURE 7.1. A wolf that had just been released into the Apache National Forest of eastern Arizona, 1998. Photo by George Andrejko, Arizona Game and Fish Department.

multiple and contradictory images of animals that continue to be presented to the American public. Wolves have been a critical species for representing conflicting claims about human relationships to the lands of the United States, serving as the "other" to be reviled or championed—an icon of threat and disorder to some and beauty and harmony to others. It is my contention that at stake in the competing iconographic significance of wolves is the construction and reconstruction of human identity in relation to the larger biotic community. Popular wolf iconography is not only a matter of politics or science, but also a powerful expression of the perceived natural order. In relation to human understandings of animality, wolves have featured prominently. Conceived negatively, this understanding of animality has been used to condemn wolves while legitimating human control and killing of wolves. More recently, however, animality has been conceived of in more positive terms,[6] and wolves have been looked to as beacons of the wild spirit that humans have forsaken in their rush to tame the forces that sustain biotic processes. Understanding the historical contexts that made such different meanings possible can shed light on the ways in which people continue to utilize other animals, especially large predator animals like wolves, to express their sense of the human place in nature.

Wolf Iconography

> The representation is one thing, and that which it represents is another.
> —St. John of Damascus, Third Discourse in Defense of the Holy Icons[7]

Images of animals and the narratives and various experiential associations attached to them are often powerful tools to advertise allegiance and affirm a sense of moral territory. The use of such images may collectively contribute to an iconic role for any given animal: a means for people to think about their lives and communities, ostensibly with greater precision and clarity.[8] Similar to the way a religious icon directs and focuses an adherent's attention, aiding the viewer in contemplating something beyond the icon itself, so too have wolves become an icon for many persons, representing much more than the animals themselves.[9] Religious studies scholar David Chidester, in his analysis of the relationships between religion and popular culture, provides a helpful definition of icons that I will rely upon here: icons, he argues, are ordinary objects that are nonetheless transformed into "extraordinary magnets of meaning with a religious cast . . . [for which] the term *religion* seems appropriate because it signals a certain quality of attention, desire, and even reverence for sacred materiality."[10]

Indeed, the profound emotions and imaginative associations that wolves stir for many Americans make their images significant "magnets of meaning." I suggest that there are three primary reasons that the term "icon" is a valuable way to spotlight the significance of wolves in the public imagination. First, the term is heuristically valuable for analyzing the ways in which wolves function as a source and lure of meaning for various constituencies, particularly in focusing people's attention on issues beyond wolves' immediate physical presence (e.g., land management, government intervention, ethical obligations to nondomestic species). Moreover, the term captures the religious or quasi-religious qualities that people attribute to wolves, based upon valuations of wolves either as a species of sacred value (often tied to understandings of "nativism") or as a profane species (a "deviant misfit" with nefarious intention). Finally, as the title of this chapter indicates, wolves have consistently been associated with the notion of wilderness and oftentimes serve as an icon of wildness, along with its many extra-ordinary connotations such as freedom, authenticity, and untamed spirit.

The controversial status of wolves is embedded in a rich and significant shift in public perceptions of animals in America, particularly predator animals that were and are believed to conflict with human interests. Once one of the most vilified animals in North America (their association with thievery, cunning, malfeasance, and bloodlust led to their near eradication from the continental United States), during the latter decades of the twentieth century wolves came to be valued by many as a signifier of ecological holism and as the paradigmatic symbol of wilderness.[11] This iconographic significance is far from settled, but by observing how various groups of people have selectively narrowed the way in which wolves *should* be perceived, we gain perspective about how a number of people in the United States conceive of their relationships to animal others and to the lands that together they attempt to co-inhabit.[12]

On the Other Side of the Fence

The iconic pedigree of wolves has deep historical roots. From the colonial period until the early twentieth century, the fate of wolves and the meanings assigned to them were imaginatively tethered to landscapes that were considered to be in need of the pacifying hand of civilization. Wilderness, wolves, and beastliness formed an unholy symbolic triumvirate that reinforced the colonizing and domesticating missiology of early European settlers.[13]

In the narratives and rituals of many Native American societies that depended on coordinated hunting as a means of subsistence, wolves were often
recognized as positive examples of familial loyalty, paragons of physical endur-
ance, and beings of great intelligence.[14] By way of contrast, a wealth of folklore
and pastoral and agrarian-influenced religious metaphors crossed the Atlantic
with various European peoples, preparing them to view the "new world"
through the mythologies they had inherited from the old. In these European
mythologies, wolves were overwhelmingly endowed with a negative symbolic
mystique.[15] Forced to dwell beyond the boundaries of cultivated lands, wolves
became transgressors when they crossed the lines meant to keep them "in their
place," threatening human dominance, security, property, and domestic animals valued for their utility.[16] The transgression could go the other way, too:
some believed humans could slip back into a degenerate, wild condition, cor-
rupted by the wilderness and its savage inhabitants.[17]

Even as other animals began to receive attention as subjects of benevolent religious and ethical concern beginning in the mid-nineteenth century, wolves remained imaginatively confined to realms too unwholesome for empathy. Wolves,
it seemed, were not innocent enough, nor did they have the genteel manners that
America's middle-class wished to see reflected in their animal charges.[18]

As American wildlife that once seemed abundant became visibly imperiled,
however, some people began to focus their attention on conserving wild species. Limited protections for "game animals"—protections meant to conserve
animal populations for perpetual hunting or scientific study—received particular attention. Because of the politically well-positioned figures who supported this effort, some of the first lands set aside for conservation purposes
were the product of these concerns.[19] Despite these early calls for animal protection and conservation, *predator animals* remained ensconced in the category
of the unworthy. Wolves in particular continued to represent the epitome of
the "bad" animal, a quintessential varmint with neither sporting manners nor
moral qualms about their "violent" acts. As one early Coloradan put it, if
nothing were done to quell wolves' eating habits, the plains were likely to re-
vert back to their former condition, "a howling wilderness with a vengeance."[20]
As in New England, wolves were a despised villain and their howls a reminder
of what humans had yet to subdue.

Although early colonists relied largely on biblical metaphors to justify
wolf killing, by the late nineteenth and early twentieth centuries there were
additional ideological claims added to such providential sources. With un-
apologetic disdain for both wolves and indigenous nations, wolf hunter Ben
Corbin reasoned in his book *Corbin's Advice or the Wolf Hunter's Guide* (1900),

"I can not believe that Providence intended that these rich lands . . . should forever be monopolized by wild beasts and savage men. I believe in the survival of the fittest. . . . The wolf is the enemy of civilization, and I want to exterminate him."[21] This blend of Social Darwinism and Manifest Destiny combined to form a powerful brew of human hubris that spread from the imagination to the landscape, where wolves and native communities were targeted for the perceived affront they posed to American economic progress. Wolf deaths were often gruesome affairs: wolves were roped and then dragged behind horses, they were poisoned and suffered prolonged death throes from strychnine, they were hamstrung by hunters and farmers who then used trained dogs to tear them apart, they were lured into swallowing meaty baits with hooks inside of them, and whole litters of their pups were "denned."[22]

Influenced by the interests of Western livestock ranchers and increasing federal power in Western land management, the bureaucratization of wolf control proved an efficient means to obtain the desired goal of "intensive organized effort until the last animal [wolf] is taken."[23] As early as 1907, the U.S. Biological Survey (USBS) provided pamphlets for distribution that detailed the most effective ways to kill wolves; by 1915, the USBS acquired congressional funding and responsibility for the task; by 1928, 500 men were employed by the USBS for predator control.[24]

With dramatic license that reflects the ideological milieu of that time, the *Rocky Mountain News* described this government-sponsored mission against wolves and other wild animals in Manichean terms, an ultimate contest between good and evil:

> NOT YET is the wilderness won. Grim, relentless, trammeled, yet untamed, the spirit of nature battles against encroaching civilization. . . . Mighty in its untutored majesty is the out-of-doors, but mightier is man. . . . Man's progress is ever onward, forward. He is impeded, never stopped.
>
> The history of civilization is written in terms of its struggle against enemies. Thru immemorial aeons there have been forces to contend against—forces which have threatened at times to overcome even the ever-conquering deity which is the spirit of man.[25]

In the nineteenth and early twentieth centuries, the fate of wolves was yoked to a larger national project to make the United States secure for domestic animals, safe for domestic crops, and well-stocked with the maximum number of "desirable" species. Ideas about American "progress" demanded enfleshment, and wolves' bodies were used to visually illustrate an achievement of progress that still remained uncertain. The displacement and then display of wolf carcasses and other predators offered visual confirmation of the conquest over the "untamed" and the "uncivilized," insinuating that if indeed the wilderness was "not yet won," then the wait would not be long (figures 7.2 and 7.3).

As an icon of wilderness, wolves were the savage other that defied by their very presence the ambition to remake the American landscape in conformity to human interests. At stake, as figure 7.2 indicates, was the "control" of the land and notions of human identity as nature's rightful manager. The defeat of wolves was constructed as a victory for humans under the assumption that wolves and humans were incompatible species.

Significantly, the latter photograph (figure 7.3), taken during the waning stages of wolf eradication efforts, openly links wolf (and coyote) deaths with another American icon: the automobile. The car, and its association with speed, convenience, and the "progress" of roads into areas once inaccessible, here serves also as a trophy display of those animals that stood in the way of such "civilized" amenities.

FIGURE 7.2. U.S. Biological Survey predator-control exhibit, 1926. Denver Public Library, Western History Collection. A sign on the back display wall reads: "Conservation, Utilization and Control of Wildlife."

FIGURE 7.3. Animal carcasses on an automobile, between 1919 and 1929. Denver Public Library, Western History Collection. Stamped on back of photoprint: "If this picture is used in any manner for publicity purposes, please see that proper credit is given to the Bureau of Biological Survey."

These photographs, and numerous others like them, offered visual confirmation of the defeat of one icon (wolves/wilderness/nature) and its replacement by another (car/civilization/culture). Visual culture scholar David Morgan calls such ritualized displays "soft iconoclasm," an act or series of acts in which "the image is not physically destroyed but redeployed as an example of a new and decidedly negative taxonomic classification."[26] Though writing about the context of colonial Peru, Morgan makes a point about iconoclasm that holds for those who sought to "win the West":

> The idea was to mount a spectacle, a theatrical staging of violence that would enact an ideological transfiguration of the past. . . . It was an effective, memorable, and brutal means of publicly dethroning one image or symbol and replacing it with another. As such violence marked the end or death of one regime and heralded the triumph of a new order.[27]

The replacement of native fauna with domestic stock in the West was never a fait accompli; it was an act of "soft iconoclasm" that required continuous exertion. By hanging the skins of wolves on fences, displaying them in government-sponsored dioramas, or draping them over an automobile, ranchers and federal employees were advertising and reinforcing the boundaries that they sought to establish. Wolf skins and carcasses were used to give physical heft to those ideological boundaries. The effectiveness of such boundary-making efforts was starkly realized in state after state in the twentieth century: Arkansas had its last wolf killed in 1928; Washington and Wyoming in 1940; Colorado in 1945; Oregon in 1947; Texas and New Mexico in 1970; and Arizona in 1976. In many of these places, an effective breeding population had been absent since the mid-1920s, many decades prior to these last deaths.

Wolves were not the only predator animals targeted for extermination in the United States. Bears, mountain lions, coyotes, and innumerable "nontarget" animals that were victims of the liberal use of poisons were extirpated from parts of their historic range by the first decades of the twentieth century. Animals that "preyed" on agricultural profit margins, like prairie dogs, birds, and insects, also provoked government involvement. Underlying such exterminations was a pervasive moral anthropology that, Darwinian assertions to the contrary, humans were different not only in degree but in kind from other animals. The fate of wolves was a shared one, a piece of a larger national project. Unlike most of their nondomestic animal kin, however, wolves were largely unable to survive the control efforts of government agents.[28]

Green Fire and Thinking Like a Mountain

Yet in the midst of these last deaths, and even because of them, increasing numbers of Americans were beginning to doubt the supposed need for landscapes divested of predator animals like wolves. Wolves continued to be associated with wilderness, but with the separation incurred by a rapidly urbanizing America a new set of values began to intrude upon the old, transforming the associations that were attached to wilderness and bestowing a positive value upon both uncultivated lands and the undomesticated creatures that most concretely represented these lands. An ecologically motivated movement for landscapes with a full complement of native species began to take shape in the late 1960s. At this critical juncture, one story above all others captured the imaginations of Americans who were more willing than ever to regard wolves as a symbol of loss instead of danger.

Aldo Leopold's essay "Thinking Like a Mountain," though only modestly appreciated upon its initial release in *A Sand County Almanac* (1949), eventually became a foundational reference point and inspiration for environmentalists, ecologists, ethicists, and many others.[29] It is no mistake that wolves were central to this short essay. Because wolves had long borne the brunt of animosity toward predators and other "useless" animals in the United States, they were also the ideal animal icon for symbolizing a possible sea-change in public sentiment.

In the essay, Leopold recollects his early days in the U.S. Forest Service, a time when he was young and "full of trigger itch." He describes how he and a group of colleagues were eating lunch above a river in eastern Arizona when their interest was piqued by what they thought was a doe fording the stream. They soon realized their mistake: below them, a mother wolf and her pups were greeting one another, oblivious to the government workers above. "In those days," Leopold reflected, "we had never heard of passing up a chance to kill a wolf. In a second we were pumping lead into the pack, but with more excitement than accuracy. . . . When our rifles were empty, the old wolf was down, and a pup was dragging a leg into impassable slide-rocks." When Leopold and his crew arrived, they bore witness to a "green fire" as it died in the mother wolf's eyes, a moment that impressed itself upon his memory and led him to reflect upon its deeper significance: "I thought that because fewer wolves meant more deer, that no wolves would mean hunters' paradise. But after seeing the green fire die, I sensed that neither the wolf nor the mountain agreed with such a view."[30]

This experience not only marked a change in Leopold's view of predator species, but also contributed to altering his view of the human place in the biotic community. In order to "think like a mountain," Leopold averred, one had to consider the wolf's integral role in the larger landscape. In the absence of natural predators, deer would denude the mountain, encouraging erosion that, if left unchecked, would degrade the entire ecosystem. "I now suspect," he wrote, "that just as a deer herd lives in mortal fear of its wolves, so does a mountain live in mortal fear of its deer."[31] The lesson Leopold drew from this, stated later in the book, was that humans have a great responsibility—not to assume a self-defeating "conqueror role" but to be merely a "plain member and citizen" of the biotic community.[32]

While there is little doubt that Leopold's reflections on "thinking like a mountain" were powerfully expressed, he was not the first to articulate a holistic understanding of earthen processes,[33] nor was he the first scientist to argue for tolerance toward predators.[34] One of the reasons Leopold remains an intriguing figure is that he was among those who existed on the threshold of changing land management policies, from managing undesirable individual species for the sake of improving desirable game animal numbers, to viewing all species as part of a larger land community in which each had a vital function.[35]

For Leopold, the eradication of wolves was a gut response, a too-quick effort to conform the land to the desires of a few. As he lamented, he had been an "accessory" to the wolf's destruction and therefore contributed to the dissolution of the wilderness: "Here my sin against the wolves caught up with me."[36]

Leopold effectively wedded scientific understandings of the natural world with an ethical mandate that proved a foundational source for the arguments of future conservation advocates, and, for many, he grounded holistic spiritual intuitions in empirical evidence. Unlike the wilderness advocates before him, Leopold had the science of ecology on his side, and thus his arguments were more persuasive. According to historian Roderick Nash, this made Leopold "the prophet of a new order," an order that included predators within its purview.[37]

The Green Fire Spreads

In the affluent and increasingly urban and suburban context of a post–World War II America, people were becoming more receptive to ideas like Leopold's, more willing to question the role of the government in "controlling" wildlife according to Progressive-era management philosophies, and more interested in visiting the wildlands that constituted America's "natural heritage" in order to see such creatures and escape the "artificiality" of citified existence.[38] The immediate threat of wolves, both real and perceived, had largely passed into legend. A trickle of disapproval from select scientists would turn into a flood of public sentiment. Wolves became the icon of choice to represent endangered species, ecologically threatened lands, and a new vision of the human that laid less emphasis on dominance over the nonhuman world.

The passage of the Endangered Species Act (ESA) in 1973 remains a legislative milestone, reflecting a rising public consciousness regarding animal extinction. It proved a pivotal turning point for wolves, which were listed soon after for protection.[39] With the Endangered Species Act, "The heart of Leopold's land ethic," writes Michael Robinson, "was partially written into federal law."[40] As discussions began about carrying out the mandate of the ESA, part of which is "to provide a means whereby the ecosystems upon which endangered species and threatened species depend may be conserved,"[41] wildlife and wilderness advocacy groups seized upon the high-profile image of wolves to advertise their causes.

The elevation of wolves as a species that was to be vigilantly protected often carried connotations of a larger hoped-for healing between Americans and the

natural world. Indeed, many people anticipated a resurrection of sorts, understanding wolves to pose a quintessential moral test as to whether humans
could coexist with large predators and thus with "wild" nature.

In 1995, the same year that wolves were reintroduced into portions of Idaho
and Yellowstone National Park, preeminent wolf biologist L. David Mech remarked that since the wolf had come to symbolize disappearing wilderness,
"the creature now symbolizes [all] endangered species and has become the
cause célèbre of numerous animal-interest groups," resulting in "wolf deification."[42] "Deification" may be a poetic flourish, but wolves certainly gained an
iconographic significance that was used to challenge conventional, extractive
ways of conceiving of human-land relationships. Wolf reintroduction represented
a confluence of interests—ecological, ethical, cultural, and even spiritual—with
a common unifying theme: if wolves could be "saved," or at least partially re-
stored to portions of their former historic habitat, then humans too might
discover ways of living that supported the flourishing of life rather than its
destruction.

Wild Animals with Green Fire

Leopold's "green fire" trope wended its way into environmental discourse as a
means of drawing attention to these issues.[43] By the early 1980s, a new movement in environmentalism had begun, and newly formed "radical" groups like
Earth First! unashamedly proclaimed an ideology based on ecological ideas
and reverence (sometimes worship) of the earth. Rallying around the motto
"no compromise in defense of Mother Earth," Earth First! brought together
activists who championed the protection of wild habitats and many who were
willing to engage in civil disobedience or illegal activities (ecotage/monkey-
wrenching) in order to curtail what was perceived as anthropocentric arrogance.[44] These activists' use of wolf narratives and imagery underscores how
the symbolic value of wolves shifted, for within the radical environmental
movement wolves represented the wild, primal forces that humans needed to
recover in order to "come to their senses" and better resist the industrial and
corporate forces that threatened to unweave the biotic fabric of life.

By the time Earth First! formed, *A Sand County Almanac* was well known
in conservationist circles. Dave Foreman, a co-founder and charismatic leader
in the budding radical environmental movement, became one of Leopold's
foremost evangelizers. According to social ethicist Bron Taylor, for radical

environmentalists Leopold's "green fire" experience "evolved into a mythic moral fable in which the wolf communicates with human beings, stressing interspecies kinship [and became] a symbol of life in the wild, incorporated into the ritual of the tradition . . . with the idea that an authentic human life is lived wildly and spontaneously in defense of Mother Earth."[45] For Foreman, who often wove his own dramatic revision of Leopold's "Thinking Like a Mountain" into his folksy orations, the howl of a wolf awakened a larger human need. He asserted, for example:

> The wolf's howl is the cry of defiant contempt. But it's also something more. It's the cry of joy, of pleasure in being alive. No matter how bad it gets, it's wonderful to be alive on earth. . . . No matter how depressed we get, how angry, we still have to be full of joy, happiness. That's what keeps us going. So, yeah, howl with contempt for adversity. Howl with defiance. But howl with joy, too. . . . Robots don't howl. But animals do. Free, wild animals with green fire.[46]

Such sentiments were complemented by many iconic illustrations in the *Earth First!* journal, as well as other radical environmental publications that contrasted the deadly impacts of industrial civilization to the freedom and authenticity represented by wild wolves. In the image in figure 7.4, the juxtaposition of an industrially polluted, mechanized world and a thriving, yet threatened wilderness is mediated by the dying wolf, who represents the death of liberty itself, as the caption indicates: "Hear the warning." The image visually echoes Foreman's speech, rejecting the anthropocentrism of the industrial human ("Robots don't howl") while appealing to wolves as paragons of authentic ecological and spiritual virtue ("But animals do"). Similar themes were evoked in other images, with wolves as the chosen figure to represent the death or near-death of the wild in order to stoke the consciences of viewers (figure 7.5).

For radical environmentalists, however, wolves were not just representatives of the natural world's victimization and exploitation. More fancifully, renegade wolves who thwarted the minions of development were also popular icons in radical environmental publications (figures 7.6 and 7.7). Depictions of wolves howling in triumph atop an overturned bulldozer and loping away from the scene of their monkeywrenching exploits conform to a type of animal imagery that critical theorist Steve Baker dubs "vengeance cartoons," in which animals "turn the tables on the society which so readily marginalizes them,"[47]

FIGURE 7.4. "As Wolves Die . . .," in Graybill (ed.), *Beware! Sabotage! Black Cat Manual* (Eugene, OR: Unknown, 1996), 16.

FIGURE 7.5. "Do you understand . . . ?," in Graybill (ed.), *Beware! Sabotage! Black Cat Manual* (Eugene, OR: Unknown, 1996), 9.

FIGURE 7.6. Artist: Brush Wolf; *Earth First!* 8, no. 5 (May 1, 1988), back cover.

FIGURE 7.7. Artist: TWASHMAN; *Earth First!* 10, no. 2 (December 21, 1989), back cover.

and "the values of the dominant culture are undermined."[48] For radical environmentalists, such images, complemented by the view that the wild is the true home of all biological life, reinforced their biocentric beliefs that "wild" human and nonhuman animals were justified in resisting industrial development that threatened sacred wilderness areas.[49] Throughout the 1980s, such ideas were actively promoted through "Green Fire Roadshows," in which activists and musicians traveled the country in order to spread this message.[50]

Especially during the 1990s, the interests of those within the radical environmental movement came to include broader issues such as corporate globalization, solidarity with third-world peoples, and anarchist social philosophy, but wolves' images remained potent icons of resistance, as evidenced on the covers of the twentieth (2000) and twenty-fifth (2005) anniversary editions of the *Earth First!* journal, where wolves are prominently featured. Many radical environmentalists believe that attentiveness to the needs of these and other threatened animals can encourage deeper environmental and metaphysical interconnection, as well as lead to direct resistance on their behalf.[51] Critical to such perceptions is the supposition that humans are not biologically, or even morally, superior to other animals. Thus, the decentering of humans as environmentally omniscient that Leopold described in the story of his wolf epiphany has been adopted and extended within the radical environmental milieu as part of a larger social critique—and wolves have become a primary icon in representing what radical activists believe to be the profound disconnect between humans and their environments.

Conserving Green Fire

This feeling, of course, is not confined to radical environmental activists. Since the 1970s, one of the sources from which both radical and more mainstream environmentalists have drawn a great deal of their ecological information has been the field of conservation biology. Conservation biology is marked by a strong sense of urgency, a product of these scientists' feelings that natural systems are being compromised globally by human abuses. Though conservation biologists generally have been more cautious about announcing their personal values than nonscientists have, in many ways conservation biologists follow in the tradition of Leopold, who in the latter years of his life was explicit about the obligation he believed scientists had to inform the public not just with quantitative data but with an "ecological education" that induced a sense of wonder regarding evolutionary processes.

Part of the mission of conservation biologists has been to promote ideas about biodiversity, and one key to conceptualizing biodiversity has been to draw attention to animals that are considered "strongly interacting species" in order to highlight their critical contributions to ecosystem resiliency.[52] Wolves have received attention in this respect, since they influence the numbers of herbivores, like elk, moose, and deer, whose population densities can impact vegetation, significantly degrading the habitat needs of other species.[53] Beyond their physical charisma, wolves are thus looked to as ecological indicators, a top predator whose presence is likely to enhance species diversity. In the long term, conservation biologists are interested in preserving evolutionary processes, but they rely on the iconic appeal of certain species to inform the public about larger issues regarding biodiversity.

There is more to conservation biology than ecological arguments, however. Scientists like Michael Soulé and Reed Noss, for example, contend that "by insuring the viability of large predators, we restore the subjective, emotional essence of the 'wild' or wilderness."[54] Wolves, in other words, are not merely an ecological artifact; when wolves are absent, possible subjective connections to the land, as well as biodiverse environments, are impoverished. Wolves, in this sense, are a window through which to think about what ecologically rich landscapes demand of humans, for though large carnivores can be "politically troublesome," anything less than their restoration is a "betrayal to the land."[55]

Wildlife conservation and restoration groups, such as the Wildlands Project, the Rewilding Institute, the Center for Biological Diversity, WildEarth Guardians, and Defenders of Wildlife,[56] have been heavily influenced by conservation biologists whose work they have drawn upon to advocate for the establishment, protection, and restoration of large wilderness areas and endangered species.[57] Because of their high profile as an endangered species, wolves have become a "political animal" in the more literal sense of the phrase, an effective and affective means of putting a nonhuman face to these conservation efforts.

How to Manage Green Fire? The Dilemmas of Wolf Reintroduction

The meanings assigned to wolves, despite their recent celebrity status, remain unstable and contested. The presence (or threat of the potential presence) of wolves in the American landscape continues to represent a host of competing values. As the iconic associations people have with wolves meet the practical realities of coexisting with them—realities that are shared unequally between those who dwell near reintroduction sites and those who do not—difficult questions arise over what human-created boundaries are appropriate for an icon of wildness.

For some, wolf restoration efforts signal a willingness to accept a humbler human role as part of the larger biotic community. Trish Stevenson, Aldo

Leopold's granddaughter, expressed this well when she addressed a small crowd that was present to witness the release of Mexican gray wolves into the Blue Range Wilderness Area in January 1998. "It was the land of his first job," Stevenson said, referring to Leopold's early work in the Apache National Forest (the forest in which the Blue Range is located), "where he fully learned what wild country was and where the binding power between landscape and mind became an irrepressible factor in his life." She continued:

> The mountain and the wolf showed him something new, that the Earth is here not only for the use of people, but also that the Earth is a whole organism. . . . The wolf reintroduction program is part of rebuilding the organism. . . . Thanks for returning the "green fire" to the mountain.[58]

If Stevenson was correct, then human self-understanding had shifted: humans were now less defined by their ability to master and more by their ability to rebuild "nature." Being human was still defined by an ability to control the lives of other animals—a striking constant—but what this control meant (for other animals and the imagination of the human) was transformed.

Not everyone shared Stevenson's sentiments. Especially in the areas most impacted by wolf recovery efforts, challenges to wolf reintroduction have been consistent and oftentimes acrimonious. The fears that people express are not always directly related to potential livestock losses. One common sentiment is that wolf reintroduction represents a federal ploy to divest private-property owners of their land. People who feel this way often ask: Why should the psychological burdens and economic costs of wolf reintroduction be borne most directly by those who are least supportive of these introductions? Wolf advocates counter: Why should the public bear the ecological costs of a landscape absent of predators, particularly when government subsidies support the livestock industry?[59] Behind these arguments are not only economic interests but also competing visions of the relationship between humans and the larger biotic community.

One advertisement that offers a vivid example of the stakes involved for wolves amidst such reintroduction controversy is worth dwelling on here, especially in contrast to previous photographs (figures 7.2 and 7.3). The Center for Biological Diversity (CBD) has been heavily involved in wolf reintroduction efforts, and its publications have consistently pointed out what those at the CBD consider the dubious actions of the livestock industry. In an advertisement printed in the *New York Times* (figure 7.8), the CBD accused the livestock industry of being "unwilling to share even a tiny portion of America's vast public lands," noting especially what it believed were the frivolous lawsuits

FIGURE 7.8. Center for Biological Diversity, advertisement in the New York Times, 1999. The full advertisement is available at http://www.biologicaldiversity.org/swcbd/activist/images/wolf .pdf (accessed August 26, 2011).

of cattle associations and the more serious threats of some ranchers to shoot wolves on sight.

The image and the accompanying text (all of which is not shown in figure 7.8) place before the viewer a scene of violence. Comparing this image with figures 7.2 and 7.3, one can discern that their themes have been reversed. Whereas the wolves hung as trophies in the 1920s were intended to reinforce the "just" cause of ranchers in protecting "innocent" livestock, in the CBD advertisement viewers are provoked to ask why an "innocent" wolf was unjustly shot and why the perpetrators of this violence had not yet been punished for their misdeeds.

In both cases, the carcasses of wolves are used to give concrete weight to abstract ideas about policy, justice, ethics, and, ultimately, humanity. In figures 7.2 and 7.3, wolves are "sacrificed" (justly, it is implied) for the teleological good of American progress; they visually substantiate this abstract notion. In the CBD advertisement, the broken wolf body serves a very different function, with the accompanying text explicitly accusing the perpetrator of murder. The wolf has become the "pure" animal that has been defiled, and the criminals are those who abuse the land for ill-gained profit. Using iconographic language, one might say that the CBD advertisement depicts an act of violent iconoclasm, except the image denotes not a victory cry, but a lament over the failed protections that allowed for the destruction of this iconic animal. At the same time, the advertisement condemns what is considered a regressive human unwillingness to accept a role as "plain member and citizen" of the land community, as Leopold envisioned.

From these contrasting images (figures 7.2, 7.3, and 7.8), similar in their subject matter but vastly different in their connotations, one gains a sense not only of the possible difficulties in reintroducing wolves to areas from which they have been eliminated, but also of the differences between what various groups consider proper human interaction with the natural world. On the one hand, for those in favor of wolf reintroduction, wolves, as the essence of "wildness," provide an opportunity to "redress past mistakes," as one U.S. Fish & Wildlife Service fact sheet put it (USFWS 1995), and their presence is tangible confirmation that humans, as Trish Stevenson averred, are learning that they are only one part of a greater Earth organism. On the other hand, resistance to wolf reintroduction is defended as protecting local interests and rural communities, but is equally a defense of a different, more dominance-oriented understanding of the human being.[60]

Frequently caught in the political crossfire are government employees responsible for carrying out the mandate of the Endangered Species Act. Wildlife and wilderness advocates, like cattle ranchers and sportsmen before them, appeal to the power of Washington to enforce a new set of values and a new set of boundaries. Yet because the movements of wolves continue to be constrained by bureaucratic orders, those who associate wolves with the essence of wildness find invasive management practices difficult to accept.[61] Doug Honnold, an attorney for the Sierra Club Legal Defense fund, writes:

We have the mediagenic Fish & Wildlife Service translocation effort, heralded in virtually every newspaper and television station in the country. The images, as we have seen today, are the images of wolves captured, wolves darted, wolves translocated, and wolves set "free" by man. Big government moving chess pieces on the land. I can't help but wonder whether this is nothing but another variation of the human desire to control nature that led—in an earlier incarnation—to the extirpation of the wolf from the western landscape.[62]

Others place the blame on the public's shoulders more generally, lamenting that humans are not able to live with unmanaged wolves, and have settled for what writer Charles Bowden has called a "Robo Wolf."[63] For critics, such intensive management is an adulteration of wolves' wildness and a reflection of an inability to accept the presence of other creatures on their own terms.[64] Wolves, once fenced out of domestic spaces as undesirables, are currently fenced in, so to speak, by the boundaries of their recovery zones, which raises serious questions for some people about whether ideologies are truly changing or if wolf management is merely a more benign alternative to a long-standing theme of human dominion.

Wolf reintroductions have revealed that the meanings assigned to wolves are frequently incompatible, as they collide and refract through various iconographic prisms. As political scientist Martin Nie suggests, the debate over these reintroductions drives home the point that wolves are not merely an ecological or economic problem; they are a democratic problem, exposing power differentials related to variant views about how humans "fit" in nature.[65]

Concluding Remarks: Reflecting on Green Fire

> A deep chesty bawl echoes from rimrock to rimrock, rolls down the mountain, and fades into the far blackness of the night. It is an outburst of wild defiant sorrow, and of contempt for all the adversities of the world.
> —Aldo Leopold, *A Sand County Almanac*[66]

Ed Bangs, a U.S. Fish & Wildlife Service biologist deeply involved in Yellowstone reintroduction efforts, once noted, "Wolves and their management have almost nothing to do with reality, which makes working on any wolf issue hard on biologists, who are trained as scientists and not as psychologists."[67] No doubt Bangs meant that very little of the rhetoric about wolves turns out to be about the biology of wolves. However, far from having "nothing to do with reality," the complaints that various constituencies raise have everything to do with perceptions of reality that have very real impacts. This is why icons—their construction, their destruction, and their strategic deployment—remain important tools as imaginative markers of identity and shapers of public perception.

In the history of the United States, the presence of wolves often defined the boundary between the "civilized" (i.e., settlement, ranches, domesticated animals and landscapes) and the "wild" (i.e., indigenous communities, nondomesticated animals and lands). The presence of fewer wolves was taken as a sign of economic and moral progress. Today it is increasingly the case that more wolves (not fewer) are believed to signify moral progress, a sign of humans' coming to terms with animals in a non- (or neo-) dominionist manner, even recognizing the "intrinsic worth" of animals that were once despised as useless or evil. Wolf eradication and reintroduction reveals a set of very tangible efforts to inscribe these values on animal bodies and the American landscape.

Perhaps there is something of value to be learned about wolf iconography from the traditional usage of religious icons. Though crafted to mediate a transcendent reality, religious icons also were intended to offer opportunities for personal introspection and self-critique. To meditate on the wolf is simultaneously to meditate on ourselves. It is possible that wolves may now bring people together to reflect upon both the future of their local communities and the biotic community as a whole. If so, the "green fire" that Leopold saw fading away may yet burn brightly.

Notes

1. To view the full advertisement, see "Historical Campaign Ad: Wolves (Bush/Cheney '04)," http://www.youtube.com/watch?v=MU4t9O (accessed November 15, 2010).

2. For a sample of objections to the advertisement, see Schlickeisen 2004; Estés 2005; Edward 2005. For an excellent analysis of animal imagery and its use to caricature "the enemy" while glorifying the "good guys," especially in wartime poster propaganda, see Baker 2001:33–48. For iconic material artifacts in the context of American civil religion, particularly in relation to "othering," see Morgan 2005:240–244.

3. For examples of the different negative labels applied to wolves, see Lopez 2004:137–199; Robinson 2005:150–162; Worster 1994:258–290.

4. This image has appeared in U.S. Fish and Wildlife Services (USFWS) literature and Arizona Game and Fish Department (AGFD) brochures on wolf reintroduction in the Southwest, as well as in the pamphlets of some wildlife advocacy groups. See, for example, the USFWS welcome page for Mexican wolf recovery, http://www.fws.gov/southwest/es/mexicanwolf/ (accessed November 15, 2010) and the cover of its brochure entitled "Mexican Gray Wolf: Restoration in the Southwest" (2004); the AGFD's Mexican wolf reintroduction and management Web page, http://www.azgfd.gov/w_c/es/wolf_reintroduction.shtml (accessed November 15, 2010); the Blue Range Primitive

Area topographic map, produced by the U.S. Forest Service (1998); and the cover of the Southern Rockies Wolf Restoration Project's trifold pamphlet "Restore the Balance, Return the Wolf!" (2000).

5. Holaday 2003:128.

6. See chapter 6 in this volume, by Michelle Superle, for an example of a positive conception of animality.

7. Quoted in Ouspensky and Lossky 1969:34.

8. See especially David Morgan's chapter "Defining Visual Culture" (Morgan 2005), which provides a nice overview of the scholarly twists and turns of visual studies, as well as his emphasis on the practice of seeing ("the ocular dimension of religion") as socially constructed though not reducible to such constructions.

9. The term "icon" is occasionally used in literature about wolves (e.g., Grambo 2005; Coleman 2004), though typically without sustained reflection about the term's connotations.

10. Chidester 2005:34.

11. Considerations of space in this article prevent me from detailing the debate over the concept of wilderness. Some scholars have argued that wilderness is a dangerous term, which creates socially oppressive or romantic dualisms linked to notions of human absence (Guha 1989; Cronon 1995). Others believe that the term is apt, since it evokes a sense of the proper humility required of humans who enter into biodiverse or sacred spaces that are relatively free of human impacts (Nash 2001; Foreman 2004). Still others distinguish between wilderness areas and the quality of wildness that is associated with them (Snyder 1990; Turner 1996; Shepard 1998:131–151). For edited volumes that provide detailed attention to these debates, see Soulé and Lease 1995; Callicott and Nelson 1998. I believe the term remains valuable for a number of reasons, not the least of which is that many people continue to use it in popular contexts to denote areas that they consider to be exceptional, whether for ecological or spiritual reasons, or both.

12. Wolves, like humans, are entwined in a network of relationships, only one of which has to do with our narrative and visual discourses about them. Though all experiences of wolves are mediated by cultural context and individual experience, wolves are obviously not *mere images*, nor are they fated to be bound by visual or narrative stereotypes—even if we receive a good deal of information about them through various media. Animals have agency that should not be ignored, even if—and perhaps because—we, as humans, are constantly reinterpreting the meanings of that agency. See Waldau (2006), who discusses the "eminently human challenge" of accessing "nonhuman realities," and Ingram (2000), who draws on philosopher Kate Soper's conception of "critical realism" to argue that there is a nonhuman nature that remains external to any human discourses about it and that "some social constructions of animal ethology are more accurate than others" (2000:x, 71–72).

13. When European explorers and settlers first landed on the shores of what would come to be known as America, one of the first things that was noticed was the potential

of the continent for their domestic stock, which foreshadowed important changes that would be enacted upon the New World landscape, as well the coming conflict between colonists, wolves, and domesticated animals. See, for example, Crosby 1972, especially pages 74–111; Gerbi 1985:50–54, 96; Anderson 2004.

14. For general information on Native American relationships with wolves, see Hampton 1997; Lopez 2004; Fritts et al. 2003; Grambo 2005. Deeper treatments of such relationships are more difficult to find, but Schlesier (1987) provides at least one well-detailed anthropological analysis of wolves within the larger ritual matrix of the proto-Cheyenne (Tsitsitsas), and Coleman (2004) offers interesting historical material about Algonquians in New England.

15. Of course, the pastoral culture of the early Israelites provided many potent animal metaphors that were picked up later by Jewish, Christian, and Muslim traditions. Especially important for the way in which wolves were conceived in Christian thought was the predominant animal image used to represent Jesus: the Lamb of God. "Innocent" lambs beset by wolves was a common metaphor to describe persecution in the early church (e.g., Matt. 7:15), and early Christians and Renaissance artists alike made use of such symbols in depicting the other on the prowl (Rowland 1973:161; Kienzle 2006:106–108).

16. For a classic treatment of the relationship between colonists, livestock, and Indians, see Cronon 1983; for more recent treatments of these relationships in New England, see Anderson 2004, as well as Coleman 2004, which focuses on wolves and also includes chapters on the Midwest and Mormon territory.

17. For excellent descriptions of aurally inspired fears of the "howling" wilderness see Nash 2001:16, 26, 32, 36, 62–63; also, for Puritan ambivalence and New World typologies, see Albanese 1990:35–40. For more positive representations of Puritan views about wilderness, see Gatta 2004. For the connection between human "savagery" and wolf-like behavior in colonial times, see Coleman 2004:31–32, 59, 62; Albanese 1990:34–35; for a philosophical treatment of the "beast within," see Midgley 1995:36–44.

18. Protection for animal species in general in the United States was a process of gradual extension that radiated outward from urban dwellings: first to domestic animals, later to certain aesthetically pleasing birds, then to larger charismatic mammals (Mighetto 1991; Dunlap 1988; cf. Thomas 1996). The wolf, however, would have to wait to receive such moral consideration. The first organizations in the United States that lobbied for animal protections, such as the Society for the Prevention of Cruelty to Animals, were focused primarily on the humane treatment of domestic and draft animals.

19. The Boone and Crockett Club, for example, was founded in 1887 by Theodore Roosevelt and others to promote honorable hunting practices and preserve the lands that hosted game animals that were of interest to hunters. John J. Audubon led the charge in bird preservation, and the Audubon Society, founded in his honor, became an influential organization in public policy. William T. Hornaday was another influen-

tial and tireless early twentieth-century wildlife advocate and scientist. He served as director of the New York Zoological Park, founded the American Bison Society, and authored several books that promoted his ideas regarding wildlife protection, including *Our Vanishing Wildlife* (1913). For these men, wolves were still a nuisance at best and a scourge in need of eradication at worst. Hornaday's comments can be taken as representative: "Of all the creatures in North America, none are more despicable than wolves"; they are "insatiable in appetite, a master of cunning and the acme of cruelty" and as a "four-footed fiend . . . wherever found, the proper course with a wild gray wolf is to kill it as quickly as possible" (1904:140–142).

20. Quoted in Robinson 2005:35.

21. Corbin 1995:123–24. Corbin further expounded upon his religious reasoning: "In Genesis we read that [Abraham] was rich in cattle, in silver and in gold—something like the ranchmen and stockmen of North Dakota. Indeed the pastoral life preceded every other profession. . . . In the New Testament, the parable of the Good Shepherd shines like a star. . . . Largely my life has been spent in protecting these flocks against the incursions of ravenous beasts of prey. I know it is but a step and the first step, which counts in the march of civilization. God made the country, but man made the town" (1995:123).

22. For details about these methods and their historical precedents, see Young and Goldman 1944:286–368; Brown 2002:31–108. For an interpretation of why such methods were used, see Lopez 2004.

23. Quoted in Brown 2002:63. For how this relates to the Progressive political movement as a social and moral campaign, see Worster 1994:262–274.

24. For an excellent historical study of the links between federal involvement and livestock associations of the West, and a detailed portrait of Stanley Young, the most influential early leader of the USBS, see Robinson 2005. Young (with co-author Arthur Carhart) penned some of the final "last stands" of the wolves that were brought to justice on his watch. Though traces of regret can be found in his writing, what he believed to be economically desirable ultimately trumped his occasionally more generous assessments of wolves, and he remained convinced that the wolf was "one hundred percent criminal" (Worster 1994:277).

25. Quoted in Robinson 2005:157–158.

26. Morgan 2005:129.

27. Morgan 2005:123–124.

28. In the lower forty-eight states, wolves continued to survive only in remote areas of Minnesota, largely due to migrating populations of wolves from Canada. Physiological and social factors account, in part, for wolves' inability to endure the eradication campaigns. For example, in comparison with coyotes, wolves have more specific prey needs and reproduce more slowly (for a nice summary of these adaptive discrepancies, see Coleman 2004:94, 184, 229). As Robinson puts it, wolves are "canny and adaptable but not omnipotent" (2005:103).

29. I cover some of Leopold's influences on environmentalism and ecology. For readers interested in the influence of Leopold on environmental ethics, the work of Baird Callicott is essential. Callicott taught the first environmental ethics class in 1971 and established the first academic program in environmental philosophy, and has written extensively on Leopold, including in books such as *Companion to a Sand County Almanac* (editor, 1987), *In Defense of the Land Ethic* (1989), *The River of the Mother of God and Other Essays* (1991, co-edited with Susan Fladler), and *Beyond the Land Ethic* (1999). Since the 1970s, the field of environmental ethics has blossomed, and Leopold's land ethic has provided the ethical and ecological pylons for subsequent construction. As of 1998, according to Michael Nelson, there were "4 environmental ethics journals, courses in environmental ethics taught at hundreds of universities and colleges throughout the world, various graduate programs specializing in environmental philosophy, 2 dozen anthologies in the area, 2 international societies for environmental ethics and philosophy, and thousands of articles and books on environmental ethics written by philosophers and nonphilosophers alike" (1998:742). Sophisticated treatments of the ethical factors involved in wildlife management are becoming more prevalent, and one can expect to see more work in this area as ethicists seek to call attention to and offer prescriptions for bridging the gaps between ideas, policy, and practice. For examples, see Jickling and Paquet 2005; Lynn 2006, 2002; Gore et al. 2011.

30. Leopold 1989:129–130.

31. Leopold 1989:130.

32. Leopold 1989:204.

33. See, for example, Clarence Glacken's encyclopedic tome *Traces on the Rhodian Shore: Nature and Culture in Western Thought from Ancient Times to the End of the Eighteenth Century* (1967). In a post-Darwinian context, Americans like popular turn-of-the-twentieth-century nature writer John Burroughs appealed to an "indwelling, mysterious power that physics or chemistry cannot analyze" as the driving force and connective tissue of evolutionary processes (Worster 1994:17). This unified vision of the natural world, later known as organicism, both influenced and was influenced by early twentieth-century ecologists (Worster 1994:17–21). Also worth noting is a book with which Leopold was familiar, Pyotr Ouspensky's *Tertium Organum* (1911), which proposed that the earth was "an entire organism." Fladler notes that it remains a mystery when and where Leopold first discovered Ouspensky's writings, but Ouspensky's organicism had a direct influence on Leopold as he attempted to piece together a conceptual framework for the ecological principles he saw at work in his field experience (see Fladler 1974:18).

34. The American Society of Mammalogists included several scientists that questioned government policies of predator extermination. Although most scientists did not object to predator control, they did seek to reign in the rush toward the complete elimination of predator species. One of the first arguments for selective control, as

opposed to indiscriminate killing, came from Yellowstone ranger Milton Skinner in 1924 (Skinner 1995:292–295).

35. In his sundry forestry positions in the southwestern United States (1909–1924), Leopold showed an aptitude for bringing together various constituencies for game protection under the same banner, but as a faithful forester of his time, part of his public outreach initially included a focus on "raising a fight on predatory animals" (Fladler 1974:13). From the mid-1930s, and especially toward the end of his life, Leopold increasingly began to question the breadth of human foresight in management decisions. For an excellent treatment of this topic, see Fladler 1974:36–75; Meine 1988. For a concise summary of Leopold's literary development and output, see Meine 1998.

36. Quoted in Fladler 1974:102.

37. Nash 2001:197. Nash suggests something deeper underlying the burgeoning wilderness movement by calling Leopold a prophet. Science may have helped frame wilderness arguments, but among wilderness advocates there was a motivation that went beyond scientific theory. This was indicated when Robert Marshall's father described his wilderness lobbying as "missionary work," when Leopold called wilderness preservation "an act of national contrition," and when Robert Sterling Yard claimed a "gospel of wilderness" among a core group of wilderness "believers" (Nash 2001:201, 199, 207). Wilderness was not a mere resource for these and other advocates; it was an ultimate reference point and a long-term baseline with which to compare degraded lands.

38. Such sentiments preceded Leopold, of course, most notably expressed in Henry David Thoreau's claim that a civilization's vitality was directly dependent on its root in "wildness" (2001 [1862]:225, 239), but this stream of thought became increasingly prominent in a rapidly industrializing America. For the relationship between urbanization, affluence, and the increased popularity of National Parks, see Nash 1970. See also Nash's emphasis on the importance of "scarcity value" in preserving wilderness areas (Nash 2001:xiv, 249), a value that applies in parallel fashion to wolves. For how Hollywood films incorporated such social changes in their storylines, even though most wild animal heroes reflected "sanitized" human values of "natural" benevolence and altruism, see Ingram 2000:69–136. on wolves in particular, see pages 102–113.

39. Nie (2003) provides a solid overview of how the ESA has been tested and modified because of wolf reintroduction efforts (see particularly pages 90–104, 119–123). See also Dunlap 1988:142–146, 152–154.

40. Robinson 2005:304.

41. Endangered Species Act 1973, Sec. 2b.

42. Mech 1995:271.

43. Leopold struggled for some time to find a publisher for *A Sand County Almanac*, and even after its posthumous publication in 1949, it took still longer for the book to receive acclaim. The book was rejected by three different publishers before Oxford University Press picked it up. Knopf's editors played with the idea of publishing the

book, but ultimately felt that it was "far from being satisfactorily organized" and that it was "unlikely to win approval from readers" (Meine 1998:704). They were correct—at least initially. The book went out of print in the mid-1950s. It was rediscovered in the 1960s as environmental issues became a growing concern.

44. "Ecotage" is a conjoining of the words "economic" and "sabotage," a neologism denoting extralegal actions that involve attempts to protect wild places and creatures. A little less fancy but no less common, "monkeywrenching" is a term used interchangeably with "ecotage" by radical environmentalists. Though there has always been considerable debate among radical environmentalists about the efficacy of illegal direct action tactics, radical environmentalists maintain that ecotage—in contrast to terrorism or ecoterrorism—is directed against inanimate objects or property and therefore should be considered nonviolent. For more on this subject, see Foreman and Haywood 2002:1–16; Foreman 1991:119–143.

45. Foreman 1991:260.

46. Quoted in Zakin 1993:198.

47. Baker 2001:152.

48. Baker 2001:156.

49. Taylor has analyzed the religious dimensions and political impacts of radical environmentalists in a series of articles (including Taylor 2005b, 2002, 2001a, 2001b, 1995, 1991), which can be reviewed at http://www.brontaylor.com/environmental_articles /journal_articles.html (accessed November 15, 2010).

50. Taylor 2002:30–32, 39–40.

51. Numerous examples can be found in the *Earth First!* journal. See, as one example, Coronado 2005. In relation to wolves, one activist noted, "They are social like humans, but they are also wild. *Wild* (emphasis in original). I just spent five days in jail for protesting a ski resort in Colorado. I thought about wolves—and about jaguars—the whole time. We used to have wild jaguars in Arizona and New Mexico. I felt just like a trapped wolf or jaguar in its zoo or breeding pen" (Russell 2005:154). For an interesting encounter with two activists associated with Earth First! and involved in the early push for Mexican wolf reintroduction, see Burbank 1990:161–171. Burbank notes that the more deeply he became involved in the politics of wolf reintroduction in the Southwest, the more he found that radical environmentalists were instrumental in pushing the process forward.

52. See Takacs 1996; cf. Soulé 1985:727–734.

53. See, for example, Ripple and Beschta 2004; Ripple and Larsen 2004; Terborgh et al. 1999.

54. Soulé and Noss 1998:24.

55. Soulé and Noss 1998:24–25.

56. Defenders of Wildlife provides a paradigmatic example of how wolf imagery can be utilized in this respect. Founded in 1947, the conservation purview of Defenders of Wildlife—a national conservation organization with a membership in the hundreds of thousands—encompasses many species of wildlife, yet wolves remain the primary iconic

animal for its promotional efforts. In addition to such regular fund- and awareness-raising campaigns as their adopt-a-wolf program, through which contributors receive a stuffed animal and a certificate of "adoption," Defenders has disseminated images of wolves on postcards, T-shirts, coffee mugs, mousepads, backpacks, and especially through their iconic logo.

57. Revealing the overlap between those from grassroots environmental groups and from the academy, Foreman and Soulé were among those who founded the Wildlands Project in 1991, following Foreman's departure from Earth First! in 1990. Though Foreman has since gone on to devote his time to the Rewilding Institute, a conservation "think tank" he helped found in 2003, conservation biologists like Soulé, John Terborgh, Paul Paquet, and others continue to serve as science advisors for both the Wildlands Project and the Rewilding Institute.

58. Quoted in Moody 2005:166.

59. For an excellent breakdown of the "symbol and surrogate" issues that orbit around wolf reintroduction, see Nie 2003:73–78, 93, 101.

60. Polling surveys have consistently noted the tendency for urban and suburban dwellers to favor wolf reintroduction, with numbers in favor of reintroduction increasing over time. For an annotated bibliography to dozens of surveys, see Browne-Nuñez and Taylor 2002. For additional survey references, see Fritts et al. 2003:295–97; Nie 2003:76.

61. Robinson writes that radio-collaring, used on grizzlies as early as 1961, began with good intentions and led to attempts to define the boundaries of ecosystems by animal movement. However, now radio collars are more likely to be used for apprehending problem wolves. According to Robinson, as a part of the protocol for the Yellowstone reintroduction, the USFWS attempted to have at least one collared animal in each pack in case of livestock depredation; this wolf was known as a "Judas wolf" (2005:345).

62. Honnold 1998:129.

63. Bowden 1995:432.

64. Unlike human-designated wilderness areas or national parks and forests, the boundaries of which are defined by political fiat, wolves do not stay put. Wolves are mobile animals, and given the opportunity they will disperse to new territories, disregarding the lines that humans have carefully drawn in their minds and on their maps. Perhaps surprising to many for whom the wolf is a wilderness icon, wolf biologists agree that wolves, among the most highly adaptive of large mammals, do not need wilderness areas to survive. In the United States, wilderness came to be associated with wolves because historically wolves were driven to places less inhabited by humans. However, in other parts of the world (and increasingly in the contiguous United States, in areas of Minnesota, Wisconsin, and Michigan), wolves thrive close to human settlement (Mech 1995:272–73; Fritts et al. 2003:300–301; Boitani 2003:324–327, 335, 340; Brown 2005:140–142).

65. Nie 2003:210–211.

66. Leopold 1989 [1949].

67. Bangs 1995:397.

References

Albanese, Catherine L. 1990. *Nature Religion in America: From the Algonkian Indians to the New Age*. Chicago: University of Chicago Press.

Anderson, Virginia DeJohn. 2004. *Creatures of Empire: How Domestic Animals Transformed Early America*. New York: Oxford University Press.

Baker, Steve. 2001. *Picturing the Beast: Animals, Identity, and Representation*, 2nd ed. Urbana: University of Illinois Press.

Bangs, Ed. 1995. "Wolf Hysteria: Reintroducing Wolves to the West." In *War Against the Wolf: America's Campaign to Exterminate the Wolf*, ed. Rick McIntyre, 397–410. Stillwater, MN: Voyageur Press.

Boitani, Luigi. 2003. "Wolf Conservation and Recovery." In *Wolves: Behavior, Ecology, and Conservation*, ed. L. David Mech and Luigi Boitani, 317–340. Chicago: University of Chicago Press.

Bowden, Charles. 1995 [1992]. "Lonesome Lobo." In *War Against the Wolf: America's Campaign to Exterminate the Wolf*, ed. Rick McIntyre, 421–433. Stillwater, MN: Voyageur Press.

Brown, David E., ed. 2002. *The Wolf in the Southwest: The Making of an Endangered Species*. Silver City, NM: High-Lonesome Books.

——. 2005 [1992]. "A Tale of Two Wolves." In *El Lobo: Readings on the Mexican Gray Wolf*, ed. Tom Lynch, 138–142. Salt Lake City: University of Utah Press.

Browne-Nuñez, C. and J. G. Taylor, eds. 2002. *Americans' Attitudes Toward Wolves and Wolf Reintroduction: An Annotated Bibliography*. Information Technology Report USGS/BRD/ITR 2002–0002. Denver, CO: U.S. Government Printing Office.

Burbank, James. 1990. *Vanishing Lobo: The Mexican Wolf and the Southwest*. Boulder, CO: Johnson Books.

Callicott, J. Baird and Michael P. Nelson, eds. 1998. *The Great New Wilderness Debate: An Expansive Collection of Writings Defining Wilderness from John Muir to Gary Snyder*. Athens: University of Georgia Press.

Chidester, David. 2005. *Authentic Fakes: Religion and American Popular Culture*. Berkeley: University of California Press.

Clifford, Hal. 2005. "Saved by Wolves." In *Comeback Wolves: Western Writers Welcome the Wolf Home*, ed. Gary Wockner, Gregory McNamee, and SueEllen Campbell, 190–194. Boulder, CO: Johnson Books.

Coleman, Jon T. 2004. *Vicious: Wolves and Men in America*. New Haven, CT: Yale University Press.

Corbin, Ben. 1995 [1900]. "Corbin's Advice, or the Wolf Hunter's Guide." In *War Against the Wolf: America's Campaign to Exterminate the Wolf*, ed. Rick McIntyre, 123–129. Stillwater, MN: Voyageur Press.

Coronado, Rod. 2005. "Howling Like a Wild Wolf." *Earth First!* 26, no. 1 (November–December): 40–42.

Cronon, William. 1983. *Changes in the Land: Indians, Colonists, and the Ecology of New England*. New York: Hill and Wang.

——. 1995. "The Trouble with Wilderness; or, Getting Back to the Wrong Nature." In *Uncommon Ground: Toward Reinventing Nature*, ed. William Cronon, 69–90. New York: W. W. Norton.

Crosby, Alfred W. 1972. *The Columbian Exchange: Biological and Cultural Consequences of 1492*. Westport, CT: Greenwood Press.

Dunlap, Thomas. 1988. *Saving America's Wildlife: Ecology and the American Mind, 1850–1990*. Princeton, NJ: Princeton University Press.

Edward, Rob. 2005. "Howling Back." In *Comeback Wolves: Western Writers Welcome the Wolf Home*, ed. Gary Wockner, Gregory McNamee, and SueEllen Campbell, 170–175. Boulder, CO: Johnson Books.

Estés, Clarissa Pinkola. 2005. "Wild Wolf—Wild Soul." In *Comeback Wolves: Western Writers Welcome the Wolf Home*, ed. Gary Wockner, Gregory McNamee, and SueEllen Campbell, 91–94. Boulder, CO: Johnson Books.

Fladler, Susan. 1974. *Thinking Like a Mountain: Aldo Leopold and the Evolution of an Ecological Attitude Toward Deer, Wolves and Forests*. Madison: University of Wisconsin Press.

Foreman, Dave. 1991. *Confessions of an Eco-Warrior*. New York: Harmony Books.

——. 2004. *Rewilding North America: A Vision for Conservation in the 21st Century*. Washington, DC: Island Press.

Foreman, Dave and Bill Haywood [pseudo.], eds. 2002. *Ecodefense: A Field Guide to Monkeywrenching*, 3rd ed. Chico, CA: Abbzug Press.

Fritts, Steven H., Robert O. Stephenson, Robert D. Hayes, and Luigi Boitani. 2003. "Wolves and Humans." In *Wolves: Behavior, Ecology, and Conservation*, ed. L. David Mech and Luigi Boitani, 289–316. Chicago: University of Chicago Press.

Gatta, John. 2004. *Making Nature Sacred: Literature, Religion, and Environment in America from the Puritans to the Present*. New York: Oxford University Press.

Gerbi, Antonello. 1985. *Nature in the New World: From Christopher Columbus to Gonzalo Fernandez de Oviedo*. Pittsburgh: University of Pittsburgh Press.

Glacken, Clarence. 1967. *Traces on the Rhodian Shore: Nature and Culture in Western Thought from Ancient Times to the End of the Eighteenth Century*. Berkeley: University of California Press.

Gore, Meredith L., Michael P. Nelson, John A. Vucetich, Amy M. Smith, and Melissa A. Clark. 2011. "Exploring the Ethical Basis for Conservation Policy: The Case of Inbred Wolves on Isle Royale, USA." *Conservation Letters* 0:1–8.

Grambo, Rebecca L. 2005. *Wolf: Legend, Enemy, Icon*. Buffalo, NY: Firefly Books.

Guha, Ramachandra. 1989. "Radical American Environmentalism and Wilderness Preservation: A Third World Critique." *Environmental Ethics* 11 (Spring): 71–83.

Hampton, Bruce. 1997. *The Great American Wolf*. New York: Henry Holt and Company.

Holaday, Bobbie. 2003. *The Return of the Mexican Gray Wolf: Back to the Blue.* Tucson: University of Arizona Press.

Honnold, Doug. 1998. "Wolves, Bears, and the Spirit of the Wild." In *Reclaiming the Native Home of Hope: Community, Ecology, and the American West*, ed. Robert B. Keiter, 127–133. Salt Lake City: University of Utah Press.

Hornaday, William T. 1904. *The American Natural History.* New York: Charles Scribner and Sons.

Ingram, David. 2000. *Green Screen: Environmentalism and Hollywood Cinema.* Exeter, UK: University of Exeter Press.

Jickling, Bob and Paul C. Paquet. 2005. "Wolf Stories: Reflections on Science, Ethics, and Epistemology." *Environmental Ethics* 27, no. 2 (Summer): 115–134

Kienzle, Beverly. 2006. "The Bestiary of Heretics: Imaging Medieval Christian Heresy with Insects and Animals." In *A Communion of Subjects: Animals in Religion, Science, and Ethics*, ed. Paul Waldau and Kimberley Patton, 103–116. New York: Columbia University Press.

Leopold, Aldo. 1989 [1949]. *A Sand County Almanac, and Sketches Here and There.* New York: Oxford University Press.

——. 1995a [1930]. "Game Management in the National Forests." In *Aldo Leopold's Southwest*, ed. David E. Brown and Neil B. Carmony, 125–131. Albuquerque: University of New Mexico Press.

——. 1995b [1920]. "The Game Situation in the Southwest." In *War Against the Wolf: America's Campaign to Exterminate the Wolf*, ed. Rick McIntyre, 180–192. Stillwater, MN: Voyageur Press.

Lopez, Barry. 2004 [1978]. *Of Wolves and Men.* New York: Scribner Classics.

Lynch, Tom, ed. 2005. *El Lobo: Readings on the Mexican Gray Wolf.* Salt Lake City: University of Utah Press.

Lynn, William S. 2002. "Canis Lupus Cosmopolis: Wolves in a Cosmopolitan Worldview." *Worldviews* 6, no. 3: 300–327.

——. 2006. "Between Science and Ethics: What Science and the Scientific Method Can and Cannot Contribute to Conservation and Sustainability." In *Wildlife Conservation: In Pursuit of Ecological Sustainability*, ed. David Lavigne, 191–205. Limerick, Ireland: University of Limerick Press.

McIntyre, Rick, ed. 1995. *War Against the Wolf: America's Campaign to Exterminate the Wolf.* Stillwater, MN: Voyageur Press.

Mech, L. David. 1995. "The Challenge and Opportunity of Recovering Wolf Populations." *Conservation Biology* 9, no. 2 (April): 270–278.

Meine, Curt. 1988. *Aldo Leopold: His Life and Work.* Madison: University of Wisconsin Press.

——. 1998. "Moving Mountains: Aldo Leopold and a Sound County Almanac." *Wildlife Society Bulletin* 26, no. 4: 700–705.

Midgley, Mary. 1995. *Beast and Man: The Roots of Human Nature*, rev. ed. New York: Routledge.

Mighetto, Lisa. 1991. *Wild Animals and American Environmental Ethics.* Tucson: University of Arizona Press.

Moody, Joan. 2005 [1998]. "El Lobo's Homecoming." In *El Lobo: Readings on the Mexican Gray Wolf*, ed. Tom Lynch, 164–168. Salt Lake City: University of Utah Press.

Morgan, David. 2005. *The Sacred Gaze: Religious Visual Culture in Theory and Practice.* Berkeley: University of California Press.

Nash, Roderick Frazier. 1970. "The American Invention of National Parks." *American Quarterly* 22, no. 3 (Autumn): 726–735.

——. 2001. *Wilderness and the American Mind*, 4th ed. New Haven, CT: Yale University Press.

Nelson, Michael P. 1998. "Aldo Leopold, Environmental Ethics, and the Land Ethic." *Wildlife Society Bulletin* 26, no. 4: 741–744.

Nie, Martin. 2003. *Beyond Wolves: The Politics of Wolf Recovery and Management.* Minneapolis: University of Minnesota Press.

Ouspensky, Leonid and Vladimir Lossky. 1969. *The Meaning of Icons.* Trans. G. E. H. Palmer and E. Kadloubovsky. Boston: Boston Book and Art Shop.

Ripple, William J. and Robert L. Beschta. 2004. "Wolves, Elk, Willows, and Trophic Cascades in the Upper Gallatin Range of Southwestern Montana, USA." *Forest Ecology and Management* 200 (October): 161–181.

Ripple, William J. and E. J. Larsen. 2004. "Wolves and the Ecology of Fear: Can Predation Risk Structure Ecosystems?" *BioScience* 54 (August): 755–766.

Robinson, Michael J. 2005. *Predatory Bureaucracy: The Extermination of Wolves and the Transformation of the West.* Boulder: University of Colorado Press.

Rowland, Beryl. 1973. *Animals with Human Faces.* Knoxville: University of Tennessee Press.

Russell, Sharman Apt. 2005 [1993]. "The Physics of Beauty." In *El Lobo: Readings on the Mexican Gray Wolf*, ed. Tom Lynch, 143–155. Salt Lake City: University of Utah Press.

Schlesier, Karl H. 1987. *The Wolves of Heaven: Cheyenne Shamanism, Ceremonies, and Prehistoric Origins.* Norman: University of Oklahoma Press.

Schlickeisen, Rodger. 2004. "Defenders of Wildlife Action Fund Reacts to Bush-Cheney Political Campaign Ad 'Wolves.'" Wolf Song of Alaska, October 22. http://www.wolfsongalaska.org/news/Alaska_current_events_920.htm (accessed April 6, 2007).

Shepard, Paul. 1998. *Coming Home to the Pleistocene.* Washington, DC: Island Press.

Skinner, Milton P. 1995 [1924]. "The Predatory and Fur-Bearing Animals of Yellowstone National Park." In *War Against the Wolf: America's Campaign to Exterminate the Wolf*, ed. Rick McIntyre, 292–296. Stillwater, MN: Voyageur Press.

Snyder, Gary. 1990. *The Practice of the Wild.* New York: North Point Press.

Soulé, Michael and Reed Noss. 1998. "Rewilding and Biodiversity: Complementary Goals for Continental Conservation." *Wild Earth* 8, no. 3 (Fall): 18–28.

Soulé, Michael E. 1985. "What Is Conservation Biology?" *BioScience* 35:727–734.

Soulé, Michael E., James A. Estes, Brian Miller, and Douglas L. Honnold. 2005. "Strongly Interacting Species: Conservation Policy, Management, and Ethics." *Bio-Science* 55, no. 2 (February): 168–176.

Soulé, Michael E. and Gary Lease, eds. 1995. *Reinventing Nature? Responses to Postmodern Deconstruction*. Covelo, CA: Island Press.

Takacs, David. 1996. *The Idea of Biodiversity: Philosophies of Paradise*. Baltimore, MD: John Hopkins University Press.

Taylor, Bron. 1991. "The Religion and Politics of Earth First!" *The Ecologist* 21, no. 6 (November/December): 258–266.

——. 1995. "Resacralizing Earth: Pagan Environmentalism and the Restoration of Turtle Island." In *American Sacred Space*, ed. David Chidester and Edward Linenthal, 97–115. Bloomington: Indiana University Press.

——. 2001a. "Earth and Nature-Based Spirituality from Deep Ecology to Radical Environmentalism, Part I." *Religion* 31, no. 2: 175–193.

——. 2001b. "Earth and Nature-Based Spirituality from Earth First! and Bioregionalism to Scientific Paganism and the New Age, Part II." *Religion* 31, no. 3: 225–245.

——. 2002. "Diggers, Wolves, Ents, Elves, and Expanding Universes: Bricolage, Religion, and Violence from Earth First! and the Earth Liberation Front to the Antiglobalization Resistance." In *The Cultic Milieu: Oppositional Subcultures in an Age of Globalization*, ed. Jeffrey Kaplan and Heléne Lööw, 26–74. Lanham, MD: Altamira/Rowman and Littlefield.

——. 2005a. "Conservation Biology." In *Encyclopedia of Religion and Nature*, ed. Bron Taylor, 415–418. London: Thoemmes Continuum.

——. 2005b. "Earth First! and the Earth Liberation Front." In *Encyclopedia of Religion and Nature*, ed. Bron Taylor, 518–534. London: Thoemmes Continuum.

Terborgh, John, James A. Estes, Paul Paquet, Katherine Ralls, Diane Boyd-Heger, Brian J. Miller, and Reed F. Noss . 1999. "The Role of Top Carnivores in Regulating Terrestrial Ecosystems." In *Continental Conservation: Design and Management Principles for Long-Term, Regional Conservation Networks*, ed. Michael Soulé and John Terborgh, 39–64. Washington, DC: Island Press.

Thomas, Keith. 1996. *Man and the Natural World: Changing Attitudes in England, 1500–1800*. New York: Oxford University Press.

Thoreau, Henry David. 2001 [1862]. "Walking." In *Henry David Thoreau: Collected Essays and Poems*, ed. Elizabeth Hall Witherell, 225–255. New York: Library of America.

Turner, Jack. 1996. *The Abstract Wild*. Tucson: University of Arizona Press.

U.S. Congress. 1973. Endangered Species Act of 1973. 16 U.S.C. 1531–1544, 87 Stat. 884.

U.S. Fish & Wildlife Service and U.S. Department of the Interior. 1995. "Gray Wolf: Canis Lupus." Biologue Series.

Waldau, Paul. 2006. "Seeing the Terrain We Walk: Features of the Contemporary Landscape of Religion and Animals." In *A Communion of Subjects: Animals in Religion,*

Science, and Ethics, ed. Paul Waldau and Kimberly Patton, 40–64. New York: Columbia University Press.

Worster, Donald. 1994. *Nature's Economy: A History of Ecological Ideas*, 2nd ed. Cambridge: Cambridge University Press.

Young, Stanley and Edward A. Goldman. 1944. *The Wolves of North America*. New York: Dover Publications.

Zakin, Susan. 1993. *Coyotes and Town Dogs: Earth First! and the Environmental Movement*. New York: Viking.

eight

Thinking with Surfaces

Animals and Contemporary Art

Ron Broglio

How different their eye and ear! How different the world to them!
—William Blake, *Visions of the Daughters of Albion*

THINKING ABOUT ANIMALS MEANS TAKING SERIOUSLY THE possibility that everything takes place "on the surface." That is, after all, what we are usually told about animals, isn't it? Animals are all body, soulless and speechless creatures whose lives lack the meaning associated with depth or the spirit associated with heights. Animals don't know how to think like we do; they don't know that they are going to a veterinarian or a slaughter house; they don't even know that they are animals! In sum, dominant streams of Western thought construe the animal, including the biological element of the *animal rationale*, as that which exists on the surface alone.

Both following and critiquing this dominant understanding of animality, this chapter will contrast the work of animal portrait artists of the eighteenth century and contemporary art such as the work by the collaborative artists known as Olly Suzi to explore the meaning of animality. I use the term "animality" to refer to transformations on surfaces—that is, the active becoming rather than the established being or essence of a living entity. Humans through arts, economy, politics, and culture soar to heights and plumb depths in attempts to escape this animality, to escape their own and others' animal surfaces. Similarly, humans deploy the differentiation of inside and outside in an attempt to go beyond their animal surface; we treasure the construction of a privileged interiority by which one says "I" and simultaneously denies animals any parallel "inner life."

To take up the animal means giving surfaces their place. It means valuing this place despite the overvaluation of the heights of culture and the depths of interiority. By contrasting animal portrait artists of the eighteenth century and contemporary artists such as Olly Suzi, this chapter will make a place for two kinds of surfaces: the surfaces of canvases and the surfaces of animal bodies.

Animal Portraits

Animal portraits of the eighteenth century consider the animal body as simply surface in order to enframe it within the human domain. The paintings of sheep, cattle, horses, hogs, and dogs are occasioned by the celebration of an animal's domestication and its "improvement" as a breed. Animal portraits primarily functioned to advertise and advance a breed as well as to commemorate a particular animal's significance to the breed. Agricultural animals, the topic of so many animal portraits, are enframed by domestication before they are ever framed as paintings. Domestication was understood to "enlighten" animals and bring them within the folds of culture. As William Youatt explains in his 1832 manual for cattle rearing: "when he [cattle] receives a kind of culture at our hands, he seems to be enlightened with a ray of human reason, and warmed with a degree of human affection."[1] In this chapter cattle breeding will serve as an example of how eighteenth- and nineteenth-century breeders and animal portrait artists ply the surface of the animal for social benefit. Breeding in this context means reading the surface of the animal body in order to expose the interior of the animal as subsurface, as lacking interiority, as product—as meat. In this modern understanding of breeding, the animal grazier reads the bodies of cattle as cuts of meat and selects the animals that will be bred so that the shape and size of their offspring yield more of the desired sections.

In the eighteenth century, paintings of beef cattle helped build and establish cattle breeds, enframing the animal as agricultural product. By way of contrast, in the work of many contemporary artists, canvas and body surfaces are the place where animals leave their marks by biting back, as it were, and provide a glimpse of a world other than our own—a world outside of human rationalization and enlightenment. For example, rather than paint in a studio,

Olly Suzi work in the "wilds," the domain of the animal, where they paint the animal's form on canvas in the presence of the animal and encourage the animal to interact with the canvas as well. Their canvases offer up a surface for human-animal exchange where the human animals and animal animals trade marks. Their paintings counter the livestock portraits used to discern and to promulgate the cultivation and enculturation of livestock for human use. Animals move from enframed to unframed. Olly Suzi's paintings suggest a rethinking of marks of significance and what they mean within the economy of art, language, and culture. Further, their work suggests another sort of writing, another language, and a unique means of (re)presenting animals.

In-In

Cattle portraiture serves as an example of how art illustrates and helps to transform the natural world. The story of cattle surfaces goes back quite some ways and is at least as old as cave paintings. The birth of modern breeding practices marks one of the most important turns in the story of animal surfaces. Breeding is the measuring and manipulating of surfaces. Visible points and characteristics distinguish groupings of animals as within the same species as distinct breeds. The story of modern cattle breeding begins in the British Midlands in the 1760s at Dishley Farm, run by Robert Bakewell. As an agricultural innovator, Bakewell focused on improving the form, flesh, and propensity for fattening of his beasts. He developed "in-in" (same family lineage) breeding of his cattle, which helped him to ensure the purity of the desired characteristics.[2] Under the in-in breeding method, animals would gain flesh and fat in less time and consequently increase the grazier's productivity and profits. Offspring that did not meet his standards of form and flesh were removed from the breeding stock. Deciding which animals to breed and which characteristics of each animal were desirable traits to be inherited depended upon Bakewell's preconceived image of what cattle should ideally look like. Having an ideal type to breed toward allowed Bakewell to read the body of his cattle as desirable or undesirable surfaces.

Bakewell's ideal was realized on canvas by livestock artists of the period, a history that is detailed in Elspeth Moncrieff's *Farm Animal Portraits*.[3] Artists would draw idealized beasts by using prize cattle as their study, then ever so slightly exaggerate the features: a straightened and elongated back for the most famous *Durham Ox* (figure 8.1), a few more bulges of fat on canvas for *The White Heifer That Travelled*, a white heifer raised by Robert Colling, and a

FIGURE 8.1. John Boultbee's *The Durham Ox*, after John Boultbee, engraved by I. Whessel, 1802.

corrected tail and rump of fat in Shakespeare and his sire, D.[4] Beginning in the late eighteenth century, paintings of prized cattle were made into prints that circulated to illustrate the standard toward which graziers should breed their beasts. These bovine pinups changed the way farmers looked at and fashioned their animals. As a result of new breeding practices and the new art of cattle portraiture, cattle in the field became instances designed to actualize the fictions found on the canvas. The surface of the animal body is transposed onto the artist's canvas only to have the artistic image in turn transform the physical body of cattle. The beginning of cattle breeding is a play of surfaces from cattle exteriors to canvas then back to cattle.

Inside Out

Optical supremacy enables the circulation between canvas and cattle body. Since the fundamental means of evaluating and categorizing animals during the eighteenth century was by their lines and surfaces—i.e., by what can be seen—artists had a privileged position in the promotion of breeds.[5] With a primacy placed on line and form by breeders, the artist was able to employ his skills toward creating a visual argument for the value of an animal. In painting, the cattle's surface communicates its value; one need simply look at Boultbee's painting to see the desired traits: a formidable neck, broad shoulders, the well formed dewlap, the fine ribs, and so on. Lest the two-dimensional image not convince, then the inscription of dimensions at the bottom of many paintings and prints will advance the point.

Yet, more important than the visual representation itself is the "spacing" that takes place in the act of codifying the animal. The artist and grazier both judge the animal while maintaining a distance. Furthermore, the eye as window positions the viewing subject as a human with privileged interiority in contrast to the outward surface of the viewed object, the cattle's corpulence. Through sight, we possess in our minds the animal that is seen from a distance. The animal surface is contrasted with and co-opted by the human who uses his own reflexive interiority (i.e., "thinking") to divide the animal surface into cuts of meat and then to project the schematic cuts onto the body of the beast. The cattle, now imagined as meat, have been turned inside out. Since these animals are not considered to have an interiority and since they do not speak in our language, their inside is symbolically made an outside, a mere surface to be exposed for human use, even before this is done literally, in the process of slaughtering and consuming them.

Real animals do, of course, look back, and in this look the dominant schemas that order our world and regulate our relations with animals are upset. What is understood to be at the center and what at the periphery, what is understood as interior and what exterior, gets misplaced. John Berger in "Why Look at Animals?" and more recently Jacques Derrida in *The Animal That Therefore I Am* both leverage the look of the animal toward a rethinking of the human:

> The animal scrutinizes him [man] across a narrow abyss of non-comprehension. This is why the man can surprise the animal. Yet the animal—even if domesticated—can also surprise the man. The man too is looking across a similar, but not identical, abyss of non-comprehension. And this is so wherever he looks. He is always looking across ignorance and fear. And so, when he is *being seen* by the animal, he is being seen as his surroundings are seen by him.[6]

Animals look at us, and we are confounded both by their radical otherness and by their uncanny sameness. We are struck by the realization that we may be objects in their world as much as they are objects in ours. And when we acknowledge that animals look back at us, we are forced to grant that there may be something of the animal's "self" that we do not know. Derrida in his autobiographical book *The Animal That Therefore I Am* argues that the moment when he finds himself looked at naked by his cat is when thought renews itself and thus properly begins. In Derrida's deconstructive[7] analysis of this exchange of glances between his naked self and an animal, he constructs a bridge that allows one to cross the human/animal divide without forgetting the otherness of the animal. The cat under his roof reminds the thinker of the otherness of all animals, human and nonhuman, and simultaneously reveals the otherness forgotten within the human. Each kind of otherness supplements the other, undoing the old Cartesian idea that the interior "thinking 'I'" is the center of the self. As Steve Baker explains in *The Postmodern Animal*: "Precisely as an alternative to Descartes's 'I think therefore I am,' Derrida proposes the formulation: 'The animal looks at us, and we are naked before it. And thinking perhaps begins there.'"[8] The "there" in Derrida's statement works as a deferral and displacement of the ground that authorizes thought. In the look of the animal, the center of the environment moves outside the human and gets placed upon the multiple centers of the many "eyes" out "there." As a consequence, human identity finds its "I" in the eyes of the Other.[9]

Perhaps even more pressing than the look from animals is their physicality. To the extent we understand the power and immediacy of raw physical contact between bodies as "animal," our physicality is imagined to be among our most animal characteristics. Physicality operates outside human symbol systems and is largely unintelligible within human cultural codes. The shock of physicality found in actual contact with animals may counter the enframing that occurs within traditional animal portraiture. This physical contact has the potential to enliven the surface of the animal body as something other than an object enframed by human desires. If for Derrida human thinking begins in the regard of the animal, to move this notion further, contact with animals provides a possibility to think *with* them.[10]

Outside Out

Martin Heidegger's work on the notion of "world," elaborated in this volume by Brett Buchanan (chapter 9), proves an important starting point for thinking through and with the animal surface. Heidegger's sense of a limited animal world—animals, he argues, are "poor in world" (*weltarm*) when compared to the "world-building" (*weltbildend*) human—encapsulates much of philosophy's history with the animal question. Heidegger's most discussed topography of the animal's world appears in his 1929–1930 seminar published as *The Fundamental Concepts of Metaphysics*: "the stone is worldless; the animal is poor in world; man is world-forming."[11] Animals certainly have environments (*Umwelt*), but they are not aware of their environments in the same way that humans are. Derrida summarizes Heidegger's position by explaining: "As for the animal, it has access to entities, but, and this is what distinguishes it from man, it has no access to entities *as such*."[12] Heidegger's lizard, for example, sits on a rock and enjoys the sun but does not know the rock as rock nor sun as sun. Heidegger elaborates by saying, "When we say that the lizard is lying on the rock, we ought to cross out the word 'rock' in order to indicate that whatever the lizard is lying on is certainly given *in some way* for the lizard, and yet is not known to the lizard *as* a rock."[13] The animal is caught up in its series of relations to other entities without an ability to remove itself from the "captivation" that such a series presents.

Heidegger draws his notion of an animal world from the work of Jakob von Uexküll, a founding figure in ethnology and semiotics. In "Stroll Through the Worlds of Animals and Men," Uexküll moves beyond mechanistic biology to develop a line of inquiry into the animal's sense of its surroundings, something close to an animal phenomenology.[14] For Uexküll, the animal's environment is constituted by the "carriers of significance" or "marks" that captivate the animal. All other elements in the world drop off and have no place in the animal world, or what Uexküll calls *Umwelt*.[15] Caught within the series of relations that is their *Umwelt*, animals simply can't get outside their surroundings to have a look around.

By way of contrast, the human world has heights and depths—from Plato's ascent out of the cave to Empedocles's refusal to climb out and insistence on digging in and digging deeply.[16] It is human uprightness, our verticality, that sufficiently displaces us from our surroundings so that we can see the rock at a distance, a rock as rock. Animals, so understood, do not have this distance. "Their whole being is in the living flesh," as J. M. Coetzee characterizes this understanding.[17] In contrast to human verticality, animals live horizontally. The eagle does not reach heights nor the mole plumb depths; rather they live on the surface.[18] As Derrida has explicated in *Of Spirit*, world is for Heidegger only possible for humans, those beings who have spirit. As much as they are poor in spirit, animals are left "poor in world." The "uprightness" of humans is both physical and metaphysical while the animal world is decidedly flat. Without heights and depths, the animals are left with marks on the surface, as seen in Heidegger's lizard on a rock. The animal surface provides a crossing out or erasure of interiority and language that (re)marks in our language the place of their relations.[19] To consider animals and take seriously the role of surfaces to thought and language therefore means reevaluating physical and metaphysical uprightness of humans.

Giles Deleuze in *Logic of Sense* counters the verticality of Plato and Empedocles with the horizontal animality of Diogenes; the cynic philosopher "is no longer the being of the caves, nor Plato's soul or bird, but rather the animal which is on the level of the surface."[20] Known as the dog of Athens, Diogenes lived on the surface. If he wrote anything, none of it survives; we have only anecdotes: he ate without discernment whatever he happened upon in the streets, masturbated in public, took to insulting his contemporaries, and lived in a tub. Plato could not coax "the dog" into a dialogue, a conversation meant to invite Diogenes within the Academy where he would be refuted by the masters of language, Plato and Socrates. Fed up with words, always more words, Diogenes would offer his detractors food, something to stuff their mouths with and stop the babble of culture. Food could stop the philosophical abstraction and recall the animal body of the speaker. Fredrick Young in his essay "Animality" explains:

> Plato had no *idea* how to deal with Diogenes. For Diogenes refused to argue on Platonic grounds, refused dialectics and the rational "voice" that goes with it by means of which "man" speaks. With Diogenes, there's a different modality of argumentation, if we can even call it that, the performative[,] and animality. The Diogenic is more than a literal abject attack on Plato. More significantly, Diogenes' strategies are irreducible to any modality of dialectics or philosophy proper. Again, what we have is the problematics of the surface, of animality—a physiognomic performance that unleashes the performativity of animality into the Platonic landscape and architecture.[21]

The performative *is* thought for Diogenes. His actions with his body in space are his thinking. In like manner, Coetzee in *The Lives of Animals* explains that "the living flesh" of the animal is its argument. When Coetzee's protagonist Elizabeth Costello is asked if life means less to animals than to humans, she retorts that animals do not respond to us in words, but rather with gestures of the living flesh. Its argument from its flesh is its "whole being."[22] In like manner, the world for Diogenes is not that of the culture that surrounds him and that seeks to incorporate his corpus, if he would ever get around to writing one. Instead, he offers corporality, bodies and surfaces that evade the ins and outs and ups and downs of his contemporaries. It comes, then, as no surprise that Diogenes lived his life in exile from Sinope, his birthplace.

Diogenes's performative thought indicates an other world, something other than the distanced observation by which humans understand an environment through a privileged interiority and reflexive consciousness. Collapsing heights and depths to surface, there is no space for interiority and reflexivity. In this collapse, Diogenes sides with the animals. Although for Heidegger animals cannot see objects in themselves, they nevertheless see and interact with the world around them. If not a Heideggerian clearing—reserved for humans alone—then is it possible that animals have some other sort of clearing and revealing available to them and not to humans? Even Heidegger in addressing the poverty of the animal admits this. The living flesh of animals and life itself, Heidegger argues, is not "something inferior or . . . at a lower level in comparison with human *Dasein*. On the contrary, life is a domain which possesses *a wealth of being-open, of which the human world may know nothing at all*."[23] If human knowledge is that of distances and interiorities (our heights and depths), it is possible that one way of knowing that has been closed off to us is the knowing given to us by surfaces, a space where animals have often been relegated in their "poverty."

It is under the context of physicality, surfaces, and performance that the work of contemporary artists Olly Suzi gains currency. Their paintings jostle the *Umwelt* of the animal and the world of the human through the particular set of parameters under which the paintings are executed. Olly Suzi work as a team in the environment of animals under conditions that are threatening and difficult for the human as they execute drawings of the animals in the animals' presence. From Arctic waters to African deserts, the two artists place themselves in extreme environments—sites that are at the limits of human dominion and are more likely to be important to the animal's domain and world. Whether in an underwater cage designed to protect divers from sharks, squatting within range of a polar bear, or a few paws length from a lion, the artists work "hand over hand" creating sparse, strong, moving lines in the shape of the animal before them.[24] The artists feel "helpless" and "out of our depths" by working within the environment of the animal rather than in the familiar terrain of an artist's studio.[25] Working in the animal's terrain produces a sense of fear that becomes important to Olly Suzi's art: "Fear plays a vital role in our art-making process. We are constantly challenged by and confronted with environments and animals, especially predators (polar bears, white sharks, big cats), that trigger adrenaline, a primal response that alerts us to the potential of imminent danger."[26] They explain that "[t]he knowledge we gather [about the animal] arms us, but fear is still present; a warm glow, keeping us warm."[27] Fear is something that rises to the surface and keeps the artists in contact with the surface, preventing them from slipping into an interiority of selfhood that would provide a safe haven.

As Olly Suzi work at the surface, their physical presence becomes one of the marks within the animal domain. They are one of the "carriers of significance" captivating the animal from within its world. From the animal's world the artists are a marked surface while from the human's world the animal body is a surface to be illustrated. One surface meets another. Between these two surfaces a canvas is spread out. The blank space of the canvas is fair game from within the world of both humans and animals. The artists draw from within the domain of the animal and "encourage the animals to interact" with the canvas.[28] A white shark bites off a corner, a leopard tears at the cloth, an anaconda slithers across the surface leaving a mud-stained track (see figure 8.2). The animal as surface and the human as surface leave their mark on a mutual environment of canvas that has become the outside, the outer margin or limit of each domain. The outside finds a way out of a limited *Umwelt* and becomes evidence of a much larger world—the site of production and possibilities.

Their work is a performance. The making of their art is part of the art itself and gets documented in photographs taken by Greg Williams, Olly's brother, who accompanies the artists in their travels. The drawings are not something to be executed at the distance of a studio. Like Diogenes, their actions disavow the linguistic markers of the dialectic and the Academy with us humans on one side and the animals (caged) at the other side. Clive James observes that "[Sir Edwin] Landseer used to have his lions shot and stuffed before he drew them. Olly and Suzi, who know which side they are on, would have been more likely to shoot and stuff Landseer."[29] In their work there are no sides except, perhaps, the outside at a remove from culture and human interiority. In fact, the work of Olly Suzi is distinctly out of place in much the same way that Diogenes is: "The academic conversation among philosophers does not concede the materialist position a fitting place—indeed, it cannot because the conversation itself presupposes something like an idealist agreement. An existential materialist feels misunderstood from the start in a place where people only talk. In the dialogue of heads, only head theories will ever come up."[30] It is in the space of distant places and with a language of the body rather than talking heads that Olly Suzi explore a much larger world.

FIGURE 8.2. Shark I, Shark II, and Shark III. Photographs by Greg Williams of Olly Suzi's "Shark Bite," 1977.

Contact

The larger world that humans and animals create in alliance with one another can be considered a "contact zone." The word comes from Mary Louise Pratt's *Imperial Eyes*, in which she uses the term to describe the "social spaces where disparate cultures meet, clash, and grapple with each other, often in highly asymmetrical relations of domination and subordination."[31] The grappling between humans and animals forms a topography much like the space described by Pratt. With Olly Suzi, for example, such topography is an actual relation between bodies—a marker or carrier of significance of each other's body from within their respective domains. The marks cross, and cross out, till there is a space negotiated and shared between human and animal through their (re) marks. Such re-marks take on the character of a hybrid language similar to the origins of Pratt's term:

> I borrow the term "contact" here from its use in linguistics, where the term "contact language" refers to improvised languages that develop among speakers of different native languages who need to communicate with each other consistently, usually in context of trade. Such languages begin as pidgins, and are called creoles when they come to have native speakers of their own. Like the societies of the contact zones, such languages are commonly regarded as chaotic, barbarous, lacking in structure.[32]

It is exactly the asignifying scrawls across the canvas spread out by Olly Suzi that bear witness to and constitute the pidgins and forked tongues of the animal-artist alliance.

Olly Suzi have drawn animals. Rather, they have formed alliances that become the agents of painting.[33] Foremost, the artists talk about respect for the animal, a respect that makes alliance possible. They glean from experts in the field the various information needed to stand up to and survive within the *Umwelt* of the other. How far to stand from a polar bear, how to not look afraid in front of a large cat, and how to handle an anaconda is a knowledge leading to physical comportment. Olly Suzi's physical bearing in the world of the animal and how the animal reacts to their actions serves as a syntax for a pidgin language between species.

Their work with the white wolves of Canada's Ellesmere Island serves as a fine example of this pidgin language. The artists explain: "We wanted to meet the wolf in its natural habitat. We wanted to take the human-animal and artistic interaction that stage further, to feel its spirit. We wanted to co-exist."[34] In this particular human-animal interaction, Olly Suzi were extending Joseph Beuys's 1974 performance *Coyote: I Like America and America Likes Me*. Beuys spent a week with a coyote inside the Rene Block Gallery in New York. The artist and animal negotiated space and communication: Beuys threw his glove at the animal, offering it the artist's creative hand; the coyote tore at newspaper on the floor and even tugged at the blanket wrapped around Beuys. Props, bodies, time, and space created a contingent language. Steve Baker explicates the interaction quoting Beuys: "Beuys was acting out the limits of his own control of the situation, with the coyote figuring for him as 'an important cooperator in the production of freedom.' The animal enabled the artist to edge closer to that which 'the human being cannot understand.'"[35] Out of his depths, the artist is forced to take on a new language that moves between the human and the animal. Olly Suzi describe their own wolf encounter with special attention to body language as a means of collaborating and negotiating space:

> As we started to draw and film, the wolf approached us inquisitively, observing our movements, curious and completely unafraid. She came to within ten feet and we drew first her head then her slender flank. . . . By crouching down we had signaled to the wolf that we were not a threat, and she had acknowledged our submissive act. We knew now that the wolves were here, but for how much longer it would be hard to say.[36]

Each of the sections in *Olly & Suzi: Arctic Desert Ocean Jungle* is filled with tales of how they navigated extreme environments. Details of bodily motion—buoyancy under water, cautious wading in the marshy domain of an anaconda, rapid brush strokes in the minus forty degrees Celsius weather of the polar bear's icy habitat—are more than adventurous tidbits meant to titillate the admirers back home. Motion and environment contribute to the individuality of the pidgin language and the space in which this language is formed.

Beuys failingly tried to use his performance with a wolf as a metaphor for American politics, U.S. treatment of Native Americans, and American ecology. The event was more successful in its literalism. Metaphor takes us back to the already codified language of the Academy. If we are to fashion a new space and a new language in the canvas shared by humans and animals, metamorphosis should replace metaphor.[37] It may be helpful to recall here the opening chapter of this volume by Tim Ingold, in which he argues against a metaphorical understanding of what hunter-gatherers mean when they say things like "the forest is our parent." Just as Ingold says we would misunderstand the Cree or Mbuti if we took their statements that they have social relations with animals metaphorically, when James proclaims that Olly is something of a bull seal and Suzi a gazelle, there is more than metaphor at work.[38] Density and lightness, slowness and speed, thick and thin are states of being inhabited by the lines on canvas, the flight and repose of the animals, and the corporality held by the human-animal alliance. The surfaces and bodies refuse linguistic signification and in doing so take us elsewhere, to the "poor in world" of the animal that is rich in its own textures: "*signification may be undone*, with both literal and metaphorical attempts to fix meaning giving way to 'a distribution of states'; and that *individual identity may be undone*, with both human and animal subjects giving way to 'a circuit of states.'"[39] The canvas bears witness to the "distribution of states." The "hand over hand" method of the artists, along with the interaction of the animal, diffuses the agency of the artwork and creates an event structure.

It is certainly possible to read the work of Olly Suzi as a naïve, hopeless effort to engage animals in a project in which the animals have no interest. Perhaps the notion that the art is an alliance is simply hazy romanticism. However, the artists themselves consider their work with predator species as a way of bearing witness to endangered ecological chains that sustain the predators and that the fierce animals help constitute. As such, it is a project in ecological awareness. But Baker counters such critiques of Olly Suzi in part by considering the authenticity or earnestness of the project, a sincerity that produces something new rather than taking refuge in art as satire or irony.[40] My own interest is in how their art shows a concern for human and animal phenomenologies. Humans and animals share the same earth, but live in different worlds. What, then, are the possibilities to think at the edge of the human world, at the place where it bumps up against the animals' worlds? What happens where skin and scales meet? Negotiating this meeting place, this contact zone, requires that the artists momentarily suspend or leave behind much of the world of culture and acquire new gestures and a different awareness of their bodies. They do not put themselves in danger as a sort of stunt; rather, they negotiate the space not only using some technological elements of culture (wet suits, shark cages, special paints, etc.) and some cultural awareness of various animals' behaviors, but also, as I'm emphasizing here, relying on bodily movements and the physicality of the environment. So, for example, when encountering a polar bear, the artists have technological equipment of transportation, warm clothing, paints that will not freeze too quickly, and a camera to document the event. However, they also must rely on knowing the proper proximity to the animal, how to crouch down, and how to maneuver in the snow.

Identity is larger than any one human or animal. Deleuze and Guattari call this distribution of states between various elements in an environment a "haecceity," Latin for "this-ness":

> There is a mode of individuation very different from that of a person, subject, thing, or substance. We reserve the name "haecceity" for it. A season, a winter, a summer, an hour, a date have a perfect individuality lacking nothing, even though this individuality is different from that of a thing or a subject. They are haecceities in the sense that they consist entirely of relations of movement and rest between molecules or particles, capacities to affect and to be affected. When demonology expounds upon the diabolical art of local movements and transports of affect, it also notes the importance of rain, hail, wind, pestilential air, or air polluted by noxious particles, favorable conditions for these transports. Tales must contain haecceities that are not simply emplacements, but concrete individuations that have a status of their own and direct the metamorphosis of things and subjects.[41]

The tales told in *Olly & Suzi: Arctic Desert Ocean Jungle* form an important part of the art and read like lines from Deleuze and Guattari: "It's very cold, about –10C on the surface and only slightly warmer in the water. . . . The blackness of the water felt like swimming through night, inky impenetrable darkness. . . . The sound was astonishing, a barrage of squeaks and chirps, the physical ping of echo sonar as the Orcas swirled around us, encircling us in their trap of bubbles."[42] Olly Suzi log the "diabolical art" of passing over from the human into movement, tension, gesture, sound, and response. It is not simply that the artists have moved their studio outdoors and into another's domain; rather, they have crossed into other worlds, other *Umwelts*. The pidgin language formed in contact zones is one of crossing and marking, double crossing and re-marking.

Hand and Claw

Crossing and marking: the artists' bodies become carriers of significance in the animal's world. Along with cold, dark waters and amid sonar pings, the human body is an environmental element in the world of the orcas. The sense of self unfolds, unravels, becoming like canvas. We are markers of significance in a world that is not our own: a whale shark glides along the length of Olly's body, a great white shark bumps the diving cage, an alligator's tail pushes against Suzi's hand, a snake's scales rub against their skin. The animals leave their marks. Double-crossing: Being astute to the way animals work in their terrains, Olly Suzi do not give in to the animal. They understand enough to maneuver in the animal world. They also know how to use a blank white surface. Let the shark bite the canvas and the anaconda slither across paper (figure 8.3). The paper will record one of the many crossings in the "inky, impenetrable darkness." The recording becomes the double-crossing, the betrayal and portrayal of an event that cannot be fully captured but that leaves traces of its passing. The canvas bears witness to the event. In a gallery, it functions like a map indicating an experiential terrain that has been traversed. The canvas is both presence and absence, a production and a loss. It points to the animal's "wealth of being-open, of which the human world may know nothing at all." The artists have extended themselves to the limits of the human world to bump up

FIGURE 8.3. Anaconda on Painting. Photograph by Greg Williams of Olly Suzi's "Green Anaconda," 2000.

against this wealth. As viewers we stand in the shadows of this other and foreign openness and we wonder at its surfaces.

Who is making the work of art? Who signs it and in a signature invests the art with language and value? Contrary to Heidegger's insistence, one does not need "hand" to write. For Heidegger, the hand (in the singular and in its singularity) functions like the distance of the artist's gaze and the grazier's eye in cattle portraiture. Hand allows humans to both be in touch with things and to manipulate them from a transcendental distance. Derrida explicates Heidegger's hand in "Geschlecht II":

> The nerve of the argument seems to me reducible to the assured opposition of *giving* and *taking*: man's hand *gives and gives itself, gives* and *is given*, like thought or like what gives itself to be thought and what we do not yet think, whereas the organ of the ape or of man as a simple animal, indeed as an *animal rationale*, can only *take hold of, grasp, lay hands on the thing*. The organ can *only* take hold of and manipulate the thing insofar as, in any case, it does not have to deal with the thing *as such*, does not let the thing be what it is in its essence. The organ has no access to the essence of the being *as such*.[43]

The shark biting into a canvas certainly seems to want to take hold of the thing, to grasp it. The animal organs, including the human animal's organs, fail for Heidegger to "give" and allow themselves to be given over to thought. The nudging and bumping and gnawing of animals shows a relationship between an animal and its environment. Heidegger wants to cut short this relationship and cut off any opportunity for the claw or paw to be hand. Relationship is not thinking, for Heidegger. As Derrida turns Heidegger, the hand becomes shorthand for metaphysical thinking, an investment in the human's ability to speak in our language. Heidegger's hand writes itself as human only. Yet, what is thought if it is not the relationships among things made visible? The animal in marking a canvas doubles the double-crossing. Its mark is both the relationship between teeth and canvas, fur and white surface, scale and paper and is the visible sign of this relationship. It is both mark and remark at once. The canvas is made useful and purposeful within the *Umwelt* of the animal. As such, the animal uses the canvas as "hand" to write and think with and to think on, like a scratch pad.

Contact zones and pidgin language leverage a rift within the human between the cultural humanity of man and our animality. It is our cultural humanity that creates heights and depths and ins and outs that distance us from surroundings. Nevertheless, the animality of man beckons: "It is possible to oppose man to other living things, and at the same time to organize the complex—and not always edifying—economy of relations between men and animals, only because something like an animal life has been separated within man, only because his distance and proximity to the animal have been measured and recognized first of all in the closest and most intimate place."[44] Olly Suzi circulate within the "economy of relations between men and animals." They are able to cross over to the "wealth of being open" in the "poor in world" of the animal because of the "diabolical art" by which their animal bodies mingle with other elements in the animal *Umwelt*. As part of the event structure that is their art, the artists ply their animality. They think -orca, –great white, and -anaconda in order both to be a part of animal worlds and to double-cross the animal's world while bringing something back, a scratch pad of animal-human surfaces that circulates in a double economy as "marker of significance" for animality and culture.

Throughout this chapter, surfaces are shown to have a power of production by leveraging their negative place in philosophy to think outside typical philosophical architecture, which privileges human interiority over and against objects of inquiry. At the heart of this essay is a claim by Coetzee's character Elizabeth Costello who explains that animals don't think like us nor speak like us but rather "Their whole being is in the living flesh."[45] I have employed Uexküll's biosemiotics of *Umwelt* to further Costello's claim about the flesh of animals as well as the visceral and tactical qualities implicit in the notion of "living flesh." If, as Coetzee claims (through Costello), there is something meaningful in the living flesh of the animal, which is precisely to challenge our usual understanding of flesh, and if Uexküll's work bears this out, then what are the implications for the visual arts?

I have focused on cattle portraits as a unique representative of art's historical uses of animals. These paintings employ the artistic rhetoric of picturesque landscapes, but rather than placing small groupings of animals in a scene, the artists represents a single animal in the foreground or middle ground. By doing so, the breeders' agricultural needs are placed directly in the middle of the painting. Art as consumption of the landscape meets the animal as an object of consumption. These animal portraits are not simply mimetic; rather they are intended to be productive by suggesting an ideal animal toward which grazers can breed their beasts. In these representations the animal's surface, its form and hide, are taken as indicators of its insides—meat and fat. The flesh and the inside of the animal become another exterior—cuts of meat—for human consumption.

Turning to a notion of *living* flesh changes the object of cultural consumption into a meaningful agent with an *Umwelt*. One way of exploring this

Umwelt is by taking philosophy at its word and thinking with the poverty and
"mere" surface of the animal. Indeed, since the world of the animal remains
foreign to humans, or as Thomas Nagel says, we will never know "what it is like
to be a bat" from the bat's perspective, we can only know the animal through
surfaces. We know it through contact with the surface of the animal and the
surface of the animal's world, or "bubble," as Uexküll explains. And perhaps
this is not radically different from how we know other humans. Olly Suzi
work with the animal surface, its living flesh, as well as the surface of the animal bubble as it meets our own in contact zones. The resulting marks on paper
are instructively different from animal portraiture and the history of animal
painting. The pieces of paper bear witness to animals' worlds. This witnessing
is not a knowing and consuming like cattle portraits that subsume the animal
and its world and subsequently deprive animals a space outside human understanding. These works leave the mystery of the animal—or rather animals—
and their worlds intact while calling attention to their existence.

Notes

1. Youatt 1834:4.
2. Ritvo 1987:34–81.
3. Moncrieff, Joseph, and Joseph 1988.
4. These examples of "correcting" the look of the animal through representation
include, respectively, John Boultbee's *The Durham Ox* (1802); Thomas Weaver's *The
White Heifer That Travelled* (1811); and descriptions of Shakespeare and D in William
Marshall's *Economy of the Midland Counties* (1796:324).
5. Foucault 1994:137.
6. Berger 1991:3 (emphasis in original).
7. For a succinct explanation of what Derrida means by "deconstruction," see Brett
Buchanan's essay (Chapter 9 in this volume).
8. Baker 2000:186.
9. The language of "the look" remains problematic insofar as it reinscribes the animal interior and its Otherness within the domain of visual culture. Unfortunately, "the
look" already points to human interiority, the depths and heights of our highly coded
special languages from linear perspective to Cartesian perspectivialism and on to the
Lacanian Imaginary and Symbolic (Jay 1988:4–11).
10. Derrida 1987:370.
11. Heidegger 1961:185.
12. Derrida 1991:51.
13. Heidegger 1961:198 (emphasis in original).
14. Uexküll 1957. For discussion, see Ingold 2000:176.

15. Uexküll 1957:10–11; Agamben 2004:52–55.

16. Deleuze 1990:128–29; Young 2003:10.

17. Coetzee 1999:65.

18. Blake 1982:3.

19. Derrida 1991:53.

20. Deleuze 1990:133.

21. Young 1834:16 (emphasis in original).

22. Coetzee 1999:65.

23. Heidegger 1961:255 (emphasis added).

24. Olly Suzi, Williams, and Baker 2003:8. Readers may find it useful to see examples of how Olly Suzi work in the wild. Clips are available from a Clive James interview at http://www.clivejames.com/gallery/painting/olly-suzi, a shorter clip at http://clivejames.com/video/library/1, or by following links on the artists' Web site, http://www.ollysuzi.com/projects/index.php.

25. Olly Suzi, Williams, and Baker 2003:184.

26. Olly Suzi. Williams, and Baker 2003:162.

27. Olly Suzi , Williams, and Baker 2003:162.

28. Olly Suzi, Williams, and Baker 2003:145.

29. James 2003:2.

30. Sloterdijk 1987:104.

31. Pratt 1992:4.

32. Pratt 1992:6.

33. Baker 2000:126.

34. Olly Suzi, Williams, and Baker 2003:67.

35. Baker 2003:149–51.

36. Olly Suzi, Williams, and Baker 2003:64.

37. Baker 2000:117.

38. James 2003:2.

39. Baker 2000:117–118 (emphasis in original).

40. Baker 2000:24–25, 38.

41. Deleuze and Guattari 1987:261.

42. Olly Suzi, Williams, and Baker 2003:176.

43. Derrida 1987:175 (emphasis in original).

44. Agamben 2004:16.

45. Coetzee 1999:65.

References

Agamben, Giorgio. 2004. *The Other: Man and Animal*. Stanford, CA: Stanford University Press.

Baker, Steve. 2000. *Postmodern Animal*. London: Reaktion Books.

——. 2003. "Sloughing the Human." In *Zoontologies*, ed. Cary Wolfe, 147–164. Minneapolis: University of Minnesota Press.

Berger, John. 1991. *About Looking*. New York: Vintage.

Blake, William. 1982. *The Book of Thel*. In *The Complete Poetry and Prose of William Blake*, ed. David V. Erdman, 3–6. New York: Anchor.

Coetzee, J. M. 1999. *The Lives of Animals*. Princeton, NJ: Princeton University Press.

Deleuze, Gilles. 1990. *The Logic of Sense*. New York: Columbia University Press.

Deleuze, Gilles and Felix Guattari. 1987. *A Thousand Plateaus: Capitalism and Schizophrenia*. Minneapolis: University of Minnesota Press.

Derrida, Jacques. 1987. "Geschlecht II: Heidegger's Hand." In *Deconstruction and Philosophy*, ed. John Sallis, 161–196. Chicago: University of Chicago Press.

——. 1991. *Of Spirit*. Chicago: University of Chicago Press.

——. 2001. "The Animal That Therefore I Am (More to Follow)." *Critical Inquiry* 28, no. 2: 369–380.

——. 2008. *The Animal That Therefore I Am*. New York: Fordham University Press.

Foucault, Michel. 1994. *The Order of Things*. New York: Vintage Books.

Heidegger, Martin. 1961. *The Fundamental Concepts of Metaphysics: World, Finitude, Solitude*. New York: Doubleday.

Ingold, Tim. 2000. *Perception of the Environment*. New York: Routledge.

James, Clive. 2003. "Introduction." In *Olly & Suzi: Arctic Desert Ocean Jungle*, 2. New York: Harry N. Abrams.

Jay, Martin. 1988. "Scopic Regimes of Modernity." In *Vision and Visuality*, ed. Hal Foster, 3–23. Seattle: Bay Press.

Marshall, William. 1796. *Economy of the Midland Counties*. London: G. Nicol.

Moncrieff, Elspeth, Stephen Joseph, and Iona Joseph. 1988. *Farm Animal Portraits*. Woodbridge, Suffolk: Antique Collector's Club.

Olly Suzi, Greg Williams, and Steve Baker. 2003. *Olly & Suzi: Arctic Desert Ocean Jungle*. New York: Harry N. Abrams.

Pratt, Mary Louise. 1992. *Imperial Eyes*. New York: Routledge.

Ritvo, Harriet. 1987. *The Animal Estate*. Cambridge, MA: Harvard University Press.

Sloterdijk, Peter. 1987. *Critique of Cynical Reason*. Minneapolis: University of Minnesota Press.

Uexküll, Jakob von. 1957. "A Stroll Through the World of Animals and Men: A Picture Book of Invisible Worlds." In *Instinctive Behavior: The Development of a Modern Concept*, ed. Claire H. Schiller, trans. D. J. Kuenen, 5–80. New York: International Universities Press.

Young, Fredrick. 2003. "Animality: Notes Towards a Manifesto." In *Glossalalia*, ed. Julian Wolfreys and Harun Karim Thomas, 9–22. Manchester, UK: Edinburgh University Press.

Youatt, William. 1834. *Cattle: Their Breeds, Management, and Diseases*. London: Baldwin and Cradock.

PART III

Animal Others

Theorizing Animal/Human

PART III CONCLUDES THIS VOLUME WITH AN EXPLORATION OF the theoretical ground upon which the animal/human binary has been contemplated, disputed, pondered, and weighed over the past century and upon which the nascent field of animal studies is now taking root. It serves as an introduction both to the richness of the emergent field and to the ideas of some of the most celebrated thinkers of the 20th century. The reader is immediately confronted with the complexity of the categories of human and animal, their robustness for human thought and exploration, and their resilience.

Brett Buchanan's essay "Being with Animals: Reconsidering Heidegger's Animal Ontology" (chapter 9) provides a sweeping assessment of the nonhuman animal in the history of Western philosophy. He concludes that it has generally been afflicted by a persistent need to see in animals the base from which humans dramatically ascend. Buchanan explores how animals have typically been characterized in ways that support human distinction and exceptionality, often laying the foundation for a kind of apotheosis of the human. Only in the post-Darwin era, when the human "rupture" from all other animate life lost much of its plausibility and in its stead an idea of a continuum across animal life was gaining ground, did the real philosophical dilemma of understanding what it means to be human and its relationship with "the animal other" begin. Buchanan situates Martin Heidegger's oeuvre at this juncture.

Heidegger's writings on human existence reveal animal life to be fundamental, if only implicitly so, to his philosophical project. In his clearing, or "destruction," of Western metaphysical assumptions, undertaken in order to create a space to explore the question of Being, he sets out to interrogate how we are in the world, in relation to other beings in the world, including other animal beings, and more foundationally, to "the primordial nature of Being itself."

At times, Heidegger makes the animal question his explicit concern, and here Buchanan skillfully steers us through a dense and difficult topography of ideas. Buchanan weighs Heidegger's identification of the animal as "poor in the world," characterized by its "captivation" by things, along with his more positive insistence that all living beings "have a world" as a relational structure that is variably disclosed and revealed.

Buchanan's essay reveals why Heidegger's work, though not without difficulties, marks a significant departure from earlier Western philosophical thinking about animals. Heidegger's rejection of the primacy of the conceptual and his insistence on the relational structure of our existence allow for the possibility of a "fundamental relationship" with other beings, including animals.

Ashley E. Pryor's essay "Heidegger and the Dog Whisperer: Imagining Interspecies Kindness" (chapter 10) makes a strong claim, similar to Buchanan's, for taking seriously Heidegger's insights on animals, although she is more inclined to view these insights as an inadvertent result of Heidegger's philosophy, rather than its reasoned outcome. Because Heidegger's work sets aside a priori metaphysical categories (that have fueled questions of a "what is?" nature, e.g., "*What* is a human?" "What is an animal?") and focuses instead on the "how" we are in the world, it necessitates an exploration of how we are in relation to other beings-in-the-world, including animals.

Pryor's essay begins with a discussion of the possibility of "kindness" in animals, explored through J. M. Coetzee's fiction, as a way of leading the reader to a sense of the enormity and difficulty such discussions pose in a society where animals have traditionally been conceived as nonintentional beings, locked up in their biology. Pryor's discussion moves toward a condemnation—similar to that of Buchanan's—of Western philosophy's failure to even probe the contours of what shared grounds of communication across species might look like. She argues that the possibility of genuine communication, let alone human friendship with other animal species, is "short circuited" by assumptions of the human and the animal as radically distinct. This is where the philosophy of Heidegger proves illuminating, marking for Pryor, as for Buchanan, the beginnings of a creative exodus from a sterile terrain.

Heidegger's phenomenology provides philosophical support for Pryor's understanding of kindness as a nondiscursive way of being in the world that extends beyond the human animal. However, it is celebrity dog trainer Cesar Millan, for whom meaningful communication between species is the taken-for-granted ground of his successes, that receives the focus of her analysis. For Pryor, Millan brings to fruition "the promise of Heidegger's phenomenology of animality."

Pryor insists that kindness between animals "forms the condition of possibility of pets" insomuch as it provides the context for our basic relationships with the animals with whom we share our lives. Adopting a phenomenological philosophy that emphasizes lived intersubjective experiences over that of the discursively driven, binary-committed objective knowledge, she persuasively demonstrates that kindness is neither a logical nor a linguistic operation, but is rooted in the experience of living in a shared world where communication is the rule.

J. M. Coetzee's novella, which made a brief, but fruitful appearance in Pryor's work, is a central focus of Undine Sellbach's essay "*The Lives of Animals*: Wittgenstein, Coetzee, and the Extent of the Sympathetic Imagination" (chapter 11). Sellbach's work shares with that of Buchanan and Pryor the desire to disrupt the taken-for-granted solitudes of "humanity" and "animality," and she uses Coetzee's work effectively to that end. Sellbach begins with Coetzee's *The Lives of Animals*, which, she argues, evokes a sense of the multiplicity of animal lives, and of "life" being something that all animals *have*—a heterogeneity and fullness that is lost in the term "animal."

Sellbach acknowledges that the challenge of thinking about the multiplicity of the lives of animals is enormous and perhaps even beyond our ability to imagine, and yet it remains a crucial task. She considers this paradox of the "impossible-but-important" as a fundamental feature of our experience of the world and treats it as analogous to Wittgenstein's reflections on the possibilities and paradoxes of trying to speak ethically. Wittgenstein observed that ethics arises from an impulse to speak about the meaning of life and of the experience of wonder at its magnitude. And although we inevitability stumble before the enormity of life and the limits of our imagination, he insists the task remains vital.

Stretching the imagination to its very limits is, for Wittgenstein, a "valuable form of nonsense"—nonsense because our wonder exceeds our capacity to makes sense and valuable because it is the only means to envisage life as a miracle. With this as the backdrop, Sellbach turns to Coetzee's *The Lives of Animals* and devotes the remainder of her essay to exploring protagonist Elizabeth Costello's efforts to talk about the human capacity to imaginatively engage with the lives of animals.

Costello speaks about the shared substrate of all life and insists that encounters between humans and animals allows for an opening to the very *being* of existence. She insists that our language abounds with metaphors of animality not because they serve as analogies for self-exploration but because they arise from the embodied experiences of aliveness, love, hunger, joy, and so on that are shared by all animals. Sellbach finds support for Costello in Wittgenstein's notion of *forms of life* and also makes productive use of the works of Agamben, Cavell, Derrida, Gaita, and Lévinas for Costello's (and her own) exploration of the sympathetic imagination as the means of entering into the interconnections that lie between all life.

The last essay of this volume is meant to give us pause. Myra J. Hird, in "Animal, All Too Animal: *Blood Music* and an Ethic of Vulnerability" (chapter 12) invites us to contemplate the "big picture." Her essay leads us to consider whether our outpourings over "animal others" may be, at one level at least, insular, species-specific musings, not terribly different from the medieval debates over angels and their dances on the heads of pins. This is not to belittle that which is of crucial importance to us, but rather to situate it within a broader perspective that emphasizes our shared condition of animal life, rather than our differences.

Though each of the essays in this section have problematized the categories of human and animal, all have taken the existence and stability of animal life, both human and nonhuman, as given and have plumbed their depths in general ignorance of their utter dependence upon "a more salient relationship with the engines of life itself"—namely, those of microbial life. Hird shifts the focus of our discussion away from the concepts of "the animal" to consider the ground upon which these concepts and relationships arise in the first place. Bacteria, Hird reminds us, are responsible for generating the diversity of all living organisms on earth, and their absence would mean the immediate end of the planet. If the awesomeness of this reality were to be truly grasped, Hird suggests, our species-smugness would have to give way.

To facilitate an imaginative glimpse into the real power and nearly absolute dominion of the microbial, Hird draws upon Greg Bear's novel *Blood Music*. This science fiction account narrates the devastating (for humans) spread of bacteria as it gradually infiltrates the species to such an extent that humanity, as it now exists, is wiped out. The bacteria do not operate maliciously against humans, but only according to their own logic. Nevertheless, their spread spells our doom. The readers of *Blood Music* are left with a sense of the fragility of species life and the sober awareness that the human pretense to agency was always ephemeral. Bacteria have always been in control.

Though *Blood Music* is a work of fiction, Hird argues that the power of bacteria—and animal life's dependency on them—is not. Yet animal life stumbles along blindly, absorbed in (inter)species turf wars, oblivious to its own precariousness. Similarly, we humans construct sociopolitical, economic, and ethical sandcastles, eulogize their successes, and fret over their failures, all the while remaining oblivious to our own fragility.

Hird suggests that to think and act as if we were masters of the universe, as if we were actually in control of our fate, is pure hubris. She suggests that paying attention to the determining power the microbial has over animal existence might lead to an ethic of vulnerability, which would recognize our dependence on this far more robust engine of life and lead to a shared sense of fragility with other species. The hope is that it might also inculcate a sense of *communitas* with all life.

Anne Vallely

nine

Being with Animals

Reconsidering Heidegger's Animal Ontology

Brett Buchanan

IN ASKING THE QUESTION "WHAT DOES IT MEAN TO BE HUMAN?" we both understand and distance ourselves from the animal. Nowhere is this more explicit than in the early Latin definition of the human: humans are the animal rationale, the animal that has reason. This formulation was itself a reinterpretation of the ancient Greek view of being human, as the living being that possesses rational discourse (*zoon logon echon*). In both instances we are a living animal. But essential to this definition is the claim that we are much more than just "animal" and that it is this extra quality—whether it is reason, language, or something else—that separates us from all other living beings. The discriminating factor of reason has furthermore meant that humans, insofar as we are rational, are presumed to be closer to the divine than to the rest of nature. In the great chain of being, humans are cut off from their biological neighbors. As one example, Aristotle explains in the final book of his *Nicomachean Ethics* that if reason is divine, then humanity must strive toward immortality by exercising that god-like power of intellectual contemplation. Even if human nature is understood to be stretched between both divine and animal, both immortal and mortal, it is always the divine and immortal part of ourselves that is defined as human, not the animal part. Another way that this dichotomy has been framed is that humans have both a rational soul and a sensual body. Within the history of Western philosophy, it is the body, the animal part of the human, that, roughly speaking, is quietly swept aside as philosophically and theologically unimportant. In contrast to the logical precision and infinite reach of the soul and mind, the body is configured as the source of all our mortal problems, from inappropriate emotional and sexual urges to genocidal violence.

In this long-standing Western understanding, the solution to the problem posed by human animality is not found, as one might think, within animality but by escaping it. Plato and, in a different manner, Aristotle argue that we should free our souls from the base inclinations of the body by exercising rational thought and contemplating universal ideas. The body is just an impermanent dwelling place for the soul, which is more at home with eternal truth than animal contingency. Much later, Descartes, considered the father of modern philosophy, will intensify and extend the mind-body split, famously arguing that animals are mechanical bodies and that the sounds they emit under duress are equivalent to the sounds made by machines. There is no subjectivity behind the noise of an animal, just the whirring of a mindless mechanism.[1]

It was not until Carl Linnaeus—who devised a taxonomy of the natural world wherein *Homo sapiens* occupied a stratum along with simians—and then Charles Darwin—whose discoveries proposed not only an evolutionary line between human and nonhuman animals, but also a blind process of natural selection that contests the idea of divine providence and essentialist distinctions—that the "animal other" became a more formidable foe. Now the animal could no longer be so easily dismissed and became a more philosophically intriguing puzzle. To ask about the meaning of human nature now requires that one ask about (instead of presuming) the meaning of the animal— and vice versa. The question of the animal requires that we look in the mirror anew, and once we do, to recognize that the animal is not so other. As Peter Steeves has remarked, "we have met the animal's body, and he is us. There are no animal Others."[2]

Within and against this philosophical tradition stands an intriguing and perhaps unexpected figure. Martin Heidegger (1889–1976) is most often recognized for his contribution to rethinking the meaning of human existence beyond the metaphysical assumptions of philosophy, such as the mind-body problem and self-world dichotomy.[3] The key concern for Heidegger is the question of the meaning of Being; he is not as interested in *what* something is (the usual ontological inquiry about a being or thing [*Seiende*], what Heidegger will refer to as an "ontic" inquiry), as he is with *how* something *is* in the world (the inquiry into the Being or "to-be" [*Sein*] of a being or thing). In this respect, Heidegger stands as one of the most influential philosophers of the twentieth century, and his thought reaches into nearly every major theoretical development subsequent to him, from critical theory to post-structuralism, and from such diverse professions as nursing and architecture. But it is not his writings on human existence that are of particular interest here. Rather, his sporadic writings on animals, which are today receiving ever greater attention, provide the occasion for reconsidering animals and our relations with them.[4] In this chapter I highlight what makes Heidegger's position on animal life attractive—and also problematic—as a contemporary response to the Western philosophical tradition. Among his arguments, probably the most convincing and contemporary is that we need to approach animal others not by objectifying them through scientific explanation but by understanding animals in our "being-with" (*Mitsein*) them. In highlighting this methodological emphasis on being-with, I will also highlight some of the points of contention that have been raised with respect to his treatment of animals.

Heidegger and the Tradition

Among Heidegger's many contributions to philosophical thought is his close familiarity with and critique of the Western tradition. In his early and most famous work, *Being and Time* (1927), Heidegger advances what he calls a positive "destruction" of the history of traditional ontology.[5] This idea of "destroying" the Western tradition of thought has been made famous through Jacques Derrida's concept of "deconstruction," a term that he consciously borrows from Heidegger and reinterprets. With Heidegger, as with Derrida, the task is to expose, question, and to the extent possible overcome the problematic assumptions that underlie so much of the history of thought. As Heidegger clearly states, however, this destruction is also constructive. His intention is not simply to shatter the tradition into a rubble of discarded ideas, but rather to realize the full potential of philosophy. Heidegger maintains that throughout history no philosophical system had properly posed the question of Being. From Plato onward, he argues, the realm of ontology—that which is concerned with what *is*, namely, beings—has been interested in asking about this or that being (*Seiende*), from atoms to animals to God, but not once has the question of the meaning of Being (*Sein*) itself been raised. Heidegger argues that this question has been forgotten over the ages, and yet, crucially, it necessarily forms the primordial background to any and all concerns regarding actual beings. Thus, before asking questions about whether God exists, what exactly a mammal is, or if an amoeba is a plant or animal, all of which are ontological questions, we need to first ask what it means "to be" in the first place. What is the meaning of Being *as such*; and what does it mean to be human, to be animal, to be God? With this as his impetus, Heidegger sought to critique previous ontologies in order to call attention to the primordial question of Being itself.

Heidegger found that one of the keys to this destruction of previous ontologies was a focus on human existence, what Heidegger calls *Dasein*, literally "being-there" but ultimately untranslatable. To ask about Being itself, he reasoned, we must ask first about the kind of being that inquires about Being and, he presumes, it is only humans that ask the question of Being. We humans have an understanding of Being, no matter how faint it may be, within the very engagement of our lives. We can understand ourselves in terms of the possibility of being or not being. Thus Heidegger concludes, simply enough, that in order to arrive at the ontological presuppositions embedded within the history of philosophy and properly pose the question of Being, we must first begin with an understanding of our own concrete and everyday lives. Through a "hermeneutic of existence," an interpretation of how we live—from the simplest of acts, such as hammering a nail or walking down a road, to the more complex analyses of our mortality and finitude—we may discern the hidden meaning of what it means to be. As Heidegger will write, "We are ourselves the entities to be analyzed."[6]

In an important sense, this focus on human existence resembles the very philosophical tradition Heidegger claims to be critiquing. Doesn't Kant emphasize the anthropological dimension of our rational faculties? Wasn't it Descartes who impressed upon us the importance of the *cogito*, the thinking "I" that provides the Archimedean stability of subjectivity and thus of human existence itself? Isn't it Aristotle who claims that all living things have souls, but that humans alone have a cognitive soul enabling us to discourse rationally and thus politically? After all his criticisms of these thinkers for asking about beings (like human beings) instead of Being, hasn't Heidegger engaged in roughly the same kind of inquiry, offering a mere variation on the theme of human uniqueness?

Despite his early emphasis on human existence, Heidegger ultimately works to slide out from beneath the metaphysical assumption of the human as a substantial being residing outside any particular context. Since the nineteenth century, one of the common critiques leveled against "metaphysics," which became the term for a variety of philosophical ideas under critique, is that it has always posited an essential human nature, something that unequivocally defines us *as* human regardless of time or place. As mentioned above, this is typically taken to be a rational soul, spirit, mind, ego, even consciousness. But as Heidegger claims, such a position posits a fixed human essence and thus already assumes a definition of human beings as existent things in the world. Heidegger's startling insight is that prior to asking what it means to be we always already have an implicit understanding of what it means to be human and, more broadly, what it means to be a thing in the world. Thus, far from falling in line with the tradition, Heidegger looks to expose the prejudice of the human within our consideration of the world. It just so happens that in order to overcome a metaphysics of human subjectivity, one has to pass through an "existential analytic" of being human to reveal the origins of the meaning of Being.

For all of the praise that Heidegger deserves for challenging the idea of a fixed human essence and helping us rethink the kind of beings we are, he nevertheless maintains the idea that humans are radically unique and relegates animals (not to mention plants and all other living and nonliving things) to a secondary status in his ontology. And yet, despite Heidegger's primary interest in human *Dasein*, the question of the animal is not surrendered. A few years after the publication of *Being and Time*, Heidegger returned to the issue of animal life in his 1929–1930 lecture course, *The Fundamental Concepts of Metaphysics* (FCM).[7] Here in these lectures he asks the same question about animals that he had previously asked only of human *Dasein*: do animals have a "world"? Are they worldly? That is, can they be understood in terms of an open relation to their surroundings such that their environment opens up to them as Heidegger came to understand humans? And—to ask an even more daunting and problematic question—how would we know either way? In short, what does it mean *to be* animal?

Being-with the Animal Other

One of Heidegger's strongest features—as we shall see, perhaps his most unsuccessful as well—is that throughout all of his wrestling and grappling with the being of the animal he never manages to pin the animal down. As he himself is aware, he reaches only tentative conclusions about animal being. This does not mean that he did not seek more certainty, and he does on several occasions proclaim an animal essence, namely their captivation (*Benehmen*) by things. But when all is said and done, Heidegger will conclude that his interpretations of the animal remain "incomplete" (FCM, 385/265) and that his thesis concerning the animal "must remain as a problem."[8] This not only is true of these 1929–1930 lectures, but also holds for the references to animals throughout his later writings. In order to highlight Heidegger's approach to animal life, there are a few issues on which I wish to concentrate: (1) how Heidegger admits to the elusive nature of the animal, rather than twisting it into some formulation that obscures and diminishes the animal as other; (2) how he attempts to let the animals "be" themselves; (3) how he emphasizes our *Mitsein* and our going-along-with the animal, rather than taking a distanced and objective stance; how he, in other words, is cautious of assuming an anthropomorphic appropriation of the animal. Heidegger is not always successful in these endeavors, yet he has paved the way for how we might *be* with the animals in whose midst we live, both theoretically and physically.

By emphasizing *Mitsein*—being-with animals—Heidegger is specifically avoiding a rationalization, or even an imagination, that too often explains away and reduces the lives of animals. The problem with rationalizing or imagining is that animals are taken out of their own most immediate environment in order to be understood. From the Lascaux cave paintings to modern nature documentaries, and all the images in between, animals have been contorted as representations of our own machinations, be they rational or imaginative. This is not to dismiss the significance of these representations, but simply to recognize that, whatever their worth, they do not convey a form of intimate knowledge about animals as they are often presumed to do. Too often animals have been decontextualized—sometimes literally ripped from their environments—in the attempt to understand them. They are then reframed in this or that discourse which purports to reveal some truth about them. Heidegger, however, is influenced by biologists and ethologists such as Jakob von Uexküll and recognizes that animals, like humans, cannot be taken as things present-at-hand (*vorhanden*) that we can know, represent, and imagine, and thus master, control, and inevitably manipulate. For Heidegger, neither reason nor imagination is sufficient to genuinely approach the being of animals on their own terms. Forty years before Thomas Nagel wrote his influential essay "What Is It Like to Be a Bat?"[9] in which he showed just how difficult it is to try to imagine a bat's perceptual world, Heidegger, in a similar spirit, remarks that "the difficulty is not merely that of determining *what* it is that the insect sees but also that of determining *how* it sees. For we should not compare our own seeing with that of the animal without further ado."[10] Thus the problem for Heidegger is how to approach the animal without making it into something it is not. Previous attempts to understand the animal other have had questionable success, whether it be through a rational discourse pronouncing the animal to be this or that, through imaginative representations found in myth and art, or even through innocent imitations of what it might be like to be a certain nonhuman animal.

The discretion that Heidegger seeks is found in an alternative approach, what he calls "transposition (*Versetzen*)": "Transposing oneself into this being means going along with [*mitgehen*] what it is and with how it is. Such going-along-with means directly learning how it is with this being *with* which we are going along *in this way*."[11] The key to this formulation is that Heidegger admits it is difficult enough, if not impossible, to transpose ourselves into another human being, let alone a nonhuman animal, *if* this means trying to get "inside" the other. He does not want to assimilate the animal into anything resembling the human (or, for that matter, assimilate one human to another), because by making a comparison between the two one risks effacing any difference between them. At stake here is remaining other (*als andere*) while nonetheless gaining an understanding of the animal other *in* its otherness.[12] To succeed in transposition therefore requires that we be ourselves in going along with the animal in the animal's being.

But what does this being-with mean? It is far from simply chatting with your best friend or literally going along with your dog for a walk. Being-with means these things too, of course, but there is a more profound ontological understanding of it. In *Being and Time*, Heidegger explains that *Mitsein* is an existential dimension of our being-in-the-world (*in-der-Welt-sein*). Through his examination of human *Dasein*, we learn that his critique of the subject/object distinction and the mind/body distinction is rooted in his analysis of human *Dasein*'s being-in-the-world; we exist not in a world that is distinct from us, as though it were set over and against our own impenetrable subjectivities.[13] Rather, the very nature of our existence is one of being-in-the-world as a whole, and in which living and nonliving things are disclosed and opened to us. In this view, the world is not a being or entity to be known, but is part of a relational structure *with* human *Dasein* such that other things become meaningful.[14] Being-with, then, plays a specific role here insofar as the world is one that is shared with others, not subsequently as the result of encountering others in one's everyday activities, but as an ontological predisposition to be able to encounter others in the first place. Another way of putting this is that any epistemological attempt to know oneself or know the other is rooted in the phenomenon of being-with; knowledge of the other derives only from a more primordial understanding grounded in being-in-the-world. Thus, when we are led to wonder about the nature of transposition in being-with animals, we are informed that this "Being transposed into others belongs to the essence of human *Dasein* (*Das Versetztsein in Andere gehört zum Wesen des menschlichen Daseins*)."[15]

Yet it is true that the nonhuman animal presents a difficulty that is not necessarily present with other human beings. When Heidegger speaks of being-with-others, he is usually addressing our everyday encounters with other humans. The examples that he gives are particularly indicative of this. When we go for a solitary walk along a country path or when we sit down at our desk to do some reading or writing, we may not be in the presence of another person, but the environment as a whole is one of being-with other humans inasmuch as the path and room are what they are because they are set out in advance as belonging to others. The world as a whole is marked by the presence of other people, even if they are not encountered in person. To be human is therefore to be in the world such that one encounters things as already laid out in advance; there is a horizon in which things are understood. But, we might wonder, what about a walk through a forest that is so devoid of human life that we feel as though we are alone in the world? Here we might wonder about the insects that fly around us, the brush that cushions our step, the birds that fly above and around us, and the sounds that form the environment in which we are swept along. What sense of being-with is discernible here, and what, moreover, does this say about our understanding of animal life?

By noting that we are always already comported and transposed to being-with other people and animals, the question primarily concerns what insight we can gain about how it is to be an animal. In order to do so, let us look at what Heidegger calls the "striking example [*auffälliges Beispiel*]" of a domestic pet. There is much to be said about the following passage, and I fear that it is striking for reasons different than Heidegger's own.

> We keep domestic pets in the house with us, they "live" *with us*. But we do not live with them if living means *being* in an animal kind of way. Yet we *are with* them nonetheless. But this being-with is not an existing-with because a dog does not exist, but merely lives. Through this being with animals we enable them to move within our world. We say that the dog is lying underneath the table or is running up the stairs and so on. Yet when we consider the dog itself—does it comport itself toward the table as a table, toward the stairs as stairs? All the same, it does go up the stairs with us. It feeds with us—and yet, we do not really "feed." It eats with us—and yet, it does not really "eat." Nevertheless, it is with us! A going-along-with . . . a transposedness, and yet not.[16]

Before going any further, Heidegger's remarks about the pet dog—let's call him Fritz—hold not just for domestic animals, but for all animals, whether domestic, wild, or anything in between. What he is after here is a clarification of "animality" itself, what it means to be an animal. He is not concerned with what we know about this or that animal or how we might imagine an animal, but is pursuing a statement of essence concerning the very being of animals as such. This holds, therefore, for "*all* animals, *every* animal [alle *Tiere*, jedes *Tieren*]" from amoeba to apes, zoophytes to zebras.[17] Throughout his writings Heidegger refers to all sorts of animals; there are dogs, bees, sea urchins, lizards, larks, apes, flocks of birds, woodpeckers, bulls, and stallions. There is a full spectrum of animals implied in Heidegger's writings, but more often than not there is simply the nameless "animal," for all of these magnificent beings are always and in every case examples of one category: animal. Heidegger does this because, he argues, an animal cannot relate to something *as* something, such as Fritz apprehending the table *as* a table. Without this "as," the status of its being in relation to a world is in doubt. "If it cannot [draw this relation]," Heidegger writes, "then the animal is separated from man by an abyss."[18] And for this reason, Heidegger understands human *Dasein* as radically unique and separated by an abyss from animality.

It is precisely this issue that has raised the interest of Derrida over the course of many of his writings. In his book *Of Spirit*, and again later in his essay "The Animal That Therefore I Am (More to Follow)," Derrida questions the idea of a chasm or abyss between the two.[19] For someone who has long been preoccupied by the notion of borders and limits, the possibility of a border between human and animal—human/animal—proves too enticing a target to pass over. Writing on Heidegger, Derrida argues that he is: "Compromised . . . by a *thesis* on animality which presupposes—this is the irreducible and I believe dogmatic hypothesis of the thesis—that there is one thing, one domain, one homogeneous type of entity, which is called animality *in general*, for which any example would do the job."[20] No matter what animal Heidegger provides as an example, it is always an example of animality as such. Derrida's critique of Heidegger rests on the assumption that there *are* borders and differences between human *Dasein* on the one hand and all other animals on the other. The question, however, is why Heidegger maintains and even emphasizes differences between humans and animals—differences that, it bears repeating, are crucial to maintain for Derrida[21]—but has no problem lumping all other animals together in one category. If the difference between a chimpanzee and a human is "an abyss," then how can we ignore the differences between a flea and an ape? We might further wonder what Heidegger would make of presumably more difficult cases of "borderline" beings such as children.[22] Is a young child in the same ontological category as a "normal" adult human (that is, *Dasein*)?

Returning to the case of poor Fritz, Heidegger's position becomes more discernible. The relation between a dog and a human is a skewed one, even if both can be said to be-with each other. From Fritz's side, he *lives* with us, whereas from the human side we *exist* with Fritz. Heidegger even admits as much when he boldly declares that "a dog does not exist but merely lives." Similarly, we are invited to see that whereas humans eat, Fritz feeds. From this it is not much of a stretch to say that just as one has teeth, the other has fangs; one has hair, the other has fur; one has hands, the other may have claws or paws; one has a face, the other has . . ., well, this is never answered. Both Heidegger and Emmanuel Lévinas (the French phenomenologist, Judaic scholar, and key thinker responsible for introducing the work of Heidegger and Husserl in France) maintain that although animals have faces, they are nevertheless characterized as deficient in some manner.[23] At work, then, is the assertion of a difference between the being of human *Dasein* and the being of an animal. Is this just a conceptual wordplay? Are we really just mincing words here when we talk about the animal not existing, not eating? Heidegger contends that it is not just a terminological issue when he speaks in this way, for if it were then his position would have little strength. Instead, Heidegger maintains that these differences in language refer to differences in human and animal ways of being.

The primary concern is not what we *call* the relation—one can imagine Gershwin's words of indifference between "you say 'feed,' I say 'eat,' let's call the whole thing off"—but the relation itself. Our understanding of animal life, insofar as it is rooted in this ontological privilege of being-with, is inclined toward how animals relate to their environment. Heidegger is able to say that a dog lives and feeds, whereas a human exists and eats, because this terminology is a manner of describing the respective ways of being for both dog and human. An animal like Fritz, Heidegger argues, does not "comport [*verhalt*]" itself toward the things in its environment *as* the things they are. Even though a dog may bound up the stairs or a lizard may enjoy basking on a hot rock, Heidegger contends that an animal never relates or comports itself toward these things in their being. Insofar as this is the case, an animal is unable to transcend its own limitations, is unable to leap out of its own predicament in order to allow the environment to open up to a world. And if this is the case, the animal does not "exist"—where existence is interpreted literally as *ex-sistere*, to stand out from itself—but merely "lives."[24] Finally, if the animal does not exist in the fashion of human *Dasein*, the abyss that Heidegger mentions creeps open.

Being Animal

I would agree with Heidegger that even though we exist in the midst of other animals, we do not relate to one another, nor to the world, in the same way. It is this that Heidegger is emphasizing in the passage on the dog cited above, namely, that being human entails a fundamentally different relation to other things and the world than does the relation between any other animal and its milieu. One of the greater repercussions of the trajectory of Heidegger's thought, however, is that we may not even be capable of being-with animals properly speaking, at least not in Heidegger's sense of the word. As he suggests in the case of Fritz, which again means the case of any animal, there is a going-along-with, a transposability, and yet not really. The problem is that animals seem to be living beings with whom we can transpose ourselves, and yet their being refuses our going along with them because of their essentially different nature. More specifically, Heidegger withdraws the possibility of being-with animals because they do not seem to have a world in the same sense as human *Dasein* and thus do not allow us to *be* with them in a reciprocal fashion. But what exactly does this mean? Has he just removed the possibility of our ever gaining meaningful insight into animal life?

Over the course of his comparative examination between humans, animals, and lifeless objects (for example, a stone), Heidegger begins with a few hypotheses in order to arrive at an eventual claim concerning animals. The opening hypotheses are the following: "We can formulate these distinctions in the following three theses: the stone is *worldless*; the animal is *poor in world*; man is *world-forming*."[25] All three theses are specifically formulated in relation to the concept of world. Heidegger's primary question, and the very reason he reintroduces the question of the animal back into his thought, is to wonder whether other beings have a relation to the world in a manner similar to that of human beings. Since human *Dasein* is defined by its being-in-the-world, if animals can also be defined as world-forming, then any means of ontological distinction will surely fade away. Despite what we've seen from the passage concerning Fritz the dog, we have not yet observed any argument or illustration about the being of the animal that would shed light on this inability to relate to other things. Nevertheless, we have just seen that this does form a guiding hypothesis for Heidegger: the animal is poor in world.

Although he states this hypothesis rather matter-of-factly, Heidegger has not always been so comfortable making declarations with respect to the "world" (or lack of world) of animals. For instance, in 1925 he speaks openly about the importance of the world for animals. In his *History of the Concept of Time*, Heidegger writes: "The snail is not at the outset only in its shell and not yet in the world, a world described as standing over and against it, an opposition which it broaches by first crawling out. It crawls out only insofar as its being is already to be in a world. It does not first add a world to itself by touching. Rather, it touches because its being means nothing other than to be a world."[26] He makes a similar comment during a series of lectures in honor of Wilhelm Dilthey: "Every living creature has its environing world not as something extant next to it but as something that is there for it as disclosed, uncovered. For a primitive animal, the world can be very simple. . . . But we miss the essential thing here if we don't see that the animal has a world. In the same way, we too are always in a world in such a way that it is disclosed for us."[27] From these passages, not only does it appear that Heidegger relates animal being to the openness and disclosure of a world, but also that he does so in direct comparison to human beings. From snails to human beings, all living creatures are noted to be in a world as something intrinsic to their being. Within just a few years time, however, Heidegger withdraws this earlier assertion by instead hypothesizing that animals do not have a world, at least not in the same way as humans. By 1930, as we have just seen, animals are configured as "poor in world." Just a few more years after this in 1935, Heidegger will draw the conclusion that "the animal has no world [*Welt*], nor any environment [*Umwelt*]."[28]

What accounts for this change? We find in Heidegger's analyses an increasingly pronounced difference between humans and animals and that this difference has to do with the concept of world.[29] Again, we might be tempted to chalk this up to a terminological issue—humans are worldly, animals are environmental—but this would again miss the fundamental issue. The reason for this difference rests on the essential distinction of how each being relates to other beings and to Being as such. In the case of human *Dasein*, existence is characterized by "transcendence," though this should not be confused with an otherworldly understanding of transcending one's body or transcending this world for another. Rather, Heidegger's notion of transcendence describes how human existence always already entails being beyond itself and being outside itself, whether one wants to think of this as projecting oneself into the future, as a necessary requirement of being-in-the-world or the transcendent distinction between beings and Being.[30] Describing the transcendent character of human *Dasein* is the single most important task of *Being and Time*.[31] It is only due to the transcendent character of our being that we can be said to have a world: the world *is*, not as an existent thing out there but as the meaningful horizon in which we comport ourselves as human *Dasein*. Thus our ability to be in the world is dependent on our being able to relate to other things in their being because we can step out of ourselves. This distance is precisely what Heidegger means when he says that humans are world-forming: "Man also stands over against the world. This standing-over-against is a *'having'* of world as that in which man moves, with which he engages."[32]

By contrast, animals do not have this intrinsic ability to step beyond themselves. Although Heidegger would surely not approve of the following formulation, we might say that only human *Dasein* is a truly transcendent animal. All other animals are instead declared to be so captivated by the things within their midst that they are never capable of being open to these things as such. Heidegger therefore concludes that "captivation [*Benommenheit*]" is the fundamental essence of the animal. "To say that captivation is the essence of animality means: *The animal as such does not stand within a manifestness of beings. Neither its so-called environment nor the animal itself are manifest as beings.*"[33] The notion of captivation is not pulled out of nowhere. Heidegger draws on a number of examples to describe the behavior of animals within their natural settings, and these examples derive from a wide range of scenarios, from everyday observations, as with the case of Fritz in his relation to a table, to examples taken from contemporary scientific research, such as the behavior of bees in their relations to the hive and their own abdomens.[34] In every scenario the question is the same: does the animal have access to beings and/or Being *as such*? And in every scenario the answer seems to be the same: the animal clearly relates to beings through seeing, hearing, seizing, and so on, but never relates to these beings in their being. In other words, the animal is said to be so absorbed in itself that it is captivated by the thing and thus never really free to relate to the thing as the thing that it is. For example, the pet dog is described as unable to relate to the table *as* a table, a lizard is described as never touching the rock *as* a rock, and the bee or lark never see the sun *as* a sun. They may relate to these beings, but never to the being of these beings themselves. They never step out of themselves—out of what Heidegger calls their "encircling ring [*Umring*]" (FCM, 363/249)—and thus never comport themselves toward beings. Instead, animals remain captive and beholden to things. Animals "are never placed freely in the clearing of being which alone is 'world.'"[35] For this reason Heidegger claims that animals are poor in world; their "environment" consists of a sphere wherein other beings may "disinhibit" them but there is not a transcendent opening to beings or Being as such. The ontological difference between beings and Being is not transparent.

Now, as Heidegger asserts, these claims concern the "essence" of animality, what it means *to be* an animal. The essence of the animal as captivation differs fundamentally, according to Heidegger, from the essence of human *Dasein*. Accordingly, the animal subsequently lacks many of the defining features characteristic of human *Dasein*. As we have seen, animals do not have a world as understood by the manifestness of beings. Heidegger continued to make similar remarks over the course of his career, all very much in the same manner. For instance, animals are said to lack language, not as a means of communication or expression, but as "the clearing-concealing advent of being itself."[36] They are likewise deprived of experiencing death, since death holds an ontological orientation within existence. While human *Dasein* entails a "being-toward-death," animal life is not defined in the same temporal manner. There is no orientation toward mortality and finitude within the very conception of their being as there is for human *Dasein*. Being-toward-death is a definitive way of being human whereby death is understood as always already the completion of our being (and not as some end point down the line); by comparison, Heidegger maintains that animals do not have the same relation to their own mortality. Indeed, they are not finite in the same existential-ontological way. Therefore, although animals might "perish [*Verende*],"[37] they do not, in Heidegger's thinking, "die [*stirbt*],"[38] just as they do not eat or exist.

No matter what reservations we may have with Heidegger's distinctions—and we may very well wish to follow Derrida and many others in calling them problematic—I have insisted that Heidegger proposes a unique way of considering animal others. Above all, I want to maintain that Heidegger's conception of being-with animals opens up many possibilities for considering the world we share with them.

Conclusion

Even though Heidegger denies that human *Dasein* can ever be with animals or go along with them in their *own* being, since we do not occupy the same worlds, this obviously does not mean that we do not share the same spaces as they do. Insofar as we exist "in a peculiar way *in the midst* of beings," it is also the case that we are charged with a new task that bears specifically on the uniqueness of our attitude and comportment toward the world and its beings. In a passage that has not received much attention, Heidegger writes:

We should merely learn to see that *from out of this everydayness*—although certainly not grounded or sustained by it—*fundamental relationships of human* Dasein *toward beings,* amongst which man himself belongs, are possible, i.e., *are capable of being awakened.* . . . In this connection we should remember this: animality no longer stands in view with respect to poverty in world as such, but rather *as a realm of beings* which are *manifest* and thus call for a *specific fundamental relationship* toward them on our part, one in which at least initially we do not move.[39]

It is interesting that Heidegger utilizes a familiar metaphor within philosophy to depict the fundamental relationship human *Dasein* can have toward animal others: an awakening to them, no matter how different they may or may not be. While philosophers such as Socrates and Kant incite us to awaken from our dogmatic slumbers and take life into our own hands, Heidegger suggests that we are capable of being awakened to a fundamental relationship that we have with other beings—including animals. This relation, which is spoken of as a new function, is no less than the opening onto an ethics as understood and interpreted via ancient Greek philosophy. Ethics "comprises everything referring to human deed and action, including man in his activity, in his conduct, in his stance, in that which the Greeks designate ηθοζ [ethos], from which our expression 'ethics' comes. 'ηθοζ' means man's stance, the stance taken by man."[40] Human *Dasein* is always already ethical due to its comportment in the world and its stance toward beings, but this "protoethical engagement," as William McNeill aptly puts it, is not enough in itself.[41] In dwelling with others, and specifically with others that have a different manner of being, as is said to be the case with animals, we are capable of being awakened to our own being as fundamentally relational.

Some commentators have taken Heidegger's analyses to be just another form of anthropocentrism, even if no longer as naïve or dogmatic as previous incarnations. As Matthew Calarco highlights, Heidegger is susceptible to this critique insofar as his assessment of animal life always comes back to an oppositional and negative depiction of animals in comparison to humans.[42] Heidegger anticipates and confirms this response when he considers human beings as the "positive side" of having a world, even if Heidegger insists we are not meant to see such a statement as a value judgment. Although I do not disagree with the charge of a subtle and latent anthropocentrism, I do want to suggest that Heidegger's analysis of being-with animals as the methodological starting point nevertheless provides the opening to a new phenomenological experience of animal others. The animal is not merely something to be captured and known, to be watched and studied, to be mastered and used or loved and protected. There is a mystery that continues to surround the being of animals that Heidegger clearly respects despite the seemingly negative pronouncements that suggest otherwise. Thus, when Michel Haar states that Heidegger's "phenomenology of animality teaches us more about man than about animals!" this need not be taken as a complete failure on the part of Heidegger.[43] Gaining greater self-understanding is surely not a bad thing, so long as we do not achieve this at the expense of animals. Our own lives are inextricably exposed to these others to the degree that we may very well learn more about ourselves than we do of the diversity of animal life, yet this does not foreclose our learning something about the lives of other animals by allowing them to be themselves.

From one perspective, then, as Derrida remarks, Heidegger insists "there is no animal *Dasein* [*Il n'y a pas de* Dasein *animal*]."[44] Didier Franck similarly reproaches Heidegger, noting that "never in the history of metaphysics has the Being of man been so profoundly disincarnated" because Heidegger's ontology necessitates "the total exclusion of [*Dasein*'s] live animality."[45] It may very well be that Heidegger imprisons the animal in a new way, not via an outside method of an epistemological grasp but from within the being of the animal itself. In this sense, it is arguably the case that Heidegger does a greater disservice to animals than previous discourses, because here he seems to exclude them not only from humanity but also from being itself, as has been suggested by the Italian philosopher Giorgio Agamben.[46] Ontologically, the animal is cut off from the freedom to be that is opened by humans alone.

From another perspective, however, I would want to emphasize that despite various criticisms of his thought, the emphasis on our being-with animals is perhaps what saves an otherwise troubling, even if nuanced, outlook. Phenomenologically, Heidegger opens the door for considering how we exist with animals even if we do not cohabit the same worlds. We are with animals every day, from the thousands of species of bacteria inhabiting our human body, as Alphonso Lingis writes, to the insects and birds, and the cats and salmon, that make up our individual lives.[47] Being-with animals keeps open the possibility of encountering the animal other in a completely new way. By not approaching them with a preconceived idea or agenda, our being-with them allows for surprising and unexpected discoveries—discoveries that can simultaneously reveal both animal and human being, or, in an extension beyond Heidegger's thought, rupture the animal/human binary altogether. For instance, I might point to how Heidegger's notion of being-with prepares the way for more contemporary reworkings of a relational ontology, such as that of Donna Haraway. Rather than "being-with" and its static implications (e.g., humans and dogs can cohabit together, but human being and animal being remain ontologically distinct), Haraway proposes a more dynamic and symbiotic relationship between beings in her term "becoming with." "To be one," she writes, "is always to *become with* many," in such a way that all beings (living and nonliving) co-constitute one another in an ontological web of companion species.[48] To become with many others entails that we dissolve the idea that there is an essence to being human and an essence to being animal. Becoming with also means that we are responsible for very real others (e.g., Fritz), as opposed to being-with the anonymous, nonexistent "animal" that always remains nameless in Heidegger's abstract accounts.[49] For all of Heidegger's faults with respect to animals – and I am not here to offer apologetics – he nevertheless asks us to reconsider how we approach the lives of animal. So while we may disagree with this or that element of Heidegger's descriptions of animal life, and while we might be tempted to describe how Heidegger's treatment of animals mimic, to a certain degree, the tradition he claims to critique, I think we can take away from his thought a particular approach to the animal that emphasizes the dimension of our being-with them.

The phenomenological dimension of Heidegger's thought entails that we come to look at the world in a new way. Through it, we discover, as Maurice Merleau-Ponty claims, that "true philosophy consists in relearning to look at the world," and specifically at how beings manifest themselves to us.[50] The phenomenological interest in animal lives situates us in a world that is alive with movement and that cannot but induce in us a sense of wonderment. There are still many more questions to be raised with regard to how we understand ourselves and others by emphasizing our being-with one another. It is surely not an easy task to cultivate something like a fundamental relationship with other animals, but there are many remarkable cases by anthropologists, philosophers, psychologists, biologists, ethologists, and so on, who provide illuminating glimpses into what it is like to be with animals without intruding in their own being.[51] Heidegger's thought therefore prepares us for investigations that take the living world as a meaningful place, worthy of scholarly attention, enjoyment, and protection. His thought needs to be considered for its impact on such specific developments as eco-phenomenology, as well as appreciated for what it has contributed to the more general domain of environmental practices.[52] With Heidegger we begin a long-awaited return to a shared environment that asks us not so much to lay claim to other animals through knowledge but to be-with others in a mutual embrace of the unknown. This may be the continually unfinished task of our fundamental relationship with animal others as a calling to which we are asked to respond.

Notes

1. On Descartes's attitude toward animals, see in particular his letters of November 23, 1646 (to the Marquess of Newcastle), and February 5, 1649 (to Henry More), in René Descartes, *Descartes: Philosophical Letters* (1970). In the latter, one reads: "I came to realize, however, that there are two different principles causing our motions: one is purely mechanical and corporeal and depends solely on the force of the spirits and the construction of our organs, and can be called the corporeal soul; the other is the incorporeal mind, the soul which I have defined as a thinking substance. Thereupon I investigated more carefully whether the motions of animals originated from both these principles or from one only. I soon saw clearly that they could all originate from the corporeal and mechanical principle, and I thenceforward regarded it as certain and established that we cannot prove at all the presence of a thinking soul in animals" (1970:243). Inasmuch as this is the case, animals are no more than "natural automata" (1970:244).

2. Steeves 1999:8.

3. Heidegger's various critiques of metaphysics are multifaceted, but for the most part his interest is in retrieving the question of the meaning of Being (*Sein*), a question that he maintains has been forgotten since the Presocratics. Metaphysics is thus not just an area of philosophy that concerns itself with the supersensuous and nonphysical (e.g., soul, mind, God); for Heidegger, metaphysics is the history of Western philosophy itself and most notably its exclusion of the question of being (that is, "what is Being?"). The history of philosophy has inquired in many ways after what any given being is (e.g., human, chair, animal, God), but not into the preconditions for how something is the being that it is.

4. Helpful recent surveys of the literature dealing with Heidegger and animals can be found in Elden 2006:273–291; Calarco 2004, 2008; Derrida 2008; Buchanan 2008; and Oliver 2009. There are almost too many publications to note here, and many more have continued to appear since the original composition of this chapter. I should note that I am adopting the language of "animal" and "human"—and not "nonhuman animal" and "human animal"—in order to keep with Heidegger's own usage. This also pertains to the language of "them" and "us," categories that I would not otherwise subscribe to; I see Heidegger's own thought beginning to problematize this anthropocentric binary in his notion of being-with even though he firmly perpetuates the distinction between human (us) and animal (them), as this chapter will highlight.

5. Heidegger 1962:44; Heidegger 2001:23. Page references within the body of the text and in the references will refer to the original German followed by the English translation, separated by a slash (e.g., 44/23).

6. Heidgeer 1962:67; Heidegger 2001:41.

7. Heidegger 1995; Heidegger 1983.

8. Heidegger 1995:273; Heidegger 1983:396.

9. Nagel 1974:435–450.

10. Heidegger 1995:231. "Die Schwierigkeit besteht aber nicht nur in der Bestimmung dessen, was das Insekt sieht, sondern auch, wie es sieht. Denn wir dürfen auch nicht ohne weiteres unser Sehen mit dem des Tieres vergleichen" (Heidegger 1983:337).

11. Heidegger 1995:202 (emphasis in original). "Sichversetzen in dieses Seiende heißt, mit dem, was und wie das Seiende ist, mitgehen—in diesem Mitgehen unmittelbar über das Seiende, mit dem wir so gehen, erfahren, wie es mit ihm steht" (Heidegger 1983:296–297).

12. Heidegger 1995:203; Heidegger 1983:297.

13. See, for example, this note from Heidegger's 1925 lecture course: "Self and world belong together in the single entity, *Dasein*. Self and world are not two beings, like subject and object, or like I and thou, but self and world are the basic determination of *Dasein* itself in the unity of the structure of being-in-the-world (Heidegger 1982:297) [Selbst und Welt gehören in dem einen Seienden, dem Dasein, zusammen. Selbst und Welt sind nicht zwei Seiende, wie Subjekt und Objekt, auch nicht wie Ich und Du, sondern Selbst und Welt sind in der Einheit der Struktur des In der-Welt-seins die Grundbestimmung des Daseins selbst]" (Heidegger 1975:422).

14. On this note, I would recommend Heidegger's 1929 lecture "On the Essence of Ground," where he is particularly succinct and clear in his analysis of the world. Found in Heidegger 1998b.

15. FCM, 307/209; cf. *Being and Time*, 118/155, 124/161.

16. Heidegger 1995: 201 (emphasis in original). "Haustiere werden von uns im Haus gehalten, sie 'leben' mit uns. Aber wir leben nicht mit ihnen, wenn Leben besagt: Sein in der Weise des Tieres. Gleichwohl sind wir mit ihnen. Dieses Mitsein ist aber auch kein Mitexistieren, sofern ein Hund nicht existiert, sondern nur lebt. Dieses Mitsein mit den Tieren ist so, daß wir die Tiere in unserer Welt sich bewegen lassen. Wir sagen: Der Hund liegt unter dem Tisch, er springt die Treppe herauf. Aber der Hund—verhält er sich zu einem Tisch als Tisch, zur Treppe als Treppe? Und doch geht er mit unds die Treppe hinauf. Er frißt mit uns—nein, wir fressen nicht. Er ißt mit uns—nein, er ißt nicht. Und doch mit uns! Ein Mitgehen, eine Versetztheit—und doch nicht" (Heidegger 1983:308).

17. Heidegger 1995:186. For German, see Heidegger 1983:275.

18. Heidegger 1995:264. "Wenn nicht, dann ist das Tier durch einen Abgrund vom Menschen getrennt" (Heidegger 1983:384).

19. Derrida 1989; Derrida 2002. The latter has appeared more recently in book form, Derrida 2008.

20. Derrida 1989:57 (emphasis in original). "Compromise plutôt par une thèse sur l'animalité qui suppose, c'est l'hypothèse irréductible et je crois dogmatique de la thèse, qu'il y a une chose, un domaine, un type d'étant homogène, qu'on appelle l'animalité en générale pour laquelle n'importe quel exemple ferait l'affaire" (Derrida 1987:71). In

"The Animal That Therefore I Am (More to Follow)," Derrida refers to "the limit about which we have had a stomachful, the limit between Man with a capital M and Animal with a capital A" (2002:398). The issue of borders is also raised by Agamben 2004:59.

21. Virtually no one (including theorists of animal rights) wants to argue that there are no differences between, for example, humans, dogs, and apes.

22. Heidegger has written little if anything about children. In comparison, one might consider the significant amount of attention that Maurice Merleau-Ponty paid to the phenomenological and ontological lives of children (Merleau-Ponty 2010). An alternative to children that also points to the blurring of lines between humans and animals might include feral humans. See, for example, Steeves 2002; Agamben 2004:30.

23. Heidegger's comment arises in the context of his 1950s lectures What Is Called Thinking? (1968, 1961). While discussing a traditional view of "man," he writes: "Thus one might also say: *homo est animal rationale*—man is the animal that confronts face-to-face. A mere animal, such as a dog, never confronts anything, it can never confront anything *to its face*; to do so, the animal would have to perceive *itself* (1968:61) [So könnte man auch sagen: homo est animal rationale: der Mensch ist das vor-stellende Tier. Das bloße Tier, ein Hund z.B., stellt nie etwas vor, er kann nie etwas vor-sich-stellen; dazu müßte er, müßte das Tier sich vernehmen]" (1961:26). In a different vein, Lévinas states the following in an interview on the specific meaning that "face" has for his thought: "One cannot entirely refuse the face of an animal. It is via the face that one understands, for example, a dog. Yet the priority here is not found in the animal, but in the human face. We understand the animal, the face of an animal, in accordance with *Dasein*. The phenomenon of the face is not in its purest form in the dog" (Lévinas 1988:169).

24. In his 1946 "Letter on 'Humanism,'" Heidegger writes: "Such standing in the clearing of being I call the *Ek-sistence* of human beings. This way of being is proper only to the human being (1998a:247) [Das stehen in der Lichtung des Seins nenne ich die Ek-sistenz des Menschen. Nur dem Menshen eignet diese Art zu sein]" (1976:325). Further on, he writes: "In terms of content *Ek-sistence* means standing out into the truth of being (1998a:249) [Ek-sistenz bedeutet inhaltlich Hin-aus-stehen in die Wahrheit des Seins]" (1976:326).

25. Heidegger 1995:177 (emphasis added). "Wir halten sie fest durch drei Thesen: 1. der Stein (das Materielle) ist weltlos; 2. das Tier ist weltarm; 3. der Mensch ist weltbildend" (Heidegger 1983:177).

26. Heidegger 1992:166. "Die Schnecke aber ist nicht etwa zunächst nur im Haus und noch nicht in der Welt, einer sogenannten gegenüberstehenden Welt, um in ein solches Gegenübersein erst durch das Herauskriechen zu kommen. Sie kriecht nur heraus, sofern sie schon ihrem Sein nach in einer Welt ist. Sie legt sich durch Tasten nicht erst eine Welt zu, sondern sie tastet, weil ihr Sein nichts anderes besagt als in einer Welt sein" (Heidegger 1979:224). For further comment on this passage, see Krell 1992:90; van Buren 1992:359, 387.

27. Heidegger 2002:163. "Jedes Lebewesen hat seine Umwelt nicht als etwas, was neben ihm vorhanden ist, sondern das für ihn erschlossen, aufgedeckt da ist. Diese Welt kann sehr einfach sein (für ein primitives Tier). . . . Hier ist aber das Wesentliche übersehen, wenn ich nicht sehe, daß das Tier eine Welt hat. Ebenso sind auch wir selbst immer in einer Welt, so daß diese für uns erschlossen ist" (Heidegger 2003:178).

28. Heidegger 2000:47. For a longer discussion on these and similar points, see Buchanan 2008.

29. For a particularly detailed reading of the 1929–1930 lectures, I would recommend McNeill 1999. This essay is also reprinted in McNeill 2006.

30. See Heidegger 1982:298–302.

31. Heidegger 1998c:371n.66. This endnote is interesting because it clearly spells out Heidegger's response to the claim that he is still anthropocentric in his approach to human *Dasein*.

32. Heidegger 1995:177 (emphasis in original). ". . . sondern der Mensch steht der Welt gegenüber. Dieses Gegenüberstehen ist ein Haben der Welt als das, worin sich der Mensch bewegt" (Heidegger 1983:262).

33. Heidegger 1995:248 (emphasis in original). "Die Benommenheit ist das Wesen der Tierheit, sagt: *Das Tier steht als solches nicht in einer Offenbarkeit von Seiendem. Weder seine sogenannte Umgebung noch es selbst sind als Seiendes offenbar*" (Heidegger 1983:361.

34. Heidegger 1995:240–248; Heidegger 1983:350–358.

35. Heidegger 1998a:248. "aber niemals in die Lichtung des Seins, und nur sie ist 'Welt', frei gestellt sind" (Heidegger 1976:326).

36. Heidegger 1998a:249. "lichtend-verbergende Ankunft des Seins selbst" (Heidegger 1976: 26). See also Heidegger, FCM, 444/307.

37. Heidegger 1962:284; Heidegger 2001.

38. Heidegger 1962:291; Heidegger 2001:247. See also Heidegger 1995:266–267; Heidegger 1971:107.

39. Heidegger 1995:276 (emphasis in original). "*Wir sollen nur sehen lernen, daß aus der Alltäglichkeit heraus—freilich nicht durch sie begründet und getragen—*Grundverhältnisse des Daseins des Menschen zum Seienden, *dazu er selbst gehört, möglich sind, d.h.* wach werden können. . . . *Dabei ist wohl zu beachten: Die Tierheit steht jetzt nicht bezüglich der Weltarmut als solcher im Blick, sondern* als ein Bereich von Seiendem, *das* offenbar *ist und somit von uns ein* bestimmtes Grundverhältnis *zu ihm erheischt, in dem wir uns gleichwohl zunächst nicht bewegen*" (Heidegger 1983:400).

40. Heidegger 1995:35–36. ". . . der all das umfaßt, was das menschliche Tun und Lassen meint, den Menschen in seinem Tun, in seinem Gehabe, in seiner Halthung, in dem, was die Griechen als als ηθος bezeichnen, woher unser Ausdruck Ethik kommt. ηθος meint die Haltung des Menschen den Menschen in seiner Haltung" (Heidegger 1983:54).

41. McNeill 2006:62. Frank Schalow has also been instrumental in highlighting an ethical reading of Heidegger's thought. See Schalow 2006.

42. Calarco 2004:29.

43. Haar 1993:29.

44. Derrida 1989:56; Derrida 1987:70.

45. Franck 1991:146.

46. Agamben 2004:91.

47. Lingis 1999.

48. Haraway 2008:4 (emphasis in original). Haraway expands on the concepts of becoming with and companion species throughout this book and in many of her earlier writings.

49. "Touch, regard, looking back, becoming with—all of these make us responsible in unpredictable ways for which worlds take shape" (Haraway 2008:36). In shaping a shared world with companion species, we also move out of Heidegger's protoethical stance and into a more concrete ethical position of responsibility.

50. Merleau-Ponty 1998:xx.

51. For a particularly Heideggerian title, one might consider Heuer 2006.

52. There are too many sources to mention here, but it is worth recommending Zimmerman 1997; Abram 1997; Brown and Toadvine 2003; Steeves 1999.

References

Abram, David. 1997. *The Spell of the Sensuous: Perception and Language in a More-Than-Human World*. New York: Vintage.

Agamben, Giorgio. 2004. *The Open: Man and Animal*. Trans. Kevin Attell. Stanford, CA: Stanford University Press.

Brown, Charles S. and Ted Toadvine, eds. 2003. *Eco-Phenomenology: Back to the Earth Itself*. Albany: State University of New York Press.

Buchanan, Brett. 2008. *Onto-Ethologies: The Animal Environments of Uexküll, Heidegger, Merleau-Ponty, and Deleuze*. Albany: State University of New York Press.

Calarco, Matthew. 2004. "Heidegger's Zoontology." In *Animal Philosophy: Essential Readings in Continental Thought*, ed. Matthew Calarco and Peter Atterton, 18–30. New York: Continuum.

——. 2008. *Zoographies: The Question of the Animal from Heidegger to Derrida*. New York: Columbia University Press.

Derrida, Jacques. 1987. *Heidegger et la question: De l'esprit et autres essais*. Paris: Flammarion.

——. 1989. *Of Spirit: Heidegger and the Question*. Trans. Geoffrey Bennington and Rachel Bowlby. Chicago: University of Chicago Press.

——. 2002. "The Animal That Therefore I Am (More to Follow)." Trans. David Wills. *Critical Inquiry* 28:369–418.

——. 2008. *The Animal That Therefore I Am*. Trans. David Wills. New York: Fordham University Press.

Descartes, René. 1970. *Descartes: Philosophical Letters*. Trans. and ed. Anthony Kenny. London: Oxford University Press.

Elden, Stuart. 2006. "Heidegger's Animals." *Continental Philosophy Review* 39:273–291.

Franck, Didier. 1991. "Being and the Living." In *Who Comes After the Subject?*, ed. Eduardo Cadava, Peter Connor, and Jean-Luc Nancy, trans. Peter T. Connor, 135–147. New York: Routledge.

Haar, Michel. 1993. *The Song of the Earth: Heidegger and the Grounds of the History of Being*. Trans. Reginald Lilly. Bloomington: Indiana University Press.

Haraway, Donna. 2008. *When Species Meet*. Minneapolis: University of Minnesota Press.

Heidegger, Martin. 1961. *Was Heisst Denken?* Tübingen: Max Niemeyer Verlag.

——. 1962. *Being and Time*. Trans. John Macquarrie and Edward Robinson. Oxford: Blackwell Publishers.

——. 1968. *What Is Called Thinking?* Trans. J. Glenn Gray. New York: Harper & Row.

——. 1971. *On the Way to Language*. Trans. Peter D. Hertz. New York: HarperCollins.

——. 1975. *Die Grundprobleme der Phänomenologie*. Frankfurt-am-Main: Vittorio Klostermann.

——. 1976. "Brief über den 'Humanismus.'" In *Wegmarken*. Frankfurt-am-Main: Vittorio Klostermann.

——. 1979. *Prolegomena zur Geschichte des Zeitbegriffs*. Frankfurt-am-Main: Vittorio Klostermann.

——. 1982. *The Basic Problems of Phenomenology*. Trans. Albert Hofstadter. Bloomington: Indiana University Press.

——. 1983. *Die Grundbegriffe der Metaphysik: Welt-Endlichkeit-Einsamkeit*. Frankfurt-am-Main: Vittorio Klostermann.

——. 1988. "The Paradox of Morality: An Interview with Emmanuel Lévinas." In *The Provocation of Lévinas: Rethinking the Other*, trans. Andrew Benjamin and Tamra Wright, ed. Robert Bernasconi and David Wood, 168–180. New York: Routledge.

——. 1992. *History of the Concept of Time: Prolegomena*. Trans. Theodore Kisiel. Bloomington: Indiana University Press.

——. 1995. *The Fundamental Concepts of Metaphysics: World, Finitude, Solitude*. Trans. William McNeill and Nicholas Walker. Bloomington: Indiana University Press.

——. 1998a. "Letter on 'Humanism.'" In *Pathmarks*, trans. Frank A. Capuzzi, ed. William McNeill, 239–276. Cambridge: Cambridge University Press.

——. 1998b. *Pathmarks*. Trans. Frank A. Capuzzi. Ed. William McNeill. Cambridge: Cambridge University Press.

——. 1998c. "On the Essence of Ground." In *Pathmarks*, ed. William McNeill, 97–135. Cambridge: Cambridge University Press.

——. 2000. *Introduction to Metaphysics*. Trans. Gregory Fried and Richard Polt. New Haven, CT: Yale University Press.

——. 2001. *Sein und Zeit*. Tübingen: Max Niemeyer Verlag.

——. 2002. "Wilhelm Dilthey's Research and the Struggle for a Historical Worldview." In *Supplements: From the Earliest Essays to* Being and Time *and Beyond*, trans. Charles Bambach, ed. John van Buren, 147–176. Albany: State University of New York Press.

——. 2003. *Les conferences de Cassel.*Trans. and ed. Jean-Claude Gens. Paris: J. Vrin.

Heuer, Karsten. 2006. *Being Caribou: Five Months on Foot with an Arctic Herd.* Toronto: McClelland & Steward.

Krell, David Farrell. 1992. *Daimon Life: Heidegger and Life-Philosophy.* Bloomington: Indiana University Press.

Lévinas, Emmanuel. 1988. "The Paradox of Morality: An Interview with Emmanuel Lévinas." In *The Provocation of Lévinas: Rethinking the Other*, trans. Andrew Benjamin and Tamra Wright, ed. Robert Bernasconi and David Wood. New York: Routledge.

Lingis, Alphonso. 1999: "Bestiality." In *Animal Others: On Ethics, Ontology, and Animal Life*, ed. N. Peter Steeves, 37–54. Albany: State University of New York Press.

McNeill, William. 1999. "Life Beyond the Organism: Animal Being in Heidegger's Freiburg Lectures, 1929–30." In *Animal Others: On Ethics, Ontology, and Animal Life*, ed. H. Peter Steeves, 197–248. Albany: State University of New York Press.

——. 2006. *The Time of Life: Heidegger and Ethos.* Albany: State University of New York Press.

Merleau-Ponty, Maurice. 1998. *Phenomenology of Perception.* Trans. Colin Smith. New York: Routledge Press.

——. 2010. *Child Psychology and Pedagogy: The Sorbonne Lectures 1949–52.* Trans. Talia Welsh. Evanston, IL: Northwestern University Press.

Nagel, Thomas. 1974. "What Is It Like to Be a Bat?" *The Philosophical Review* 83, no. 4: 435–450.

Oliver, Kelly. 2009. *Animal Lessons: How They Teach Us to Be Human.* New York: Columbia University Press.

Schalow, Frank. 2006. *The Incarnality of Being: The Earth, Animals, and the Body in Heidegger's Thought.* Albany: State University of New York Press.

Steeves, H. Peter. 1999. "Introduction." In *Animal Others: On Ethics, Ontology, and Animal Life*, ed. H. Peter Steeves, 1–14. Albany: SUNY Press.

——. 2002. "The Familiar Other and Feral Selves: Life at the Human/Animal Boundary." In *The Animal/Human Boundary: Historical Perspectives*, ed. Angela N. H. Creager and William Chester Jordan, 228–264. Rochester, NY: University of Rochester Press.

Van Buren, John. 1992. *The Young Heidegger: Rumor of the Hidden King.* Bloomington: Indiana University Press.

Zimmerman, Michael. 1997. *Contesting Earth's Future: Radical Ecology and Postmodernity.* Berkeley: University of California Press.

ten

Heidegger and the Dog Whisperer

Imagining Interspecies Kindness

Ashley E. Pryor

> There are people who have the capacity to imagine themselves as someone
> else, there are people who have no such capacity (when the lack is extreme,
> we call them psychopaths), and there are people who have the capacity but
> choose not to exercise it.
>
> —J. M. Coetzee, *The Lives of Animals*

Why Can't We Be Friends?

This paper defends a simple thesis: kindness occurs not only between humans
but between species. Everyone agrees that I can choose to be kind or cruel to
my dog by attending to or ignoring her needs. I argue that this kindness is
not the one-way street it is often thought to be; my dog can be kind to me too.
Many people today attribute a capacity for kindness to their canine companions,
but, following a long-standing Western idea that animals are capable of neither
kindness nor cruelty, many other people would protest that such an attribution
is sentimental or confused. In his book *Elizabeth Costello*, Nobel laureate and
novelist J. M. Coetzee weighs in on this debate through an imagined dialog
between the book's heroine, a famous novelist who gives the book its title,
and the character of Professor Thomas O'Hearne, a hard-boiled academic
philosopher of the Anglo-American tradition. Costello, who often seems to
be speaking for Coetzee himself, appeals for a quasi-phenomenologically
grounded ethics of animal rights based on an experience of the kindness that
human and nonhuman animals share. For her, "kindness" extends beyond a

subjective and volitional attitude of cheerful solicitude or tenderhearted sympathy for our animal "others" and names a more fundamental relationship. Kindness is "an acceptance that we are all of one kind, one nature."[1] To the delight of Professor O'Hearne and to the consternation of her potentially sympathetic audience, Costello leaves her "concept" of kindness lamentably undeveloped, providing ample fodder for O'Hearne's counter-attack. O'Hearne accuses Costello of being hopelessly naïve in her belief that humans might "live in a community with animals."[2] O'Hearne remarks that although animal rights proponents "talk a great deal about our community with animals," rarely do they specify how they "actually live that community."[3] O'Hearne continues:

> Thomas Aquinas says that friendship between human beings and animals is impossible, and I tend to agree. You can be friends neither with a Martian nor with a bat, for the simple reason that you have too little in common with them. We may certainly wish for there to be community with animals, but that is not the same thing as living in community with them. It is just a piece of prelapsarian wistfulness.[4]

O'Hearne is certainly correct to find a certain "abstract" and even "idle" quality about Costello's appeal to kindness in the absence of any real descriptions of it. But as those of us who have experienced "kindness" with other animal species know, O'Hearne's claim that living in community with animals is "just a piece of prelapsarian wistfulness" is counterintuitive and refuses a dimension of the experience of kindness toward and friendship with animals that Costello recognizes but cannot adequately articulate.

In the history of continental philosophy, much of which Coetzee engages through Costello and O'Hearne, the possibility of human friendships with other species is short-circuited by the assumption that the twin abstractions of "the human" and "the animal" provide an adequate starting point for a discussion of the different modes of relationships that humans experience with different animal species. In this conception, the human being becomes a kind of super animal, or "animal plus," with human uniqueness grounded in a particular capacity or faculty, such as reason, self-consciousness, language, political activity, or, more subtly, a capacity for self-creation that flows from the lack of a fixed human nature. In such conceptions, the nature of human being becomes visible in contrast to a nebulously determined animal "other," where "animal" appears as a catchall term for all self-moving life forms that do not bear essential human features. There is little room in this for a discussion of what Costello calls the possibility of kindness between humans and other animal species, let alone of friendship. For although many philosophers are content to recognize a biological common ground between humans and other animal species, they generally have been hesitant to characterize human relationships with animals—or theirs with us—in terms of mutual kindness, friendship, or other terms usually reserved for human-human relations.[5] This hesitancy stems from two concerns: the first is a belief that humans' rationality and use of symbol foreclose the possibility of the intimate and reliable knowledge of another that is presupposed in any robust definition of an intersubjective relationship like kindness or friendship. The second concern, the problem of anthropomorphic projection onto animals, is anticipated in the first. In the perceived absence of any shared medium of communication, philosophers have worried that attempts to characterize interactions between humans and other animal species using a vocabulary of social relationships risks "a homonization of the animal."[6]

Is it really the case, though, that human beings have no real access to the character and personality of the animals we share our lives with? Is it the case that when we speak of our cats' distinctive personalities, or talk about the mutual joy we share with our dog in the "flow" of our game of fetch, that we are merely projecting our human conceptions upon them? Is our dog merely following its instinctive appetite for food when she learns a new trick at the dog agility center or sidles up to us to lay her head in our lap when we are tired and sad? Should we question the depths of Mark Doty's grief, when he memorializes his two dogs, "My two speechless friends . . . they were the secret heroes of my own vitality."[7]

My answer to these questions is that kindness between species not only is possible, but also forms the condition for the possibility of companion animals, or pets. That is to say, kindness constitutes our basic relationship with the animals with whom we share our lives, and conversely, it informs the relationship of these animals to us. Kindness is not primarily a concept, word, or sign, but an observable disposition. Phenomenological thought and its attempt to "bracket" the subjective contribution to cognition and knowledge is a good starting place for considering what I mean by kindness because phenomenology allows us to investigate lived experience and its meaning from a place that questions and disrupts the primacy of the detached and objective point of view.

Central to my understanding of kindness is the presumption that kindness between different animal species involves a "sense" of commonality between beings, as Costello suggests, and that this sense precedes any logical or rational determination and is more likely rooted in complexly related somatic sensitivities to moods and expressions of energy. Kindness, as I am imagining it here, does not necessarily include a subjective attitude such as cheerful solicitude or generosity of spirit. Thus, I want to distinguish three kinds of kindness: (1) an attitude of cheerful solicitude, (2) the vague sense or idea of sharing a kinship with other animals, in the sense that Costello suggests "that we are all of one kind," and finally, (3) the nonsubjective and prediscursive mutual suspension of customary attitudes, instincts, or ways of thinking in order to act responsively to another living being in such a way that supports their well-being. Although the first and second kinds of kindness might often accompany the third experience of kindness, neither has been established definitely as belonging to another animal's social repertoire.[8] While a dog's wagging tail and licks do seem to express among many things a feeling of cheerful alacrity, it is rather unlikely that the dog entertains such abstract notions of "shared kinship" or of belonging to "one nature." What is phenomenologically demonstrable are the varying degrees human beings and their would-be pets suspend their habits and usual ways of thinking in order to establish a harmonious living or working relationship with another being. Thought of in this sense, kindness is only possible between beings who can find something in common with one another—except this "finding in common" is not a logical or linguistic operation whereby identity is wrested from difference or derived from the idea of living in a shared world, but is rooted in many possible modes of communication, including, but not limited to, a receptivity to touch, scents, and the ability to "read" changing expressions of energy, mood, and voice. The question is whether these modes of communication are foreclosed to the animal. Should we think of the animal as not only "reading" but also engaged in a suspension of a habit or way of thinking, or deny the animal this capacity?

As we will see, Martin Heidegger's discussion of the animal can help us to understand this way of thinking of kindness as something other than anthropomorphism. For our purposes Heidegger's phenomenological account of "seeing" in his discussion of the determination of the animal and the human in the 1942–1943 Parmenides lecture course—borrowed from a more extensive treatment of the lecture course from 1929–1930, subsequently published as *The Fundamental Concepts of Metaphysics: World, Finitude, Solitude*—provides the conceptual resources and language for thinking about a nonsubjective and nondiscursive suspension of habits and routine ways of thinking that potentially expose human beings to a sense of kindness with other animal species. In Heidegger's *Parmenides* he argues that our being-with (*Mitsein*) animals is not an "existing-with." Yet Heidegger, at least in his better moments, shows that there are two senses of, and ways of apprehending, being. There are flashes of "insight" (*Einblick*) on the one hand and the ability to "see something *as* something," or *apophansis*, on the other. Heidegger strictly reserves the capacity for *apophansis*, for "seeing *as*," to human beings. In *The Fundamental Concepts of Metaphysics*, he explains that "when we consider the dog itself—does it comport itself to the table *as* table, to the stairs *as* stairs . . . it feeds with us, but it does not really 'feed.' It eats with us—and yet, does not really 'eat.' Nevertheless, it is with us! A going-along-with . . . a transposedness, and yet not."[9] Here Heidegger disregards or downplays his own argument that there is a "flash" of insight, prematurely foreclosing the possibility of an attuned dispositional and prelogical relationship that defines or might come to define the relation between Heidegger and dog.

Might dogs and humans share that first kind of insight—the flash in which a being's relationship with the world is suspended in such a way that one can change one's behavior or "transpose"? What I am calling kindness can only happen if both human and dog can break their captivated state. Surprisingly, works in phenomenology after Heidegger have not explored this possibility. Thus I undertake just such an exploration here, bringing together this stream of reflection in continental philosophy with on-the-ground insights provided by the work of dog trainer Cesar Millan, aka "the dog whisperer."

Watching dog trainers, particularly those who are attuned to the kinds of issues I am discussing, one can see more clearly the importance of the transpositional "flash" that is central to kindness. As we will see, Millan's approach could be described broadly as phenomenological insofar as he is concerned with and able to suspend his human subjectivity in such a way that he begins not with a presupposed matrix of expected behavior, but with meeting a dog at its own level (both physically, often by crouching down into the dog's space, and psychologically by imitating the dog's gestures and social habits)—the dog-in-itself. Millan also attempts to exude the energy that he sees displayed by the alpha dog in a pack, suspending his own more human characteristics.[10] In his ability to suspend momentarily his own routinized behaviors and habits, week after week Millan demonstrates what dog lovers everywhere know already—dogs routinely manifest a mode of insight. That is, dogs show themselves capable of breaking their captivation with an object (such as a rock, sock, person, or other dog) by shifting their experience and reaction to that object; that is, they are capable of "seeing" or experiencing the object in another way. Thus Millan's work seems to carry out the promise of Heidegger's phenomenology of animality.

Heidegger and Human/Nonhuman Kindness

To think being is very simple, but the simple is for us the most arduous.
—Martin Heidegger, *Parmenides*

Heidegger's discussion of human-animal difference is embedded in an ongoing critique of the modern understanding of human subjectivity and the consequences that this conception of human being as subject has for "planetary consciousness" and "man's historical destiny." In an addendum to the Parmenides lecture course, Heidegger writes:

> Modern man has a "lived experience" of the world and thinks the world in those terms, i.e., in terms of himself as the being that, as ground, lies in the foundation of all explanation and ordering of beings as a whole. . . . Only when man becomes the subject do nonhuman beings become objects. Only within the domain of subjectivity can a dispute arise over objectivity, over its validity, its profits and loss, and over its advantages and disadvantages.[11]

A direct consequence of this mode of subjective thinking is a distorted characterization of the nonhuman animal, for the meaning of the animal is always determined in contrast to the human. "Since, in metaphysics, man is experienced and thought of as the rational animal, animality is then interpreted against the measuring rod of rationality, as what is irrational and without reason, i.e., interpreted against human intellectuality as what is instinctual."[12] Heidegger argues that at the heart of most metaphysical representations of the human is a deep anthropomorphism that seeks to find human traits in the animal—traits such as logic, language, rationality, and even sociability—and instead discovers its opposites: irrationality, mute silence, autistic self-enclosure, and instinct. Heidegger identifies the costs that this anthropocentric way of grasping the world has for nonhuman animal life: it leaves nonhuman animals susceptible to the "assaults of chemistry and psychology." Heidegger writes:

> In this way, in metaphysics and in its scientific repercussions, the mystery of the living being goes unheeded; for living beings are either exposed to the assault of chemistry or are transferred to the field of "psychology." Both presume to seek the riddle of life. They will never find it; not only because every science adheres only to the penultimate and must presuppose the ultimate as the first, but also because the riddle of

life will never be found where the mystery of the living being has already been abandoned.[13]

Given this critique of anthropocentrism and the problematic anthropomorphism of the nonhuman, on the one hand, and the techno-scientific domination of animal life via chemistry and psychology, on the other, we might expect to find Heidegger's own discussion of animals would draw from concrete discourses of observed animal behaviors. But, in fact, Heidegger rarely turns to such discourse. Moreover, when he does turn to direct observation of animals—for example, in his phenomenological description of a uniquely human access to the world that he calls "the open" (*das Offene*) and that he contrasts with animal "captivation" (*Benommenheit*)—he does so on the basis of an invasive laboratory experiment conducted by dissecting living bees. Despite Heidegger's caveats about the problem of determining the animal vis-à-vis the human, he concludes in *Parmenides* that animals lack access to the open. This seems to violate his intention to avoid defining the animal by the "measuring rod" of the human—to avoid defining the animal as, so to speak, a "human minus" (minus rationality, the open, etc.).

Heidegger may fail to live up to the rigorous requirements of a nonanthropomorphic approach to animals—a failure that he himself acknowledges at points in the 1929–1930 course—but his phenomenological analysis of the human being's access to the "open," to which I shall now turn, provides resources for thinking about kindness between humans and other animal species. In *Being and Time* Heidegger challenged the structure of the modern subject by identifying the more primordial ways in which human beings relate to the world. In *Parmenides*, Heidegger extends and focuses his analysis of the human subject (*Dasein*) by considering the way that the human being is related to being *as* such (sometimes capitalized as Being) rather than individual beings. Heidegger elucidates this relationship of the human to the very ground of being that makes it possible to see any particular being by way of a discussion of freedom, which Heidegger connects closely with what he calls "the open." "The open is the light of the self-luminous. We name it the 'free,' and its essence 'freedom.' 'Freedom' has a primordial sense here, alien to metaphysical thinking."[14] The open is the "primordial" space that makes seeing beings possible; it is the ground out of which the world of beings becomes unveiled in what Heidegger calls "*alêtheia*," a Greek word usually translated as "truth." Moreover, for Heidegger only humans have access to the open and thus freedom.

I want to propose that the experience of being itself—of the open—and the related moment when the experience of being gives way to some kind of

engagement with beings—what Heidegger calls the "unmediated and immediate irruption of Being into beings"[15]—is shared by human and nonhuman
animals alike. It is the flash of insight that enables us (among other things) to
suspend behaviors, thoughts, or instincts for the sake of living harmoniously
with other beings, what I have thematized as kindness. This position would
not imply that nonhuman animals engage in a "thinking that attempts to
think being itself,"[16] something Heidegger rightly restricts to the human.
However, it does presuppose that nonhuman animals have access to some
kind of freedom or openness—some kind of insight that allows them to leap
out of habitual ways of perceiving and acting.

Like Heidegger's description of the irruption of the thought of being, the occurrence of such insight occurs independently of and often in spite of any volitional or subjective structure of thought. However, unlike what Heidegger calls
thinking, I am suggesting that such insight does not presuppose the (uniquely
human) word. We can appreciate this point when we consider how we come to
have a moment of insight, such as when we are engaged in nondiscursive activities, for example, working out a color scheme for a painting or choreographing
the sequences of a dance. As many artists or thinkers acknowledge, such creative
tasks are often made possible through flashes of insight, moments away from the
problem during which preconceived ideas suddenly give way in order to allow
for the emergence of a new form, idea, or way of being.

As I read Heidegger's Parmenides lecture, the sudden irruption of Being
into beings parallels this notion of insight. Like Heidegger's description of being, insight occurs as a nonvolitional occurrence, a nonsubjective happening
that has the capacity to break through a routinized pattern of dealing with
beings and to transform our relationships. Where this conception of insight
differs from Heidegger's is that it does not presuppose in any way a relationship
with the word. All that is required to have insight is the capacity to suspend a
customary pattern of thinking or acting long enough to transform a relationship with another being. I argue that insight is prior to thinking as it requires
only a sense of the open or openings but does not need to think them as such,
to *think* (where thinking requires words and discursive language) the open as
such.

Heidegger does not extend even this minimal sense of openness to nonhuman beings, or at least never explicitly. When it comes to discussing why it
is that animals lack access to thinking being, he says that the sign of animals'
essential exclusion is that no animal or plant has the word. His proof of this is
not a discussion about humans and language or even an elaboration of why we
should consider animals as being devoid of language. Instead, he reverts back

to a discussion that occurs earlier in the Freiburg lectures of 1929–1930, where he determines animal behavior as being essentially captivated behavior.[17] There, Heidegger sketches his central phenomenological description of animality on the basis of work derived from the twentieth-century zoologist Jacob Johann von Uexküll, and then from a single experiment on bees. The experiment involves placing a bee in front of a huge bowl of honey. The researcher then cuts the bee's abdomen away and watches as the bee continues to suck the honey. Heidegger reads the bee's continual sucking as a kind of "captivation."[18] This use of the bee is strange in at least two ways: first, Heidegger is silent about the techno-scientific determination that the experiment implies. But more problematic still is that Heidegger determines from this experiment the nature of animality as such—as if the radical diversity of animal life could be fully represented by experimental observations of bees.

"Captivation" fails to grasp the relationship to the "open" that makes the mutual responsiveness humans can share with some animals possible. As we will see in the next section, both human and nonhuman animals are in their togetherness already and always in a mutual suspension of ways of thinking and of relation that support their well-being and that constitute their world.

The Dog Whisperer and the Problem of the American Pet

> We are the only species that follow unstable pack leaders.
> —Cesar Millan, *Dog Whisperer*

Each week Cesar Millan demonstrates in his television program what dog lovers know already—that dogs routinely manifest a mode of *insight*. That is, dogs (and other animals), when guided by another being who is attuned to their problem, be it a phobia or fixated behavior, demonstrate the ability to break a captivated or fixated state with an object (such as a rock, sock, person, or other dog), so as to "see" or to experience the object in another way. Drawing upon his years of experience observing dogs' behaviors in a variety of settings, Millan offers a significant correction to Heidegger's determination of the "essence" of animality as being "captivated."

Millan is not himself an academic philosopher and he does not attempt to develop a rigorous conceptuality of animal behavior, but his work with dogs could be described as "phenomenological," which is to say he observes dogs as they are embedded in their own particular environments and forms of relationships. Consequently, Millan also shares with Heidegger a real suspicion of and disdain for anthropomorphic projections that wrench animals from the environments most proper to them:

> Most animal lovers insist on trying to relate to their dogs using human psychology. . . . I suppose it is natural to humanize an animal, because human psychology is our first frame of reference. We've been raised to believe the world belongs to us, and that it should run the way we want it to. . . . Humanizing a dog, the cause of many problem behaviors I am called in to correct, creates imbalance, and a dog who is out of balance is an unfulfilled and, more often than not, troubled dog.[19]

Millan's phenomenology of dogs is grounded in his insight that the vast majority of problem dog behaviors stem directly from their human owner's tendency to treat dogs like human beings. A central premise of Millan's dog training philosophy is that humans' tendency to treat dogs as if they were humans is the root cause of most canine "issues"—what Millan jokingly refers to as the problem of "humans who love too much." From years of working with "problem dogs," Millan concludes that the natural expression of a dog's nature is not captivation (what Millan calls an obsessed or fixated mind), but rather "a calm-submissive" energy. Millan describes this "calm-submissive" energy as a state of mental balance that is at once "open-minded," receptive, and responsive to other beings in the world (and especially to the pack leader).[20] Millan is careful to distinguish this "calm-submissive" mind from concepts of canine behavior that describe dogs as sophisticated machines or mere bundles of instinct.

Millan describes the dog's "calm-submissive mind" not in terms of biological mechanisms or processes but modes of human social interaction. Millan writes:

> The word *submissive* carries with it negative connotations, just as the word *assertive* does. *Submissive* doesn't mean pushover. It doesn't mean you have to make your dog into a zombie or a slave. It simply means *relaxed* and *receptive*. It's the energy of a group of well-behaved students in a classroom, or of a church congregation.[21]

Millan considers dogs to be first and foremost social creatures like humans. Dogs' sense of identity as well as the development of their personalities is intimately tied to their interactions with the other members who constitute their pack. "Your dog's *pack mentality* is one of the greatest natural forces involved in shaping his or her behavior," writes Millan. "A dog's pack is his life. The pack is his primal instinct. His status in the pack is his self, his identity."[22] Indeed, what Millan calls "the power of the pack" is so crucial to a dog's identity, any behavior that threatens the harmony of the pack is understood as a threat to the individual dogs that constitute the pack. In the absence of human intervention, a bitch who exhibits a tendency to isolate herself or proves otherwise unable to fit in with the pack will quickly be corrected by the pack leader. If the problem behavior does not change, the asocial dog is eliminated, one way or another, from the pack.[23] The captivated state that Heidegger describes in the Freiburg lecture (and which informs his later discussion of the difference between "animals" and humans in the Parmenides lecture) in which an animal is obsessed, fixated, or exclusively related to an object, as the bee with the honey, would never be tolerated within a dog pack. Fixated, obsessed, or otherwise "closed-off" behavior is, rather, "read" by the pack as signs of a pathological imbalance. Significantly, when dogs do manifest asocial or antisocial behavior, the cause of this imbalance is rarely a problem within the dog's innate disposition but, as Millan demonstrates each week on *Dog Whisperer*, it is almost always attributable to the dog's human companion's failure to provide the dog adequate outlets to expend its energy. In a phrase reminiscent of Freud on human neurosis, or Nietzsche on the origin of *ressentiment*, Millan writes, "A fixation is wasted energy."[24]

A central premise behind Millan's dog training philosophy is his observation that dogs and humans (and indeed all animals) share a "universal. . . . interspecies" language of "energy."[25] As Millan describes it, the "language" of energy is innate or instinctual to all animals and is given prior to the development of any subsequent formal logic or discursive languages. Although this language may be communicated vocally, it is not exhausted nor primarily expressed through the voice, but expressed through the ever-changing rhythmic vibrations of the earth and in the many scents and smells by which animals communicate their desires and emotions to one another. Animals, writes Millan, "are speaking to one another all of the time."[26] Millan gives the concrete example of the ongoing communication of energy between animals: the first is the way that animals in the African savannah or jungle, but also in an American backyard, will intermingle effortlessly, "peaceful, despite the many different species sharing the same space."[27] These same animals, however, will quickly disperse, if they perceive the approach of a predator, even before the predator enters their space:

> Animals immediately recognize when a predator is projecting hunting energy, sometimes even before they spot the predator itself. As humans we are often blind to these nuances in animal energy—we think the tiger

is dangerous at all times, when, really, if he has just eaten a three hundred pound deer, he's probably more tired than treacherous. The moment his tummy gets empty, however, he is a different animal. . . . Even
your backyard squirrel will pick up on this subtle difference. Yet we humans tend to be blind to what, in the animal kingdom, is pretty much a
flashing red light.[28]

The success of Millan's training program trades on humans' ability to tap
into this universal language to communicate energetically with their dogs. The
key to successful dog training and the key to successful human and dog relationships is to cultivate a mutually responsive energetic relationship between
the dog and his human companion through cultivating a "calm-assertive" energy in the pet owner (or pack leader), on the one hand, and the "calm-submissive" energy of the dog, on the other. Millan's project requires both the human
and the dog to undergo a mutual suspension of their habits, instincts, and
ways of thinking for their mutual benefit. The human must suspend her tendency to understand her dog as either a human subject, such as child trapped in
a dog suit, or as a mere object for manipulation or selfish gratification. The
canine must give up its fixated, inappropriately dominant, or antisocial behavior in order to rejoin its pack. In each case, the shift that occurs is primarily
communicated through a shift in energy: the human learns to assert calm-
dominant leadership by adjusting his or her posture, tone of voice, and emotional tonality, and the dog learns to adopt the calm-submissive mind required
to replace old fixated behaviors with socially responsive ones. Thus for Millan
the key to successful interactions with dogs is to recognize and respond to
their particular form of sociability, the pack structure that requires and revolves around a firm and stable pack leader. What Millan names "the power of
the pack" consists of very specific sets of social relationships that are established and reinforced through an initial act or imposition of leadership through
"calm and assertive force," which Millan likens to the way the mother dog in-
teracts with her pups, an imposition that is subsequently spread out and maintained laterally throughout the pack. Millan's cardinal observation is that dogs
crave the order instituted by the pack leader and maintained by the pack, and
in lieu of any clear leader in their environment, they will attempt to usurp the
role for themselves. In situations where humans do not act as the pack leader
to provide firm and clear guidelines of acceptable behavior for the pack (which
in Millan's version now includes the human), the dogs inevitably manifest
unwanted, often destructive behavior. Extreme fixation or captivation, what

Millan names "obsession," is one of the most common ways that dogs manifest energies that are out of balance.

In his book *Cesar's Way: The Natural, Everyday Guide to Understanding and Correcting Common Dog Problems*, and also on his National Geographic Channel show *Dog Whisperer*, Millan offers concrete evidence of this diagnosis in his "rehabilitation" of Punkin, a mixed breed dog who is dangerously captivated by rocks, and his training of Amanda, Punkin's overly aggressive owner. The segment begins with Millan's premise that "a pack leader never allows obsessions, or insecurity, or instability: dogs only develop these side effects when they live with us." Within minutes of his session with Amanda and Punkin, Millan establishes both Punkin's obsession with rocks, as well as Amanda's tendency to use an aggressive, as opposed to a "calm-assertive" energy with the dog. Punkin exhibits classic obsessive behavior when he sees rocks; he strains at his leash to get a rock until he gets it in his mouth and will not drop the rock when commanded, barking and snarling furiously at anyone who attempts to remove the rock. His connection with the rock is immediate, absolute, and exclusive. There is no space for any form of negotiation or relationship outside Punkin's desire to control the rock. For her part, Amanda feeds the dog's fixation by increasing the dog's anxiety both by projecting aggressive and angry energy and through her use of the choke-collar. So intense is Punkin's fixation with the rocks that Punkin will strain against the choke holder even at the risk of his own well-being. As Amanda herself observes, "When he is interested in a rock he knows no pain." Punkin and Amanda are thus embroiled in a classic vicious circle: Punkin's fixation is intensified by Amanda's aggressive attempts to correct his fixation, which in turn creates more aggression in Amanda, and more fear, anxiety, and pain for the dog. Millan initially uses a twofold strategy to correct the problem. His first task is to break Punkin's obsession with the rocks by creating the "calm-submissive" state of mind in the dog so that the dog is open to a new relationship with the rocks (in this case the rocks are just one more object in the environment and no longer act as a trigger for unwanted behavior). To do this, Millan both literally and figuratively assumes the role of the dominate pack-leader as he crouches down to the dog's level and mimics the action of a light nip with his hands, such as a mother dog might use to correct her pups, or a pack leader would use to control another pack member. For forty-five minutes Millan works with Punkin to break his fixation with the rock by first challenging Punkin's right to have the rock. Each time Punkin makes a move for the rock, Millan lightly corrects Punkin by making a nip-like action with hand, just as another dog would use

to defend its territory. As Millan explains, in using the nip-like touch his purpose is never to try to harm the dog in either "body, mind, or spirit," but
rather, "I want the mind to become weaker or sensitive to the presence of my
physical touch." In this way, Millan states, "I create an opening in order for
him to calm down. . . . it's a physical touch that makes the brain react." As
important as this repeated gesture is for creating "an opening" through which
Millan can shift the dog's fixated state, it is the calm-assertive energy that Millan uses with Punkin that is central to the success of the dog's rehabilitation.
Unlike Amanda, whose use of brute force coupled with aggressive energy only
fuels the dog's obsession with the rock, Millan's projection of calm-assertive
energy enables him to make the familiar connection of a pack leader with a
member of his pack. Having established that the rock is his, through the projection of calm-assertive energy backed up with a light physical correction that
mirrors that of a balanced pack leader, Millan then works to substitute the
physical correction with a vocal correction. And we see, as if by magic, that
Punkin is able to walk with Millan past rocks without incident. Unfortunately,
Millan is less successful in his rehabilitation with Amanda, who by the end of
the show has not yet mastered the ability to use the "calm-assertive" energy of
a pack leader, but reverts instead to random and aggressive acts of controlling
Punkin by tugging on her choker collar. Not surprisingly, while Punkin is able
to shift his attention away from rocks to engage in a social relationship with his
stable pack leader, Millan, he reverts to his fixation when he is reunited with
the energetically imbalanced Amanda. "There are no quick fixes for the obsessive mind," Millan observes, however the show ends on a brighter note: the
promise that Cesar's "balanced pack" will more quickly affect the change that
Amanda cannot yet accomplish herself.

Although most of the dogs and owners that Millan works with are capable
of making the energetic shift needed to achieve the desired behavior results,
for those who cannot, Millan established the Dog Psychology Center. The
Dog Psychology Center is composed of a pack of thirty to forty well-balanced
dogs, many of whom have been with Millan since he first opened the center,
and some of whom Millan's family take home with them and consider to be
part of their family. The central premise of the Dog Psychology Center is that
dogs learn from other dogs, and particularly they learn how to balance their
energies and behaviors so that they may live harmoniously with the rest of the
pack. Although Millan functions as the pack leader of the group, his central
job at the center is to ensure that the dogs get the vigorous exercise they need
in order to maintain a calm-submissive energy. Most of the work of socializing
dogs and correcting obsessed behavior is undertaken by the dogs themselves.

In general, the "power of the pack" coupled with adequate exercise overwrites the neuroses and fixations of most dogs. And indeed, in his many years of working with dogs, Millan states that he has met only two dogs that could not be rehabilitated as social animals, and he estimates that 1 percent of dogs have a "mental imbalance, or are so deeply damaged by humans that they can't safely be returned to society."[29]

Apart from providing excellent, transparent examples of dogs who suspend their captivation to change their relationship to their trigger, the cases presented on *Dog Whisperer* help to develop a set of as yet underdeveloped intuitions concerning the problem of the "humanization of the animal," or what Millan elsewhere diagnoses as the "problem with America's pets." In short, they help us to understand how treating dogs like human beings dressed up in fur suits is essentially unkind and risks damaging the psychological health of our dogs.

We can extend the fluidity of deconstructive phenomenological determination of the human and animal relation to think about what is at stake in Millan's method of "retraining humans" and "rehabilitating dogs." One way of understanding Millan's work is to assume that it is embedded in a traditional "substantialist" approach to the human/animal distinction. On this reading, Millan is training human beings to assert *their* "human" dominance *over* the (merely) "animal" world. I suggest this reading misses what is most interesting in Millan's work with dogs and distorts the character of the remarkable transformation that occurs in both the dogs and the humans he "rehabilitates." As suggested above, Millan's method involves the human in an imaginary projection into the dog's sense of sociability. This requires that the human draw upon the calm, but assertive energy of a canine pack leader by manipulating movements, tonality, and most of all, energy. In short, at the heart of Millan's work is a belief in the possibility of a reciprocal transformation of both dog and human that is possible because of "the open" space in which the world manifests itself to both species. Making each of these transformations possible is a moment of suspension and insight: the dog suspending its relationship to its trigger and the human suspending its habitual way of relating to the dog. In this reciprocal movement a new opening occurs, an opening that we have thought of here as kindness.

Notes

1. Coetzee 1999:61.
2. Coetzee 1999:65.
3. Coetzee 1999:65.

4. Coetzee 1999:65.

5. For example, Jacques Derrida has argued in an uncharacteristically sweeping conclusion that the denial of the ability of animals to see us, rather than simply be seen by us, "is probably what brings together *all* philosophers and all theoreticians *as such*" (Derrida 2008:13 [emphasis in original]). "Elle est sans doute celle qui rassemble tous les philosophes et tous les théoriciens en tant que tells" (Derrida 1999:264). For discussion, see Gross 2010:224.

6. I borrow this term from Martin Heidegger, who charges that the poet Rilke risks a "homonization" of animals and "animalization of humans" in the "Eighth Duino Elegy." Heidegger 1992:152.

7. From Mark Doty's *Dog Years: A Memoir*, as quoted in Chapman 2007.

8. Ethologists may, in fact, not be too far from documenting in controlled studies something like what I have called "kindness." For example, the highly regarded primatologist Frans de Waal has recently argued that nonhuman great apes have a robust capacity for "empathy" (de Waal 2009). De Waal speculates that this capacity for empathy may also be possessed by a range of social mammals (de Waal 2009).

9. Heidegger 1995:210 (emphasis in original). In German the entire passage reads: "Haustiere werden von uns im Haus gehalten, sie 'leben' mit uns. Aber wir leben nicht mit ihnen, wenn Leben besagt: *Sein in der* Weise des Tieres. Gleichwohl *sind wir mit* ihnen. Dieses Mitsein is aber auch kein *Mitexistieren*, sofern ein Hund nicht existiert, sondern nur lebt. Dieses Mitsein mit den Tieren ist so, daß wir die Tiere in unserer Welt sich bewegen lassen. . . . Er ißt mit uns—nein, er ißt nicht. Und doch mit uns! Ein Mitgehen, eine Versetztheit—und doch nicht" (Heidegger 1982:308).

10. Milan and Peltier 2006:28.

11. Heidegger 1992:165. "Der moderne Mensch 'erlebt' die Welt und denkt sie erlebend, d.h. von sich aus als demjenigen Seienden, das aller Erklärung und Einrichtung des Seinden im Ganzen als der Grund zugrunde liegt. . . . Nur wo der Mensch zum Subjekt geworden, wird das nicht menschliche Seiende zum Objekt. Nur im Bereich der Subjektivität kann ein Zwist über die Objektivität und ihre Geltung und ihren Nutzen und Schaden entstehen und darüber verhandelt werden, ob die Objektivität jeweils einen Nutzen oder Schaden bringe" (Heidegger 1982:247).

12. Heidegger 1992:160. "Weil nun aber der Mensch in der Metaphysik als das vernünftige Tier erfahren und gedacht wird, deshalb wird die Tierheit jedesmal am Maßstab der Vernünftigkeit als das Unvernünftige, Vernunftlose, und d.h. zugleich in der Entsprechung zur menschlichen Verständigkeit und Triebhaftigkeit, ausgelegt" (Heidegger 1982:238).

13. Heidegger 1992:160. "So bleibt in der Metaphysik und in ihrem Gefolge für alle Wissenshaft das Geheimnis des Lebendigen außer der Acht; denn entweder werden die Lebewesen dem Angriff der Chemie ausgesetzt oder sie werden in den Gesichtskreis der "Psychologie" versetzt. Auf beiden Wegen gibt man vor, das Rätsel des Lebens zu suchen. Man wird es niemals finden; nicht nur deshalb nicht, weil jede Wissenschaft

nur immer an das Vorletzte gefesselt bleibt und das Letzte als Erste voraus-setzen muß, sondern auch deshalb wird man das Rätsel des Lebens so nie finden, weil man zuvor das Geheimnis des Lebendigen preisgegeben hat" (Heidegger 1982:238–239).

14. Heidgger 1992:148. "Darnach ist das Offene das Lichte des Sichlichtenden. Wir nennen es 'das Freie' und sein Wesen 'die' Freiheit. Dies Wort hat hier einen anfänglichen Sinn, der dem metaphysischen Denken fremd ist" (Heidegger 1982:221).

15. "Diesem wesenhaft unvermittlten und unmittelbaren Ein-fall des Sein" (Heidegger 1982:223).

16. "The essence of the open reveals itself only to a thinking that attempts to think being itself" (Heidegger 1992:149). "Enthüllt sich das Wesen des Offenen nur dem Denken, das versucht, das Sein selbst zu denken" (Heidegger 1982:222).

17. See especially, chapter 4, sections 58–61. The philosopher, Giorgio Agamben, has undertaken a brilliant reading of the role of captivation in the Freiburg lectures in his work, *The Open: Man and Animal* (2004). Agamben's conception of potentiality inherent in the open has been a crucial influence in developing my phenomenology of kindness here.

18. For a comprehensive and well-argued presentation of the role of the bee experiment in Heidegger's theory of animal captivation, see Calarco 2004:24–27.

19. Millan and Peltier 2006:82–83.

20. Millan and Peltier 2006:73–74.

21. Millan and Peltier 2006:73.

22. Millan and Peltier 2006:111.

23. Millan is quick to remind us that the pack leader is always concerned with the survival of the pack over that of any particular member (Millan and Peltier 2006:117).

24. Millan and Peltier 2006:159.

25. Millan and Peltier 2006:61.

26. Millan and Peltier 2006:62.

27. Millan and Peltier 2006:62.

28. Millan and Peltier 2006:62.

29. Millan and Peltier 2006:173. This gives pause in light of the fact that according to the American Humane Society, many of the 9.6 million animals who are put to death each year, are "unrehabilitable."

References

Agamben, Giorgio. 1999. *Potentialities: Collected Essays in Philosophy*. Stanford, CA: Stanford University Press.

——. 2004. *The Open: Man and Animal*. Stanford, CA: Stanford University Press.

Calarco, Matthew. 2004. "Heidegger's Zoontology." In *Animal Philosophy: Ethics and Identity*, ed. Peter Atterton and Matthew Calarco, 18–30. London: Continuum.

Chapman, Danielle. 2007. "Howl." *New York Times Review of Books*, June 3.

Coetzee, J. M. 1999. *The Lives of Animals*. Princeton, NJ: Princeton University Press.

De Waal, Frans. 2009. *The Age of Empathy: Nature's Lessons for a Kinder Society*. New York: Harmony Books.

Derrida, Jacques. 1999. "L'animal que donc je suis (á suivre)." In *L'animal autobiographique: Autour de Jacques Derrida*, ed. M. L. Mallet, 253–261. Paris: Galilee.

——. 2008. *The Animal That Therefore I Am*. Trans. David Wills. Ed. Marie-Louise Mallet. New York: Fordham University Press.

Gross, Aaron. 2010. "The Question of the Animal and Religion." PhD diss., University of California, Santa Barbara.

Haraway, Donna. 2003. *The Companion Species Manifesto: Dogs, People, and Significant Otherness*. Chicago: Prickly Paradigm Press.

Heidegger, Martin. 1982a. *Gesamtausgabe Bd. 29/30: Die Grundbegriffe der Metaphysik: Welt, Endlichkeit, Einsamkeit*. Frankfurt am Main: Klostermann.

——. 1982b. *Gesamtausgabe Bd. 54: Parmenides*. Frankfurt am Main: Vittorio Klostermann.

——. 1992. *Parmenides*. Trans. André Schuwer and Richard Rojcewicz. Bloomington: Indiana University Press.

——. 1995. *The Fundamental Concepts of Metaphysics: World, Finitude, Solitude*. Trans. William McNeil and Nicolas Walker. Bloomington: Indiana University Press.

Krell, David. 1992. *Daimon Life: Heidegger and Life Philosophy*. Bloomington: Indiana University Press.

Lévinas, Emmanuel. 1990. "The Name of a Dog or Natural Rights." In *Difficult Freedom: Essays on Judaism*. Trans. Sean Hand, 151–153. Baltimore, MD: Johns Hopkins University Press.

Millan, Cesar, and Mellissa Jo Peltier. 2006. *Cesar's Way: The Natural, Everyday Guide to Understanding and Correcting Common Dog Problems*. New York: Harmony Books.

Santner, Eric L. 2006. *On Creaturely Life: Rilke, Benjamin, Sebald*. Chicago: University of Chicago Press.

eleven

The Lives of Animals

Wittgenstein, Coetzee, and the Extent of the

Sympathetic Imagination

Undine Sellbach

The Lives of Animals

The Lives of Animals is the title of a novella by J. M. Coetzee.[1] *The Lives of Animals*: what thoughts inhabit these words? To begin with I am reminded of the multiplicity of animal life, human life being but one of its many variants. An elaborate web of affinities and differences lies between all beings—between humans and other animals and between animals and other animals. This thought is at once obvious and difficult to imagine. It is obvious because our lives with other animals (and our lives as animals) are at once mysterious and shared. It is difficult to imagine because, as Jacques Derrida has pointed out, the word "animal" does not adequately capture this "heterogeneous multiplicity" of relations.[2] Between humanity and animality we often picture an absolute break, which deflects from the complex web of differences and affinities between life forms. Here *the animal* is cast as an abstract *other*, a device for delimiting, in negative terms, the concept of a human life. In such circumstances it is difficult to hear what Derrida calls "the plural of animals . . . in the singular," and it is difficult to imagine, as Coetzee's title invites us to imagine, the presence of many animals with many lives.[3]

But alongside the multiplicity of animal life lies a further provocation. Coetzee does not simply affirm the fact of animal life in all its variety, he designates *The Lives of Animals*—he presents *life* as something that animals *have*. But in what sense can an animal truly have a life? A life, it would seem, is something that a human being *has* and other animals simply *live*. Raymond Gaita makes this point in his discussion of Coetzee's novella when he says that although some animals possess a certain striking individuality, the stories we write about them are not properly biographical because nothing a nonhuman animal does amounts to "making or failing to make something" of its life, "nor even of life making something of it."[4] Although animals may suffer or feel happy in the course of their lives, he argues, we do not say that they "rejoice" or "despair" in life for only humans have a life that is capable of affecting them with the question of its meaning.[5]

Coetzee, by contrast, seems to challenge the ease with which we make such distinctions. Consider *The Lives of Animals* alongside the title of another of Coetzee's books, *Life and Times of Michael K*. The book's protagonist, a homeless South African gardener called Michael K, lives a life that is, in an important regard, undesignated—in literal terms the word "life" lacks an article to specify it. In *Life and Times of Michael K* the problem of life is not presented as a search for an overall significance, but an exposure to existence at the very limits of human meaning. The book raises the troubling question of whose life or what life counts? Is an undesignated life a valuable life, a life that can, in some way, be counted?[6]

In this context the title, *The Lives of Animals* might be read as an attempt to give expression to the singular affecting quality of life insofar as it exceeds human categories of value and meaning. To designate undesignated life, to imagine the multiplicity of the word "lives" and at the same time the particularity of *each life* specified by the word "the"—this is the book's provocation.

But how might we even begin such an undertaking? Empirically, an account of the lives of animals seems impossible to provide in full. Coetzee's novella refers in detail to a bat, some apes, a gathering of humans, a rooster, some horses, a panther, cattle, and sheep, but surely even a longer more encyclopedic text would struggle to describe animal life in all its diversity and singularity. Furthermore, our accounts of other animals are always, to a certain extent, anthropomorphic for they are mediated by human perceptions, concepts, gestures, feelings, and imaginings. An exploration of the possibilities and paradoxes entailed by words "the lives of animals" is what the philosopher Ludwig Wittgenstein might have considered an ethical task.

A Valuable Form of Nonsense

In his "Lecture on Ethics," Wittgenstein observes that ethics, insofar as it comes from a desire to speak about the meaning of life or about absolute right, wrong, or value, has no foundation in the empirical world. Rather than making a moral dictum or general principle his main focus, he describes the sensation of going for a walk on a fine summer day. In this situation, he tells his audience, he has an experience that might best be captured by the words: "I wonder at the existence of the world."[7] Through these words an engagement with this or that detail gives way to a vision of life as a whole. The difficulty is that although it is quite possible to wonder at a particular state of affairs (to feel wonder that it is sunny and not raining today), it seems impossible to fully understand what it would be to wonder at the existence of the world as a whole. To do so, Wittgenstein suggests, would be to feel wonder at the world whatever be the case—something that would be tantamount to feeling wonder towards a tautology.[8]

The words "the lives of animals" may also be taken as an expression of wonder. Wonder toward the unfolding web of life and perhaps also wonder at the extraordinary singularity of each encounter between lives. But the difficulty is that the wonder we feel toward other animals tends to be selective—some animals are considered exotic, others ordinary or banal. It seems difficult to move from this or that remarkable fact of nature to a feeling of wonder toward animal life as a whole.

Wittgenstein insists that when we speak ethically, we stretch our imagination to its very limits. "My whole tendency and I believe the tendency of all men who ever tried to write or talk Ethics or Religion was to run against the boundaries of language."[9] Ethics is not a set of ineffable truths that words fail to capture, for it is nonsensical by its "very essence."[10] According to Wittgenstein, ethics *is* the strain of the imagination against itself, against its own limits, and as such he sees it as "a document of a tendency in the human mind which I personally cannot help respecting deeply and I would not for my life ridicule it."[11]

The impulse to run up against the limits of meaning, says Cora Diamond in her reading of Wittgenstein, is something we must acknowledge—both in ourselves and in others—if we are to understand what it is we do when we speak ethically. Here Diamond suggests that although we cannot fully comprehend the content of certain ethical claims, it may still be possible to understand the predicament of the speaker of ethics by imaginatively reenacting their impulse to run up against the limits of language.[12]

In a further attempt to give imaginative shape to the wonder he feels at life, Wittgenstein asks his audience to imagine an unexpected incident.

> Take the case that one of you suddenly grew a lion's head and began to roar. Certainly that would be as extraordinary a thing as I can imagine. Whenever we should have recovered from our surprise, what I would suggest would be to fetch a doctor and have the case scientifically investigated, and if it were not for hurting him, I would have him vivisected. And where would the miracle have got to? For it is clear that when we look at it in this way, everything miraculous has disappeared.[13]

Wittgenstein is not suggesting that science has proven that there are no miracles, but rather that "the scientific way of looking at a fact is not the way to look at it as a miracle."[14] To recognize the scene in the lecture hall as a miracle would be to open oneself to a form of wonder that is not driven by the scientific demand for a final explanation. The lion-headed man is at once an emblem of wonder Wittgenstein feels toward life as a whole and a reminder of the nonsensicality of its articulation.

But in telling this story Wittgenstein also introduces beastliness into a space where it ought not to be—in an academic lecture hall and in a philosophical discourse on ethics.

Could ethics, understood as an imaginative encounter with the limits of sense, unsettle, as Wittgenstein's example seems to suggest, the boundaries between the anthropological and the zoological, philosophy, and animality? And what (or whom) do we understand to be affected by these unsettled boundaries—the human being or the animal?

In an effort to respond to these questions, I will read Coetzee's novella *The Lives of Animals* in conjunction with the thought of Wittgenstein. In particular, I will draw on Wittgenstein to distinguish two interrelated approaches to the notion of *life*. On the one hand, there is the task of discovering distinctions and affinities in *forms of life*. On the other hand, there are the feelings of orientation and disorientation that comes from being in the *midst of life,* of living with humans and other animals. The title of Coetzee's novella troubles current ways of construing the human/animal divide, I will argue, precisely because it asks us to think about differences and similarities in forms of life alongside the possibility that all animals (human and nonhuman) have, at least in some respect, an orientation to life that contains the possibility of its own disturbance.

The Sympathetic Imagination

Coetzee's novella *The Lives of Animals* tells the story of Elizabeth Costello, an Australian novelist of small fame who is invited to Appleton College in the United States to give some guest lectures. The story is composed of her lectures and the surrounding conversations with academic staff, her son (who works at the college in an unrelated field), and his family. From the outset the intellectual unfolding of Elizabeth Costello's thought cannot be separated from the difficulty of its expression. She feels exposed before her audience and struggles to present her ideas in a compelling way, lacking the reassurance of feeling understood. The topic she has chosen to discuss is the breadth of the sympathetic imagination.

In the course of her first lecture, she quotes a well-known article by the philosopher Thomas Nagel, describing his attempts to imagine what it would be like to be a bat.

> It will not help to try to imagine that one has webbing on one's arms, which enables one to fly around . . . catching insects in one's mouth; that one has very poor vision, and perceives the surrounding world by a system of reflected high-frequency sound signals; and that one spends the day hanging upside down by one's feet in an attic. Insofar as I can imagine this (which is not very far), it tells me only what it would be like for me to behave as a bat behaves. But that is not the question. I want to know what it is like for a *bat* to be a bat. Yet if I try to imagine this, I am restricted by the resources of my own mind, and those resources are inadequate to the task.[15]

In response Elizabeth Costello tells her audience about the "sympathetic imagination," something in which she believes Nagel puts little faith.

> For instants at a time . . . I know what it is like to be a corpse. The knowledge repels me. It fills me with terror; I shy away from it, refuse to entertain it.
>
> All of us have such moments, particularly as we grow older. The knowledge we have is not abstract—"all human beings are mortal, I am a

human being, therefore I am mortal"—but embodied. For a moment we *are* that knowledge. We live the impossible: we live beyond our death, look back on it, yet look back as only a dead self can.

"When I know, with this knowledge, that I am going to die, what is it, in Nagel's terms, that I know? Do I know what it is like for me to be a corpse or do I know what it is like for a corpse to be a corpse? The distinction seems to me trivial. What I know is what a corpse cannot know: that it is extinct, that it knows nothing and will never know anything anymore. For an instant, before my whole structure of knowledge collapses in panic, I am alive inside that contradiction, dead and alive at the same time."[16]

At stake is the breadth of the sympathetic imagination. According to Nagel, we do not have a bat's sense modalities and this makes the bat "a fundamentally alien form of life."[17] But for Elizabeth Costello the sympathetic imagination has no absolute bounds. As a novelist she can imagine characters who have never lived. "If I can think my way into the existence of a being who has never existed," she explains, "then I can think my way into the existence of a bat or a chimpanzee or an oyster, any being with whom I share the substrate of life."[18] Differences and similarities in animal and human forms of life, although important, she tells her audience, are ultimately of "secondary consideration" for what is most important in the encounter is not this or that particular type of life, but an opening to the very *being* of life.[19]

In a collection of philosophical commentaries published in a volume alongside Coetzee's story, Peter Singer argues that the analogy Elizabeth Costello makes between our ability to understand characters in novels and our ability to understand other animals is highly misleading.[20] We can sympathetically portray a fictional person, a person who actually does not exist, he argues, because their way of life is similar to our own. But no such resource is available when we try to imaginatively understand the lives of beings very different from ourselves.

If, as Singer suggests, the ability to understand another stops where our shared ways of life stop, then expressions of sympathy or understanding that try to go beyond these limits are unfounded. In the face of this confusion, it would seem that the task of the philosopher is to identify exactly what forms of life—what practices, abilities, or perceptual apparatus—we do and don't share with animals. For Nagel the answer would be very little, for although it is true that we share more with a monkey than a bat, and more with a bat than a Martian, we cannot say, in the case of the bat, what it would be like to *be* a bat because we do not share their sense modalities.[21] Singer, by contrast, says that we share the capacity to feel pain with most animals (and on this basis alone we have a moral obligation to consider their interests), but that there are many other ways of being—looking to the future, reasoning, using sophisticated language, telling stories, reflecting on death—that we do not share.[22] Singer has so little confidence in Elizabeth Costello's account that he doubts that Coetzee takes her views seriously. He implies that the people who object to her views in the story are used by Coetzee as distancing devices, to enable him to avoid taking authorial responsibility for the intellectual implications of the ideas he puts forward via her character.[23]

In her essay "The Difficulty of Reality and the Difficulty of Philosophy," Diamond proposes that Singer fundamentally misunderstands Coetzee's story by treating it as a "fictional frame" for a series of arguments about animal rights.[24] According to Diamond, what Singer fails to recognize is that Elizabeth Costello resists the language of philosophy because she "sees our reliance on argumentation as a way we make unavailable to ourselves our sense of what it is to be a living animal."[25] Elizabeth Costello does not present herself as a participant in an intellectual debate, whose job it is to identify shared attributes and general principles. The disorientation she feels before her audience is not a matter of mere conceptual confusion. In Diamond's words, Elizabeth Costello should be understood as "a woman haunted by the horror of what we do to animals. We see her as wounded by this knowledge, this horror, and by the knowledge of how unhaunted others are."[26] By framing our relationship with other animals in terms of a debate about what we can and cannot legitimately know, moral philosophy "deflects" us from the vulnerability and mortality we share with other animals, and from the "difficulty" of expressing this "reality," of keeping it in view.[27]

It is in this context, that we should understand Elizabeth Costello's insistence on an opening to the embodied life we share with other animals. And if, as she also says, we can imagine ourselves beyond this life into death, into a *living death*, then the question becomes: what is it that we understand about human and animal existence when we imagine these things—when we imagine both the fullness of life and the life of the dead?

The Crossed-Out Metaphor of Animality

In "Prehistory of the Postanimal," David Clark describes Western philosophy as a tradition of thought haunted by the animal. But whereas Elizabeth

Costello *feels* this haunting—she is wounded by other people's lack of horror at how we use other animals and by her own animal vulnerability—philosophy exhibits an "unacknowledged attachment *to* animality"—an *unconscious haunted-ness* that emerges from the repetitiveness of the need to deny the animal.[28] "What we are . . . witnessing here is . . . an underlying and interminable *an-thropological melancholia* . . . expressed in the form of ongoing foreclosures and erasures of the imagined animal, acts of renunciation whose repetitiveness and whose axiomatic nature puts to us that philosophy cannot have done with ani-mals but *cannot have done with having done with them either.*"[29] The repetitive-ness of the need to deny the animal, the fact that every denial is incomplete for it is followed by further imaginings—imaginings that in turn are dis-avowed—is melancholic, in Freud's sense of the term, for the loss of animality is repeatedly played out without being acknowledged, an ungrieved form of mourning.

This repetitive pattern of "incomplete denials" is also something that Eliza-beth Costello identifies in her discussion of the role of animals in everyday dis-course.[30] She points out that we often find in the being of other animals powerful expressions of many of our important experiences—suffering, love, friendship, hunger, mindlessness, fear, aliveness, purpose, trauma, and joy. These expressions have emerged through the shared history of our interactions with animals. As analogies they help articulate various aspects of human expe-rience. But their full implications—as efforts to imagine animal life and to try to understand what it is to undertake such an imaginings—are often cur-tailed.[31] Metaphor making between the human and animal realms is tolerated insofar as it services our task of self-description, but these metaphors are cor-rected, or crossed out if they threaten to unsettle the boundary that sets hu-manity over and above nature.

In her lecture, Elizabeth Costello draws on public discourse surrounding the horror of the Nazi concentration camps to make her point. Our descrip-tions of the camps, she says, resonate with the metaphorics of the stockyard—"They went like sheep to the slaughter"; "They died like animals"; "The Nazi butchers killed them."[32] But at another level, she believes, the full implications of this comparison are denied, for we condemn the citizens of the Third Reich for their complicity in their regime's horrific crime, but we do not condemn ourselves for the degradation and violent extermination going on in factory farms or meat processing camps. At such points, she suggests, we refuse to take our own words seriously, and the terrible fate of animals becomes a metaphor entirely in the service of something beyond itself.[33] For ultimately, "in our chosen 'metaphorics' it turns out to be 'they,' the citizens of the Third Reich, who were the beasts. By treating fellow human beings, beings created in the image of God, like beasts, they had themselves become beasts."[34] The comparison between the human and the animal is made then crossed out.

Elizabeth Costello tries to undo this violent pattern of borrowing and denial by taking seriously the analogy between the industrialized farming of animals and the industrialized harvesting of human labor and bodies in death camps. But in so doing she risks collapsing all distinction between human and animal, a collapse that made possible the mechanized slaughter of the Jewish people by Nazi Germany. Is there a way of understanding Elizabeth Costello's attempt to think the horror of factory farming side-by-side with the horrors of the Holocaust, without reducing this relation to a dangerous assertion of sameness?

Embodied Souls

In his book *The Philosopher's Dog*, Raymond Gaita responds to the portrait of animal human relations put forward by Coetzee in his story. Like Coetzee, Gaita is concerned with the wrong of animal suffering and exploitation. But he does not believe that Elizabeth Costello's efforts to understand the industrialized farming of animals through the metaphors of the Holocaust is a genuine way to overcome this wrong. Gaita writes: "One need not be susceptible to such extravagant comparisons in order to fully acknowledge that our cruelty to animals is abominable and to hope that future generations will find it so."[35]

According to Gaita, the degradation and exploitation of animals through industrialized farming rests on a refusal to view animals as conscious, sensate beings. This denial is much broader than the refusal to attribute a particular mental state to an animal. Rather, it is the claim that in no circumstances can we be sure that nonhuman animals feel genuine pain or joy, believe things, show concern for others, have expectations, and so forth.

Underpinning this skeptical stance, Gaita argues, is the presumption that we are justified in attributing states of consciousness to other beings only insofar as we have evidence for these states. Radical skepticism calls in to doubt the existence of all other minds, for no amount of behavioral evidence seems capable of letting us know for certain what, if anything, is going on inside the heads of others. But for many philosophers, the shared human capacity for language is reassurance enough that we are capable of understanding each other, and the problem of skepticism only reemerges in relation to the apparently language-less domain of nonhuman animals.

Drawing on Wittgenstein's work in *Philosophical Investigations*, Gaita points out that although it is impossible to give the skeptic the watertight behavioral evidence she or he requires, it is possible to show that the skeptic's demands for absolute foundations are misplaced. When confronted with the suffering of another person, Wittgenstein says, we do not first calculate whether he is likely to be an automaton exhibiting only the outward markings of pain, rather "my attitude towards him is an attitude towards a soul."[36] Here the soul of another being is not a spirit hidden within a behavioral shell. Instead *to see the behavior of another living thing is to see its soul*.[37]

Although Gaita is resistant to Elizabeth Costello's "extravagant comparisons," he finds in her account an understanding of the embodied life of concepts and feelings that might be used to overcome the skeptical tendency that underpins denials of animal suffering.[38] Gaita writes:

> Like Wittgenstein, [Coetzee] seems to believe that we misunderstand the importance of the infinitely subtle inflexions and demeanours of the body, the many forms of its expressiveness, if we take them only as the basis for hypothetical attributions of states of consciousness to animals. Rather (I take him to suggest) [that other animals] partly determine the meaning that words like "knowledge" and "belief" . . . and "fear" have in our life with language. Out of such unhesitating interactions, between ourselves, and between us and animals there developed—not beliefs, assumptions and conjectures about the mind—but our very concepts of thought, feeling, intention, belief, doubt.[39]

As Gaita makes clear, such remarks are not intended to provide the skeptic with evidence to *prove* that animals (or indeed other humans) have feelings, doubts, intentions, and so forth, for there is no evidence that will provide the absolute foundation she or he requires. Instead, they imply that the demand for absolute empirical foundations is out of place, that our willingness to use a particular psychological term to describe another is primarily a *conceptual* rather than an *empirical* matter. Gestures of sympathy and understanding are not mere empirical calculations. Instead they explore the possibilities of thought and action entailed by our concepts, concepts that have emerged, in part, from a long history of shared interactions with other animals.

This is not to deny that we often need to draw on this or that piece of evidence, but rather that the appeal to evidence in a given circumstance only makes sense insofar as there is "no room for serious doubt" that other animals are sentient creatures.[40] To seriously doubt that animals feel pain, Gaita concludes, is as absurd as claiming "I have pain in my pocket."[41] In both cases we disconnect ourselves from the fabric of human and animal relations that makes it possible for us to put these words forward in the first place.

Although Gaita recognizes in Elizabeth Costello a nuanced understanding of the bodily interactions between humans and animals that make concepts such as *pain* and *sympathy* possible, he thinks that in her effort to empathize with animal suffering, she extends the analogy too far. At the end of his book, he writes: "I cannot, and I know no one else who can, respond to the killing of animals as though it were mass murder."[42] Gaita does not immediately spell out his reasons, perhaps because he too expresses a conviction that cannot be adequately captured at the level of argument.[43] But although Gaita does not directly elaborate on his words, the book as a whole might be understood as an attempt to give background and reason to them. To liken the industrialized farming of animals to the Holocaust, he suggests, is as absurd as the claim that animals have no thoughts or feelings.[44] Like the skeptic, Gaita implies, Elizabeth Costello ultimately loses sight of the complex network of affinities and differences that underpin human and nonhuman forms of life, a history that seems to give both meaning and limit to the expression "the lives of animals."

A Profound Bodily Disturbance of the Soul

I think that Gaita is right to draw attention to the many forms of life we "unhesitatingly" share with other animals, but it does not seem true to say that there is nothing in "the infinitely subtle inflexions and demeanours" of our lives with other animals that is capable of provoking the terrible horror Elizabeth Costello feels. For Elizabeth Costello, to understand other animals as embodied souls is to feel horror at how we treat them as mere things. In "pressing" herself to acknowledge this, she suffers from "a profound disturbance of the soul," a disturbance that leaves her isolated from her family, her colleagues, and even divided from herself.[45]

As Cary Wolfe observes, the disturbance Elizabeth Costello suffers is not just "the unspeakability of how we treat animals in practices such as factory farming but also the unspeakability of the limits of our own thinking in confronting such a reality."[46] Gaita takes this unspeakability as an indication that Elizabeth Costello has lost sight of the complex forms of life underpinning the concepts we share. I think there is an important truth to Gaita's response. As Diamond observes, in drawing on the Holocaust as an image that expresses the horror of our treatment of other animals, she seems unable to keep in full

view what the Holocaust shows us about human beings treatment of one another.[47] But by framing the analogy Costello draws as an illegitimate use of
language, Gaita misses the sense in which she experiences her own departure
from shared social understandings as a form of animal vulnerability.

To better understand the animal vulnerabilities at stake in *The Lives of Animals*, I will turn to Wittgenstein's account of *forms of life*, a notion that Gaita
utilizes in his reading of Coetzee. In particular I want to consider the relationship between Wittgenstein's account of forms of life and his attempts to imagine a life lived in absence of these shared forms.

Forms of Life and Forms of *Life*

Wittgenstein emphasizes that our ability to project concepts into new situations and be understood is not due to a preestablished agreement in opinions
or rules, but to an agreement in *forms of life*, a familiarity with the complex
weave of possibilities opened up by bodies, language, and environment. His
Philosophical Investigations, with its proposals of criteria for what we do (and do
not) do and say in different circumstances, can be understood as Wittgenstein's personal exploration of these possibilities. By appealing to *forms of life*,
Wittgenstein appears to evoke a realm at the intersection of biology and culture that delimits our conventions, our concepts, and our behavioral responses.
This realm could provide a foundation to Gaita's insistence that Elizabeth
Costello has extended her sympathetic imagination too far. In my view, Wittgenstein's thought takes shape in its effort to resist the inevitability of this
conclusion. To help explain why, I turn to Stanley Cavell's account of the way
Wittgenstein's *forms of life* is used as a concept that spans the relation between
different patterns of being and a shared being of life.

According to Cavell, Wittgenstein's criteria (his proposals of what we do
and say) are not intended as proof or explanation for an "attunement" in form
of life. Rather they are "only another description of the same fact," for "nothing is deeper than the fact, or the extent, of agreement itself."[48] This "agreement" is not a priori, but rather made and remade made through sympathetic
leaps. This is not to say that all affirmations of shared life are legitimate, for
our capacity to read the behavior of others rests on a familiarity with the web
of possibilities opened up by bodies, words, and environment. It does mean
that the forms of life we share with others are sometimes open to contestation
or transformation. There is an underlying ambiguity in Wittgenstein's use of
the term "forms of life." It functions—whether in regard to all living beings or

in the context of human life—both as an affirmation of agreement and as a mark of difference.

Cavell describes this ambiguity when he says that in Wittgenstein's work forms of life can be given an "ethnological" or a "biological" direction.[49] The ethnological reading stresses the importance Wittgenstein gives to the conventional or social dimension of life as opposed to our private, inner lives. On this reading, Wittgenstein's insistence that "what has to be accepted, the given, is—so one could say—*forms of life*"[50] is taken to reinforce the social nature of humanity, for understanding between individuals is made possible through shared conventions.[51] Thus, although the ethnological reading promises understanding between beings that share the same conventions and social practices, it also implies that, in the absence of shared conventions, no understanding is possible.

However, Cavell believes that Wittgenstein's insistence that we must accept forms of life should also be pursued in "its biological direction," when, for example, Wittgenstein speaks of our natural reactions or imagines an alternative "fictitious natural history" in place of our own.[52] Here the emphasis is placed not on *forms* of life but on forms of *life*, on life being a given that indicates "the limit and gives the conditions of the use of criteria as applied to others."[53] "The criteria of pain," for example, "do not apply to what does not exhibit a form of life."[54] One can imagine a wriggling fly in pain, Wittgenstein says, but how might we even begin to imagine what it would be to think the same thing of a stone? We are not familiar with the *criteria* for a stone being in pain, and this suggests that we assign sensations only to "what behaves like a human being," namely to a "body" or to a "soul which some body *has*."[55]

If the social and the biological notions of "forms of life" are both possibilities Wittgenstein raises, then one must account for their interaction. In Cavell's view, the "mutual absorption of the natural and the social" means that we must pay attention not only to differences in the social realm—"differences between promising and fully intending, or between coronations and inaugurations, or between barter and a credit system"—but also to differences between the human form of life and other forms of biological life—"between, say, poking at your food, perhaps with a fork, and pawing at it, or pecking at it."[56]

As this passage suggests, differences between biological forms of life are also indicators of a certain convergence or "attunement" within and between biological life forms.[57] As Wittgenstein points out, even language cannot form an absolute boundary between human beings and other life forms. In order to make language the dividing line between humans and animals, he suggests, we would have to be willing to subtract from our definition of language the many "primitive forms of language" used by various animals—such as "commanding, questioning, recounting" and "chatting"—practices which human beings would have enormous difficulty doing without.[58]

The central focus of Cavell's reading is the possibilities of existence opened up within a human life; nevertheless, his remarks give valuable insight into the way that human and nonhuman animal lives intertwine. Cavell's understanding of forms of life resonates with Coetzee's title *The Lives of Animals*, with its provocation to think about the multiplicity of the concept "lives," alongside the singularity of the designation "the." Wittgenstein's idea that shared forms of life are not fixed, but made and unsettled via sympathetic leaps might be understood as an expression of the particularity of each attempt to traverse the relation between beings.[59] There are more nuances to the act of understanding (and failing to understand) than a simple contrast between comprehension and miscomprehension suggests.[60] For this reason, appeals to community based on shared forms of life will sometimes entail both an affirmation of agreement and an acknowledgment of difference.

Acknowledging this may involve the recognition that sometimes in the attempt to articulate the experiences of other animals we run up against the limits of language. In *Philosophical Investigations*, Wittgenstein writes: "If a lion could talk, we could not understand him."[61] Traditionally these words have been interpreted as an emblem of the absolute gulf between human and animal and a warning that the human imagination has reached its limit. But it is important to remember that Wittgenstein refers not only to a speaking lion but also to a roaring man. Perhaps there is room in the lecture hall for a whole series of remarkable hybrids. This leads me to suggest that the figure of the talking lion might also be read differently, as an emblem of the open, yet enigmatic relation between beings and as a reminder of the nonsense we must at times be willing to risk if we are to embark in conversation.

Hybrid Creatures

In the opening remarks of her lecture, Elizabeth compares herself to Red Peter, an educated ape who in Franz Kafka's *Report to an Academy*, "stands before the members of a learned society telling the story of his life—of his ascent from beast to something approaching man."[62] This comparison, she tells her audience, is not a lighthearted anecdote intended to put them at ease at the outset of an academic discussion. "I am not a philosopher of mind," she insists, "but an animal exhibiting, yet not exhibiting, to a gathering of scholars, a wound, which I cover up under my clothes but touch on in every word I speak."[63] In an effort to find words to express the animal vulnerability she shares yet conceals, she tells the story of Sultan, an educated ape whose life is first recorded by the early nineteenth-century psychologist Wolfgang Köhler in his book *The Mentality of Apes*. Sultan, she proposes might be thought of as the real-life counterpart to Kafka's Red Peter. In the scene Elizabeth Costello relates, Sultan is hungry, but his trainer does not feed him. Instead he throws three crates into his cage and dangles a bunch of bananas from a wire three meters above the ground.

> Sultan knows: Now one is supposed to think that is what the bananas up there are about. The bananas are there to make one think, to spur one to the limits of one's thought. But what must one think? One thinks: why is he starving me? One thinks: What have I done? Why has he stopped liking me? One thinks: Why does he not want these crates anymore? But none of these is the right thought. Even a more complicated thought— for instance: What is wrong with him, what misconception does he have of me, that leads him to believe it is easier for me to reach a banana hanging from a wire than to pick up a banana from the floor?—is wrong. The right thought to think is: how does one use the crates to reach the bananas? . . .
>
> At every turn Sultan is driven to think the less interesting thought. From the purity of speculation (Why do men behave like this?) he is relentlessly propelled toward lower, practical, instrumental reason (how does one use this to get that?) and thus towards acceptance of himself as primarily an organism with an appetite that needs to be satisfied.[64]

My proposal is that Elizabeth Costello's story about the ape Sultan resembles a reading Cavell proposes of the opening scene of *Philosophical Investigations*.

In "Notes and Afterthoughts on the Opening of Wittgenstein's *Investigations*," Cavell points out that Wittgenstein begins his book not with an account of shared forms of life, but with an imaginative experiment. He asks his readers to imagine a world where words and gestures are simply the outer casing of inner meanings. According to Wittgenstein, this picture of language and world is implicit in Saint Augustine's recollection of his childhood.

> When they (my elders) named some object, and accordingly moved towards something, I saw this and I grasped that the thing was called by the sound they uttered when they meant to point it out. Their intention

was shown by their bodily movements, as it were the natural language of all people: the expression of the face, the play of the eyes, the movement of other parts of the body, and the tone of the voice which expresses our state of mind in seeking, having, rejection, or avoiding something. Thus, as I heard words repeatedly used in their proper places in various sentences, I gradually learnt to understand what objects they signified; and after I had trained my mouth to form these signs, I used them to express my own desires.[65]

This scene of early learning, Wittgenstein goes on to remark, does not provide reassurance that the child is understood. It is as though, through the sheer force of its will, the child must decode the gestures and signs of his elders and then find some way to attach his own wants to these symbols.

This suggests that there is something deeply mistaken about the idea that words and gestures are the outer expression of private will. But Cavell does not take Wittgenstein to be dismissing the scene on this basis. Instead he continues Wittgenstein's imaginative experiment by inventing possible contexts for its nonsensical aspect.

In the account I intend to focus on, Cavell imagines that the child is the hero of the *Investigations*, whose "language games" open up the philosophical landscape of the book. As Cavell points out, the child hero's first encounters with the adult world leave him in a "state of derangement." One might say that he experiences the *force* of words (*that* an order is made, *that* a desire is expressed), without yet fully grasping their meaning (*what* is ordered or expressed).[66]

Cavell likens this state of derangement to an account of childhood given by psychoanalyst Jean Laplanche. According to Laplanche, we all begin life thrown by the *enigmatic desires* of those around us.[67] The messages, signs, and symbols of the world are impossible to fully comprehend and so as children we are marked by a sense of disorientation, an *inner strangeness*. This inner strangeness becomes an unconscious residue within the self, which we cover over in adult life.[68]

To acknowledge this inner strangeness—to break the pattern of disavowal— entails a certain willingness to reimagine ourselves and our relation to others. Inherent in Laplanche's account is the possibility that the others we encounter may be troubled by their own sense of inner strangeness.[69] I propose that the story of Sultan might be thought of as an effort to imaginatively raise this possibility. Like Wittgenstein's child, Sultan begins his life surrounded by "enigmatic messages" that he cannot fully comprehend. Like the child, Sultan is thrown by the troubling question of his place in the desires of those around him. Like the child, the very *being* of Sultan's life is left torn, perturbed; and the same order that produces this disturbance covers it over, by submitting Sultan to a regime of reason that drives him always to the "less interesting thought."

Although these possibilities resonate with Cavell's portrait of Wittgenstein's child, the analogy is cut short when he concludes that the "state of derangement" the child feels "marks" its "turn to the human" and thus its renouncement or "perversion" of the "unending circle of the animal, the realm of the un-talking subjects, of the repetitive cycles of need as satisfaction."[70] In his tale of the advent of the speaking, desiring subject, animals are assigned a purely instrumental mode of existence.[71]

This claim is striking because it works against the tenor of Cavell's whole understanding of Wittgenstein's forms of life notion, with its attentiveness to the complex web of continuities and differences between beings. Here we see a further formation of the unacknowledged pattern of attachment and disavowal that Clark calls *anthropological melancholia*. One damaging effect of this pattern is that humans seem to discover their lack of essence, their openness to becoming other, only by virtue of a violent denial of the possibilities of animal life.[72]

Clark writes: "When we are told that animals *both* lack speech and are unable to keep a secret, that is, when non-human creatures are said both to be unable to say something and to be unable *not* to say something, we start to realize that there is potentially no limit to what is kept from or denied to animals—the sure sign of which is that they are finally said . . . to lack *lack*; constitutive absences and troublesome nothingness are reserved, for better or for worse, for human beings."[73]

In this regard Elizabeth Costello's story about Sultan can be understood as an attempt to imaginatively unbind our attachment to this violent pattern of denial in a way that makes explicit its damaging effects. Whereas Cavell insists that life's perturbation coincides with the human passage beyond the "repetitive cycles of need and satisfaction" characterizing the animal, Sultan the ape *begins* with the troubling question of his place in the desires of others and his instrumental existence is gradually *made*, manufactured by the scientist's humanization experiments and regimes. This suggests a further way of reading Cavell's tale: for when he consigns animals to an instrumental existence, he brings into proximity two possibilities that are conventionally held separate—the compulsion to repeat inherent in human societies (a compulsion that conceals our own animal vulnerability) and the compulsive repetition that quite literally describes the life of a trained animal.[74]

The Roaring Man and the Talking Lion

To conclude, I want to briefly tie these thoughts back to Wittgenstein. Most of the creatures running up against the limits of sense in Wittgenstein's writing are his human interlocutors, but the hybrid creatures are an exception. This leads me to suggest a further way of reading the aphorism that we cannot understand the talking lion. For it is quite possible that the talking lion makes no sense to its lion neighbors. To imagine this may be to imagine that the talking lion is unable to fully understand itself. Like the roaring man that interrupts Wittgenstein's "Lecture on Ethics," the talking lion may be troubled by its own inner strangeness, a strangeness manifest as a profound bodily sense of disorientation. Whether these creatures—part human, part beast—are best understood as Wittgenstein's self-portraits or portraits of the nonhuman animals whose lives are caught by the procedures of human institutions and conversation is a question that I intend to leave open.

Notes

1. Coetzee 1999.
2. Derrida 2004:124.
3. Derrida 2004:125.
4. Gaita 2002:77.
5. Gaita 2002:77.
6. As Giorgio Agamben argues, the distinction between natural and political life established by Ancient Greek thought has broken down such that biological life (the life of both individuals and species populations) is now the main focus of power. The intensified management of natural life has given rise to a form of *biopolitical* existence—an existence where the problem of *whose or what life counts* becomes urgent to the point that life itself seems perturbed by the question of its legitimacy (Agamben 1989). Agamben is drawing upon and revises Michel Foucault's work on biopolitics.
7. Wittgenstein 1965:8.
8. As if we were to feel wonder at "the sky being blue or not blue" (Wittgenstein 1965:9).
9. Wittgenstein 1965:11–12.
10. Wittgenstein 1965:11.
11. Wittgenstein 1965:11–12.
12. See Diamond 2000.
13. Wittgenstein 1965:10.
14. Wittgenstein 1965:10–11.

15. Nagel 1979:169.

16. Coetzee 1999:49.

17. Nagel 1979:168.

18. Coetzee 1999:49.

19. Coetzee 1999:45.

20. Singer 1999:85–92.

21. Nagel 1979:170.

22. Singer 1999:91.

23. Singer's reading is at odds with Coetzee's own reflections on the paradoxes entailed by animal stories. In a short critical essay, "What Does It Mean to 'Understand'?," written several years after the publication of *The Lives of Animals*, Coetzee reflects on the predicament of authors who inhabit the thoughts and experiences of an animal. His remarks resonate with Wittgenstein's account of ethical language as a valuable kind of nonsense. When a beast talks in a story, Coetzee says, the author knows, at some level, that they are not actually recording the creature's real thoughts or experience, but at the same time, in order to be able to write the tale, the author must believe that they are really inhabiting the mind of the beast. The storyteller's stance is paradoxical; nevertheless, he adds, "it does appear to be a position of some importance to human societies, which, in a paradoxical movement of their own, both (a) entertain it, and (b) dismiss it as nonsense" (Coetzee 2003:133).

24. Diamond 2008:48.

25. Diamond 2008:53.

26. Diamond 2008:46.

27. Diamond 2008:57.

28. Clark's analysis suggests that the abjection of the animal as other is more than a simple affirmation of difference. For the animal is never wholly separate from the human, but functions, to borrow a notion from Derrida, as a *constitutive outside*—an outside that is at some level internal to our very concept of humanity.

29. Clark n.d.:8 (emphasis in original).

30. Clark n.d.:8.

31. See also Baker 1993.

32. Coetzee 1999:20.

33. Like Elizabeth Costello, Stanley Cavell is concerned with what it is to be tethered to our words. See Cavell 1979b.

34. Coetzee 1999:21.

35. Gaita 2002:211.

36 Wittgenstein 1958:§357.

37. Wittgenstein 1958:§283. As Stanley Cavell elaborates, our main way of engaging with the world is not in fact knowing or not knowing particular facts for certain, but rather acknowledging (or neglecting to acknowledge) the claims others make on me. "It is not enough that I know (am certain) that you suffer," he writes, "I must do or

reveal something (whatever can be done). In a word, I must acknowledge it, otherwise I do not know what '(your or his) being in pain' means" (Cavell 1979b:263).

38. Notice how there is a distinction between Elizabeth Costello and Coetzee the author.

39. Gaita 2002:69.

40. Gaita 2002:61.

41. Gaita 2002:53.

42. Gaita 2002:210.

43. Whereas Elizabeth Costello feels a mix of astonishment and horror at the failure of the people around her to see the meat industry as "mass murder," Gaita expresses astonishment and horror that anyone could assimilate human and animal life in this way.

44. The subtle interrelations between human and nonhuman animals are ironed over, in the name of a reductive assimilation or an absolute difference.

45. Diamond 2008:54.

46. Wolfe 2008:3.

47. Diamond 2008:55.

48. Cavell 1979a:34, 32.

49. Cavell 1989:40–43.

50. Wittgenstein 1958:§226 (emphasis in original).

51. Some readers of Wittgenstein, Cavell adds, also take this as a refutation of skepticism for "the very existence of, say, the sacrament of marriage, or of the history of private property, or of the ceremony of shaking hands, or I guess ultimately the existence of language, constitutes proof of the existence of others" (Cavell 1989:42). Cavell is referring to authors such as Norman Malcolm, G. P. Baker, P. M. S. Hacker, and Rogers Albritton. See, for example, Malcolm 1966:543.

52. Wittgenstein 1985:§185, 230.

53. Cavell 1989:42–43.

54. Cavell 1989:43.

55. Wittgenstein 1958:§283 (emphasis in original).

56. Cavell 1989:44, 41, 42.

57. Hence the phrase "shared forms of life" does not designate this or that convention or "opinion" in common, but rather a whole range of possibilities opened up by certain facts of nature.

58. Here Wittgenstein might also be asking if the model of language, as the outward symbol of private thoughts, can really capture the true workings of words or thoughts. To imagine a form of language, he tells us, is to imagine a whole form of life, a way of acting and behaving. Simon Glendinning makes a similar point about this passage in *On Being with Others: Heidegger, Derrida, Wittgenstein* (1998:73).

59. In his book *On Being with Others*, Glendinning relates one such leap to mutual understanding: "There is (what I definitely want to call) a game I used to play with my mother's dog Sophie, in which we would run around a small pond. My aim was to

catch her; hers to avoid being caught. Sometimes we would find ourselves facing each other, on either side of the pond, each of us watching the other for movements indicating a direction of pursuit or flight. I would try faking a movement; starting to the left but running to my right. Sophie would sometimes be foxed, but would always correct her run when she saw me coming the other way. . . . Sophie has a lot of collie in her and I never caught her. But one day while (we) were playing this game I slipped as I tried to change direction too quickly on damp grass. Almost immediately Sophie ran straight up to me. I was unhurt, but she licked my face anyway. I do not see why this cannot be counted as a case of 'mutual intelligibility.' The dog could see my distress and I could see her sympathy" (1998:142). Glendinning emphasizes that the "mutual intelligibility" between himself and Sophie does not amount to a straightforward "match" of behavior/ response. Instead, he suggests the experience of understanding between humans and other animals tends to partake of the uncanny. "In my view, or at least, in my experience, it is precisely when animals are most like humans that they are most uncanny. And they are so in virtue of not simply and not quite matching; that is, in virtue of so closely resembling humans while remaining cats or apes or whatever, and so, in another way, still being very distant indeed. What I want to say is: The human is open here to another which it simply cannot fully appropriate into 'the same.' And I also want to say: In their own ways many other animals are, in their relations with humans, 'the same too,' uncannily" (1998: 72).

60. Glendinning emphasizes there are no ideal instances of self-comprehension or mutual comprehension. Being with others, in his view, involves a willingness to remain open to these (less than ideal) instances of mutual understanding without covering over the heterogeneities that exist both within and between different forms of life. This implies that there is no single formulation of the relation between human and nonhuman animals but rather a multiplicity of near/far relations—some unsettling, others that falter and others unhesitating leaps of affirmation. Even when we encounter a form of life that is resolutely different from our own, Glendinning argues, we may still in some sense be "at home" with its behavioural traits, for it is only in circumstances when we meet a "radical alien," when we are barely able to recognise or read something as a form of life, that it is possible to say that the criteria for a body-soul are unsatisfied. To turn to another as an embodied soul, he writes, is to make a "spontaneous or originary apostrophe . . . in advance of evidence or reasons which might ground it" (Glendinning 1998: 146).

61. Wittgenstein 1958:§223.

62. Coetzee 1999:15.

63. Coetzee 1999:31–32.

64. Coetzee 1999:34–37.

65. Extract from Augustine's *Confessions* quoted in Wittgenstein 1958:§1.

66. For Wittgenstein the "advent" of language and/or our entry into the sociosymbolic order more broadly seems to coincide with this excess of force over significance.

67. Laplanche 1999.

68. In his book *On the Psychotheology of Everyday Life*, Eric. L. Santner links the intensified political regulation of life to the emergence of psychoanalysis and the subject with an unconscious. "To borrow a term from Giorgio Agamben, we might say that the life that is of concern to psychoanalysis is biopolitical life, life that has been thrown by the enigma of its legitimacy, the question of its place and authorization within a meaningful order" (2001:30). According to Santner, an inner strangeness or unconscious residue emerges in the subjects through their exposure to biopolitical existence. Santner's focus is on the crisis of meaning and legitimacy suffered by human life, but in light of Agamben's suggestion that the biological life itself is torn apart by the question of its own authorization, it becomes possible to ask whether this crisis of legitimation instills in some nonhuman animals an inner strangeness or unconscious.

69. Laplanche 1999:80.

70. Cavell 1995:170. Cavell's discussion draws heavily on his earlier essay "Declining Decline" (1989).

71. In "Companionable Thinking," Cavell's contribution to *Philosophy and Animal Life* (a collection that includes Diamond and Wolfe's discussion of *The Lives of Animals*), he reflects on his past work and concludes that he has largely avoided the question of our obligations to other animals. Provoked by Diamond's reading of his ideas in the context of Coetzee's novella, he asks whether "soul-blindness"—the failure to see ourselves and others as human beings—might have an equivalent in our treatment of other animals (Cavell 2008:93).

72. As Agamben argues, animality has been traditionally cast as a realm beyond sense, language, and reason—the indefinite, open, and multiple domain of bodies. Humanity, by contrast, was aligned with the positive attributes of rationality and meaning. However, with the emergence of the biological sciences and their new vocabularies for cataloguing the interconnections between different forms of life, it became increasingly difficult to pinpoint any attribute that could definitively separate humans from other animals. Our efforts to define humanity in positive terms (man is a rational animal, humans are animals who can speak, etc.) have been gradually replaced by an abstract mechanism, which posits humans as those creatures without any essence or defining characteristic. Animals—the beings who initially played the role of Reason's "other"—are now recast as creatures whose mechanical drives and instincts lack even the aporias of nonsense. Agamben calls this abstract mechanism of human self-definition "the anthropological machine" (Agamben 2004).

73. Clark n.d.:6 (emphasis in original).

74. This may mean, as Agamben has suggested, that a realm of ambiguity between humanity and animality comes into being through a shared exposure and abandonment to the institutions that regulate life (Agamben 2004:47, 70).

References

Agamben, Giorgio. 1989. *Homo Sacer: Sovereign Power and Bare Life*. Trans. Daniel Heller-Roazen. Stanford, CA: Stanford University Press.

——. 2004. *The Open: Man and Animal*. Trans. K. Attrel. Stanford, CA: Stanford University Press.

Baker, Steve. 1993. *Picturing the Beast: Animals, Identity, and Representation*. Champaign: University of Illinois Press.

Cavell, Stanley. 1979a. *The Claim of Reason*. Oxford: Oxford University Press.

——. 1979b. *Must We Mean What We Say?* Cambridge: Cambridge University Press.

——. 1989. "Declining Decline." In *This New Yet Unapproachable America: Lectures After Emerson After Wittgenstein*, 29–76. Albuquerque, NM: Living Batch Press.

——. 1995. "Notes and Afterthoughts on the Opening of Wittgenstein's *Investigations*." In *Philosophical Passages: Wittgenstein, Emerson, Austin, Derrida*, 125–186. Oxford: Blackwell.

——. 2008. "Companionable Thinking." In *Philosophy and Animal Life*, ed. Stanley Cavell et al., 43–126. New York: Columbia University Press.

Clark, David. n.d. "Towards a Prehistory of the Postanimal: Kant, Lévinas, and the Regard of Brutes." Seminar paper, Center for Cultural Analysis, Rutgers University.

Coetzee, J. M. 1999. *The Lives of Animals*, 2nd ed. Princeton, NJ: Princeton University Press.

——. 2003. "What Does It Mean, 'to Understand'?" *Philosophy, Psychiatry and Psychology* 10 (June): 133–134.

Derrida, Jacques. 2004. "The Animal That Therefore I Am (More to Follow)." In *Animal Philosophy: Ethics and Identity*, ed. Matthew Calarco and Peter Atterton, 113–128. London: Continuum.

Diamond, Cora. 2000. "Ethics and the Method of Wittgenstein's *Tractatus*." In *The New Wittgenstein*, ed. Alice Crary and Rupert Read. London: Routledge.

——. 2008. "The Difficulty of Reality and the Difficulty of Philosophy." In *Philosophy and Animal Life*, ed. Stanley Cavell et al., 43–126. New York: Columbia University Press.

Gaita, Raymond. 2002. *The Philosopher's Dog*. Melbourne: Text Publishing.

Glendinning, Simon. 1998. *On Being with Others: Heidegger, Derrida, Wittgenstein*. London: Routledge.

Laplanche, Jean. 1999. *Essays on Otherness*. Ed. J. Fletcher. London: Routledge.

Malcolm, Norman. 1966. "Wittgenstein's *Philosophical Investigations*.'" In *Wittgenstein: The Philosophical Investigations*, ed. G. Pitcher. London: Macmillan.

Nagel, Thomas. 1979. "What Is It Like to Be a Bat?" In *Mortal Questions*, 169–180. Cambridge: Cambridge University Press.

Santner, Eric L. 2001. *On the Psychotheology of Everyday Life*. Chicago: University of Chicago Press.

Singer, Peter. 1999. "Reflections." In *The Lives of Animals*, 83–92. Princeton, NJ: Princeton University Press.

Wittgenstein, Ludwig. 1958. *Philosophical Investigations,* 2nd ed. Trans. G. E. M. Anscombe. Ed. G. E. M. Anscombe and R. Rhees. Oxford: Blackwell Publishers.

——. 1965. "A Lecture on Ethics." *The Philosophical Review* 74:3–12.

Wolfe, Carey. 2008. "Exposures." In *Philosophy and Animal Life,* ed. Stanley Cavell et al., 1–42. New York: Columbia University Press.

twelve

Animal, All Too Animal

Blood Music and an Ethic of Vulnerability

Myra J. Hird

Animal, All Too Animal

"He isn't ready." Untroubled by the fact that their companion calls them parasites, the bacteria recently inhabiting Vergil Ulam's body talk with each other. Ions slide from cell to cell expeditiously, almost instantaneously communicating. The bacteria know they need to infuse slowly so that their lumbering companion does not become anxious or, worse, crazy.

In Greg Bear's novel *Blood Music*,[1] Vergil is a geneticist employed by the bioengineering company Genetron. Vergil develops a line of lymphocytes—white blood cells—that can function autonomously. He begins by constructing strings of DNA bases to form codons. Considered junk DNA by molecular biologists, Vergil thinks the codons may be useful. And besides, he rationalizes, by using Genetron castoffs his extracurricular laboratory activities are more likely to fall below his employer's radar.

Vergil inserts the DNA strings into *E. coli* bacteria—already so familiar to humans as part of the diverse flora of the gut—which absorb the circular plasmids and incorporate them into their DNA. The bacteria then duplicate and release the plasmids, passing on DNA—their biologic—to other cells. Using the process discovered by Nobel laureate Barbara McClintock, Vergil then fixes the DNA-RNA feedback loop by using viral reverse-transcriptase. The bacteria deploy ribosomes and RNA as encoders, readers, and tape. Now equipped with a genetic loop, the bacterial cells develop their own memory and the ability to understand, process, and respond to their environment.

* * *

Blood Music may be more fact than fiction. Evolutionary theorists and microbiologists know bacteria produced and infuse all life on earth. They are highly adaptable: some scientists go so far as to use words like social, self-organized, and sentient.[2] In this chapter, I provide an account of our intimacy with these nonspecies companions. I want to push our important analyses of how nonhuman animals are used to define what is distinctly human , to include our more salient relationship with the engines of life itself. As such, this chapter offers an extension of the excellent chapters in this volume that focus on human relationships with other animals: an invitation to consider the principal organisms on this planet.

Our relationship with bacteria, I contend, suggests an urgent need to build an ethics of vulnerability. Instead of the more familiar formulations of Otherethics based on face-to-face interaction, and its often attendant confluence with rights discourses,[3] an ethics of vulnerability begins from the starting point of entangled relationality, radical asymmetry, and indissoluble openness. I begin the project of building an ethics of vulnerability by considering metabolism.

Metabolism is a necessary condition for autopoiesis.[4] Autopoiesis defines the self-maintaining agency of a given living system, from cells to whole organisms.[5] All plants and animals on earth are metabolically defined as consumers; we must use already available organic and inorganic compounds. Some bacteria, by contrast, are defined metabolically as producers.[6] Through this production, the recycling of organic and inorganic matter, bacteria provide a hospitable environment for plants and animals. This metabolic asymmetry defines our relationship to bacteria as one of vulnerability and of a need to meet-with bacteria in ways that are not ultimately dependent upon the renunciation of human-bacterial entanglement familiar within formulations of the parasite. Such an ethics of vulnerability contributes to materialist theories critiquing Kant's separation of humans from the universe.[7]

In the Beginning

Overconfident as he is, Vergil cannot help but notice that his research seems to proceed rather easily:

> More than once, he had the spooky feeling that his work was too easy, that he was less a creator and more a servant. . . . This, after having the molecules seem to fall into their proper place, or fail in such a way that he clearly saw his errors and knew how to correct them. The spookiest moment of all came when he realized he was doing more than creating little computers. Once he started the process and switched on the genetic sequences, which could compound and duplicate the bio-logic DNA segments, the cells began to function as autonomous units. They began to "think" for themselves and develop more complex "brains."[8]

Genetron soon discovers the surreptitious experiments and Vergil is fired, unaware that in a desperate attempt to save his labors, Vergil injects himself with his still fledgling lymphocytes. Now out of the test tube and into a multicellular animal body, the bacteria are able to explore expanded lines of flight. Over the next weeks, Vergil begins to notice changes. He no longer needs eyeglasses; his asthma disappears. His taste in food and appetite change, and he loses weight. The surface of his skin becomes crisscrossed with delicate lines as the bacteria infuse throughout Vergil's body, strengthening and transforming his bones, organs, and tissues.

* * *

Even the more innovative Western philosophers have disavowed the nonhuman.[9] Their analyses propose rationalizations for human distinction: language, rationality, consciousness, and the like are harnessed to endorse Kant's separation of human from universe. The chapters in this volume provide important and timely insights that challenge this separation and some of the consequences it has had for both human and animal well being.

It says something important about the limits of our philosophical horizon that humans *are* animals. A broader view of our living planet reveals this separation to be rather trivial. How might we meet-with—to use Donna Haraway's provocative term[10]—living organisms who do not have the kind of faciality we recognize, who are not, as evolutionary theorist Lynn Margulis says, "big like us"?[11]

We are, like all animals, so entangled with bacteria that their relative invisibility within our theoretical approaches to sociable life should incite reflection. To say that bacteria are ubiquitous to life (and nonlife) means not only that they proliferate throughout the biosphere and within all of its inhabitants, but also that bacteria are essential to life as we know it.[12] Referring to the "unseen majority," William Whitman, David Coleman, and William Wiebe[13] estimate there are about 5×10^{30} bacterial cells on earth: that's 5000000000000000000000000000000 bacterial cells. Another estimated 10^{18}—1000000000000000000—circulate in the atmosphere attached to dust.

Moreover, there must be something enduringly advantageous about being small, says microbiologist Betsy Dexter Dyer: most organisms on earth are bacteria, they have the greatest diversity, and they dominate evolutionary history.[14] And because they are the smallest of living organisms, bacteria enjoy a much more intimate relationship with the environment than their sluggish, lumbering animal offspring: "a little moisture or dryness, slightly more concentrated salt, an elevated temperature or pH are all sensed directly by single cells."[15] In comparison with bacteria, then, human beings are rare, strangely huge, and cumbersome. Humans also suffer from a limited metabolism and it takes us years to sexually reproduce; creating a new organism every twenty minutes or so, bacterial reproduction is much more efficient. R. A. Lafferty's short story "Slow Tuesday Night" imagines a human world at microbial speed: fortunes are made and lost within minutes, transportation and manufacturing are practically instantaneous, people meet, fall in love, marry, have children, and divorce in a matter of hours.[16]

Stephen J. Gould once remarked, "With respect to the old belief in steady progress, nothing could be stranger than the early evolution of life—for nothing much happened for ever so long. . . . The oldest fossils are some 3.5 billion years old . . . but multicellular animals appeared just before the Cambrian explosion some 570 million years ago."[17] Gould, of course, has animals in mind. But deep time is when everything happened. During the pre-Cambrian era, bacteria created all major forms of metabolism, multicellularity, nanotechnology, metallurgy, sensory and locomotive apparatuses (the flagellum wheel), reproductive strategies and community organization, light detection, alcohol, gas and mineral conversion, hypersex, and apoptosis. From a big-like-us perspective, humans may believe animals (and more specifically humans) are the greatest show on earth, but Hermann von Helmholtz reminds us that bacteria are the "less glamorous backstage machinery that actually produces the show."[18]

Bacteria are LUCA—our Last Universal Common Ancestor—generating the diversity of all living organisms on earth.[19] Along with multicellularity and metabolism, bacteria created symbiosis and symbiogenesis. Symbiosis is defined as the living together of two separately named organisms for the greater part of at least one of those organism's lives.[20] The term "differently named organisms" is used rather than "species" because bacteria are not readily defined as species insofar as species are defined as organisms that produce organisms that can reproduce. Ceylon cats are a species because they can reproduce more cats through sexual reproduction, whereas a female horse and a male donkey may sexually reproduce but the male mule offspring will be sterile. Bacteria, by contrast, exchange DNA readily with many different kinds of bacteria as well as other organisms (cats, chrysanthemums, and mules included).

Symbiosis frequently occurs amongst living organisms. Lichen is a symbiosis of algae or cyanobacteria and fungi. The cyanobacteria or algae provide the photosynthetic metabolism, and the fungus can reorganize its membranes to sustain the lichen in extreme weather changes, such as frozen tundra and desert rocks.[21] Another common example is *Mixotricha paradoxa*. Hundreds of these microscopic protists live in the hindguts of the Australian termite *Mastotermes darwiniensis*, digesting the wood that the termite eats.[22] Not only do these protists live in symbiotic relationship with the termites, but also other microorganisms—small and large spirochetes—cover their surfaces, enabling motility (the ability to move), and attach to the protists via specific attachment sites. Moreover, *M. paradoxa* with its symbionts have five genomes, and their DNA is transferred horizontally when protists are transferred between termites. *Asobara tabida* wasps have an obligate relationship with *Wolbachia* bacteria: without *Wolbachia*, the wasp cannot reproduce offspring.[23]

Symbiogenesis refers to the appearance of a new phenotype, trait, tissue, organelle, organ, or organism from a symbiotic relationship.[24] Lynn Margulis won the American National Medal of Science for synthesizing evidence showing that mitochondria and chloroplasts were once free-living bacteria that became symbiogenetically incorporated into eukaryotic cells. Evolutionary theorists and microbiologists alike accept symbiogenesis as an evolutionary phenomenon, but its overall role in evolution remains controversial. For neo-Darwinists such as Richard Dawkins and Thomas Cavalier-Smith, symbiogenesis is a rather rare phenomenon compared with random mutation.[25] For Margulis and others, it is the driving force of evolution. Symbiogenesis theory suggests an inheritance of contagion rather than linear vertical transmission from generation to generation, and its attraction for material, Deleuzian, and other social theories is well established and growing.[26]

Along with LUCA, the majority of evolutionary schemas accept bacteria as both base and trunk of the tree of life (TOL).[27] Stephen Jay Gould's *Wonderful Life*[28] provides a history and critique of the arboreal metaphor within evolutionary theory, from the pre-arboreal Great Chain of Being, Charles

Darwin's "great Tree of Life," Ernest Haeckel's blooming tree, William Hennig's single-branch emphasis, and computational method developments to molecular sequencing.[29] Bacteria complicate this TOL because it is based on replication and vertical inheritance, and bacteria exchange genes horizontally through lateral gene transfer (LGT) as well as vertically. Thanks to bacteria, the base of the TOL is a polytomy, and some scientists now refer to the TOL as a web or ring of life.[30] Marla Rivera and James Lake, for instance, argue that two prokaryotes fused their genomes (through symbiogenesis), closed the ring of life, and created the first eukaryote.[31] Molecular biology, notes Scott Gilbert,[32] shows that animal-bacterial co-evolution through horizontal gene transfer is the rule, not exception. And Ford Doolittle argues that within-species genomic variation is produced through the diversity of microbial life.[33]

Our last universal common ancestor, generators, and master players in the web of life and inventors of metabolism, motility, reproduction, and genetic exchange, bacteria are not some rogue organisms to which we might gesture in some attempt at inclusivity. Studying bacteria in all of their proliferation and diversity suggests humans and other animals to be oddities of nature.

In Between

Having worked out how to pass the brain-blood barrier, the bacteria explore Vergil's mind, tapping into the viscidities of his cognitive and affective states. And when they think he is ready, his companions begin to speak with Vergil. In a sense, Vergil has anticipated this, and by now he knows the bacteria mean him no harm. He's curious about their intentions and how far they want to go:

> What kind of psychology or personality would a cell develop—or a cluster of cells, for that matter? He tried to recall all his schooling on cell environments in the human body. Blood, lymph, tissue, interstitial fluid, cerebrospinal fluid. . . . He could not imagine an organism of human complexity in such surroundings not going crazy from boredom. The environment was simple, the demands relatively simple, and the levels of behavior were suited to cells, not people.[34]

Vergil learns that his companions have moved across and within his girlfriend, who is being transformed by the bacteria over an open shower drain. "Let the buggers out, Vergil had said. Show them what the world's about."[35] In a desperate attempt to stem the bacterial tide, his friend and confidant kills Vergil, and so he dies unaware that the bacteria have moved rapidly through other vectors (such as tap water) infusing animals, fungi, plants, and exchanging DNA with other bacteria. Most humans go along with this infusion, this companionship. Of course, they have little choice: their bodies have been literally designed through and through, by and for this kind of evolution. A few choose to remain separate, and the bacteria make provisions for these individuals to exist outside. North America goes silent, as radio, telephone, television, and Internet communications cease. Russia takes center stage as the only super power (the book, after all, was published in the 1980s) and proposes to nuke the entire United States. Of course, the focus is on who is to blame: the bio-tech industrial complex, the slow-to-act Centers for Disease Control, industrial scientists, government policy, a public consumed with technological consumption. But all of this blame slinging simply rearranges the *Titanic*'s deck chairs.

Michael Bernard, scientist turned entrepreneur and Genetron mouthpiece, is infected via Vergil Ulam's damp handshake. Bernard smuggles himself to a friend's high containment laboratory in Germany and offers himself up to experimentation to find a way to stop the bacteria: to find a cure. Through blood tests and scans, the German scientists easily discern what is happening to Bernard's body, but they have no idea how to stop the bacteria from their course.

Bernard begins to talk with the noocytes—the intelligent bacteria—in his body:

> BACTERIA: We have studied INDIVIDUAL in your conception. We do not fit the word.
>
> BERNARD: There are no individuals?
>
> BACTERIA: Not precisely. Information is shared between clusters of ********.
>
> BERNARD: Not clear.
>
> BACTERIA: Perhaps this is what you mean by INDIVIDUAL. Not the same as a single mentality. You are aware that cells cluster for basic structuring; each cluster is the smallest INDIVIDUAL. These clusters rarely separate for long into single cells. Information is passed between clusters sharing in assigned tasks, including instruction and memory. Mentality is thus divided between clusters performing a function. Important memory may be diffused through all clusters. What you think of as INDIVIDUAL may be spread throughout the totality.[36]

All eukaryotic cells are heterogenomic (their genomes have more than a single type of ancestor). That is, eukaryotic cells are communities rather than individual entities.[37] Of all the cells in a human body, 10 percent are eukaryotic (derived from bacteria) and 90 percent are bacteria. As Dorian Sagan notes, "The human body . . . is an architectonic compilation of millions of agencies of chimerical cells."[38] Any definition of *Homo sapiens* must take into account the "provisional configuration of elements," writes Lewis Thomas. "A good case can be made for our nonexistence as entities. We are not made up, as we had always supposed, of successively enriched packets of our own parts."[39] In *When Species Meet*, Donna Haraway details the community of the human body:

> I love the fact that human genomes can be found in only about 10 percent of all the cells that occupy the mundane space I call my body; the other 90 percent of the cells are filled with the genomes of bacteria, fungi, protists, and such, some of which play in a symphony necessary to my being alive at all, and some of which are hitching a ride and doing the rest of me, of us, no harm. I am vastly outnumbered by my tiny companions; better put, I become an adult human being in company with these tiny messmates. To be one is always to become with many.[40]

Becoming-with species, for Haraway, means that relating precedes identity: the relating itself forms constituent identities. In other words, relating *is* identity. As Haraway points out, species have ontologies-in-themselves "sometimes-separate heritages both before and lateral to *this* encounter."[41] But there is contagion at work in Haraway's species-meeting: kin and kind defined less through neo-Darwinian "arboreal descent" and more through "the play of bodies."[42] Haraway's companion species impregnation is metaphoric to be sure in its weaving of histories of co-dependence and production; but it is more than this. It is a literal enmeshing of bodies and all of their resident companion species (and those species themselves) in a recursive cascade; "turtling all the way down" as Haraway[43] and Isabelle Stengers[44] put it, drawing on the mythological image of the world sitting on top of a turtle, which is in turn on top of another turtle, and another, ad infinitum.

Symbionts all the way down as I have called it, encapsulates our bacterial identities.[45] The web or ring of life is both made possible by and entangled with bacteria. Through deep time we are more than connected to bacteria. We are kin through symbiogenetic mergers. Human bodies are symbionts: 600 kinds of bacteria in our mouths and 400 kinds of bacteria in our guts, and the countless more bacteria that inhabit our orifices and skin. Indeed, the number of bacteria in our mouths is comparable to the total number of human beings that have *ever lived* on earth.[46] The number of microbes in our bodies exceeds the number of cells in our bodies by 100 fold. The human distal gut contains more than 100 times as many genes as our human genome (which has 2.85 billion base pairs): "Human animals live in symbiosis with thousands of species of anaerobic bacteria, six hundred species in our mouths, which neutralize the toxins all plants produce to ward off their enemies, four hundred species in our intestines, without which we could not digest and absorb the food we ingest."[47]

Every living thing that exists now, or has ever lived, is bacteria. Asking what bacteria have to do with humans is, in Gould's terms, asking the wrong question, or as Cary Wolfe puts it referring to humanism, "the 'human' that we know now, is not now, and never was, itself."[48]

In the End

"Vergil Ulam was turning into a galaxy."[49] Vergil is not dead, as his friend supposed. Instead, through hypersex and remarkable communication and information sharing, Vergil is *becoming-bacteria*. His memory—including all memory traces of his body—join all of the other human traces throughout North America and commune within what the bacteria call the *thought universe*.

Brown-colored microbial mats spread across and through buildings, along sidewalks, across fields. Rivers and lakes sparkle and become bioluminescent with bacterial activity. Eventually the buildings disappear completely.

Half a million protestors from European countries surround the Pharmek laboratories in Germany where Michael Bernard offered himself up to scientific monitoring and experimentation. The protestors want Bernard killed and the whole complex torched. The scientists are doing their best to stave off the thronging mass, but many of the scientists themselves have been evacuated. The scientists, and the rabble masses outside, are unaware that the bacteria have been monitoring human communication. They know they need to transform Bernard soon if he is to survive the human panic and blood lust. Besides, these noocytes are getting ready to join their distant cousins—numbering in the tens of billions now—in North America, whom they can sense have moved far ahead due to their less restricted environment. Far ahead indeed: when Russia fires several nuclear warheads on the United States, the noocytes temporarily alter space-time and defuse the missiles. Bernard does the math:

If I multiply this crude number [the two trillion fully developed intelligent individuals that exist within me] times the number of people in

North America—half a billion, another rough guess—then I end up with a billion trillion, or on the order of 10^{20}. That is the number of intelligent beings on the face of the Earth at this moment—neglecting, of course, the entirely negligible human population.[50]

* * *

Bacteria, not plants or animals, are the most important actants sustaining the biosphere. Bacteria maintain the chemical elements crucial to life on earth—oxygen, nitrogen, phosphorous, sulphur, carbon, and some twenty-five other gases—through ongoing (re)cycling processes that enable plants and animals to thrive.[51] While animal metabolism is defined by consumption (animals must consume already-made organic matter), bacteria evolved earth's metabolic production economy: phototrophs convert solar energy; chemotrophs convert chemical energy; lithotrophs gain electrons from elements (such as hydrogen and sulphur) or simple organic compounds (such as water and hydrogen sulphide); and organotrophs convert complex organic substances (such as proteins in dead biomass and carbohydrates in grasses and grains).[52] In short, bacteria provided, and continue to provide, the environment in which different kinds of living organisms *can* exist.

Bacteria also sustain the biosphere through rapid replication, both vertical heritable genetic exchange and horizontal gene transfer within and across species. They produce the biosphere through quick reproduction. Unimpeded by environmental constraints, a reproducing *E. coli* bacterium would equal the weight of the earth's crust in 1.75 days; a single cyanobacterium on a sterile earth could oxygenate the atmosphere in forty days. And bacteria sustain the biosphere through their organization into highly communicative and adaptive colony structures.[53] In community form, bacteria "form one global, exceedingly diversified, yet functionally unified peculiar being."[54]

Bacteria are also crucial to the biosphere because they create and sustain symbiotic relationships. Symbiosis is an intimate relationship between organism and environment: in the case of symbiogenesis, the environment literally becomes the organism, because what begins as the environment (another organism, for example) becomes incorporated into the organism to create, indeed, a new organism.[55] A vast number of planetary symbioses involve bacteria. For instance, cyanobacteria exist in both unicellular and colonial forms (their blooms can be seen from space) and live symbiotically with protists, worms, sponges, and other land and aquatic plants.[56] Bacteria fix nitrogen for more than 17,000 kinds of leguminous plants.[57] Without hindgut bacteria, these "tropical cows" would not be able to process (break down and make available to the biosphere in recycling) one-third to two-fifths of the phytomass in their environments.[58] The biosphere did not become a frozen wasteland thanks to bacteria that decompose cyanobacteria living in ocean sediments, releasing methane that attracts solar energy.

Addressing the radical asymmetry between bacteria and all other living organisms on earth, Carl Woese writes, "If you wiped out all multi-cellular life forms off the face of the earth, microbial life might shift a tiny bit. . . . If microbial life were to disappear, that would be it—instant death for the planet."[59] Bacteria precede humans relating with them and the vast majority of microbial intra-actions have nothing to do with humans.[60] Humans do not even *know* about the vast majority of intra-actions that take place on earth.

How then to configure globality with these tiny messmates who dominate the biospheric "parliament of things"?[61] Such a figuration, an ethics if you will, is not simply a redistributed parliament, but one whose totality is excessive to human domains. As Graham Harman reminds us, "All reality is political, but not all politics is human."[62]

An Ethic of Vulnerability

Russian biologist Vladimir Vernadsky, writing in the early 1900s, would perhaps recognize the bacteria transforming the planet in Bear's *Blood Music.* Vernadsky conceived of the *noosphere,* which he defined as a phase in the earth's history. Nonliving matter characterizes the geosphere phase; living matter the biosphere phase. During the noosphere stage, humans create new resources (such as global consciousness) by transforming the biosphere.

In *Blood Music* the twenty-five or so humans in North America who, through chemical incompatibility did not initially become part of the bacterial galaxy, are monitored, and the bacteria ensure these humans have plenty of food and comfortable shelter. Trusted family and friends rebuild themselves into human form to visit these last vestiges of humankind, to help them feel safe, and to entreat them to join the transformation. Some decide to join while others remain apart. The few humans who stay apart are well provided for by the bacteria, who mean them no harm.

The bacteria continue to learn, transform, and transmute. Michael Bernard's bacteria try to explain to their (now) barely recognizable human messmate:

BACTERIA: Symbiotic bacteria and transfer viruses—naturally occurring in all animals and specific for each species—are implanted with molecular memory transcribed from the intron. They exit the individual and pass on to another individual, "infect," transfer the memory to somatic cells. Some of the memories are then returned to chemical storage status, and a few return to active memory.

BERNARD: Across generations?

BACTERIA: Across millennia.

BERNARD: The introns are not junk sequences . . .

BACTERIA: No. They are highly condensed memory storage.

Vergil Ulam had not created bio-logic in cells out of nothing. He had stumbled across a natural function—the transfer of racial memory. He had altered a system already in existence.[63]

A bacterial history of the present.

* * *

One way to build an ethics of vulnerability is by thinking about metabolism. Eating and digesting are mundane, central, and sustaining activities that define us to our core:

> The way we eat represents our most profound engagement with the natural world. Daily, our eating turns nature into culture, transforming the body of the world into our bodies and minds. . . . Our eating also constitutes a relationship with dozens of other species—plants, animals, and fungi—with which we have coevolved to the point where our fates are deeply entwined. . . . Eating puts us in touch with all that we share with the other animals, and all that sets us apart. It defines us.[64]

All organisms on earth rely on just two sources of energy: light energy from the sun and/or energy derived from chemicals. All animals are, metabolically, consumers (heterotrophs live off others, relying on the ingestion of other organisms and their products). Autotrophic bacteria, by contrast, do not eat (they fix or otherwise convert elements).

Photoautotrophs (such as plants, algae, and cyanobacteria) use light, carbon dioxide, and water to produce their own food:

$$\text{Light energy} + CO_2 + H_2O \longrightarrow \text{sugar} + O_2 \text{ (waste)}$$

Photoautrophic waste is what animals use to breathe. Plants use carbon dioxide, and combine it with hydrogen (from water) to make carbon-hydrogen compounds such as wood, starch, and sugar.[65] Purple sulfur bacteria use carbon dioxide combined with the hydrogen from hydrogen sulfide to make carbon compounds. Purple nonsulfur bacteria use carbon dioxide from the air and hydrogen gas or organic molecules like lactate. Together, photosynthetic organisms deplete the atmosphere of about 250 billion tons of carbon annually. Photosynthetic metabolism "really runs the entire biosphere."[66]

Chemolithotrophy occurs in a few groups of bacteria. These organisms manufacture their own food by using chemicals (rather than light) as a source of energy and, specifically, minerals found in rocks, soils, and dissolved in water. Methanogen metabolism looks like this:

$$\text{Chemical bond energy} + CO_2 + H_2 \longrightarrow \text{sugar} + CH_4 \text{ (waste)}$$

Methanogens get their name because they produce the greenhouse gas methane as metabolic product.[67] Some methanogens are autotrophs. Although most autotrophs are photoautotrophs (they use light as an energy source), autotrophic methanogens are chemoautotrophs, using carbon dioxide and hydrogen (gases considered waste products by most organisms).

Autotrophic bacteria are producers, engaging in a different economy of relating with the world through metabolism than all other organisms on earth. Other kinds of bacteria, such as those found in rumens, termite guts, and human intestines, live symbiotically with animals and other organisms, enabling animal food digestion. So we animals can only eat well—only eat at all—with our bacterial companions. Eating well with bacteria challenges hegemonic characterizations of our bacterial messmates as pathogenic and the logic of our ongoing attempts to dominate and eradicate them. And as I have outlined, this dependence is radically asymmetrical: we need bacteria, but they don't need us.

I like to think about this asymmetry in terms of metabolism because eating is such a fundamental part of who we are. Eating well is all about survival and more besides: eating invokes and reflects fundamental desires and sociality at its core. We never, as Derrida reminds us, eat alone:

One never eats entirely on one's own: this constitutes the rule underlying the statement "one must eat well." It is a rule offering infinite hospitality. And in all differences, ruptures and wars (one might even say wars of religion), "eating well" is at stake. Today more than ever. One must eat well—here is a maxim whose modalities and contents need only be varied, ad infinitum. . . . A discourse thus restructured can try to situate in another way the question of what a human subject, a morality, a politics, the rights of the human subject are, can be, and should be. Still to come, this task is indeed far ahead of us.[68]

An ethics of vulnerability attempts to push current analyses of human-animal relations. Centering bacteria in formulations of the human-Other, I argue, does more than expand the universe of things we must take account of. It asks us to consider ourselves as vulnerable to, and with, our environments in a quantitatively and qualitatively different way. First, in comparison with autotrophic bacteria, we find ourselves to be metabolically vulnerable: our metabolism based on consumption defines our metaphysics of being as vulnerable. Second, our entanglement with bacteria, as symbionts-all-the-way-down *literally* configures us. Given metabolism is a necessary condition for autopoiesis, and autopoiesis defines the self-maintaining agency of a given living system, from cells to whole organisms, this primary metabolism may well be humans' first agential cut.[69] Symbiogenesis, described by evolutionary theorists as failed digestion, speaks as well of our evolutionary heritage as metabolic entanglement and thus vulnerability.

Third, an ethics of vulnerability challenges the very notion that there is an outside to ourselves: a symbiogenetic heritage means environments are incorporated and become our selves at genetic, morphological, physiological, and developmental levels. This profound relationality challenges catatonic and hedonistic responses to bacteria's ubiquity and power unseen (bacteria regulate the biosphere, so we might as well pollute).[70] An ethics of vulnerability means that we have no choice in our originary and generative entanglement with bacteria. We might then, as Vergil Ulam does in *Blood Music*, tread with equal parts caution and curiosity, recognizing the unpredictability and unforeseen opportunities of bacteria's corporeal generosity from micro (cell) to macro (planetary) scales.[71]

Notes

1. Bear 1985.
2. Bassler 2002; Ben-Jacob et al. 2004; Ben-Jacob and Levine 2005; Shapiro and Dworkin 1997.
3. For example, Lévinas 1969.
4. Thompson 2010.
5. Maturana and Varela 1980.
6. Hird 2009.
7. Harman 2009.
8. Bear 1985:17.

9. Hird 2009.

10. Haraway 2008.

11. Hird 2009.

12. Portions of this and the next sections are modified from Hird 2009.

13. Whitman, Coleman, and Wiebe 1998.

14. Dexter Dyer 2003.

15. Dexter Dyer 2003:14.

16. Lafferty 1999.

17. Gould 1989:309–310.

18. CBC Radio 2007.

19. Cracraft and Donoghue 2004.

20. Margulis 1981.

21. Hird 2009.

22. Dolan 2001.

23. Margulis 1981.

24. Margulis 1981.

25. Cavalier-Smith 2003; Dawkins 1986.

26. See Deleuze and Guattari 1988; Parisi 2004; Protevi 2008; Thompson 2010.

27. Cracraft and Donoghue 2004.

28. Gould 1989.

29. Hird 2009.

30. Penny and Poole 1999; Philippe 2004.

31. Rivera and Lake 2004.

32. Gilbert 2002.

33. Doolittle 2004.

34. Bear 1985:79.

35. Bear 1985:91.

36. Bear 1985:164 (emphasis in original).

37. Gilbert 2002; Margulis 1981; Sonea and Mathieu 2000.

38. Sagan 1992:368.

39. Thomas 1974:86–87.

40. Haraway 2008:3.

41. Haraway 2008:25.

42. Haraway 2008:25.

43. Haraway 2008:25.

44. Stengers 1981.

45. Hird 2009.

46. Margulis and Sagan 2007.

47. Lingis 2003:166.

48. Wolfe 2003:ix.

49. Bear 1985:79.

50. Bear 1985:155.

51. Sagan and Margulis 1993.

52. Smil 2002.

53. Ben-Jacob 1995, 1998, 2003; Ben-Jacob et al. 2004; Ben-Jacob, Shapira, and Tauber 2006; Crespi 2001; Vernadsky 1926/1997:64.

54. Sonea and Mathieu 2000:9–10.

55. Hird 2009.

56. Dexter Dyer 2003.

57. Smil 2002.

58. Smil 2002.

59. In Blakeslee 1996.

60. Barad 2007.

61. Latour 2000:144.

62. Harman 2009.

63. Bear 1985:212 (emphasis in original).

64. Pollan 2007:10.

65. Sagan and Margulis 1993:61.

66. Sagan and Margulis 1993:61.

67. Sagan and Margulis 1993:61.

68. Derrida 1995:282, 274.

69. Thompson 2010; Maturana and Varela 1980.

70. Dixon 1994.

71. Diprose 2002.

References

Barad, K. 2007. *Meeting the Universe Halfway: Quantum Physics and the Entanglement of Matter and Meaning.* Durham, NC: Duke University Press.

Bassler, B. 2002. "Small Talk: Cell-to-Cell Communication in Bacteria." *Cell* 109:421–424.

Bear, G. 1985. *Blood Music.* New York: Ace Books.

Ben-Jacob, E. 1995. "Complex Bacterial Colonies." *Nature* 373:566–567.

——. 1998. "Bacterial Wisdom, Godel's Theorem and Creative Genomic Webs." *Physica A* 248:57–76.

——. 2003. "Bacterial Self-Organization: Co-enhancement of Complexification and Adaptability in a Dynamic Environment." *Philosophical Transactions of the Royal Society A: Mathematical, Physical and Engineering Sciences* 361:1807.

Ben-Jacob, E., I. Becker, Y. Shapira, and H. Levine. 2004. "Bacterial Linguistic Communication and Social Intelligence." *Trends in Microbiology* 12, no. 8: 366–372.

Ben-Jacob, E. and H. Levine. 2006. "Self-Engineering Capabilities of Bacteria." *Journal of the Royal Society Interface* 3, February 22: 197–214.

Ben-Jacob, E., Y. E. Shapira, and A. I. Tauber. 2006. "Seeking the Foundations of Cognition in Bacteria: From Schrödinger's Negative Entropy to Latent Information." *Physica A* 359:495–524.

Blakeslee, S. 1996. "Microbial Life's Steadfast Champion." *New York Times*, October 15.

Cavalier-Smith, T. 2003. "Microbial Muddles." *BioScience* 53, October 10: 1008–1013.

CBC Radio. 2007. "How to Think About Science." http://www.cbc.ca/ideas/features /science/index.html (accessed March 2008).

Cracraft, J. and M. Donoghue, eds. 2004. *Assembling the Tree of Life*. Oxford: Oxford University Press.

Crespi, B. J. 2001. "The Evolution of Social Behavior in Microorganisms." *Trends in Ecological Evolution* 16:178–183.

Dawkins, R. 1986. *The Blind Watchmaker*. New York: W. W. Norton.

Deleuze, G. and F. Guattari. 1988. *A Thousand Plateaus: Capitalism and Schizophrenia*. New York: Athlone Press.

Derrida, Jacques. 1995. *Points . . . Interviews, 1974–1994*. Stanford, CA: Stanford University Press, 255–287.

Dexter Dyer, B. 2003. *A Field Guide to Bacteria*. Ithaca, NY: Cornell University Press.

Diprose, R. 2002. *Corporeal Generosity: On Giving with Nietzsche, Merleau-Ponty, and Lévinas*. Albany: State University of New York Press.

Dixon, B. 1994. *Power Unseen: How Microbes Rule the World*. New York: Freeman.

Dolan, M. 2001. "Speciation of Termite Gut Protists: The Role of Bacterial Symbionts." *International Microbiology* 4, no. 4: 203–208.

Doolittle, F. 2004. "Bacteria and Archaea." In *Assembling the Tree of Life*, ed. J. Cracraft and M. Donoghue, 86–94. Oxford: Oxford University Press.

Gilbert, S. 2002. "The Genome in Its Ecological Context: Philosophical Perspectives on Interspecies Epigenesis." *Annals of the New York Academy of Sciences* 981:202–218.

Gould, S. J. 1989. *Wonderful Life: The Burgess Shale and the Nature of History*. New York: W. W. Norton.

Haraway, D. 2008. *When Species Meet*. Minneapolis: University of Minnesota Press.

Harman, G. 2009. *Prince of Networks: Bruno Latour and Metaphysics*. Melbourne: Re.press.

Hird, M. J. 2002. "Indifferent Globality." *Theory, Culture and Society* 27, no. 2–3: 54–72.

——. 2009. *The Origins of Sociable Life: Evolution After Science Studies*. Houndmills, Basingstoke, UK: Palgrave Press.

Lafferty, R. A. 1999. "Slow Tuesday Night." In *Nine Hundred Grandmothers*, 134–142. Berkeley Heights, NJ: Wildside Press.

Latour, B. 2000. *Pandora's Hope: Essays on the Reality of Science Studies*. Cambridge, MA: Harvard University Press.

Lévinas, E. 1969. *Totality and Infinity*. Trans. A. Lingis. Pittsburgh: Duquesne University Press.

Lingis, A. 2003. "Animal Body, Inhuman Face." In *Zoontologies: The Question of the Animal*, ed. D. Wolfe, 165–182. Minneapolis: University of Minnesota Press.

Margulis, L. 1981. *Symbiosis in Cell Evolution*, 2nd ed. San Francisco: W. H. Freeman.

Margulis, L. and D. Sagan. 2007. *Dazzle Gradually: Reflections on the Nature of Nature*. White River Junction, VT: Chelsea Green Publishing.

Maturana, H. and F. Varela. 1980. "Autopoiesis and Cognition: The Realization of the Living." In *Boston Studies in the Philosophy of Science*, ed. R. S. Cohen and M. W. Wartofsky, 42. Dordrecht, the Netherlands: D. Reidel Publishing.

Parisi, L. 2004. *Abstract Sex: Philosophy, Bio-Technology and the Mutations of Desire*. London: Continuum.

Penny, D. and A. Poole. 1999. "The Nature of the Last Universal Common Ancestor." *Current Opinion in Genetics & Development* 9, no. 6: 672–677.

Philippe, H. 2004. "The Origin and Radiation of Eucaryotes." In *Assembling the Tree of Life*, ed. J. Cracraft and M. Donoghue, 95–106. Oxford: Oxford University Press.

Pollan, M. 2007. *The Omnivore's Dilemma*. New York: Penguin Press.

Protevi, J. 2008. "3 Lectures on 'Deleuze and Biology.'" http://www.protevi.com/john /Deleuze_biology_lectures.pdf (accessed December 3, 2010).

Rivera, M. and J. Lake. 2004. "The Ring of Life Proves Evidence for a Genome Fusion Origin of Eukaryotes." *Nature* 431 (September): 152–153.

Sagan, D. 1992. "Metametazoa: Biology and Multiplicity." In *Incorporations*, ed. J. Crary and S. Kwinter, 362–385. New York: Urzone Books.

Sagan, D. and L. Margulis. 1993. *Garden of Microbial Delights: A Practical Guide to the Subvisible World*. Dubuque, IA: Kendall/Hunt Publishing.

Shapiro, J. A. and M. Dworkin. 1997. *Bacteria as Multicellular Organisms*. Oxford: Oxford University Press.

Smil, V. 2002. *The Earth's Biosphere: Evolution, Dynamics, and Change*. Cambridge, MA: MIT Press.

Sonea, S. and L. Mathieu. 2000. *Prokaryotology: A Coherent View*. Montreal: Les Presses de L'Université de Montréal.

Stengers, I. 1981. *Power and Invention: Situating Science*. Trans. P. Bains. Minneapolis: University of Minnesota Press.

Thomas, L. 1974. *The Lives of a Cell: Notes of a Biology Watcher*. New York: Viking Press.

Thompson, E. 2010. *Mind in Life: Biology, Phenomenology, and the Sciences of Mind*. Cambridge, MA: Belknap Press of Harvard University Press.

Vernadsky, V. I. 1926/1997. *The Biosphere*. Ed. M. McMenamin. New York: Copernicus/ Springer-Verlag.

Whitman, W., D. Coleman, and W. Wiebe. 1998. "Prokayotes: The Unseen Majority." *Proceedings of the National Academy of Sciences* 95:6578–6583.

Wolfe, C. 2003. "Introduction." In *Zoontologies: The Question of the Animal*, ed. C. Wolfe, ix–xxiii. Minneapolis: University of Minnesota Press.

Epilogue

Making Animals Vanish

Wendy Doniger

WE KNOW VERY WELL HOW TO MAKE ANIMALS VANISH. WE HAVE made so many species vanish entirely from the earth. We make them vanish when we treat them as merely food, or as something to experiment on, or as hunted trophies. There are so many ways. Most pervasive, and almost impossible to notice, is the way that we have made them vanish from our human world by the words and categories we have herded them into. What this remarkable present volume of essays achieves is to make animals visible in our language—more precisely, to point out how we have made them vanish in this way and how we might bring them back into our collective vision again. By making us understand how we have made animals absent, this volume shows us how we might render them present.

Aaron Gross, in his introduction, notes that in order to do this we must first understand how animals are embedded in our concept of what it is to be human. And he concludes that we must not forget "actual" animals in our scholarly work and that to do this, "we might create a clearing where it is possible to see, and maybe be seen, by those others that we all too quickly name animals." This requires us to problematize the word "animals" in such a way that our subsequent considerations are all, in a sense, "post-animal" discussions;

and then, Gross asks, "What's beyond the 'post'?" He ends by citing the historian of religions J. Z. Smith, who speaks of "an urgent civic and academic agendum," which is that difference—such as the vision that draws a sharp ethical as well as ethological line between humans and animals—"be negotiated but never overcome."[1]

As a historian of religions myself, I'd like to get into this fight. The essays in this book demonstrate the blindness with which some cultures, including, of course, our own, have viewed the relationship between humans and animals, a blindness made all the more obvious when we see the ways that other cultures did not make this basic mistake. But how did we miss it? Our stubborn refusal to see what now seems so obvious borders on the kind of cognitive dissonance that Leon Festinger made us see: ignoring the evidence piling up on all sides, we hung on to our ancient and often theological assumptions about the difference between animals and humans.[2] Since language is the lens through which we view the world, it is easy to understand how we failed to see, through those lenses, that our lenses—our categories, our words for humans and for animals—were badly skewed. But how did we miss the connection between human-ness and humane-ness? This book not only will, I believe, clarify and inspire more scholarly work on animals, but will also supply fuel for activists who hope to treat animals more humanely—not to say humanly—in the world outside the academy.

There is an amazing scope of knowledge in this book, which sheds light on the subject through a wide range of disciplines: science, literature, anthropology, religion, and many more. If you know the cultural representations of a certain animal, this book shows you that there are things in the scientific understanding of that animal that you didn't know you didn't know; and if you know the science, it opens your eyes to the cultural implications, uses, and misuses of that science. So, too, there is a fine balance between data and speculation; the specific, factual reports, each one stunning in itself and all the more stunning cumulatively, are interleaved with more philosophical discussions, each informing the other.

There is a lot about anthropomorphism in this book, but little is said about its counterpoint, zoomorphism. Animal symbolism works in two directions, anthropomorphism—projecting human qualities upon animals—and zoomorphism—imagining humans as animals. Anthropomorphism, though more common than zoomorphism, tells us comparatively little about animals; an anthropomorphic text assumes a basic identification, such as lion as king, and then, although the object of discourse is, theoretically, an animal, the text imagines the animal as behaving the way the human does, betraying the fact that the interest lies more in kings than in lions. Zoomorphism is more complex: although this time a human being is the explicit object, the bestial qualities imputed to the human usually reveal an observation of animals more detailed (if no more accurate) than that of anthropomorphism, and the text teaches us simultaneously what sort of person it thinks that sort of animal is like and what sort of animal it thinks that sort of person is like. And where anthropomorphism simply leaps over our knowledge that most animals cannot speak (there are, significantly, relatively few anthropomorphic stories about parrots), zoomorphism seizes upon language as a point of potential difference between humans and animals, and worries that point in various ways, imputing human speech to certain individual animals and either muteness or the ability to understand animals to certain individual humans. Anthropomorphism and zoomorphism are two different attempts to reduce the otherness between humans and animals, to see the sameness beneath the difference. But sameness, just like difference, may lead to the inhuman treatment of both humans and nonhumans;[3] this is part of what Smith had in mind when he warned that difference should not be overcome. The ethical decision to treat animals according to the basic standards of human decency is one that must be taken regardless of whether we prefer to emphasize the qualities they share with us—such as their instincts and drives—or those they do not—their systems of communication. For language is, again, the sticking point.

The belief that animals are like us in some essential way is the source of the enduring and widespread myth of a magic time or place or person that erases the boundary between humans and animals. The place is like the Looking-Glass forest where things have no names, where Alice could walk with her arms around the neck of a fawn. The list of people who live at peace among animals would include Enkidu in the epic of *Gilgamesh* and the many mythical children who are raised as cubs by a pack of animals, like Romulus and Remus, Mowgli, and Tarzan, like Pecos Bill (suckled by a puma) and Davy Crockett (raised among mountain lions).[4] T. H. White, translator of a medieval bestiary, imagined the young King Arthur's education by Merlin the magician as taking place among ants and geese and owls and badgers.[5] Often, the myth of the human among wild animals tells us how the people and animals manage to speak to one another and how they manage not to attack one another (two closely related problems). It is language that ultimately separates us from the animals, even in myths. Only by speaking their language will we really be able to know how we would think and feel if we were fish or horses.

Ludwig Wittgenstein argued, "If a lion could talk, we could not understand him."[6] And language is the place from which compassion springs. It is harder (though not, alas, impossible) for us to torment the people we speak with. Elaine Scarry made this point, in reverse, when she argued that torture takes away speech.[7] And the language that inspires compassion need not be even the signing of chimps, let alone the whistles of dolphins or the body language of primates; it may be no more than the silent language of the eyes. Emmanuel Lévinas once said that the face of the other says, "Don't kill me."[8] This is the language that we must learn to read and the language that is denied by people who defend the right to treat animals as things, through a self-serving tautology.

The many cultures represented in this volume have ostensibly presented their own feelings about animals, but in order to do so they have often vividly imagined how animals feel about them, about us. This is where art must illuminate science. We cannot *know* even how another human being feels about pain, or hunger, or playfulness, or dedication to one's young; how then can we *know* how animals feel? We cannot, of course, but there is an irresistible urge to try. And that is the impulse that drives this book.

Notes

1. Smith 2004.

2. Festinger 1957.

3. For this argument, see Doniger 1999:93–106; Doniger 2005:17–36; Doniger 2010 [1998]:31–33; Doniger O'Flaherty 1995 [1988]:75–96.

4. As Alan Dundes has pointed out, Jesus, following this pattern of the birth of the hero already established by Oedipus, Cyrus, and many others, is abandoned by his noble parents (in this case, God) and nurtured by animals before being raised by parents of lower birth (Dundes 1990). The Rosicrucian Reuben Winburne Clymer, in his translation of Sinistrari's commentary on Genesis, went so far as to explain the birth of Jesus by arguing that Mary was impregnated by a salamander.

5. White 1962. The culmination of the animal education comes in chapter 23.

6. Wittgenstein 1958:223.

7. Scarry 1985.

8. Lévinas 1979:198–199.

References

Doniger, Wendy. 1999. "Compassion Toward Animals." In *The Lives of Animals*, by J. M. Coetzee. Ed. Amy Gutmann, 93–106. Princeton, NJ: Princeton University Press.

——. 2005. "Zoomorphism in Ancient India: Humans More Bestial Than the Beasts."

In *Thinking with Animals: New Perspectives on Anthropomorphism*, ed. Lorraine Daston and Gregg Mitman, 17–36. New York: Columbia University Press.

———. 2010. *The Implied Spider: Politics and Theology in Myth*, 2nd ed. New York: Columbia University Press.

Doniger O'Flaherty, Wendy. 1995 [1988]. "Other People as Animals: Rudra, Lord of Sacrificial Beasts." In *Other Peoples' Myths: The Cave of Echoes*, 75–96. Chicago: University of Chicago Press.

Dundes, Alan. 1990. "The Hero Pattern and the Life of Jesus." In *Quest of the Hero,* by Otto Rank et al., 179–223. Princeton, NJ: Princeton University Press.

Festinger, Leon. 1957. *A Theory of Cognitive Dissonance.* Stanford, CA: Stanford University Press.

Lévinas, Emmanuel. 1979. *Totality and Infinity: An Essay on Exteriority.* Trans. Alphonso Lingis. The Hague: Martinus Nijhoff.

Scarry, Elaine. 1985. *The Body in Pain: The Making and Unmaking of the World.* New York: Oxford University Press.

Smith, J. Z. 2004. *Relating Religion: Essays in the Study of Religion.* Chicago: University of Chicago Press.

White, T. H. 1962. *The Once and Future King: Part 1, The Sword in the Stone.* London: Fontana Books.

Wittgenstein, Ludwig. 1958. *Philosophical Investigations.* Trans. G. E. M. Anscombe. New York: Macmillan.

Contributors

Ron Broglio is an assistant professor in the Department of English at Arizona State University and Senior Scholar at the university's Global Institute of Sustainability. His research focuses on how philosophy and aesthetics can help us rethink the relationship between humans and the environment. He is the author of *Surface Encounters: Thinking with Animals and Art* (University of Minnesota Press, 2011) and *Technologies of the Picturesque* (Bucknell University Press, 2008). He is currently working on an artistic and theoretical treatise on post-humanism and animal studies called *Animal Revolutions: Events to Come* as well as a book on bio-power and animality in the British Romantic period.

Brett Buchanan is an associate professor of philosophy at Laurentian University (Canada). Recent publications have appeared in the *Journal for Critical Animal Studies* and *Phaen-Ex*. He is the author of *Onto-Ethologies: The Animal Environments of Uexküll, Heidegger, Merleau-Ponty, and Deleuze* (SUNY Press, 2008).

Cynthia Chris is an associate professor in the Department of Media Culture at the College of Staten Island, City University of New York. Her book *Watching*

Wildlife (University of Minnesota Press, 2006), is a critical history of nonfiction images of animals in film and television. She is also coeditor, with Sarah Banet-Weiser and Anthony Freitas, of *Cable Visions: Television Beyond Broadcasting* (New York University Press, 2007) and is currently coediting a volume on media authorship with David Gerstner. She has published articles on contemporary television in the journals *Television and New Media*, *The Communication Review*, and *Feminist Media Studies*, and numerous essays and reviews on film, performance, photography, and video for *Afterimage*, *Art Lies*, and *Springerin*, among others.

Wendy Doniger has taught at Harvard, Oxford, the School of Oriental and African Studies at the University of London, and the University of California at Berkeley, and, since 1978, at the University of Chicago, where she is at present the Mircea Eliade Distinguished Service Professor of the History of Religions in the Divinity School, the Department of South Asian Languages and Civilizations, and the Committee on Social Thought. In 1984 she was elected president of the American Academy of Religion, in 1989 a fellow of the American Academy of Arts and Sciences, in 1996 a member of the American Philosophical Society, and in 1997 president of the Association for Asian Studies. She serves on the International Editorial Board of the Encyclopedia Britannica and has been awarded six honorary degrees (most recently, one from Harvard), as well as the Radcliffe Medal, the Medal of the Collège de France, the PEN Oakland literary award for excellence in multicultural literature, and the Rose Mary Crawshay prize from the British Academy for the best book about English literature written by a woman. In November 2008 she was awarded the American Academy of Religion's Martin E. Marty Award for extraordinary contributions to the public understanding of religion. Among her many books are three Penguin Classics—*Hindu Myths*, *The Rig Veda*, and *The Laws of Manu*—and an Oxford World Classic (the *Kamasutra*) as well as *Siva: The Erotic Ascetic*; *The Origins of Evil in Hindu Mythology*; *Women, Androgynes, and Other Mythical Beasts*; *Dreams, Illusion, and Other Realities*; *Tales of Sex and Violence*; *Other Peoples' Myths*; *Splitting the Difference: Gender and Myth in Ancient Greece*; *The Bedtrick: Tales of Sex and Masquerade*; *The Implied Spider: Politics and Theology in Myth*; *The Woman Who Pretended to Be Who She Was*; and *The Hindus: An Alternative History*. In press is *Hinduism*, for the Norton Anthology of World Religions (2011). In progress are *Rings and Ringers: The Masquerades of Circular Jewelry*; a novel, *Horses for Lovers, Dogs for Husbands*; a translation of the last four books of the Mahabharata; and a memoir, *The Late Rita Doniger*.

Jonathan Safran Foer is a bestselling novelist described by *Time* aagazine as a "voice of this generation." His bestselling first book, *Everything Is Illuminated*, won numerous awards, including the *Guardian* First Book Prize and the National Jewish Book Award. His second book, *Extremely Loud and Incredibly Close*, also a bestseller, was hailed by Salman Rushdie as "ambitious, pyrotechnic, riddling, and above all . . . extremely moving." His third book, *Eating Animals*, offers a critique of factory farming and was written in close collaboration with Aaron Gross, coeditor of this volume. The *Los Angeles Times* described *Eating Animals* as possessing "the kind of wisdom that, in all its humanity and clarity, deserves a place at the table with our greatest philosophers." Foer has taught writing at Yale and is on the faculty of NYU's Creative Writing Program. His works have been translated into more than thirty-five languages.

Aaron Gross is a professor of theology and religious studies at the University of San Diego and holds a MTS from Harvard Divinity School and a Ph.D. from the University of California, Santa Barbara. He co-chairs the American Academy of Religion's Animals and Religion Group and has played a leading role in a wide variety of national and international animal-welfare campaigns since the mid-1990s. He founded the nonprofit group Farm Forward in 2007.

Myra J. Hird is Professor, Queen's National Scholar, and Graduate Studies Coordinator in Sociology/Environmental Studies/Obstetrics and Gynecology at Queen's University. She is the author of *Sociology of Science* (Oxford University Press, 2011), *The Origins of Sociable Life: Evolution After Science Studies* (Palgrave, 2009), *Sex, Gender and Science* (Palgrave, 2004), and *Engendering Violence* (Ashgate, 2002), and coeditor of *Queering the NonHuman* (Ashgate, 2008), *Questioning Sociology*, 2nd ed. (Oxford University Press, 2011), and *Sociology for the Asking* (Oxford University Press, 2002). She is also the author of some fifty articles and book chapters on topics related to science studies. Hird is currently working on a project with Kerry Rowe and Nigel Clark on garbage and waste management.

Tim Ingold is Professor of Social Anthropology and Head of the School of Social Science (2008–2011) at the University of Aberdeen. He has carried out ethnographic fieldwork among Saami and Finnish people in Lapland and has written extensively on comparative questions of environment, technology, and social organization in the circumpolar North, as well as on evolutionary theory in anthropology, biology, and history, on the role of animals in human society, and on issues in human ecology. His recent research interests are in the anthropology of technology and in aspects of environmental perception. He has edited the *Companion Encyclopedia of Anthropology* (1994) and was editor of *Man* (the Journal of the Royal Anthropological Institute) from 1990 to 1992. He is a Fellow of the British Academy and of the Royal Society of Edinburgh. His major publications include *Ways of Walking* (coedited with Jo Lee Vergunst, 2008), *Creativity and Cultural Improvisation* (coedited with Elizabeth Hallam, 2007), *Lines: A Brief History* (2007), *The Perception of the Environment* (2000), *Key Debates in Anthropology* (1996), *Tools, Language and Cognition in Human Evolution* (coedited with Kathleen Gibson, 1993), *The Appropriation of Nature* (1986), and *Evolution and Social Life* (1986). He is currently writing and teaching on the comparative anthropology of the line and on issues on the interface between anthropology, archaeology, art, and architecture. He has supervised thirty-two doctoral students to completion and is currently supervising a further ten, on subjects ranging from thinking like a river in northern Finland to traditional craft in Japan.

Carla Nappi is an assistant professor in the Department of History at the University of British Columbia. Her recent book, *The Monkey and the Inkpot: Natural History and Its Transformations in Early Modern China* (Harvard University Press, 2009) treats belief-making in early modern Chinese natural history through the lens of the *Bencao gangmu* (1596), a compendium of *materia medica*. Her current research focuses on the media of exchange of natural objects among the Chinese empire and its borderlands in the fourteenth through eighteenth centuries, paying special attention to Chinese-Islamic scientific and medical exchange in early modernity.

Joel Novek is a professor of sociology at the University of Winnipeg in Winnipeg, Manitoba. He also teaches in the environmental studies program at the same university. His research and teaching interests focus on the social context of technological change and the sociology of environmental issues. His studies examine pulp and paper megaprojects, hospital-based medical information technology, and, most currently, animal and horticultural production systems. Recent publications include articles in *Science, Technology and Human Values*, *Society and Natural Resources*, *Canadian Review of Sociology*, *Alternatives Journal*, and *Society and Animals*.

Anand Pandian is an associate professor in the Department of Anthropology at Johns Hopkins University. He is the author of *Crooked Stalks: Cultivating*

Virtue in South India (Duke University Press, 2009), coeditor of *Race, Nature and the Politics of Difference* (Duke University Press, 2003) and *Ethical Life in South Asia* (Indiana University Press, 2010), and author of numerous articles and essays on subjects related to the present essay.

Ashley E. Pryor is an associate professor of women's and gender studies and philosophy at the University of Toledo. She is now writing a book on the role that the "non-human" voice has played in a variety of Western philosophic texts (Heidegger, Agamben, Plato, Cavarero) as well as in a variety of works drawn from meditative and contemplative traditions (especially within Zen Buddhist lineages). Her most recent articles on these themes are forthcoming in *Epoché: A Journal for the History of Philosophy* and in *Silence and Listening as Rhetorical Arts*, ed. Cheryl Glenn and Krista Ratcliffe (Southern Illinois University Press).

Undine Sellbach is a writer, performer, and associate lecturer in the School of Philosophy at the University of Tasmania. Her work draws on philosophical and aesthetics techniques to reimagine the relationship between instinct, humans, animals, and the environment. She has published in the fields of animal studies, aesthetics, and architecture and is coauthor of the philosophical performance work "A Whirlwind of Insects" presented at *Sexuate Subjects: Politics, Poetics and Ethics*, University College London, 2010. She is the author of *The Floating Islands*, a philosophical fairytale, and cocreator and performer of the cabaret show *The Honeymoon Suite*, which toured in Australia, the United States, Canada, and the United Kingdom in 2007 and 2008. She is currently researching the role of insects in our ethical imagination.

Michelle Superle is a professor in the English and Communications departments of Okanagan College. She has taught children's literature, creative writing, and composition at the University of the Fraser Valley and interdisciplinary courses in the children's studies program at York University. Her recent publications include the children's novel *Black Dog, Dream Dog* (Tradewind Books, 2010) and the critical work *Contemporary, English-Language Indian Children's Literature: Representations of Nation, Culture, and the New Indian Girl* (Routledge, 2011). She received her PhD in children's literature from Newcastle University.

Anne Vallely is a professor of religious studies at the University of Ottawa. She earned her PhD from the University of Toronto, and her research focuses on the anthropology of South Asian religiosity, especially that of Jainism, and on the symbolic construction of human/non-human boundaries across cultures. She is the author of *Guardians of the Transcendent: An Ethnography of a Jain Ascetic Community.*

Gavin Van Horn is director of Midwest Cultures of Conservation at the Center for Humans and Nature, a nonprofit organization dedicated to exploring and promoting moral and civic responsibilities to human communities and to natural ecosystems and landscapes. He received his doctorate from the University of Florida, with a specialization in religion and nature. His dissertation research examined the religious, cultural, and ethical frameworks involved in the reintroduction of wolves to the southwestern United States. He continues to explore cultural perceptions of wildlife and the values embedded in the practices of ecological restoration, urban agriculture, and wildlife management.

Index

Note: Page numbers followed by *f* indicate figures. Page numbers followed by n and nn indicate endnotes.

Aadland, Chris, 163
Acuña, Jason "Wee Man," 159–160
Adams, Carol, 19nn6,12
Africa Speaks (travelogue), 160
Agamben, Giorgio, 6, 18n2, 280; biopolitics, 80, 88, 324n6; human/animal binary, 7, 17, 19n9, 21n23, 328nn72,74
"Always already" paradox, 8–9, 17
American Society of Mammalogists, 228n34
Androgynous men and women, 57, 71nn9,12
Animal abuse, linked to interpersonal violence, 19n12
Animal agency, 20n20

"Animal-Cruelty Syndrome, The" (Siebert), 19n12
"Animality" (Young), 245
Animal matters: animals and the contemporary West, 12–14, 113–119; canine characters in contemporary children's literature, 116–117, 174–202; contemporary art and surfaces, 118–119, 238–258; factory farms, discipline and distancing, 4, 12, 19n5, 20n17, 113–115, 121–151; *Wildboyz*, the animal and the abject, 6, 13, 115–116, 152–173; wolves, iconic nature and changing status of, 117–118, 203–237
Animal others: bacteria and ethics of vulnerability, 262–263, 331–345;

Animal others (*continued*)
  Heidegger's animal ontology, 259–260,
    265–288; interspecies kindness and
    phenomenological thought, 260–261,
    289–306; sympathetic imagination
    and, 261–262, 307–330; theorizing
    animal/human, 14–15, 259–263
Animal studies: absent referents and
    post-animal discourse, 15–18; "always
    already" paradox, 8–9; human self-con-
    ception and, 1, 4–7, 18n1; as location of
    resistance to human/animal binary, 2–4;
    male/female binary and, 5–6, 19nn6,12
Animal That Therefore I Am, The
    (Derrida), 242–243, 273
Animal Welfare Act, 16, 20n22
Animal welfare science, factory farms
    and, 122, 129
Anthropological melancholia, 323
Anthropomorphism, 291, 294–295, 299,
    350–351
Applebaum, Anne, 142, 143
Aristotle, 265–266
Armbruster, Karla, 192–193
Art, surfaces and animals in, 118–119,
    238–258; animal portraits and breed-
    ing, 118–119, 239–242, 241f, 255;
    animals looking back at humans,
    242–243; hand, claw, and artists'
    bodies as carriers of significance,
    252–255; Olly Suzi and physicality of
    animals in exotic locations, 246–253;
    philosophy and animals living
    horizontally, 242–246
Atavism, 91, 106n51
Attenborough, David, 156, 157
Audubon, John J., 226n19
Autopoiesis, bacteria and, 332, 344

Bacteria, 262–263, 331–348; in Bear's
    Blood Music, 262–263, 331–333,
    336–337, 339–340, 341–342; ethics

of vulnerability and, 332, 342–344;
    as most important actants sustain-
    ing biosphere, 340–341; numbers
    and diversity of, 333–336, 337–339
Baker, Steve, 175, 215, 243, 250, 251
Bakewell, Robert, 240
Bangs, Ed, 223
Batek Negritos, of Malaysia, 36
Bear, Greg, 262–263, 331–333, 336–337,
    339–340, 341–342
Because of Winn-Dixie (DiCamillo),
    186–191
Being and Time (Heidegger), 267, 271,
    277, 295
Bencao gangmu (Li Shizhen), 27–28, 55–56,
    71nn5,6; eating habits and medicinal
    use of human body parts, 59, 63,
    65–69, 74nn45,46,48,50,53, 75n62,
    76nn65,66; ethics, analogy, and
    classifications in, 58–65, 72nn20,21,
    73nn29,34; euphemisms for eating
    habits, 69–70, 76nn69,71; human
    oddities, 56–58, 71nn9,12
Berger, John, 165, 242
Bergson, Henri, 166
Bersani, Leo, 165
Bestiality, 152, 153, 169nn1,3
Beuys, Joseph, 250
Bill of rights, for animals, 129
Biopolitical existence, 324n6
Biopolitics, anthropology of. *See* Pastoral
    power
Bio-power, factory farms and, 114, 123,
    132–133
Bird-David, Nurit, 36–37, 40, 48, 51n22
Blood Music (Bear), 262–263, 331–333,
    336–337, 339–340, 341–342
Boone and Crockett Club, 226n19
Boultbee, John, 240, 241f, 242
Bowden, Charles, 223
Brambell Commission, in Great Britain,
    129

Breeding, and animal surfaces depicted in art, 118–119, 239–242, 241f, 255

Broglio, Ron: essay of, 238–258; references to, 13, 118–119

Bromyard, John, 86

Buchanan, Brett: essay of, 265–288; references to, 14, 259–260

Burbank, James, 230n51

Calarco, Matthew, 3, 17, 279

Callicott, Baird, 228n29

Canine characters, in contemporary children's literature, 116–117, 174–202; binary opposition and dogs as transforming substances, 174–177, 199nn2,4; dogs as agents of emotional transformation, 186–192; dogs as superior beings and social integrators, 181–186, 192; methodology of research, 94–198, 177; wildness and civility, children and dogs against adults, 178–181, 192

Cannibalism: euphemisms for, 69–70, 76nn69,71; Li Shizhen's recording of and medicinal uses of human body parts, 59, 63, 65–69, 74nn45,46,48, 50,53, 75n62, 76nn65,66

Cavell, Stanley, 318–319, 321–323, 324nn33,37, 326n51, 328n71

Center for Biological Diversity (CBD), 219, 220–222, 221f

Cesar's Way: The Natural, Everyday Guide to Understanding and Correcting Common Dog Problems (Millan), 301

Chemolithotrophy, bacteria and, 342, 343

Chen Cangqi, 66–68, 76n65

Chidester, David, 205–206

Child, concept of, 199n4

Children's literature. *See* Canine characters, in contemporary children's literature

China. *See* East Asia

Chris, Cynthia: essay of, 152–173; references to, 6, 13, 115–116

Chrysostom, 85–86

Chuogenglu (Notes Made on a Rest from Ploughing), 69

Clark, David, 313–314, 323, 324n28

Coetzee, J. M., 6, 8, 244; *Elizabeth Costello*, 260, 289–292; *The Lives of Animals*, 245, 255, 260–262, 307–308, 310–318, 320–324, 325n23, 326n43

Colbeak, Martyn, 156

Coleman, David, 334

Colling, Robert, 240

Colonialism, pastoral power and, 87, 89

Communication. *See* Kindness, between species

Conservation biology, 218–219, 230n56, 231n57

Corbin, Ben, 206–207, 227n21

Corwin, Jeff, 157

Coyote: I Like America and America Likes Me (Beuys), 250

Cree Indians, and animals hunted by, 41–47

Criminal Tribes Act (India), Piramalai Kallar caste and, 29, 89–93, 95, 97–98, 106nn45,53

Critchely, Simon, 153, 166–167, 168, 169

Critical realism, concept of, 225n12

CSI (television program), 169n3

Cultural milieus, pastoral power and, 82, 88

Danda, 99

Darwin, Charles, 106n50, 266

Davis, Susan G., 168

Defenders of Wildlife, 219, 230n56

DeGeneres, Ellen, 152, 168–169

Deleuze, Giles, 245, 252

Derrida, Jacques, 3–4, 6, 8, 14, 18, 20nn15,16,17, 304n5, 307–308, 325n28, 343–344; *The Animal That Therefore*

Derrida, Jacques (*continued*)
  I Am, 242–243, 273; "Geschlecht II,"
  254; Heidegger and, 267, 273–274, 280;
  Of Spirit, 244, 273
Descartes, René, 266, 282n1
Desmond, Jane, 168, 171n31
Devor, Robinson, 169n3
De Waal, Frans, 304n8
Diamond, Cora, 309–310, 313, 317–318
DiCamillo, Kate, 186–191
Difference, biopolitics of, 87
"Difficulty of Reality and the Difficulty
  of Philosophy, The" (Diamond), 313
Diogenes, 245–246, 247
Discipline, factory farms and, 113–114,
  123–124, 130–134, 142–143; bio-power
  and, 114, 123, 132–133; labor process
  theory and, 114, 123, 130–132; post-
  humanism and, 114, 123–124, 133–134
Distancing, factory farms and, 114,
  134–142; modernity and, 138–139;
  political economy of consumption,
  135–136; social geography and, 136–138
Dog Friday (McKay), 186, 187–188
Dog Love (Garber), 185–186
Dog on Barkham Street, A (Stolz), 181–185
Dog Psychology Center, 302–303
Dog stories. *See* Canine characters, in
  contemporary children's literature
Dog whisperer. *See* Millan, Cesar
Dog Whisperer (television program), 14
Dolphin Luck (McKay), 180
Doniger, Wendy, essay of, 349–352
Doolittle, Ford, 336
Doty, Mark, 291
Douglas, Mary, 165
Durham Ox, The (Boultbee), 240, 241f, 242
Dyer, Betsy Dexter, 334

Earth First!, 214, 215, 218, 230n51
East Asia, 6, 11, 27, 55–70. *See also Bencao
  gangmu*

Eating, ethics of vulnerability and,
  343–344. *See also* Cannibalism
Ecological movement, wolves and,
  117–118
"Ecotage," 214, 230n44
Edison, Thomas Alva, 155
Electrocuting an Elephant (film), 155
Eliade, Mircea, 174, 199n3
Elizabeth Costello (Coetzee), 260,
  289–292
Empedocle, 244–245
Endangered Species Act (ESA), 213, 222
Equal Music, An (Seth), 185
Endicott, Kirk, 36
Ethics, 279; ethics of vulnerability, 332,
  342–344; imagination and imagined
  boundaries, 309–310; pragmatic
  concern with animal suffering, 8, 11–12,
  18, 19, 129, 137, 141, 314–317. *See also
  Bencao gangmu*; Factory farms;
  "Lecture of Ethics"; *Nicomachean
  Ethics*

Factory farms, 4, 12, 19n5, 20n17, 113–115,
  121–151; costs of, 141–144; discipline
  and, 130–134, 142–143; discipline and
  distancing as human strategies, 113–114,
  123–124; distancing and, 114–115,
  134–142; industrialization of Canadian
  hog production, 121–123, 124–127;
  industrial paradigm, functional and
  cultural problems, 127–130; sympathetic imagination and death camp
  analogy, 313–318; use of Gulag analogy,
  127, 140–141
"Faith and Knowledge: The Two Sources
  of 'Religion' at the Limits of Reason
  Alone" (Derrida), 20n15
Falwell, Jerry, 169n1
Fanon, Frantz, 87
Farm Animal Portraits (Moncreiff), 240
Feifei, 63, 64f

Feit, Harvey, 41, 42, 43
Festinger, Leon, 350
Fladler, Susan, 228n33
Foraging, hunter-gatherers and, 47–50
Foreman, David, 214–215, 231n57
Foucault, Michel: bio-power and, 114, 123, 132–133; conception of normalization, 139; pastoral power and, 28–29, 80, 83–88, 90, 97, 100, 105n17
France, Anatole, 192
Franck, Didier, 280
Fraser, David, 128, 129
Freud, Sigmund, 169
Fundamental Concepts of Metaphysics, The: World, Finitude, Solitude (Heidegger), 14, 244, 269–270, 277, 292–293

Gaita, Raymond, 308, 315–318, 326n43
Garber, Marjorie, 185–186
Genesis, book of, 227, 352
Genetic preformation, doctrine of, 45
Gertler, M., 135–136
"Geschlecht II" (Derrida), 254
Giddens, Anthony, 124, 138–139, 142
Gilbert, Scott, 336
Glendinning, Simon, 326nn58,59, 327n60
Glover, Stephen (Steve-O), 154, 159–165, 163f, 164f, 167, 170–171n12
Goffman, Erving, 166
Goodall, Jane, 156
"'Good Dog': The Stories We Tell About Our Canine Companions and What They Mean for Humans and Other Animals" (Armbruster), 192–193
Gould, Stephen J., 334, 335
Graden, Brian, 159
"Green Anaconda" (Olly Suzi), 243f
Grinker, R. R., 50n10
Gross, Aaron: essay of, 1–23; references to, 349–350
Guailei, 58
Guattari, Felix, 252

Gudeman, Stephen, 37–40, 43, 51n22
Guoran, 59, 61–62, 62f, 73n29

Haar, Michel, 280
"Haecceity," 252
Hair, medicinal use of human, 66, 68, 75n64
Hall, Lynn, 182–183, 185
Halverson, Marlene, 129
Haraway, Donna, 6, 87, 123, 281, 333, 338
Harman, Graham, 341
Harrison, Ruth, 129
Harvey, David, 137
Hastrup, Kirsten, 34
Heidegger, Martin, 3–4, 6, 14, 18n2; animal surface and art, 243–246, 254. *See also* Heidegger, Martin, animal ontology and
Heidegger, Martin, animal ontology and, 259–260, 265–288; animals and concept of being, 275–278; criticisms of, 279–280; encountering animals in new way, 280–282; humans and meaning of Being, 267–269; *Mitsein* and *Dasein* and being-with animals, 267, 269–275, 279
Hesse, Karen, 182–184
Hird, Myra J.: essay of, 331–348; references to, 15, 262–263
History of the Concept of Time (Heidegger), 276
Hoefler, Paul L., 160
Hogs. *See* Factory farms
Holaday, Bobbie, 204
Honnold, Doug, 222–223
Hornaday, William T., 226n19
Houston, Pam, 176–177
Human/animal binary, animal studies and, 2–4, 6–7
Humane Methods of Slaughter Act, 16, 20n22
Human existence, levels of, 42

Humanity and animality, boundaries between. *See Bencao gangmu*

Hume, David, 114, 129, 135

Humor, animal/human boundaries and, 115–116, 152–154, 166, 168–169

Hunting and gathering, and ontological dualism of environment, 25–27, 31–54; Cree Indians and animals hunted by, 41–47, 49; foraging, production, and procurement, 47–50; forest pygmies and forest as parent, 35–41, 39*f*, 49, 50n10; nature as cultural construction, 31–35, 35*f*

Hurricane Katrina, 102–103

Huxley, Julian, 160

"I," human identity in eyes of Other, 118, 243

Ichikawa, M., 50n10

Imagination. *See* Sympathetic imagination

Imperial Eyes (Pratt), 249

India. *See* South Asia

Industrial farming. *See* Factory farms

Ingold, Tim: essay of, 31–54; references to, 2, 8, 9–11, 25–27, 250–251

"In-in" breeding, 240–241

Intentional worlds, nature and culture, 32–35

Interagentivity, 41

Irwin, Steve "Crocodile Hunter," 153–154, 157, 162

Jackass (television series and films), 153, 158–159, 167, 170nn10,12

Jackson, Michael, 44

Jaffe, J., 135–136

James, Clive, 247, 251, 257n24

Jilebian (Chicken-Rib Stories), 69–70

Johnson, Martin and Osa, 155

Jonze, Spike, 158, 159

Jue, 59, 61*f*

Jung, Carl, 176

Kafka, Franz, 320

Kant, Immanuel, 86, 87

Kindness, between species, 260–261, 289–306; Coetzee and, 260, 289–292; Heidegger on human/nonhuman kindness and concept of "insight," 261, 292–297; kinds of, 292; Millan and calm-submissive and calm-assertive energy, 297–303

Knoxville, Johnny, 158, 159, 170n12

Köhler, Wolfgang, 321

Koller, Jackie French, 180–181

Korda, Alexander, 160

Koskei, James, 160

Kratt, Martin, 157

Kristeva, Julia, 115, 154, 168, 170n5, 171n31

Labor process theory, factory farms and, 114, 123, 130–132

Lafferty, R. A., 334

Lake, James, 336

Language: dividing line between humans and animals, 319–324; as lens through which humans view world, 349–352; Tamil language and pastoral care, 99, 108n73

Laplanche, Jean, 322

Latour, Bruno, 122–123, 133–134, 141

Laws of Manu, 99

"Lecture of Ethics" (Wittgenstein), 309–310, 324

Leopold, Aldo, 117–118, 211–213, 228n29, 229nn35,37,43

Lévinas, Emmanuel, 3–4, 274, 284n23, 352

Levi-Strauss, Claude, 87

Life and Times of Michael K (Coetzee), 308

Lingis, Alphonso, 280

Linnaeus, Carl, 266

Li Shizhen, 27–28, 56–57. See also *Bencao gangmu*

Little, Jean, 186–191

Lives of Animals, The (Coetzee), 245, 255, 260–262, 307–308, 310–318, 320–324, 325n23, 326n43

Living Desert, The (film), 155, 170n7

Lo, Vivienne, 74n44

Logandurai (Indian cultivator), 95–97

Logic of Sense, The (Deleuze), 245

Logotheti, K., 41

Lombroso, Cesare, 106n51

Lost and Found (Little), 186–191

LUCA (Last Universal Common Ancestor), bacteria as humanity's, 334–335

Lü Kun, 56, 71n2

Lüshi chunqiu (Master Lü's Spring and Autumn Annals), 61–62, 73n29

Maakkal, 108n73

MacCormack, Carol, 34

Majing (Horse Classic), 59

Male/female binary, 5–6, 19nn6,12

Malkki, Liisa, 88

Manasu, 108n73

March of the Penguins (film), 155, 170n7

Margera, Bam, 170–171n12

Margulis, Lynn, 333, 335

Materia medica. See Bencao gangmu

Mbuti Pygmies, relation to forest environment, 35–41, 39f, 50n10

McDonaldization, Ritzer's notion of, 141

McKay, Hilary, 180, 186, 187–188

McNeill, William, 279

Mech, L. David, 214

Meerkat Manor (television program), 158

Meeythal/meeyththal, 99

Melson, Gail, 178, 180, 193

Menstrual blood, medicinal use of, 59, 64, 68

Mentality of Apes, The (Köhler), 321

Merchant, Carolyn, 127–128

Merleau-Ponty, Maurice, 281, 284n22

Metabolism, bacteria and, 332, 344

Microbial life. *See* Bacteria

Mihou, 59, 60f, 72nn20,21

Millan, Cesar, 261, 297–303

Modernity: factory farms and, 123, 124, 138–139; pastoral power and, 81–82, 86–88

Moncreiff, Elspeth, 240

Monkeywrenching, 214, 230n44

Moral conscience, as emblem of full humanity, 90–91, 106n50

Morgan, David, 210, 225n8

Moss, Cynthia, 156

Most Extreme, The (television program), 158

MTV, 6, 13, 115, 153, 158–159, 171

Mukkutal Pallu, 100

Murphy, Ray, 129

Mutual of Omaha's Wild Kingdom (television program), 156, 158

Myth, 174–175, 199n3

Myth and Reality (Eliade), 199n3

Nagel, Thomas, 256, 270, 311–312

Nappi, Carla: essay of, 55–78; references to, 6, 11, 27–28

Nash, Roderick, 213, 229nn37,38

Nature: association of children and animals with, 116, 175–176, 178; classification of, 57–68; Coetzee on, 290–292, 314; colonization of, 126–128; ethology and, 225n12; great chain of being and, 265; human place in, 68–70, 205, 220; governance or control of animal, 82–83, 91, 100–101, 104, 134, 139, 142–143, 162, 208–209, 223; networks of animate and inanimate, 114, 123; philosophical reflection on, 260, 265–270, 275, 314; post-humanism and, 133; public perceptions of, 118, 123, 127, 129, 138–139, 192, 205,

Nature (*continued*)
228n33; socialized, 139, 192; television programming on, 156–159, 161–162, 270

Nature/culture binary, 8, 10, 25–27, 31–50, 116, 129, 141, 159, 167, 171n31, 176, 178, 342; Coetzee on, 314; dogs' ability to bridge, 181–182, 192–193; wolves and, 210

Nayaka, of India, 36

Nehamas, Alexander, 58

Nelson, Michael, 228n29

Nicomachean Ethics (Aristotle), 265–266

Nie, Martin, 223

Nodelman, Perry, 199n4

Noosphere, 341

Normalization, Foucault's conception of, 139

Noske, Barbara, 130–131

Noss, Reed, 219

"Notes and Afterthoughts on the Opening of Wittgenstein's *Investigations*" (Cavell), 321–322

Novek, Joel: essay of, 121–151; references to, 5, 12–13, 113–115

Of Spirit (Derrida), 244, 273

Olly & Suzi: Arctic Desert Ocean Jungle, 252

Olly Suzi (collaborative artists), 13, 119, 238, 239–240, 243f, 246–253, 248f, 255, 256, 257n24

On Being with Others: Heidegger, Derrida, Wittgenstein (Glendinning), 326nn58,59, 327n60

O'Neill, John, 123

On the Psychotheology of Everyday Life (Santner), 328n68

Ontological dualism. *See* Hunting and gathering, and ontological dualism of environment

Ontology of dwelling, 26–27, 34–35

Organicism, 228n33

Oswald, Lori Jo, 175–176, 199n6, 200n20

Other animals: animal others across cultures, 9–11, 25–30; boundaries between animality and humanity in early modern China, 27–28, 55–78; hunting, gathering, and ontological dualism 25–27, 31–54; pastoral power and ethnographic encounters with animals in south India, 28–30, 79–111

Ouspensky, Pyotr, 228n33

Oxen, India and image of criminal, 81f, 93–98, 94f

Pandian, Anand: essay by, 79–111; references to, 11, 28–30

Parmenides Lecture Course (Heidegger), 14, 294–296, 299

Pastoral power, 28–30, 79–111; animal reason of colonial power in India, 88–93; freedom, power, and politics of pasturage, 83–88; grazing as practice of rule, 30, 79–80, 98–102, 108n73; human governments' indebtedness to animal care, 102–105; and image of criminal oxen, 81f, 93–98, 94f

Pastorale Rationale (Stephano), 86

Perkins, Marlin, 156

Pets, Heidegger and being-with animals, 272–275

Philosopher's Dog, The (Gaita), 315–318

Philosophical Investigations (Wittgenstein), 316, 318–324

Photoautotrophs, 342–343

Picturing the Beast: Animals, Identity, and Representation (Baker), 175

Pigs. *See* Factory farms

Piramalai Kallar caste: as "criminal tribe," 29–30, 82, 89–93, 97–98; "grazing" as practice of rule and, 30, 79–80, 98–102, 108n73

Placentas, medicinal use of human, 67

Plato, 244–245

Pleasures of Children's Literature, The (Nodelman), 199n4

Police: doctrine of, 84–85, 105n17; "grazing" of Piramalai Kallar caste and, 98–99, 101–102

Political economy of consumption, factory farms and, 135–136

Pontius, Chris, 154, 159–165, 163f, 164f, 167

Post-animal discourse, 17–18

Post-humanism, factory farms and, 114, 123–124, 133–134

Postmodern Animal, The (Baker), 243

Practice of care, 82, 87–88, 96–98; "grazing" as practice of rule, 30, 79–80, 98–102, 108n73

Pratt, Mary Louise, 249

"Prehistory of the Postanimal" (Clark), 313–314

Preserve Arizona's Wolves (P.A.W.S.), 204

Private Life of the Gannet (film), 160

Procurement, hunter-gatherers and, 47–50

Promise, The (Koller), 180–181

Pryor, Ashley E.: essay of, 289–306; references to, 14, 260–261

Puig, Manny, 159

Rappaport, R. A., 33

Regan, Tom, 128

Religion, study of. *See* Eliade, Mircea; Smith, J. Z.

Religious traditions: alliance with science, 20n15; human/animal binary and, 2–3

Report to an Academy (Kafka), 320

Ritzer, G., 141

Rivera, Marla, 336

Robinson, Michael, 213, 227n28, 231n61

Rocky Mountain News, 208

Roosevelt, Theodore, 226n19

Rose, Nikolas, 104

Sable (Hesse), 182–184

Sagan, Dorian, 338

Sahlins, Marshall, 32, 39–40

Same-sex contact, of *Wildboyz* and animals, 162–165

Sand County Almanac (Leopold), 211, 214, 229n43

Santner, Eric L., 328n68

Santorum, Rick, 169n1

"Scarcity value," 229n38

Scarry, Elaine, 58, 352

Schechner, Richard, 166

Schutz, Alfred, 47

Scott, Colin, 43, 44, 45, 46

Sedgwick, Eve Kosofsky, 162

Sellbach, Undine: essay of, 307–330; references to, 14–15, 261–262

Seth, Vikram, 185

Sexual Politics of Meat, The (Adams), 19nn6,12

Shanhaijing (Classic of Mountains and Seas), 72n14

"Shark Bite" (Olly Suzi), 248f

Shepard, Paul, 179, 193

Shiva, Vandana, 127

Shuihu zhuan (Water Margin), 65–66

Shweder, Richard, 32

Siebert, Charles, 19n12

Sight Hound (Houston), 176–177

Simba (film), 155

Singer, Peter, 128, 312–313, 325n23

"Slow Tuesday Night" (Lafferty), 334

Smith, E. A., 47–48

Smith, J. Z., 18, 350, 351

Social Darwinism, wolves and, 117, 208

Social geography, factory farms and, 136–138

Sociality, Schutz's definition of, 47

Soper, Kate, 225n12
Soulé, Michael, 219, 231n57
South Asia, 5, 9, 79–105
Spain, 12
Spiro, Melford, 113
Steeves, Peter, 266
Stefano, Stefano di, 86
Stengers, Isabelle, 338
Stevenson, Trish, 219–220
Stolz, Mary, 181–185
"Stroll Through the Worlds of Animals
    and Men" (Uexküll), 244
Superle, Michelle: essay of, 174–202;
    references to, 13, 116–117
Symbiogensis, bacteria and, 335–336, 340,
    344
Symbiosis, bacteria and, 334–335, 340
Sympathetic imagination, 261–262,
    307–330; animals and life versus living,
    307–308; ethics, imagination, and
    imagined boundaries, 309–310; factory
    farming and death camp analogy,
    313–318; *forms* of life and forms of *life*,
    262, 318–319; language and dividing
    line between animals and humans,
    319–324; *The Lives of Animals* and
    human/animal divide, 310–313

Taiping yulan, 70
Tamil language, pastoral care and, 99,
    108n73
Tanner, Adrian, 41–44, 46
Tao Zongyi, 67, 69
Taylor, Bron, 214
Tertium Organum (Ouspensky), 228n33
Thevar, Makkarasu, 93, 98
"Thinking Like a Mountain" (Leopold),
    211–213
Thomas, Lewis, 338
Thoreau, Henry David, 229n38
To Catch a Tartar (Hall), 182–183, 185
Tolkappiyam, 108n73

Transcendence, Heidegger's notion of,
    276–277
Tree of life (TOL), bacteria and, 335–336
Tremaine, Jeff, 158, 159
Trevarthen, C., 41
Trials of Life, The (television program),
    157
Turnbull, Colin, 35

Uexküll, Jakob von, 244, 255–256, 270,
    297
Umwelt (animal environment), 244, 246,
    247, 249, 252, 254–256, 279
Urine, medicinal uses of, 68, 76n66
U.S. Biological Survey (USBS), 208,
    209f, 210f, 227n24
U.S. Fish & Wildlife Service, 222–223

Van Horn, Gavin: essay of, 203–237;
    references to, 12–13, 117–118
Van Lawick, Hugo, 156
Vernadsky, Vladimir, 341
Vialles, Noelie, 136, 137
Von Helmholtz, Hermann, 334
Vulnerability, ethics of, 332, 342–344

Watching Wildlife (Chris), 13
Weathers, David, 159
"What Does It Mean to 'Understand'?"
    (Coetzee), 325n23
"What Is It Like to Be a Bat?" (Nagel),
    270
When Animals Attack (television
    program), 158
When Species Meet (Haraway), 338
White, T. H., 351
Whitman, William, 334
"Why Look at Animals?" (Berger), 242
Wiebe, William, 334
Wildboyz (MTV), the animal and the
    abject, 6, 13, 115–116, 152–173, 170n4,
    171n13; antics, 153–154, 158–162; antics

and slippage across species borders, 166–169; history of wildlife film and television genre, 155–158, 170n7; homoerotic interspecies contacts and, 162–165

Wilderness, concept of, 225n11. *See also* Wolves, iconic status of in the United States

Wildlife film and television genre, history of, 155–158, 170n7

Wild women (*yenü*), 55–56, 62–63, 73n35

William of Rubruck, 73n32

Williams, Greg, 247

Williams, Olly. *See* Olly Suzi (collaborative artists)

Williams, Raymond, 87

Winstanley, Suzi. *See* Olly Suzi (collaborative artists)

Winterhalder, B., 47–48

Wittgenstein, Ludwig, 316, 326nn51,58, 351; ethics, imagination, and imagined boundaries, 309–310; *forms* of life and forms of *life*, 206, 318–319; language and dividing line between animals and humans, 319–324

Woese, Carl, 341

Wolfe, Cary, 317, 339

Woloy, Eleanora, 176

Wolves, iconic status of in the United States, 117–118, 203–237; conservation biology and, 218–219, 230n56, 231n57; ecological movement and preservation of species, 211–218, 216f, 217f, 228nn29, 33,34, 229nn35,37,38; predator control and expressions of perceived natural order, 205–211, 209f, 210f, 225nn9,12,13, 226nn15,18, 227n28; wolf reintroduction and, 204f, 214, 219–224, 221f, 230n51, 231nn30,61,64

Wonderful Life (Gould), 335

Xingxing, 62–63, 63f, 73nn30,32

Yard, Robert Sterling, 229n37

Youatt, William, 239

Young, Fredrick, 245

Young, Stanley, 227n24

Yulei, 58

Zhao Xuemin, 68–69, 70

Zhong Yu, 61–62, 73n28

Zoo (docudrama), 169n3

Zoographies (Calarco), 3

Zoomorphism, 350–351